THE HASTY GOURMET™

LOW SALT FAVORITES

300 EASY-TO-MAKE, GREAT-TASTING RECIPES
FOR A HEALTHY LIFESTYLE

BOBBIE MOSTYN

NEWLY REVISED EDITION

InData Group, Inc.

Copyright @ 2005, 2014 by Bobbie Mostyn

All rights reserved. This book, or parts thereof, may not be reproduced in any form without permission from the publisher, exceptions are made for brief excerpts used in published reviews.

Published by InData Group, Inc.
P.O. Box 256
Allyn, WA 98524

Printed in the United States of America

Cover design: Gray Ponytail Studio

Visit our website:

LowSaltFoods.com

All information contained in this book is provided for informational purposes only. It should not be considered as medical advice for dealing with a health problem or a substitute for the advice of a healthcare professional. The author and publisher do not endorse, warrant, or guarantee any of the products mentioned herein, nor does any omission of such imply otherwise.

Publisher's Cataloging-in-Publication Data

Names: Mostyn, Bobbie.

Title: The Hasty Gourmet low salt favorites : 300 easy-to-make, great-tasting recipes for a healthy lifestyle / Bobbie Mostyn.

Other titles: Low salt favorites.

Description: Rev. ed. | Allyn, WA : InData Group, Inc., 2024. | Summary: Low-salt cookbook for heart-healthy eating.

Identifiers: LCCN 2024902221 | ISBN 9780967396996 (pbk.) | ISBN 9780967396934 (ebook)

Subjects: LCSH: Salt-free diet. | Salt-free diet – Recipes. | Heart – Diseases – Diet therapy. BISAC: COOKING / Health & Healing / Low Salt.

Classification: LCC RM237.8 M67 2024 | DDC 613.2/85 M67h--dc23

LC record available at https://lccn.loc.gov/2024902221

DEDICATED TO:

My husband, Mike...
for your continued love and support...
you make everything so much easier!

All my friends and family...
for enduring my recipe testing...
even when some didn't come out very well.

InData Publishing

Website:
LowSaltFoods.com

Also available
our best-selling nutritional counter:

Pocket Guide to Low Sodium Foods
4th Edition

by Bobbie Mostyn

CONTENTS

INTRODUCTION 7
  Low-Salt Lifestyle 8
  Food Labeling Guidelines 11
  Cooking Without Salt. 12
  Herbs & Spices. 16
  Sodium in Commonly Used Ingredients. 18
  Which Foods Have Less Sodium?....... 20
  About The Recipes 21
  Measurements & Abbreviations 24

APPETIZERS
  Dips & Spreads 26
  Finger Foods 31

SOUPS & CHILI
  Vegetable Soups..................... 40
  Seafood Chowders 53
  Bean Soups & Chili.................. 55

SALADS & SALAD DRESSINGS
  Side Salads 58
  Tossed Salads...................... 67
  Main Course Salads 72
  Salad Dressings 75

MAIN COURSES
  Poultry 80
  Beef, Veal, Lamb & Pork 102
  Fish & Seafood..................... 111
  Meatless Dishes 121
  Pasta Dishes & Pizza............... 131

  Asian Entrées...................... 140
  Hispanic Dishes.................... 142

SIDE DISHES
  Vegetables & Legumes 152
  Grains & Rice...................... 171
  Stuffings 174

BREAKFAST & LUNCH
  Breakfast.......................... 178
  Sandwiches & Wraps 186
  Anytime Quickies 190

BREADS & BAKED GOODS
  Breads, Buns & Doughs 192
  Other Baked Goods 198

BASICS, CONDIMENTS & SAUCES
  Basic Stuff 204
  Relishes, Salsas & Sauces 210

DESSERTS & SWEETS
  Pies, Tarts & Tortes 218
  Cakes & Cheesecakes 224
  Crisps, Strudels & Turnovers....... 230
  Puddings & Custards 234
  Fruit Desserts..................... 236
  Cookies............................ 237
  Fillings, Frostings & Toppings..... 238

COOKING TIPS & FOOD NOTES ..242

INDEX 255

INTRODUCTION

I consider myself very health conscious... I no longer eat red meat, keep fats to a minimum, and, as far as the saltshaker, I threw that out decades ago. So you can imagine my surprise when I was diagnosed with hypertension and told to cut back on salt. How could I be eating too much salt, I thought.

As it turns out, like most Americans, I was clueless about the amount of sodium I was consuming, particularly from the processed foods I routinely used in my cooking. When I checked my pantry, I was shocked... the lower-salt beans I regularly used had 220mg of sodium per half cup, my favorite bread had 250mg per slice, and the salad dressing I used most often had 650mg per 2 tablespoons!

Determined to lower my salt intake, I spent hours at the supermarket reading labels, searching for low-sodium products that could substitute for the higher salt foods I was using. Not only did I discover that nearly every food had a low-sodium alternative, but I also noticed a large disparity within brands. Take tomato sauce, for example, a ¼ cup has anywhere from 5mg to 380mg, depending on the manufacturer. Even though there is little difference in taste, by choosing the lesser brand, you eliminate 375mg of sodium.

Unfortunately, I also learned that many low-salt products have no taste; in fact, some are downright yucky! And even worse, not only did some taste awful, but many were also unhealthy... the salt had been replaced with added fat and/or sugar.

The more I learned, the more committed I became to share my findings. It became my passion and led to my first book, *Pocket Guide to Low Sodium Foods*. In my quest to raise sodium awareness, I developed a website, **LowSaltFoods.com**, where I maintain a regularly updated list of low-salt products, offer dining out tips, discuss health issues related to excess sodium, and much more.

But all was not rosy. As I began to modify my cooking to accommodate my low-sodium lifestyle, many of my salt-shaking friends and family rebelled. The truth is, some of these earlier dishes were not so good... they were bland and tasteless. In fact, one of my "salty" pals went so far as to sneak a saltshaker into the house and, while my back was turned, added salt to a sauce I was preparing.

Over the years, I am happy to say, my low-salt cooking has vastly improved. Not only is my friend no longer sneaking in a saltshaker, but he started asking for my recipes. The true test, however, was my mother-in-law... who salted everything. If she didn't enjoy something I had prepared, then it was back to the test kitchen until it was tasty enough for everyone. Eventually, not only did she find the meals I prepared pleasing, but she also was the one who first suggested I publish my recipes.

I hope you will enjoy these healthy, low-salt dishes as much as my family and friends. It has been a labor of love and I guarantee everyone will be asking for more... including your mother-in-law.

Bobbie Mostyn

LOW-SALT LIFESTYLE

Welcome to the low-salt lifestyle, a way of eating that focuses on healthy, flavorful food with a minimum of sodium. This is not a diet, but a cuisine where the natural taste of food is at the heart of each meal. If you enjoy good cooking that does not sacrifice on flavor, and with a minimum of preparation, you will love *The Hasty Gourmet™ Low Salt Favorites*.

ARE YOU SALT SAVVY?

The primary source of sodium in our diet comes from salt (also known as sodium chloride), a naturally occurring compound containing 40% sodium and 60% chlorine. (Although salt and sodium are not the same, the terms are used interchangeably throughout this cookbook.)

Sodium is essential to the body by regulating fluids, but too much sodium may cause fluid build up (water retention), putting added stress on the heart and kidneys to work harder. Over time, this can lead to high blood pressure, or hypertension, significantly increasing one's risk for stroke, heart, and kidney disease.

Although the body only needs a small amount of sodium (about 500 milligrams), for fluid regulation, the average person consumes a whopping 4,000–6,000mg per day—nearly two to three times the recommended level of 2,300mg. *NOTE: At this writing, the American Heart Association recommends most American adults limit their salt intake to 1,500mg per day.*

SALT IN OUR FOOD

Nearly everything we eat contains some sodium, even small amounts occur naturally in fruits and vegetables, but the vast majority comes off the grocery shelves and from restaurant meals. Surprisingly, less than 15% of the salt we consume comes from the saltshaker.

Thanks in part to our busy lifestyles, we have become accustomed to salty snacks and foods. Because we have less time to plan meals, we rely more on convenience and fast foods, which are loaded with salt. Unfortunately, excess sodium affects our health. In addition to hypertension, research suggests possible links to osteoporosis, dementia, asthma, edema, and other ailments.

According to the Centers for Disease Control and Prevention, nearly half of all adults—119.9 million*—have hypertension and another 59 million are considered prehypertensive (at risk of developing high blood pressure). Even more alarming, at the rate we are going, 9 out of 10 middle-aged Americans face the threat of hypertension later in life.

NOTE: In 2005 while writing the first edition of The Hasty Gourmet™ Low Salt Favorites, the number of adults with hypertension was 50 million.

So concerned, several organizations, including the American Public Health Association, urged the food industry to reduce sodium by 50% by 2010. But that did not occur. Manufacturers opposed these changes, contending that low-sodium products often do not fare well in the marketplace. Taste is the main reason people buy a particular product and when salt is removed, consumers react negatively to the loss of flavor.

Unfortunately, food manufacturers cannot be forced to produce low-salt items. It is much easier for them to stop manufacturing a product than it is to create a new item, particularly one that consumers probably will not embrace.

Perhaps one day, with enough public demand, not only will the foods we purchase have less salt, but they also will not be a detriment to our health.

It's already begun in England. An ongoing movement to reduce salt resulted in a large supermarket chain cutting the sodium in their store-brand products—12% the first year and 10% in subsequent years—with no decline in sales. They plan to continue with these cutbacks every few years until there is a 50% reduction.

Sodium & HBP

Scientists found that eating too much salt can make your blood pressure go up. This happens more often in countries where people eat a lot of salty food. Some people are more sensitive to salt than others. Especially those who already have high blood pressure or are older or black.

To keep your blood pressure in check, it's important to cut down on salty foods. This can really help, even if you're already taking medicine for high blood pressure. The *Heart Disease Journal* says eating less salt is one of the best things you can do to reduce your blood pressure.

The DASH Diet

National Heart, Lung, and Blood Institute (NIH) funded research found diet lowers blood pressure. And what you eat may also prevent and control hypertension.

Researchers looked at the Dietary Approaches to Stop Hypertension (DASH) diet. This diet helps people lower their blood pressure by eating less salt. It works for everyone, no matter their race or sex and works best with hypertensive people. And guess what? The less salt you eat, the better it is for your blood pressure!

The DASH diet is based on eating about 2,000 calories a day. It's all about eating foods that are low in fats and cholesterol... or lots of fiber, fruits, vegetables, and low-fat dairy products. What's more, following this diet may lower your chances of a stroke, cancer, heart disease, and diabetes.

NOTE: Staying healthy isn't just about what you eat. It's also staying active, keeping a good weight, and not smoking.

THE DASH EATING PLAN

Food Group	Daily Servings	Serving Sizes
Grains and grain products	7–8	1 slice bread 1 cup ready-to-eat cereal* ½ cup cooked rice, pasta, or cereal
Vegetables	4–5	1 cup raw leafy vegetable ½ cup cooked vegetable 6 oz vegetable juice
Fruits	4–5	1 medium fruit ¼ cup dried fruit ½ cup fresh, frozen, or canned fruit 6 oz fruit juice
Lowfat or fat free dairy products	2–3	8 oz milk 1 cup yogurt 1.5 oz cheese
Lean meats, poultry	2 or fewer	3 oz cooked lean meat, skinless poultry, or fish
Nuts, seeds, dried beans	4–5 per week	⅓ cup (1.5 oz) nuts 1 tbsp (0.5 oz) seeds ½ cup cooked dry beans
Fats & oils**	2–3	1 tsp soft margarine 1 tsp regular mayonnaise 1 tbsp lowfat mayonnaise 2 tbsp light salad dressing 1 tsp vegetable oil
Sweets	5 per week	1 tbsp sugar 1 tbsp jelly or jam 0.5 oz jelly beans 8 oz lemonade

*Serving sizes for ready-to-eat cereals vary between ½ cup and 1¼ cups. Check the item's nutrition label.
**Fat content changes serving counts for fats and oils, for example:
  1 tablespoon regular salad dressing = 1 serving,
  1 tablespoon lowfat dressing = ½ serving, and
  1 tablespoon fat-free dressing = 0 servings.
For additional info on The DASH Diet, visit nhlbi.nih.gov/health-topics/dash-eating-plan

TASTE IS IMPORTANT

Taste is the main reason most people find it difficult to stay on a low-salt diet. When there's less salt, the flavor isn't there, and with no taste meals are less satisfying. Also, it's hard to find flavorful, low sodium convenience foods, making it tougher to stay on track. Even with the best intentions, we end up eating more salt than recommended.

It would be a lot easier to eat less salt if food makers and restaurants didn't add so much sodium to everything. But there are things you can do to cut back on salt (see *Tips to Reducing Sodium*, pg 13, and *More Low-Salt Tips and Techniques*, pg 15).

BE SODIUM CONSCIOUS

Even though experts have warned us to eat less salt for a long time, consumers aren't paying attention. The problem is most of us don't realize how much sodium we're actually eating. Some mistakenly think what they eat is okay because they don't add salt to their food at the table or while cooking. But they might not know that a lot of the sodium we eat is already in the food we buy from the store.

Here's the important thing: if you don't know how much salt is in what you're eating, you can't take control of your diet.

As you become aware of how much sodium is in the food you buy, you will notice two things: (1) most foods have a low-salt alternative and (2) there's a large disparity among brands. For example, some pasta sauces have a ton of sodium—up to 850mg in one serving! But others have around 300mg, and no-salt-added sauces have less than 50mg. Another example is teriyaki marinade, some brands have over 600mg of salt in one tablespoon! But you can try using grilling sauces instead, which usually have less than 140mg. They might not taste exactly like teriyaki, but they'll still be yummy and better for you.

FOODS HIGH IN SODIUM

Bakery items – bagels, breads, donuts, muffins

Canned foods – soups, meats, fish, sauerkraut, beans, vegetables

Convenience foods – frozen dinners, pizza, cereals and packaged mixes, such as pancakes, food "helpers," stuffing, and rice dishes

Dairy products – cheese, cottage cheese

Deli items – bacon, luncheon meats, corned beef, smoked meats or fish, sardines, anchovies, mayo-based salads, like cole slaw and potato salad

Snack foods – crackers, chips, dips

Condiments – mustard, ketchup, mayonnaise, salad dressings, pickles, olives, capers, salsas, packaged seasoning mixes

Sauces – gravy, steak, barbecue, pasta, teriyaki, soy, and most Asian sauces

Baking needs – self-rising flour, baking and biscuit mixes, bouillon cubes, batter and coating mixes, bread crumbs, cooking wines, meat tenderizers, monosodium glutamate (MSG), baking powder, baking soda

Beverages – tomato and vegetable juices, Bloody Marys, chocolate drink mixes

FOOD LABELING GUIDELINES

The Food and Drug Administration (FDA) regulates food labeling to assure consumers the information is accurate and not misleading. Labels contain a lot of useful information to help you compare products and make healthy food choices.

WHAT THE LABEL TELLS YOU

Serving Size: Amount typically eaten, shown in familiar units (such as cups or tablespoons) followed by the metric equivalent (i.e. grams). In the label example, the serving size is ⅔ cup. If you eat twice this, double the values.

Nutrients: Listed in grams (g) except for Cholesterol and Sodium, which are in milligrams (mg). Use these figures to compare nutrients among products. If a nutrient is not shown, there is no significant amount in the product.

% Daily Value: Shows how much of the *Recommended Daily Values* (RDVs) each nutrient provides to a total daily diet. It tells you if a serving of food is high or low in a nutrient and is another way to compare similar products. Chose products with higher %DVs you want more of and lower %DVs you want less of (5% or less is considered low, 20% or more is considered high).

DUAL COLUMN LABEL

Products where you might consume more than one serving have two columns, per serving and per package. For example, a can of soup with 2 servings per can has dual columns so you can easily see the nutrient values if you eat half the can or all of the soup at one time.

LABEL CLAIMS

The FDA provides guidelines for the claims and descriptions manufacturers can use on food labeling. These requirements ensure that descriptive terms, such as *free, reduced,* or *healthy,* are used consistently to help consumers make informed choices about the foods they buy and eat.

NOTE: A product with descriptive terms, such as "50% less salt," does not mean it is low sodium. They are simply comparing this item to a similar product with twice as much sodium. Also, "low fat" and "fat free" do not mean they are low in sodium; the opposite is often true, as manufacturers frequently replace the fat with added salt and sugar.

COOKING WITHOUT SALT

Most people who enjoy my cooking marvel at how yummy everything tastes, even though I remove the salt, fat, and other not-so-healthy stuff. It's much easier to make tasty dishes when you use lots of fatty foods and salt. But the secret is finding ways to make food delicious without using those bad things. It's not hard, a few changes here and there, and of course, using plenty of herbs, spices, and other tasty things.

When you're planning meals, try to include more fresh fruits and vegetables. They hardly have any salt in them. Instead of making meat or chicken the main part of your meal, serve it on the side. Add a salad and a couple of other side dishes and you'll have lots of different foods to enjoy. Best of all, your meals will be healthier with less salt.

As you learn more about sodium, you'll see that making small changes to how you cook can help you eat less salt. I hope after you try some of my recipes, you'll feel comfortable enough to "desalt" one of your favorite dishes. Here are some of the low-salt ingredients and methods I use to make the yummy dishes you'll find in this cookbook.

1 **Replace salt with onion and garlic powder.** I use onion and garlic powder the way most people use salt. Next to pepper, I use them the most. I also use several spice mills (found in the spice section of most grocery stores). My favorites are Tuscan herbs, Provence herbs, and white pepper.

2 **Add freshly ground black pepper.** If you are not using freshly ground pepper in your dishes, now is the time to start. It is far superior to pre-ground and adds so much more flavor. I use black peppercorns most of the time, but when preparing white sauces, I often use the milder white peppercorn, mainly for appearance. Any size and type of grinder will work, as long as it allows you to adjust the coarseness. I like mine rather coarse, but you can set it to whatever coarseness you like.

3 **Use low-sodium bouillon or soup base for added taste.** This is another way to add flavor without the salt. Of the low-salt bouillons, I most often use *Herb-Ox Sodium Free,* which has a nice flavor when added to sauces and soups (both the chicken and beef have 5mg sodium per teaspoon). When more flavor is needed, I reach for one of many low-salt soup bases, which average 140mg per teaspoon.

4 **Prepare homemade broths.** Most canned broths are loaded with sodium (anywhere from 700mg to over 1,000mg per cup). There are several lower and low-salt brands, but quite frankly, their flavor is rather bland. I don't think anything beats the rich taste of a homemade broth that has simmered all day.

Freeze the strained broth into paper cups in varying amounts (¼ to 1 cup); when a recipe calls for broth, the desired amount can easily be defrosted in the microwave or under warm water.

On those occasions when I use prepared low-salt broth, I add a teaspoon or two of bouillon or soup base, which adds more flavor but little sodium.

5 **Flavor food with herbs and spices.** When I was growing up, the only seasonings in our house were salt and pepper. In recent years with the popularity of television cooking shows, gourmet magazines, and up-scale restaurants, herbs and spices are much more common than in the past.

I use both fresh and dried herbs and spices. I usually add dried at the beginning of the cooking process and fresh at the end. Adding the dried early, for example, when cooking onions or shallots, brings out more of the flavor of the seasonings. I liken the difference to roasted nuts versus raw nuts—after roasting, the nuts are more flavorful. By adding fresh herbs and spices at the end, their full flavor and fresh fragrance is brought to the dish (the exceptions are bay leaf, rosemary, and thyme, which can be added near the beginning of the cooking process).

Dried Herbs & Spices

Dried herbs and spices are more pungent than fresh — so a little goes a long ways. As a general rule, 1 tablespoon fresh equals 1 teaspoon dried. Also, because dried herbs and spices lose their flavor quickly, do not use 6 months after opening. The best way to keep track is to write the purchase date on the container. Once the date has passed, discard and purchase a new one. This is important for two reasons. First, you don't know how long it's been sitting on the shelf. Secondly, flavor comes from the freshest, most flavorful ingredients. Tired old herbs and spices without potency add little flavor to a dish.

To save time and money, you can also put together your own spice blends and keep them in an air-tight container. One of my favorite combinations is one part each tarragon, thyme, and rosemary and two parts basil.

Fresh Herbs & Spices

If you're not growing fresh herbs, now is a good time to start. Some readily available favorites are sweet basil, marjoram, rosemary, tarragon, parsley, and chives.

Plant them in a sunny spot near the kitchen or in a window. (Seeds and starts are available at garden centers and nurseries.) If you need help, there are several publications available, along with vast information on the internet, to guide you in the care and feeding of your herb family.

You can also purchase fresh herbs in the produce section of most supermarkets. Look for bright green leaves without brown spots that are not limp. They usually keep for several days in the refrigerator.

TIPS TO REDUCING SODIUM

AT HOME:

Eliminate the saltshaker – Do not salt before you taste. Break the habit of automatically reaching for the saltshaker.

Use less salt in cooking – In most recipes salt can be reduced, or in many cases omitted, without compromising the flavor. Use more herbs and spices, like onion and garlic powder. Also, low-sodium bouillon can add extra flavor, as can wine, vinegar, lemon or lime juice.

Prepare low-salt recipes – There are lots of low salt cookbooks available, as well as low-salt recipes online.

Try a new low-sodium product – There are lots of tasty options instead of highly salted foods. You won't know how yummy they are until you give them a try!

Munch on fruits or vegetables – instead of salty snacks. Not only are they healthier, but they also have very little sodium.

AT THE SUPERMARKET:

Use less prepared foods – The less processing, the less sodium. Stay away from the center aisles which are filled with salty snacks and packaged products.

Select lower salt foods – Look for foods labeled sodium free, low sodium, reduced sodium, unsalted, and no salt added. Choose brands with less than 140mg sodium per serving (or less than 5% of the recommended daily value of sodium).

Read the label – If you don't know how much sodium is in a product, you can't take control of your diet.

Know how much sodium is in each serving – The serving size listed may be smaller than what you will actually eat. Some serving sizes may be deceptive and foods that appear low in salt, may not be. For example, 1 tbsp clam juice has 60mg sodium, if there's 1 cup in a recipe, it amounts to 960mg.

Be alert to "salty" terms – like brine, cured, marinated, pickled, and smoked.

6 **Use wines, vinegars, and citric juices to add another layer of flavor.** Acidic additives like wines, vinegars, lemon and lime juice, add a sweet or sour tanginess that in some recipes is pure magic. Plus, as the liquid cooks down, its flavor intensifies. Many of my recipes have one or more acidic additives.

Red & White Wines

Because I like wine, I always have several bottles around to both drink and use in my cooking. My favorite reds are Merlot, Cabernet Sauvignon, and Zinfandel. I also prefer dry whites, such as Chardonnay, Chablis, and Sauvignon Blanc. Wines used in cooking do not have to be expensive and unless you plan to drink it within a few days, don't buy a bottle just for cooking.

Fortified Wines

These wines are fortified with liquor, such as brandy, and other flavorings, which allows for a long shelf life (up to a year in some cases). They range from sweet to full-bodied and are great for cooking, adding depth and richness. The ones I use most frequently include a dry sherry, Madeira, Marsala, vermouth, and sake; all are available in the wine department. *NOTE: Avoid so-called "cooking wines" found in the condiment section of the supermarket, as they are loaded with sodium (182mg per fluid ounce versus 2mg for most fortified wines).*

Fortified wines range in color from white to red, and depending on which one you use, will change the flavor of the dish. **Dry sherry** is light, but full-bodied and adds a richness that you don't get from white wine. **Madeira** has a distinctive rich, nutty flavor and is great with mushrooms, meats, and poultry. **Marsala** is a sweeter wine and imparts a wonderful depth to fish, meats, poultry, and desserts. **Vermouth** is fruity and perfect with lighter dishes, like fish. **Sake** has a wide-range of tastes, from sweet to dry, but most inexpensive sakes found in the supermarket have a subtle sweetness. Experiment with each of them to determine which ones you like the best.

Vinegars

There are many flavored vinegars which also affect the way a dish tastes. They range from dark and slightly sweet, like balsamic, to light and mild, like white wine vinegar. I suggest keeping at least five or six vinegars on hand. My favorites are balsamic, white balsamic, red wine, white wine, raspberry, and apple cider vinegar.

Lemon and Lime Juice

The sharp tanginess of lemon and lime juice mimics the taste of salt in many recipes. Although fresh lemon and lime juice is always preferable to bottled, you can usually substitute bottled in most recipes. Either of these adds a tang and brings out the flavor of the food, particularly vegetables.

7 **Add flavor with garlic.** Garlic plays an important part in low-salt cooking. It adds so much flavor and, in my opinion, makes or breaks many dishes (and I don't mean the plate you eat on). For those of you who don't care for garlic, you might try elephant garlic, which is very mild and has less of a garlic taste. Plus, there is an added bonus, research suggests garlic has many health benefits, including reducing blood pressure and lowering cholesterol.

8 **Make it hot and spicy.** When you add heat, the need for salt disappears. Try using minced hot peppers (like jalapeños or chipotles), dried red pepper flakes, cayenne pepper, hot paprika, some curry powders, or other hot sauces and spices in your dishes.

9 Pour a sauce on top. The flavor of many entrées is improved with the addition of a low-salt sauce. There are several sauces throughout this cookbook you can use on many different dishes. For example, a rich mushroom sauce easily goes with chicken, meat, or on mashed potatoes or rice.

MORE LOW SALT TIPS & TECHNIQUES

Substitute fresh garlic for garlic salt – if a recipe calls for garlic salt, use 1 garlic clove for every ½ teaspoon garlic salt.

Don't salt the water – when cooking pasta or rice. If you want added flavor, add a teaspoon or two of low-salt chicken bouillon.

Instead of salt, use glazes or spice rubs on poultry, meat, and fish – rub on horseradish, preserves, or chutneys before baking or barbecuing.

Avoid ready-to-eat meat or poultry – they contain too much added salt; buy fresh or frozen that has not been precooked or has no added preparations, like spices and sauces.

In old favorite recipes, reduce the amount of salt by one half – in most dishes you won't notice the difference.

Substitute sun-dried tomatoes for olives or bacon – they suggest a salty taste and you can use them in many recipes.

Replace milk with soy or coconut milk – they're rich and creamy; save 24mg or 59mg sodium, each, a cup.

In place of bread crumbs, use panko crumbs or LS crackers – Panko averages 45mg an oz, LS crackers less than 100mg, and bread crumbs average 270mg.

Try mustard powder instead of prepared mustard – in most recipes you'll get the same taste, but without the salt (some dishes may also require a little vinegar).

Use celery seed – it has a "salty" taste.

Deglaze pan drippings and reduce – this will concentrate the flavor – add brandy, wine, or vinegar to create a richer, more flavorful dish.

Watch out for "less salt" or "reduced salt" items – a can of reduced sodium soup averages 450mg a cup (and who eats just 1 cup?), canned beans with 50% less salt, have about 220mg per ½ cup.

Substitute mascarpone for cream cheese – particularly in desserts (mascarpone has 15mg per oz, cream cheese averages 110mg). *NOTE: Although very low in sodium it has a lot of fat, 13g fat and 7g sat fat.*

Stay away from canned vegetables – use fresh or frozen instead. If you do use canned, always rinse the contents; it will not remove all the salt, but it will get rid of some of it.

Experiment with low-sodium products – there are lots of other tasty options instead of foods with a lot of salt. You won't know how yummy they are until you give them a try!

Add sweetness – mix in a little sugar or sugar substitute to a pasta sauce or add apple juice to a gravy, and you won't miss the salt.

Use low-salt bread crumbs or nutritional yeast instead of cheese on top of pasta dishes – the added crunchiness is a great replacement to highly salted cheeses like Mozzarella, Parmesan, and Romano. Nutritional yeast has 10mg per tablespoon, has a nutty/cheesy taste, and is a great low-salt substitute.

Check spice blend labels – although most don't include nutritional info, the ingredients list lets you know if there is any salt in the product. If sodium or salt is listed as the first or second ingredient, avoid it.

Use salt substitutes – they contain potassium which tastes similar to salt. *NOTE: If taking hypertension drugs, check with your healthcare provider before using, as it may conflict with your medication.*

HERBS & SPICES

HERBS

Basil – Has a sweet taste, similar to licorice. There are numerous varieties, ranging from sweet to pungent (Asian), and some have a hint of lemon or cinnamon. While there is a huge difference in flavor between fresh and dried, either can be used in tomato sauces, salads, vegetable dishes, soups, eggs, fish, meats, and poultry. Basil also is an ingredient in many Italian blends.

Bay leaf – Has a spicy, woodsy flavor. There are two common varieties–California (larger and more potent) and Turkish (smaller and less potent). Often used in bouquet garni (traditionally parsley, thyme, and bay leaf), which is tied together to flavor soups, stews, and broth. Bay leaf is also used in tomato sauces.

Chervil – Similar to parsley but with a slight anise (licorice) flavor. It is one of the ingredients in Fines Herbes (see below). Use in poultry, meat, vegetable, egg, and cheese dishes.

Chives – Have a mild, onion-like flavor. Can use interchangeably with chopped green onions (green part). Use in eggs, salads, and as a topping for potatoes. Add chives at the last minute to hot dishes, as they don't hold up well to heat.

Cilantro – Similar to parsley but has a stronger flavor; commonly used in Mexican and Asian cooking.

Dill – Dill seed is the dried fruit of the herb and is similar in taste to caraway (the flavor in rye bread), dill weed is less pungent and mild. Dried dill is very different in taste than fresh. Add fresh dill at the last minute to hot dishes, as it doesn't hold up well to heat. Use with eggs, fish, soups, salads, and veggies.

Fennel – similar to anise, but sweeter. Use with fish and in Moroccan dishes.

Fines Herbes – French combination of herbs, usually tarragon, chervil, parsley, and chives. Use in French dishes, soups, stuffings, meats, poultry, and vegetables.

Herbes de Provence – Another blend that combines French herbs and lavender with Italian herbs and fennel. Use in French dishes, soups, meats, poultry, and vegetables.

Marjoram – Comes from the oregano family and has a sweet oregano-like flavor. Use with poultry, soups, veggies, beef, and fish. Marjoram is also used in Italian blends and goes well with basil and thyme.

Mint – Has a fresh minty flavor. Use with lamb, peas, or in desserts, particularly chocolate.

Oregano – More pungent, but not as sweet as marjoram. Use in Italian and Mexican dishes, soups, vegetables, meat, poultry, and pasta sauces.

Parsley – Has a fresh, mildly peppery flavor. There are dozens of varieties, the two most popular are curly-leaf (used most often as a garnish) and the more flavorful flat-leaf (or Italian) parsley. Use with eggs, fish, salads, vegetables, sauces, meats, and poultry.

Rosemary – Has a lemony, piney flavor, reminiscent of tea leaves. Most commonly used in Italian cooking. Add to poultry, meats, fish, and vegetables (especially roasted root veggies).

Sage – Originally used for medicinal purposes, it is one of the most popular herbs. It is slightly bitter with an undertone of musty mint. It is used in stuffings and savory breads, poultry, soup, vegetables, and fish.

Savory – Similar in taste to thyme, but with peppery, minty undertones There are two varieties—winter and summer—the latter is milder than winter, but both have a strong taste, so use sparingly. Add to soups, meat, and fish.

Tarragon – Has a distinctive anise-like flavor. Most frequently used in French dishes and sauces. It is one of the ingredients in Fines Herbes. Use with eggs, fish (particularly salmon), poultry, meats, and vegetables.

Thyme – Has a minty flavor with lemony undertones. Frequently used in Mediterranean cooking. Use with fish, chicken, salads, vegetables, and eggs.

SPICES

Allspice – Contrary to what most people think, is not a blend of several spices, but comes from the myrtle tree family. Its taste is similar to cloves, cinnamon, and nutmeg. It comes in whole and ground varieties and is most frequently used in savory and sweet foods, from salads to desserts.

Cardamom – Has a sweet, spicy flavor and is used in many curry blends. On its own, it makes a nice addition to many desserts. Use sparingly, a little goes a long way.

Cayenne Pepper – Also called red pepper, is very hot. Use sparingly in eggs, soups, potatoes, and other hot and spicy dishes.

Celery Seed – Tastes similar to celery and lends a "salty" taste to many dishes. Use in soups and sauces.

Chili Powder – Spicy flavor, ranging from mild to hot depending on the pepper. Often used in chili, Mexican, and other spicy dishes.

Cinnamon – Has a sweet flavor and is sold either ground or in sticks. Use in sweet or savory dishes, curries, soups, stews, and desserts.

Cloves – Have a strong, aromatic flavor. Use in sweet dishes.

Cumin – Has a distinctive peppery flavor and is used most frequently in Mexican dishes. Add to eggs, soups, chili, vegetables, meats, and poultry.

Ginger – Fresh ginger (ginger root) has a slightly sweet, pungent flavor and is used in Asian dishes; the powdered form has a different flavor than the root and is used most often with vegetables, soups, and desserts.

Mace – Has a pungent nutmeg taste. Use in custards and spicy desserts.

Nutmeg – Has a sweet, spicy flavor. Although sold whole or ground, the whole is superior in flavor when freshly ground. Use in desserts, Italian dishes, soups, and vegetable dishes.

Paprika – Comes from sweet red peppers and range from sweet and mild to hot and pungent. Most supermarkets carry the mild variety, ethnic markets carry the more pungent. Hungarian paprika is considered the best and is stronger than American. Use in most savory dishes, poultry, eggs, and as a topping on potatoes.

Turmeric – Has a pungent flavor with a hint of ginger and is a main ingredient in curry. It is bright-orange in color and can be substituted for saffron in many dishes. It is primarily used in Indian cooking, but can also be added to soups, stews, and vegetables.

SODIUM IN COMMONLY USED INGREDIENTS

Ingredient	Sod (mg)
Baking/Coating Mixes (1 oz)	
Panko crumbs	45
Plain bread crumbs	270
Seasoned bread crumbs	450
Mix (*Shake & Bake*)	800
Doughs/Pie Crusts	
Fillo dough, 1 sheet	91
Flour pie crust, ⅛	92
Graham pie crust, ⅛	108
Puff pastry, 1 sheet	1,260
Fats/Oils (1 tbsp)	
Oil, all, avg	0
Shortening/Lard	0
Butter	90
Margarine	100
Flour (¼ cup)	
All-purpose flour	0
Self-rising	360
All-purpose mix (*Bisquik*)	368
Leavening Agents (1 tsp)	
NSA baking powder	0
Baking powder	488
Baking soda	1,259
Seasonings (1 tsp)	
MSG	500
Lite salt	1,160
Meat tenderizer	1,680
Sea salt	2,280
Table salt	2,360
Sweeteners (¼ cup)	
Granulated sugar	0
Sugar substitute	0
Honey	4
Brown sugar	16
Corn syrup, light	60
Wine (1 cup)	
Table wine (red or white)	10
Cooking wine	1,456
Bouillon (1 cube or 1 tsp)	
Chicken or beef	890
LS bouillon	115
Broths (1 cup)	
Vegetable	654
Beef	782
Chicken	924
Low-sodium	140
Soups/Chili (1 cup)	
Tomato	558
Onion	635
Chicken noodle	844
Cream of mushroom	856
Clam chowder (white)	871
Vegetable beef	878
Clam chowder (red)	1,000
Chili with beans	1,080
Cheese (1 oz)	
Swiss cheese	65
Goat cheese	118
Brie	178
Cheddar	185
Mozzarella, part skim	189
Fresh mozzarella	85
Feta	316
Blue	326
American	473
Parmesan	496
Roquefort	513
Ricotta cheese, ¼ cup	65
Cream cheese	110
Mascarpone	15
Cottage cheese, ½ cup	420
Eggs	
Egg, 1 large	71
Egg substitute, 3 tbsp	85
Milk/Cream (¼ cup)	
Coconut milk	24
Milk, whole	26
Lower fat milk (2%)	29
Cream or Half-and-half	36
Evaporated milk	66
Condensed milk	70
Buttermilk	91
Sour Cream/Yogurt (¼ cup)	
Greek yogurt, plain	20
Yogurt, whole milk, plain	29
Sour cream	30
Lowfat sour cream	50
Condiments (1 tbsp)	
Mayonnaise	90
Light mayonnaise	124
Dijon-type mustard, 1 tsp	120
Yellow mustard, 1 tsp	60
Horseradish sauce	123
Ketchup	160
Capers/Olives (1 tbsp)	
Olives, ripe (black)	125
Olives, kalamata	220
Capers	310
Pickles/Relish (1 oz)	
Pickles, sweet	137
Pickles, bread and butter	190
Sweet pickle relish	244
Pickles, dill	228
Hot dog relish	328
Peanut Butter/Jelly (1 tbsp)	
Jam or jelly	6
Almond butter	37
Peanut butter	68
Salad Dressings (2 tbsp)	
Vinegar and oil	0
Honey mustard	154
Blue cheese/Roquefort	193
French	212
Ranch	270
Thousand island	289
Italian	292
Lowfat ranch	336
Caesar	363
Sauces (1 tbsp)	
Hollandaise	78
Sweet and sour sauce	86
Tartar sauce	100
Salsa	128
Cheese sauce	131
BBQ/Grilling sauce	175
Buffalo wing sauce	320
Cocktail sauce	189
Worcestershire sauce	195
Steak sauce	280
Hot pepper sauce	372
Teriyaki sauce	613
Soy sauce	878
Lite	576
Bread/Tortillas/Wraps (1)	
Bread, wheat	146
Sourdough/French	182
White	191
Rye	211
Focaccia, 2 oz	320
Tortilla/taco shells:	
Corn, soft, 6 inch	11
Corn, shelf-stable	80
Flour, 8 inch	364
Wrap (flatbread)	230

Ingredient	Sod (mg)
Pasta/Noodles (2 oz)	
Pasta (avg)	3
Fresh, refrig	33
Egg noodles	12
Grains (½ cup)	
Rice	0
Barley	18
Bulgur	24
Pasta/Pizza Sauce (¼ cup)	
Pizza sauce	240
Alfredo	360
Clam sauce, ½ cup	505
Marinara, ½ cup	577
Pesto, shelf-stable	609
Beans (½ cup)	
Canned:	
Soybeans	240
Cannellini	270
Lima beans	343
Kidney beans	370
Black beans	380
Reduced sodium	200
Garbanzo beans	420
Pork and beans	430
Pinto beans	470
Baked beans	570
Dried:	
Most beans (avg)	0
Tomatoes (canned) (½ cup)	
Tomato paste, 2 tbsp	20
Tomato purée	60
Tomatoes, whole	180
Tomatoes, diced/chopped	250
Tomato sauce	560
Vegetables (½ cup)	
Canned:	
Pumpkin	6
Sweet Potatoes/Yams	70
Beets	176
Sauerkraut, 2 tbsp	230
Peas	229
Green beans	235
Corn	273
Carrots	295
Asparagus	348
Fresh:	
Spinach, 1 cup	24

Ingredient	Sod (mg)
Celery, 1 med stalk	32
Carrot, 1 med	40
Beets	53
Artichoke (med)	120
Most other veggies	15 or less
Juices (1 cup)	
Fruit juice, avg	10
Tomato juice	585
Vegetable & fruit mix	52
Fruit (1 cup)	
Fresh:	
Honeydew, ¼	45
Cantaloupe, ¼	22
Most other fruit	6 or less
Canned:	
Most canned fruit	8 or less
Breakfast Meats (1 oz)	
Bacon	210
Turkey bacon	300
Canadian-style	214
Pork sausage, patty	285
Pork sausage, link	326
Meatless breakfast link	444
Beef/Lamb/Veal (4 oz)	
Beef, most cuts, avg	66
Beef, ground, lean	75
Corned beef, canned	1,107
Lamb, most cuts, avg	66
Lamb, shoulder, blade	71
Veal, shank, lean	96
Ham/Pork (4 oz)	
Ham steak, boneless, lean	1,240
Ham, chopped, canned	1,452
Pork shoulder, lean	86
Pork loin roast, lean	55
Chicken/Turkey (4 oz)	
Cornish game hen, ½	102
Turkey (without skin)	
Ground, lean	66
Dark meat	140
White meat	127
Chicken (without skin)	
Ground	68
Thigh	107
Breast	51
Rotisserie breast	394

Ingredient	Sod (mg)
Fish/Seafood, canned (3 oz)	
Oysters	95
Caviar, black/red, 1 tbsp	240
Sardines in oil	261
Tuna in water	320
Tuna in oil	337
Salmon, pink	324
Shrimp	360
Clams, minced/chopped	370
Crab	479
Herring, kippered, 2 oz	520
Anchovies, 1 oz	1,720
Fish/Seafood, fresh (3 oz)	
Trout	26
Tuna	35
Clams	48
Halibut or Cod	50
Salmon, Atlantic farmed	50
Smoked	571
Snapper	54
Swordfish	69
Anchovies	88
Shrimp	101
Imitation	599
Lobster	150
Oysters, Eastern farmed	151
Pacific	90
Crab, Blue or Dungeness	250
Imitation	450
Alaskan King	711
Sole (flounder)	252
Scallops	333
Hot Dogs/Sausages (1 oz)	
Italian sausage	230
Bratwurst	254
Braunschweiger	277
Chorizo	295
Meatless hot dog (1 link)	330
Kielbasa	336
Beef hot dog (1 link)	472
Turkey hot dog (1 link)	493
Luncheon Meats (2 oz)	
Roast beef	500
Turkey breast	502
Ham	530
Bologna	566
Pastrami	604
Salami	986

Sodium in Commonly Used Ingredients

WHICH FOODS HAVE LESS SODIUM?

You might be surprised to find all the places where salt sneaks into your diet. Take the following quiz to determine your sodium IQ. *NOTE: Numbers reflect generic averages. You may have a favorite that has much less than the generic!*

Which has less sodium?

1. An ounce of low salt wheat crackers, panko crumbs, or plain bread crumbs?
2. One-half cup instant chocolate pudding or regular, cooked pudding?
3. A cup of lowfat Greek yogurt or lowfat regular yogurt?
4. One cup of vegetable broth, beef broth, or chicken broth?
5. A cup of sweetened coconut flakes or shredded unsweetened coconut?
6. A cup of fresh lowfat buttermilk or a cup of buttermilk prepared from powder.?
7. A cup of instant oatmeal or a cup of quick-cooked oatmeal?
8. A slice of wheat bread, white bread, or sourdough?
9. A half cup of Marsala cooking wine or Marsala from the wine department?
10. A corn tortilla or flour tortilla?
11. Alaskan king crab, dungeness, or imitation crab?
12. A piece of frozen prepared flour pie crust or unroll pie crust?
13. A cup of coconut milk, almond milk, or rice milk?
14. ¼ cup tomato sauce or tomato purée?

Answers

1. Panko, 45mg (LS crackers 54mg; plain bread crumbs, 270mg)
2. Regular, 88mg (instant pudding has 357mg)
3. Greek, 78mg (regular lowfat has 159mg)
4. Beef broth, 493mg (vegetable, 654mg; chicken, 924mg)
5. Unsweetened, 41mg (sweetened 246mg)
6. Buttermilk powder, 34mg (fresh lowfat has 363mg)
7. Quick-cooked, 9mg (instant oatmeal has 180mg)
8. Wheat, 148mg (sourdough, 182mg, white has 191mg)
9. Wine department Marsala, 5mg (cooking wine averages 728mg)
10. 6" corn tortilla, 11mg (8" flour tortilla averages 364mg)
11. 3 oz dungeness, 250mg (imitation, 450mg; Alaskan king crab, 711mg)
12. ⅛ frozen pie shell, 92mg (⅛ unroll sheet has 140mg)
13. Rice milk, 94mg (canned coconut milk averages 96mg; shelf-stable almond milk has 145mg)
14. ¼ cup tomato purée, 30mg (¼ cup tomato sauce, 280mg)

ABOUT THE RECIPES

These recipes are all about making tasty food that's good for you and doesn't have too much sodium. Even if you're someone who usually adds a lot of salt to your food, you'll still love these dishes. They're also low in fat and cholesterol, and all have passed the "taste test" with family and friends.

As you browse the recipes, you'll see a variety of foods, including Asian, Mediterranean, Hispanic, and some good old favorites. Some are fancy enough for entertaining, but most are everyday meals that are easy to make.

A few of the recipes are more complex, but you can make most of them in 30 minutes or less. Like many of you, I don't have a lot of time to cook, so I use a lot of ready-made ingredients. If you have time to make things from scratch, I've also included recipes for pie crusts, mayonnaise, bread, and other basics.

If you're watching your salt for health reasons, your doctor may suggest you stay around 1,500mg a day. That means you should aim for about 500mg of salt at each meal (3 meals x 500mg = 1,500mg). Most of the recipes have less than 100mg of salt in a serving, so you'll have lots of yummy options to pick from.

Most ingredients are available at your local grocery store or big supermarkets, like Walmart, Kroger, Whole Foods, or Target (also included are private label/store brands from these larger retailers). For harder to find items, try Amazon or other online retailers, like Healthy Heart Market. To see a list of current low-salt products, visit **LowSaltFoods.com**.

Food manufacturers often change their products. So, it's important to check labels often, as it may have changed since the last time you used it.

Some of the low-sodium products I used in the previous edition are no longer available. And others have increased salt, which I've replaced with similar products... many with less salt than before!

Each recipe includes the brands used in the nutritional calculation, along with alternative products you can use (with an emphasis on products available nationwide). You'll find this information in the *"Total Sodium and Fat by Ingredient"* section.

The recipes are delicious when you follow them, but the final outcome depends on what products you use. You may like a different kind of flavoring, or the veggies or fruits aren't as good because of the time of year. Or the spices you use may have lost their potency. You may swap ingredients if you can't have certain foods, like milk, and use soy instead. Any of these variables can change the flavor of the dish.

So, it's a good idea to taste your food before you serve it. Once you know more about spices and which ones go well together, you can make small changes. Sometimes a bit more lemon juice or a little extra bouillon makes a big difference. And don't forget to write down what you learn from trying different things!

THE RECIPES

Recipes are divided into chapters based on courses—from appetizers to desserts. Each recipe includes:

Nutritional info – Serving analysis that shows calories, fat, saturated fat, cholesterol, carbohydrates, fiber, sugar, and sodium. All values are rounded off to the nearest whole number. Nutrients with less than 0.5 are shown as 0, those with 0.5 or greater are listed as 1.

Nutritional analysis is based on using lean meats and the lowest sodium products available. Values are determined by the USDA National Nutritional Database, food manufacturer and grocer websites, product labels, and author calculations.

Recipe Notes – Offers substitutions, cooking tips, and other helpful info.

Total Sodium and Fat By Ingredient – Shows ingredients that contain sodium or fat and the total amount in the recipe of each. For example, if a recipe calls for 4 ounces cream cheese or low fat cream cheese, the following is shown:

Sodium:
   4 oz cream cheese - 300mg
    or LF cream cheese - 480mg
Fat (Sat Fat):
   4 oz cream cheese - 36g (24g)
    or LF cream cheese - 24g (14g)

This is useful for comparing products you use to brands I use, so you can adjust the nutritional data. In this case, if you use a brand of cream cheese with 100mg sodium per ounce, the total sodium is 400mg (or 100mg more). If the recipe serves 4 people, that means each serving has an extra 25mg of sodium. This also helps you learn how much sodium is in frequently used ingredients.

Below sodium and fat numbers is *Brands used/ alternatives*. These are the products I often use plus alternative convenience items when I'm in a hurry. I've focused on using products and brands that are available nationwide.

Some recipes reference helpful hints and info on picking, storing, and cooking different foods. These are located together in *Cooking Tips and Food Notes*, pg 243.

Ingredients & Suggestions
Wine & Other Alcohols

Many dishes contain wine and other alcohol. If you prefer not using, feel free to substitute (see *Alcohol Substitutions*, pg 242, for suggestions).

Fats, Oils and Cooking Sprays

To keep fats and oils to a minimum, I suggest using a nonstick skillet when cooking. If you don't have one, coat your pan with a nonstick cooking spray. Not only does this keep food from sticking, you'll need less oil, butter, or margarine.

Olive Oil – This is my oil of choice, not only for the "healthy heart" benefits of polyunsaturated fats, but also for its subtle flavor. You can substitute vegetable oil, but it may not taste the same.

In salad dressings, I highly recommend using extra-virgin olive oil. Although more expensive than vegetable oils, to save money, use plain olive oil for cooking and extra-virgin for salad dressings. Once opened, try to use it within 6 months.

Butter and Margarine – Most recipes suggest unsalted butter or margarine. To cut down on fat, I usually pick margarine. But it can be hard to find unsalted margarine in regular stores. Luckily, you can buy some brands online, like on *Amazon*.

We calculate nutrition values using unsalted butter, unless mentioned otherwise. Both butter and margarine are shown in the *Total Sodium and Fat by Ingredient* section. If you use margarine, be sure to adjust the fat and saturated fat amounts.

Butter Spray – Another option to butter or margarine in some dishes is using a butter-like spray; it adds a butter taste but without the fat and salt. Spray it on top of potatoes, vegetables, and pastry doughs (it works well on phyllo sheets).

Eggs and Egg Substitutes

Research indicates that eating eggs may not be as bad as we once thought. According to two Harvard University studies, eating one egg or more a day posed no more risk for developing heart disease than consuming one egg a week or less. Of more concern is the amount of saturated fat consumed, which has a greater impact on raising cholesterol.

To keep fat and cholesterol to a minimum, use an egg substitute. Although some brands have no fat, they all have significant amounts of sodium (85mg or more compared to 71mg for a large egg).

FAT & SODIUM COMPARISON OF EGGS & EGG SUBSTITUTES

	Fat	Sat Fat	Sodium
2 eggs	10g	4g	142mg
1 egg and 3 tbsp egg substitute	5g	2g	156mg
6 tbsp substitute	0g	0g	170mg
4 egg whites	0g	0g	220mg

Many people use 2 egg whites instead of a whole egg, however, if you are watching your sodium intake, the whites are where the sodium resides (a large egg white has 55mg). I've found if more than one egg is needed, a combination of eggs, egg whites, or egg substitute helps keep both fat and sodium to a minimum. Below is a comparison for a recipe calling for 2 large eggs:

Unless specified, when a recipe calls for an egg, use a large size.

Sweeteners

Even though I often use sugar substitutes, the recipes are calculated using sugar. For those who don't want to use sugar, substitute your sweetener of choice.

Dairy Products

When I cook, I try to use less fat and choose low-fat or fat-free dairy products. Most dairy products have a lot of salt (varies widely within brands). For instance, one brand of lowfat sour cream may have 35mg sodium per 2 tablespoons and another, 15mg. It may not sound like much, but if you're using ½ cup, that's a difference of 80mg! So it's good to know how much salt is in different brands. That's one reason I wrote the **Pocket Guide to Low Sodium Foods**.

I understand not everyone likes using nonfat products. So, most of my recipes suggest low-fat ingredients. I've tried many of the dishes with fat-free products, and they still taste good, although some might not be as rich. Feel free to experiment. If you use a higher-fat product, it will taste more rich and creamy. And it might even have less salt... remember, when manufacturers remove fat, they usually add more sugar and salt! Below is a generic comparison of a variety of dairy products:

DAIRY PRODUCTS COMPARISON
Average sodium per ¼ cup (or 2 oz)

	Fat	Sat Fat	Sodium
Cream, heavy whipping	20g	12g	20mg
Milk, whole	2g	1g	26mg
Fat free	0g	0g	32mg
Half and half	8g	4g	36mg
Fat free	0g	0g	60mg
Yogurt, Greek	3g	1g	20mg
Sour cream	12g	6g	30mg
Lowfat	6g	4g	50mg
Fat free	0g	0g	84mg
Ricotta cheese, part-skim	5g	3g	62mg
Buttermilk	1g	0g	91mg
Cream cheese	17g	11g	230mg
Whipped	8g	6g	170mg
Light (Neufchâtel)	12g	8g	240mg
Fat free	0g	0g	504mg
Mascarpone	26g	14g	30mg
Cottage cheese	3g	1g	210mg
Lowfat	1g	0g	225mg

Adding creaminess: To make dishes creamy without too much fat or salt, there are some tricks. Instead of cream, you can mix sour cream with milk or evaporated milk. Use about 2 to 3 times more milk than sour cream.

You can also use tofu and milk. If a recipe asks for 1 cup of cream, use 5 ounces of soft tofu with ½ cup of nonfat milk or soy milk. This way, your dish will still be creamy, but with less fat and sodium.

Well, that's about it for the recipes and ingredients, now it's time to get started with the low-salt lifestyle. Hope you enjoy!

MEASUREMENTS & ABBREVIATIONS

MEASUREMENTS/EQUIVALENTS

Pinch	=	<1/16 teaspoon	=	0.01 oz	=	0.26 grams
Dash	=	<1/8 teaspoon	=	0.02 oz	=	0.58 grams
1½ teaspoons	=	½ tablespoon	=	0.25 oz	=	7 grams
3 teaspoons	=	1 tablespoon	=	0.5 oz	=	14 grams
2 tablespoons	=	⅛ cup	=	1 oz	=	28 grams
4 tablespoons	=	¼ cup	=	2 oz	=	56 grams
8 tablespoons	=	½ cup	=	4 oz	=	112 grams
12 tablespoons	=	¾ cup	=	6 oz	=	168 grams
16 tablespoons	=	1 cup	=	8 oz	=	224 grams

LIQUID

Dash	=	0.625 ml	=	2–3 drops
0.5 fl oz	=	15 ml	=	1 tablespoon
1 fl oz	=	30 ml	=	⅛ cup
2 fl oz	=	60 ml	=	¼ cup
4 fl oz	=	120 ml	=	½ cup
8 fl oz	=	240 ml	=	1 cup
16 fl oz	=	480 ml	=	1 pint
2 cups	=	1 pint	=	½ quart
4 cups	=	2 pints	=	1 quart
4 pints	=	2 quarts	=	½ gallon
8 pints	=	4 quarts	=	1 gallon

ABBREVIATIONS

carb	carbohydrates		**NF**	nonfat
chol	cholesteral		**NSA**	no salt added
envl	envelope		**oz**	ounce(s)
FF	fat free		**pkg**	package(s)
fl oz	fluid ounce(s)		**sat fat**	saturated fat
g	gram(s)		**SF**	salt free
lb	pound(s)		**sl**	slice(s)
LF	low fat		**sm**	small
lrg	large		**sod**	sodium
LS	low salt/low sodium		**tbsp**	tablespoon
med	medium		**tsp**	teaspoon
mg	milligram(s)		**w/**	with
ml	milliliter(s)		**w/o**	without

APPETIZERS

DIPS & SPREADS
Spicy Roasted Red Pepper Hummus 26
Caramelized Onion Dip............... 27
Warm Bean Dip....................... 28
Guacamole........................... 28
Chervil Cheese Dip.................. 29
Mushroom Pate with Port & Almonds .. 30

FINGER FOODS
Celery with Pimento-Walnut Cheese.... 31
Chive-Cheese Stuffed Celery.......... 31
Stuffed Mushrooms................... 32
Spicy Crab Stuffed Mushrooms........ 33
Salmon Tortilla Roll-Ups............ 34
Spicy & Cheesy Tortilla Swirls...... 34
Spinach & Goat Cheese Rolls 35
Cheesy Leek & Spinach Rolls 35
Jalapeño-Cheese Rolls 36
Spinach & Goat Cheese Wontons....... 37
Crispy Pork & Shrimp Wontons 38
   Chinese Hot Mustard.............. 38

DIPS & SPREADS

Spicy Roasted Red Pepper Hummus

Sodium Per Serving – 12mgMakes 2 cups (16 servings)

Hummus is a thick and delicious Middle Eastern sauce made from garbanzo beans and sesame paste, and whips up quickly in a blender or food processor. This version gets added zip from roasted red pepper and a jalapeño. Serve with pita bread pieces and crackers or use as a dip with veggies. This also makes a yummy spread on sandwiches and wraps.

- 1 (15-oz) can NSA garbanzo beans, drained and liquid reserved[1]
- 1 red bell pepper, roasted and chopped or 4 oz canned roasted red pepper[2]
- 2 cloves garlic, minced
- 3–4 tablespoons tahini[3]
- 1–2 tablespoons lemon juice
- 1 tablespoon olive oil
- 1 teaspoon ground cumin
- ¼ teaspoon garlic powder
- 1 jalapeño, seeded and chopped, or ⅛ teaspoon cayenne pepper[4]
- Pinch salt (optional)[5]
- 1 tablespoon chopped fresh Italian parsley or 1 teaspoon dried (optional)

1. Combine all ingredients in a food processor or blender; pulse until smooth and the consistency of peanut butter. If hummus is grainy, add ½ tablespoon olive oil. If too thick, thin with reserved bean liquid, a tablespoon at a time.
2. Serve with low-salt pita bread pieces and crackers or use as a dip with veggies.

NUTRITIONAL INFO PER 2 TBSP SERVING: Calories 58, Fat 3g (Saturated Fat 0g), Cholesterol 0mg, Carbohydrates 6g (Fiber 2g, Sugar 1g), Sodium 12mg (3mg without salt)

Recipe Notes

1 – Canned garbanzo beans (also called chickpeas) average 420mg sodium per ½ cup, low salt varieties have 1400mg, and NSA brands have 10mg-30mg (visit LowSaltFoods.com, for a list of NSA products). If NSA beans are unavailable, you can cook them from scratch using dried garbanzo beans (see *Cooking Dried Beans*, pg 243).

2 – To roast peppers, see *Roasting Peppers*, pg 251. If using canned roasted peppers, the sodium per serving increases from 12mg to about 40mg.

3 – Tahini (or sesame paste) is made from ground sesame seeds. Before using, stir thoroughly to incorporate the oil on top.

4 – If you like a lot of heat, leave some of the seeds in the jalapeño.

5 – I add a tiny bit of salt to bring out the flavors, but it tastes almost as good without it.

TOTAL SODIUM & FAT BY INGREDIENT

Sodium:
- 15 oz NSA garbanzo beans - 35mg
- 1 red pepper - 5mg or 4 oz roasted red pepper - 440mg
- 2 cloves garlic - 1mg
- 1 t cumin - 4mg
- Pinch salt - 146mg
- 1 T parsley - 2mg

Fat (Sat Fat):
- 15 oz NSA garbanzos - 7g (0g)
- 3 T tahini - 29g (5g)
- 1 T olive oil - 14g (2g)
- 1 t cumin - 1g (0g)

Brands used/alternatives:
- *Westbrae Natural* Garbanzo Beans
- *Eden Foods* Roasted Tahini
- *Mt Olive* Roasted Red Peppers

CARAMELIZED ONION DIP

Sodium Per Serving – 12mg Makes 2 cups (16 servings)

If the only onion dip you've tasted is made with dried soup mix, just wait until you try this delicious dip made with caramelized onions. Allow at least 2 hours before serving (overnight is even better), as the longer this sits, the stronger the onion flavor.

- **1 tablespoon olive oil**
- **1 tablespoon unsalted butter or margarine**
- **1 large yellow onion, finely chopped[1]**
- **1½ cups (12 oz) lowfat or regular sour cream[2]**
- **1 clove garlic, finely minced**
- **2 tablespoons finely chopped fresh chives or green onions (green part only)**
- **2 tablespoons chopped fresh basil (optional)[3]**
- **½ teaspoon lemon juice or vinegar**
- **¼ teaspoon garlic powder**
- **¼ teaspoon onion powder**
- **⅛ teaspoon ground black pepper**
- **Pinch cayenne pepper**

1. Heat oil and butter in a skillet over medium-high heat; add onions. Cook, stirring constantly, until onions begin to brown, 3 to 4 minutes. Decrease heat to medium-low; continue to cook, stirring occasionally, until onions are golden brown and caramelized, about 30 minutes. Remove from heat and let cool slightly.

2. In a bowl, mix the caramelized onions with the sour cream and remaining ingredients. Cover and refrigerate at least 2 hours or overnight. Serve with vegetables, low-salt chips, or crackers.

NUTRITIONAL INFO PER 2 TBSP SERVING: Calories 48, Fat 3g (Sat Fat 2g), Chol 9mg, Carb 2g (Fiber 0g, Sugar 0g), Sodium 12mg

Recipe Notes

1 – Yellow onions caramelize best, as they have less water than other onions (see *Caramelizing Onions*, pg 245).

2 – To minimize fat, use a combination of lowfat and regular sour cream (see *Dairy Products Comparison*, pg 23).

3 – Although optional, basil compliments the sweetness of the onions and adds another layer of flavor.

TOTAL SODIUM & FAT BY INGREDIENT

Sodium:
- 1 onion - 4mg
- 1½ c LF sour cream - 180mg
  or reg sour cream - 180mg
- 1 clove garlic - 1mg

Fat (Sat Fat):
- 1 T olive oil - 14g (2g)
- 1 T NSA butter - 12g (7g)
  or NSA margarine - 9g (4g)
- 1½ c LF sour cream - 30g (18g)
  or reg sour cream - 60g (42g)

Brands used/alternatives:
Daisy Light Sour Cream

Warm Bean Dip

Sodium Per Serving – 41mg Makes 2½ cups (20 servings)

This crowd-pleasing dip is creamy and delicious. It also is great as a spread in tacos, sandwiches, and wraps.

- **2 cups *Quick Refried Beans (pg 169)* or 1 (15-oz) can lower sodium refried beans**[1]
- **2 oz diced green chiles**
- **2 oz (½ cup) Swiss cheese, shredded**
- **2 oz (½ cup) Cheddar cheese, shredded**
- **¼ cup lowfat or regular sour cream**
- **2 tablespoons salsa (optional)**[2]

1. In a saucepan over medium-low heat, combine beans, green chiles, Swiss and Cheddar cheeses. Cook, stirring frequently, until cheese melts, about 5 minutes.
2. Mix in sour cream and salsa; heat through.
3. Serve with low-salt tortilla chips.

   NOTE: Dip thickens as it cools; reheat to return it to original consistency.

NUTRITIONAL INFO PER 2 TBSP SERVING: Calories 58, Fat 4g (Sat Fat 2g), Chol 8mg, Carb 4g (Fiber 2g, Sugar 1g), Sodium 41mg (72mg with reduced sodium refried beans)

TOTAL SODIUM & FAT BY INGREDIENT

WARM BEAN DIP
Sodium:
- 2 c *Quick Refried Beans* - 106mg or lower salt beans - 735mg
- 2 oz green chiles - 190mg
- 2 oz Swiss cheese - 100mg
- 2 oz cheddar cheese - 340mg
- ¼ c LF sour cream - 40mg or reg sour cream - 40mg
- 2 T salsa - 40mg

Fat (Sat Fat):
- 2 c *Quick Beans* - 30g (10g) or lower salt beans - 12g (0g)
- 2 oz Swiss - 18g (10g)
- 2 oz Cheddar - 18g (12g)
- ¼ c LF sour cream - 5g (3g) or reg sour cream - 10g (7g)

Brands used/alternatives:
- *Amy's Light in Sodium* Refried Beans
- *La Preferida* Organic Diced Green Chiles
- *Great Value* Swiss Cheese
- *Kraft* Shredded Cheddar Cheese
- *Daisy Light* Sour Cream
- *Frog Ranch* Salsa

Guacamole

Sodium Per Serving – 3mg Makes 1 cup (8 servings)

This guacamole is simple to make and full of flavor. Serve it as a dip with chips or as a spread in tacos, sandwiches, and wraps. Using a ripe avocado is essential, not only for taste, but also consistency. If making ahead of time, leave the avocado pit in the guacamole until ready to serve (this helps prevent the guacamole from turning brown).

- **1 ripe avocado**
- **1 tablespoon finely chopped sweet onion**
- **2–3 teaspoons salsa**
- **½ teaspoon lime juice (optional)**

1. Halve the avocado, remove pit, and scoop out flesh. Mash flesh with a fork; mix in the onion, salsa, and lime juice. Serve with low salt tortilla chips.

NUTRITIONAL INFO PER 2 TBSP SERVING: Calories 36, Fat 3g (Sat Fat 0g), Chol 0mg, Carb 2g (Fiber 1g, Sugar 0g), Sodium 3mg

GUACAMOLE
Sodium:
- 1 avocado - 11mg
- 1 tbsp sweet onion - 1mg
- 2 t salsa - 13mg

Fat (Sat Fat):
- 1 avocado - 21g (3g)

Brands used/alternatives:
- *Frog Ranch* Salsa

Recipe Notes

1 – Over the past several years the sodium in canned refried beans has slowly increased, averaging 450mg sodium in a ½ cup. LS brands are harder to find but a couple are *Amy's Light in Sodium* Refried Beans (210mg per ½ cup) and *Santiago* LS refried bean mix with 140mg a serving. Visit LowSaltFoods.com, for more low-salt options.

2 – The optional salsa in the bean dip adds more flavor, but tastes good without it. Most bottled salsa average 272mg sodium per 2 tbsp. Look for varieties with less than 80mg a serving.

CHERVIL CHEESE DIP

Sodium Per Serving – 39mg Makes 2½ cups (20 servings)

My long-time friend, Geraldine Scully, brought this dip to a gathering and it was devoured in a matter of minutes. The garlic, combined with the subtle anise flavor of the fresh chervil is scrumptious. The original had lots of sodium, which I've lowered by using mascarpone cheese. Make this several hours ahead of time to let the flavors intensify. NOTE: While dried chervil may be substituted, fresh chervil really makes this dip.

- 8 oz mascarpone[1]
- 8 oz regular or lowfat cream cheese[2]
- 2 tablespoons mayonnaise
- 2 cloves garlic, finely minced
- 2 tablespoons chopped fresh chervil or 2 teaspoons dried[3]
- 2 tablespoons chopped fresh Italian parsley

1. Mix all ingredients together until well blended. Serve with low-salt crackers or assorted fresh vegetables.

NUTRITIONAL INFO PER 2 TBSP SERVING: Calories 99, Fat 10g (Saturated Fat 5g), Cholesterol 28mg, Carbohydrates 1g (Fiber 0g, Sugar 1g), Sodium 39mg

Recipe Notes

1 – Mascarpone, or "Italian cream cheese", is creamier and richer than American cream cheese. Although it has more fat, it is low in sodium

2 – To reduce fat and keep sodium to a minimum, use a lower fat alternative or combine with regular cream cheese. See *Cream Cheese Comparison*, pg 247, for more info.

3 – Chervil is one of the components of fines herbes and is similar in taste to parsley, but with a hint of licorice. Fresh chervil is often hard to find, but if you do locate it, you're in for a treat.

TOTAL SODIUM & FAT BY INGREDIENT

Sodium:
- 8 oz mascarpone - 80mg
- 8 oz cream cheese - 600mg or LF cream cheese - 840mg
- 2 T mayo - 100mg
- 2 cloves garlic - 1mg
- 2 T chervil - 2mg
- 2 T parsley - 4mg

Fat (Sat Fat):
- 8 oz mascarpone - 96g (56g)
- 8 oz cream cheese - 80g (48g) or LF cream cheese - 48g (28g)
- 2 T mayo - 22g (3g)

Brands used/alternatives:
BelGioioso Mascarpone
Green Valley Lactose-Free Cream Cheese
Great Value Neufchâtel Cheese
Chosen Foods Classic Mayo with Avocado Oil

Mushroom Pate with Port & Almonds

Sodium Per Serving – 1mg | Makes 2½ cups (20 servings)

My neighbor, Susie Gaines, brought this delicious spread to one of our summer barbecues. Serve with low-salt crackers or baguette-size bread slices. This also makes a great pita sandwich with cream cheese and sliced apple.

- **2 tablespoons all-purpose flour**
- **¼ cup port or Marsala wine**
- **2 tablespoons unsalted butter or margarine**
- **8 oz cremini or button mushrooms, finely chopped (about 3 cups)[1]**
- **¼ cup finely chopped sweet onion**
- **1 clove garlic, finely chopped**
- **¼ teaspoon garlic powder**
- **⅛ teaspoon ground black pepper**
- **⅛ teaspoon freshly ground nutmeg**
- **⅓ cup sliced almonds, toasted[2]**
- **1 tablespoon chopped fresh chives**

1. Mix together the flour and port until smooth; set aside.
2. Melt butter in a skillet over medium-high heat; add mushrooms, onion, garlic, garlic powder, pepper, and nutmeg. Cook, stirring frequently, until mushrooms and onions are soft, 2 to 3 minutes. Mix in port mixture, stirring constantly, until liquid begins to thicken, 1 to 2 minutes.
3. Place one-half of the mushroom mixture in a blender or food processor and pulse until a smooth paste.
4. Combine the purée with the remaining mushroom mixture; stir in the almonds and chives. Cover and chill several hours. Serve with low-salt crackers or bread slices.

NUTRITIONAL INFO PER 2 TBSP SERVING: Calories 32, Fat 2g (Sat Fat 1g), Chol 3mg, Carb 2g (Fiber 0g, Sugar 1g), Sodium 1mg

Recipe Notes
1 – Cremini and button mushrooms are similar, but criminis have more flavor (see *Mushrooms*, pg 250, for varieties, cleaning, and storage).
2 – Toasting brings out the flavor of the nuts (see *Toasting Nuts*, pg 250, for toasting methods).

TOTAL SODIUM & FAT BY INGREDIENT

Sodium:
- ¼ c port or Marsala wine - 5mg
- 8 oz mushrooms - 11mg
- 2 T onion - 2mg
- 1 clove garlic - 1mg

Fat (Sat Fat):
- 8 oz mushrooms - 1g (0g)
- 2 T NSA butter - 23g (14g)
  or NSA margarine - 18g (7g)
- ⅓ c almonds - 19g (1g)

FINGER FOODS

Celery with Pimento-Walnut Cheese

Sodium Per Serving – 51mg Makes about 20 appetizers

Stuffed celery is easy to make and is a great munchie. This yummy spread was passed on to me from a close friend. Arrange on a platter and serve at your next gathering, or keep a few handy for a tasty lowfat, low-carb snack. The cheese spread is also good on crackers, finger sandwiches, and burgers.

- **8 oz whipped cream cheese**[1]
- **2 tablespoons lowfat sour cream**
- **2 tablespoons finely chopped walnuts or pecans**
- **2 tablespoons chopped pimento**
- **2–3 drops hot pepper sauce, such as Tabasco**
- **10 large celery stalks, cut in half**

1. Combine all ingredients except celery; mix well.
2. Spread onto celery and serve.

NUTRITIONAL INFO PER APPETIZER: Calories 35, Fat 3g (Sat Fat 1g), Chol 7mg, Carb 2g (Fiber 0g, Sugar 1g), Sodium 51mg

Chive-Cheese Stuffed Celery

Sodium Per Serving – 50mg Makes about 20 appetizers

Make the filling several hours ahead of time to allow the flavor of the chives to permeate the cream cheese.

- **8 oz whipped cream cheese**[1]
- **1 tablespoon chopped fresh chives**
- **½ teaspoon garlic powder**
- **½ teaspoon paprika**[2]
- **10 large celery stalks, cut in half**

1. Combine cream cheese, chives, garlic powder, and paprika; mix well.
2. Spread onto celery and serve.

NUTRITIONAL INFO PER APPETIZER: Calories 24, Fat 2g (Sat Fat 1g), Chol 6mg, Carb 2g (Fiber 0g, Sugar 0g), Sodium 50mg

---

TOTAL SODIUM & FAT BY INGREDIENT

CELERY PIMENTO-WALNUT
Sodium:
 8 oz whip cream cheese - 680mg
 2 T LF sour cream - 15mg
 2 T pimento - 3mg
 10 celery stalks - 320mg
Fat (Sat Fat):
 8 oz whipped cheese - 32g (20g)
 2 T LF sour cream - 3g (2g)
 2 T walnuts - 18g (2g)
 10 celery stalks - 1g (0g)
Brands used/alternatives:
 Philadelphia Whipped Cream Cheese
 Daisy Light Sour Cream

CHIVE-CHEESE STUFF CELERY
Sodium:
 8 oz whip cream cheese - 680mg
 10 celery stalks - 320mg
Fat (Sat Fat):
 8 oz whipped cheese - 36g (24g)
 10 celery stalks - 1g (0g)
Brands used/alternatives:
 Philadelphia Whipped Cream Cheese

Recipe Notes

1 – Whipped cream cheese is simply cheese mixed with air. It's less dense and not as rich as regular cream cheese, and has less sodium and half the fat. You can substitute it in many dishes that don't need richness and creaminess. For a comparison of cream cheese varieties, see *Cream Cheese Comparison*, pg 247.

2 – Paprika comes in sweet or hot varieties. Most American paprika is sweet, while Hungarian paprika is more pungent. Hungarian is available in ethnic or gourmet shops and some large supermarkets. Use either in this dish, but if you like a little heat, use the hot variety.

Other Veggie Stuffers
In addition to celery, other favorite stuffers are cherry tomatoes, peppadews, mini sweet peppers, and mushrooms. Scoop out the centers and stuff with the filling of your choice.

STUFFED MUSHROOMS

Sodium Per Serving – 6mg   Makes 24 appetizers

These mushrooms, stuffed with seasoned bread crumbs and topped with melted cheese, are the perfect party finger food.

- 1 cup chopped mushrooms, any type or combination, such as button, cremini, or wild varieties[1]
- ¾ cup LS plain bread crumbs[2]
- ⅓ cup chopped fresh Italian parsley
- 1 tablespoon olive oil
- 1 tablespoon unsalted butter or margarine, melted
- ½ teaspoon garlic powder
- ½ teaspoon dried rosemary, crushed
- ½ teaspoon dried sage
- ½ teaspoon dried thyme
- ¼ teaspoon ground black pepper
- 24 large (2–3 inch) button or cremini mushrooms, stemmed[1]
- 2 oz Swiss cheese, shredded (about ½ cup)

1. Preheat oven to 400°F (200°C).
2. In a large bowl, combine the chopped mushrooms, bread crumbs, parsley, olive oil, butter, garlic powder, rosemary, sage, thyme, and pepper; mix well.
3. Fill mushroom caps with bread crumb mixture; arrange in a large oven-proof dish and bake in a preheated oven for 20 minutes. Remove and sprinkle cheese on top of mushrooms; return to oven and bake another 4 to 5 minutes, until cheese melts.

NUTRITIONAL INFO PER MUSHROOM: Calories 37, Fat 2g (Sat Fat 1g), Chol 3mg, Carb 4g (Fiber 1g, Sugar 1g), Sodium 6mg

Recipe Notes

1. For info on mushroom varieties, cleaning, and storage, see *Mushrooms*, pg 250.
2. Instead of plain, use seasoned bread crumbs and reduce sage, thyme, and rosemary to ¼ tsp each. You can also make fresh bread crumbs (see *Bread Crumbs*, pg 244).

TOTAL SODIUM & FAT BY INGREDIENT

Sodium:
- 1 c + 24 mushrooms - 33mg
- ⅓ c parsley - 11mg
- 2 oz Swiss cheese - 100mg

Fat (Sat Fat):
- 1 c + 24 mushrooms - 2g (0g)
- ¾ cup NSA crumbs - 3g (0g)
- 1 T olive oil - 14g (2g)
- 1 T NSA butter - 12g (7g) or NSA margarine - 9g (4g)
- 2 oz NSA Swiss - 18g (10g)

Brands used/alternatives:
4C Salt-Free Bread Crumbs
Great Value Swiss Cheese

Spicy Crab Stuffed Mushrooms

Sodium Per Serving – 51mg Makes 24 appetizers

These spicy mushrooms were inspired by my neighbor, Bill Gaines. Although his original recipe was loaded with sodium, I think you'll agree that they are downright yummy even with a few low-salt modifications. If you like it hot and spicy, add more hot pepper sauce, cayenne pepper, or crushed red pepper flakes.

- 1 (6-oz) can crabmeat, drained
- 8 oz regular or lowfat cream cheese, at room temperature[1]
- 1 tablespoon chopped fresh Italian parsley (optional)
- 2 teaspoons finely minced celery
- 2 cloves garlic, minced
- 1 teaspoon Worcestershire sauce
- 4–5 drops hot pepper sauce, such as *Tabasco*
- 1/8 teaspoon garlic powder
- 1/8 teaspoon ground white pepper
- 24 large (2–3 inch) cremini or button mushrooms, stemmed[2]
- 2 oz Swiss cheese, shredded (about 1/2 cup)
- Pinch cayenne pepper or hot paprika (optional)

1. Preheat oven to 350°F (175°C). Spray a large oven-proof dish with nonstick cooking spray.
2. In a large bowl, combine crab, cream cheese, parsley, celery, garlic, Worcestershire, hot pepper sauce, garlic powder, and white pepper; mix well.
3. Fill mushroom caps with crab mixture and arrange in prepared baking dish; bake in a preheated oven for 15 minutes. Remove and sprinkle with cheese and cayenne; return to oven and bake another 5 minutes, or until cheese melts. Serve immediately.

NUTRITIONAL INFO PER MUSHROOM: Calories 54, Fat 4g (Sat Fat 2g), Chol 17mg, Carb 4g (Fiber 1g, Sugar 1g), Sodium 51mg

Recipe Notes

1 – To reduce fat and keep sodium to a minimum, use a lower fat alternative or combine with regular cream cheese. See *Cream Cheese Comparison*, pg 247, for more info.

2 – Cremini and button mushrooms are similar, but criminis have more flavor. For additional info on mushroom varieties, cleaning, and storage, see *Mushrooms*, pg 250.

TOTAL SODIUM & FAT BY INGREDIENT

Sodium:
- 6 oz crab - 480mg
- 8 oz cream cheese - 600mg or LF cream cheese - 840mg
- 1 T parsley - 2mg
- 2 garlic cloves - 1mg
- 1 t Worcestershire - 20mg
- 4 drops hot pepper sauce - 2mg
- 24 mushrooms - 29mg
- 2 oz Swiss cheese - 100mg

Fat (Sat Fat):
- 6 oz crab - 3g (0g)
- 8 oz cream cheese - 80g (48g) or LF cream cheese - 48g (28g)
- 24 mushrooms - 1g (0g)
- 2 oz Swiss - 18g (10g)

Brands used/alternatives:
Kroger Premium Lump Crab
Green Valley Lactose-Free Cream Cheese
Great Value Neufchâtel Cheese
Robbie's Worcestershire Sauce
Great Value Swiss Cheese

Salmon Tortilla Roll-Ups

Sodium Per Serving – 27mg Makes 60 appetizers

Prepare salmon filling the day before; cover and refrigerate to let the flavors intensify. This filling is also delicious as a spread on crackers.

- **8 oz whipped cream cheese**[1]
- **3 oz LS canned salmon or 3 oz cooked salmon**[2]
- **1 tablespoon finely chopped green onion (green part only) or fresh chives**
- **1 tablespoon finely minced celery**
- **¼ teaspoon garlic powder**
- **1–2 drops *Liquid Smoke* (optional)**[3]
- **10 LS flour tortillas**

1. Combine all ingredients except tortillas.
2. Evenly divide salmon mixture; spread onto each tortilla and roll up. Cover with plastic wrap and refrigerate at least one hour. Slice each roll into 6 pieces and serve cut-side up to display the filling.

NUTRITIONAL INFO PER APPETIZER: Calories 30, Fat 1g (Saturated Fat 1g), Cholesterol 3mg, Carbohydrates 4g (Fiber 0g, Sugar 0g), Sodium 27mg

Spicy & Cheesy Tortilla Swirls

Sodium Per Serving – 27mg Makes 60 appetizers

These tasty appetizers are simple to prepare and add color to the buffet table. The optional salsa and cilantro add even more flavor. The cheese spread is also good on crackers and in sandwiches.

- **8 oz whipped cream cheese**[1]
- **2 tablespoons chopped pimento**
- **2 tablespoons diced green chiles**
- **1 green onion, minced**
- **1 jalapeño, seeded and chopped**
- **¼ teaspoon onion powder or garlic powder**
- **2–3 tablespoons salsa (optional)**[4]
- **1–2 tablespoons chopped fresh cilantro (optional)**
- **10 LS flour tortillas**

1. Mix together all ingredients except tortillas.
2. Evenly divide cheese mixture; spread on each tortilla and roll up. Cover with plastic wrap and refrigerate at least one hour. Slice each roll into 6 pieces and serve cut-side up, showing the colorful swirls.

NUTRITIONAL INFO PER APPETIZER: Calories 29, Fat 1g (Sat Fat 1g), Chol 2mg, Carb 4g (Fiber 0g, Sugar 0g), Sodium 27mg

Recipe Notes

1 – Whipped cream cheese is simply cheese mixed with air. It's less dense and not as rich as regular cream cheese, and has less sodium and half the fat. To reduce fat and keep sodium to a minimum, combine regular cream cheese with lower fat alternatives (see *Cream Cheese Comparison*, pg 247, for more info).

2 – Canned salmon averages 465mg sodium per 3 oz, LS varieties have about 100mg (see LowSaltFoods.com, for a list of LS brands).

3 – The original recipe, which I've desalted, used smoked salmon, which is loaded with sodium (666mg per 3 oz). Instead, I add *Liquid Smoke* (available at grocers in the sauces and marinades aisle) to give it a smoky flavor.

4 – Most bottled tomato salsas average 256mg sodium per 2 tbsp, bean and corn salsa has 180mg, and fresh salsa, 142mg (visit LowSaltFoods.com, for LS products).

TOTAL SODIUM & FAT BY INGREDIENT

SALMON TORTILLA ROLL-UPS
Sodium:
- 8 oz whipped cheese - 680mg
- 3 oz LS salmon - 85mg
- 1 T celery - 1mg
- 10 LS flour tortillas - 850mg

Fat (Sat Fat):
- 8 oz whipped cheese - 36g (24g)
- 3 oz LS salmon - 4g (1g)
- 10 LS flour tortillas - 35g (15g)

Brands used/alternatives:
Philadelphia Whip Cream Cheese
Wild Planet NSA Wild Pink Salmon
La Banderita LS Flour Tortillas

SPICY & CHEESY SWIRLS
Sodium:
- 8 oz whipped cheese - 680mg
- 2 T pimento - 3mg
- 2 T green chiles - 45mg
- 1 green onion - 2mg
- 2 T LS Salsa - 40mg
- 1 T cilantro - 1mg
- 10 LS flour tortillas - 850mg

Fat (Sat Fat):
- 8 oz whipped cheese - 36g (24g)
- 10 LS flour tortillas - 35g (15g)

Brands used/alternatives:
Philadelphia Whip Cream Cheese
La Preferida Organic Diced Green Chiles
Frog Ranch Salsa
La Banderita LS Flour Tortillas

SPINACH & GOAT CHEESE ROLLS

Sodium Per Serving – 28mg   Makes 32 appetizers

Normally made with phyllo dough, these mouth-watering treats, reminiscent of spanakopita, use low-sodium egg roll wrappers.

- 1 tablespoon olive oil
- 4 cloves garlic, finely minced
- 1 shallot, finely minced
- 1 (10-oz) package frozen chopped spinach, thawed and squeezed dry, or 16 oz fresh spinach, cooked
- 3 tablespoons chopped fresh Italian parsley
- 4 oz goat cheese[1]
- 1 egg, beaten[2]
- ¼ teaspoon paprika
- ⅛ teaspoon freshly ground nutmeg[3]
- *Egg Roll Wraps (pg 205)* or 8 LS egg roll wrappers[4]
- Canola or vegetable oil, for frying

1. Heat oil in a skillet over medium heat; add garlic and shallots. Cook, stirring constantly, until shallots begin to soften, about 2 minutes. Transfer to a bowl and combine with spinach, parsley, goat cheese, and egg. Season with paprika and nutmeg.
2. Spread one-eighth filling on one side of the wrapper to within one-quarter inch of the edges; roll up like a jelly-roll, folding in sides one-quarter inch (this keeps filling from oozing out when frying). Repeat with remaining filling and wrappers.
3. Heat several tablespoons oil in a skillet over medium-high heat; fry rolls until golden on all sides. Remove and drain on paper towel. Slice into 4 pieces and serve.

NUTRITIONAL INFO PER APPETIZER*: Calories 52, Fat 2g (Sat Fat 1g), Chol 16mg, Carb 7g (Fiber 0g, Sugar 0g), Sodium 28mg (37mg with LS wrappers) *Does not include oil for frying

---

VARIATION
CHEESY LEEK & SPINACH ROLLS
1. Omit the shallot and goat cheese; substitute 1 chopped leek (white and light green parts), ⅓ cup ricotta cheese, and 3 tablespoons chopped walnuts.

NUTRITIONAL INFO PER APPETIZER*: Calories 45, Fat 1g (Sat Fat 0g), Chol 14mg, Carb 7g (Fiber 0g, Sugar 0g), Sodium 23g (32mg with LS packaged wrappers) *Does not include oil for frying

---

TOTAL SODIUM & FAT BY INGREDIENT

Sodium:
- 4 garlic cloves - 2mg
- 1 shallot - 2mg
- 10 oz spinach - 360mg
- 4 oz goat cheese - 220mg
- 3 T parsley - 6mg
- 1 egg - 70mg
- 8 *Egg Roll Wraps* - 222mg
  or LS egg roll wrappers - 520mg

Fat (Sat Fat):
- 1 T olive oil - 14g (2g)
- 4 oz goat cheese - 24g (16g)
- 1 egg - 5g (2g)
- 8 *Egg Roll Wraps* - 7g (2g)
  or LS wrappers - 0g (0g)

Brands used/alternatives:
Birds Eye Chopped Baby Spinach
Vermont Creamery Herb Chèvre
Twin Dragon Egg Roll Wrapper

Recipe Notes
1– Goat cheese can range from sweet and mild to tangy and sharp. There's a wide range of sodium from 50mg-140mg an oz, depending on the type (soft, semi-soft, etc).
2 – To keep fat to a minimum, use an egg substitute. See *Eggs and Egg Substitutes*, pg 23, for a comparison of fat and sodium in eggs and egg substitutes.
3 – Freshly grated nutmeg is far superior in taste to the pre-ground variety.
4 – The NSA wrappers I previously used are no longer available, however, a few manufacturers offer LS wraps (see *Egg Roll Wrappers*, pg 248, for more info).

Jalapeño-Cheese Rolls

Sodium Per Serving – 26mg Makes 32 appetizers

These hot and spicy treats are a big hit at social gatherings. Make ahead of time and warm in the microwave or oven before serving. The spicy spread is also good on crackers, sandwiches, and wraps.

- **8 oz regular or lowfat cream cheese, at room temperature[1]**
- **2 tablespoons chopped roasted red peppers or pimento**
- **1 jalapeño, seeded and chopped[2]**
- **Egg Roll Wraps (pg 205) or 8 LS egg roll wrappers[3]**
- **Canola or vegetable oil, for frying**

1. *Cheese Spread:* Mix cream cheese with pimento and jalapeños.
2. Spread one-eighth filling (about 2 tablespoons) on one side of the wrapper to within one-quarter inch of the edges; roll up like a jelly-roll, folding in sides one-quarter inch (this keeps filling from oozing out when frying). Repeat with remaining filling and wrappers.
3. Heat several tablespoons oil in a skillet over medium-high heat; fry rolls until golden on all sides. Remove and drain on a paper towel. Slice each roll into 4 pieces and serve warm.

NUTRITIONAL INFO PER APPETIZER*: Calories 56, Fat 2g (Saturated Fat 2g), Cholesterol 13mg, Carbohydrates 7g (Fiber 0g, Sugar 0g), Sodium 26mg (35mg with LS wrappers) *Does not include oil for frying

Recipe Notes

1 – Substitute whipped cream cheese, although it's less dense and not as rich as regular cream cheese, it has less sodium and half the fat. To reduce fat and keep sodium to a minimum, combine regular cream cheese with lower fat alternatives (see *Cream Cheese Comparison*, pg 247, for more info).

2 – On a scale of 1 to 5, jalapeños are a 3, with most of the heat contained in the seeds and veins.

CAUTION: When handling hot chiles, wear rubber gloves, as the oils of the pepper are very potent. A piece of plastic wrap or a sandwich bag also works to hold the pepper. If you touch the pepper with your bare fingers, wash your hands thoroughly and be sure to keep your fingers away from your eyes or you'll be in sheer agony!

3 – The NSA wrappers I previously used are no longer available, however a few manufacturers offer LS wraps (see *Egg Roll Wrappers*, pg 248, for more info).

TOTAL SODIUM & FAT BY INGREDIENT

Sodium:
- 8 oz cream cheese - 600mg
  or LF cream cheese - 840mg
- 2 T roasted red peppers - 65mg
- 8 Egg Roll Wraps - 222mg
  or LS egg roll wrappers - 520mg

Fat (Sat Fat):
- 8 oz cream cheese - 80g (48g)
  or LF cream cheese - 48g (28g)
- 8 Egg Roll Wraps - 7g (2g)
  or LS wrappers - 0g (0g)

Brands used/alternatives:
Green Valley Lactose-Free Cream Cheese
Great Value Neufchâtel Cheese
Twin Dragon Egg Roll Wrapper

Spinach & Goat Cheese Wontons

Sodium Per Serving – 23mg   Makes 32 wontons

These wontons are reminiscent of spanakopita and are delicious by themselves or dipped in sweet chili or tzaiki sauce.

- 1 (10-oz) package frozen chopped spinach, thawed and squeezed dry
- ½ cup *Herbed Goat Cheese (pg 84)* or LS garlic and herb goat cheese[1]
- 1 egg white, beaten
- ½ teaspoon finely minced garlic
- ⅛ teaspoon garlic powder
- ⅛ teaspoon freshly ground nutmeg
- ⅛ teaspoon ground white pepper
- 8 *Egg Roll Wraps (pg 205)* or packaged LS egg roll wrappers, each wrap cut into 4 equal pieces[2]
- Canola or vegetable oil, for frying

1. In a bowl, mix together spinach, goat cheese, egg, garlic, garlic powder, nutmeg, and pepper.
2. Place 1 tablespoon filling in center of each wonton wrapper, wet two adjacent edges with water, and fold per instructions (see *Folding Wontons*, pg 248). Place on a platter, dividing each layer with waxed paper or aluminum foil. *NOTE: If not cooking immediately, cover and refrigerate until ready to cook.*
3. Heat several tablespoons oil in a skillet over medium-high heat; fry wontons, turning once, until golden brown on both sides, about 4-5 minutes. Drain on paper towels. Serve with hot mustard sauce.

NUTRITIONAL INFO PER WONTON*: Calories 42, Fat 1g (Saturated Fat 0g), Cholesterol 8mg, Carbohydrates 7g (Fiber 0g, Sugar 0g), Sodium 23mg (32mg with LS packaged wrappers) *Does not include oil for frying

Recipe Notes

1 – The herbed feta I previously used is no longer available. Because most feta cheese is high in sodium, averaging 316mg an oz, I use a LS goat cheese (50mg-140mg an oz).

2 – The NSA wonton wrappers I previously used are no longer offered, but a few manufacturers offer LS wraps. Cutting larger egg roll wraps into 4 equal pieces is the same as 4 wonton wraps, and in some cases has less sodium (see *Egg Roll Wrappers*, pg 248, for more info).

TOTAL SODIUM & FAT BY INGREDIENT

SPINACH/CHEESE WONTONS

Sodium:
- 10 oz spinach - 360mg
- 2 oz *Herb Goat Cheese* - 95mg or LS herb goat cheese - 110mg
- 1 egg white - 55mg
- 15 Egg Roll Wraps - 563mg or LS wrappers - 975mg

Fat (Sat Fat):
- 2 oz *Herb Goat Cheese* - 14g (8g) or goat cheese - 12g (8g)
- 15 Egg Roll Wraps - 13g (5g) or LS wrappers - 0g (0g)

Brands used/alternatives:
Birds Eye C&W Baby Chopped Spinach
Vermont Creamery Herb Chèvre
Twin Dragon Egg Roll Wrapper

Crispy Pork & Shrimp Wontons

Sodium Per Serving – 20mg   Makes about 32 wontons

One of many recipes acquired while living in Hawaii. Not only do the wontons go together quickly, but they also are onolicious!

- **8 oz ground pork**
- **4 oz tiny or salad shrimp**
- **½ cup water chestnuts, chopped**
- **2 green onions, chopped (green and light green parts)**
- **1 teaspoon lite soy sauce**
- **⅛ teaspoon onion powder**
- **⅛ teaspoon ground black pepper**
- **8 *Egg Roll Wraps (pg 205)* or packaged LS egg roll wrappers, each wrap cut into 4 equal pieces[1]**
- **Canola or vegetable oil, for frying**

Dipping Sauce:
- ***Chinese Hot Mustard (recipe follows)* for dipping**
- **LS sweet-and-sour sauce for dipping[2]**

1. In a bowl, mix pork, shrimp, water chestnuts, green onions, soy sauce, onion powder, and pepper together.
2. Place 1 heaping tablespoon filling in center of each wonton wrapper. Fold per instructions (see *Folding Wontons*, pg 248) and place on platter, dividing each layer with waxed paper or aluminum foil. NOTE: If not cooking immediately, cover and refrigerate until ready to cook.
3. Heat several tablespoons oil in a skillet over medium heat; fry wontons until golden brown on both sides, 5 to 6 minutes. NOTE: Because these contain pork, it is important to thoroughly cook the pork.
4. Drain on paper towels. Serve with *Chinese Hot Mustard* and sweet-and-sour sauce.

NUTRITIONAL INFO PER WONTON*: Calories 44, Fat 1g (Saturated Fat 0g), Cholesterol 18mg, Carbohydrates 6g (Fiber 0g, Sugar 0g), Sodium 20mg (29mg with LS packaged wrappers) *Does not include oil for frying

Chinese Hot Mustard

Sodium Per Serving – 0mg   Makes about 3 tablespoons

This hot mustard is the perfect accompaniment to wontons. Although this does not make a lot of sauce, it's hot enough that a little goes a long way.

- **1 tablespoon dry mustard, such as *Coleman's***
- **2 tablespoons water**
- **4 drops lite soy sauce**

1. Mix all ingredients together and serve.

NUTRITIONAL INFO IN A SERVING: Calories 1, Fat 0g (Sat Fat 0g), Chol 0mg, Carb 0g (Fiber 0g, Sugar 0g), Sodium 0mg

Recipe Notes

1 – The NSA wonton wrappers I previously used are no longer available, but a few manufacturers offer LS wraps (see *Egg Roll Wrappers*, pg 248, for more info). Cutting larger egg roll wraps into 4 equal pieces is the same as 4 wonton wraps, and in some cases has less sodium.

2 – Most prepared sweet and sour sauces average 130mg sodium per tbsp, but there are many brands with 50mg or less (visit LowSaltFoods.com, for a list of products with the least sodium).

TOTAL SODIUM & FAT BY INGREDIENT

PORK & SHRIMP WONTONS
Sodium:
- 8 oz ground pork - 100mg
- 4 oz tiny shrimp - 250mg
- 2 green onions - 5mg
- 1 t lite soy sauce - 60mg
- 8 *Egg Roll Wraps* - 222mg
  or LS wrappers - 520mg

Fat (Sat Fat):
- 8 oz ground pork - 34g (12g)
- 4 oz tiny shrimp - 2g (0g)
- 8 *Egg Roll Wraps* - 7g (2g)
  or LS wrappers - 0g (0g)

Brands used/alternatives:
- *Kroger* Wild Caught Salad Shrimp
- *Mrs Taste* Less Sodium Soy Sauce
- *Twin Dragon* Egg Roll Wrapper
- *Mr Spice* Sweet & Sour Sauce

CHINESE HOT MUSTARD
Sodium:
- 1 T dry mustard - 1mg
- 4 drops lite soy sauce - 2mg

Fat (Sat Fat):
- 1 T dry mustard - 2g (0g)

SOUPS & CHILI

VEGETABLE SOUPS

Creamy Asparagus Soup 40
Curried Yam & Apple Bisque 41
Artichoke & Leek Soup 42
Creamed Broccoli Soup with Mandarin
    Oranges 43
Cheesy Broccoli Soup 43
Mighty Fine Borscht 44
Borscht with Beef Broth 44
Mushroom Bisque with Brandy 45
Fresh Carrot Potage 46
Curried Carrot Soup 46
Cream of Leek Soup 47
Mushroom-Leek Soup 47

French Onion Soup 48
Pumpkin Jalapeño Soup 49
Split Pea Soup 50
Spicy Split Pea Soup 50
Minestrone 51
Grandma's Lentil Soup 52

SEAFOOD CHOWDERS

Simply White Clam Chowder 53

BEAN SOUPS & CHILI

Hearty Black Bean Soup 54
Easy 4-Bean Soup 55
Meaty Bean Soup 55
Texas-Style Turkey Chili 56

VEGETABLE SOUPS

Creamy Asparagus Soup

Sodium Per Serving – 57mg Serves 4

This luscious recipe, given to me by my long-time friend, Sally Pearce, is the perfect first course for a special dinner. To keep fat to a minimum, I use lowfat sour cream and milk instead of cream.

- 2 pounds asparagus spears, trimmed and cut in 1-inch pieces[1]
- 3 cups *Chicken Broth (pg 208)* or unsalted chicken broth
- 2 teaspoons LS chicken bouillon
- 1 tablespoon unsalted butter or margarine
- 1 tablespoon olive oil
- 3 large shallots, chopped[2]
- 2 cloves garlic, minced
- 3 tablespoons all-purpose flour
- ½ teaspoon lemon juice
- ¾ teaspoon dried thyme or tarragon
- ½ teaspoon garlic powder
- ¼ teaspoon ground black pepper
- ⅓ cup lowfat milk
- ½ cup lowfat sour cream
- *Red Pepper Coulis (pg 124)* (optional)[3]
- Hot pepper sauce, such as *Tabasco* (optional)

1. In a large saucepan over high heat, combine asparagus, chicken broth, and bouillon. Bring to a boil; decrease heat to medium-low and simmer, covered, until asparagus is bright green and tender, 8 to 10 minutes. Do not overcook.
2. Meanwhile, heat butter and oil in a skillet over medium heat; add shallots and garlic. Cook, stirring frequently, until shallots are soft, 3 to 4 minutes.
3. Add flour, lemon juice, thyme, garlic powder, and pepper; cook, stirring constantly, until mixture begins to turn golden, about 2 minutes. Combine with asparagus/broth mixture, mixing thoroughly; remove from heat and cool slightly.
4. Place half of asparagus mixture in a blender or food processor and pulse until smooth; repeat with remaining mixture.
5. Return asparagus purée to pan and simmer over low heat, 5 minutes. Stir in milk and sour cream; heat through. (If soup is too thick, add a little more milk.) Ladle into soup bowls and serve with a dollop of *Red Pepper Coulis* on top. If not using coulis, grate freshly ground nutmeg on top, if desired.

NUTRITIONAL INFO PER SERVING (with coulis): Calories 260, Fat 13g (Sat Fat 4g), Chol 23mg, Carb 27g (Fiber 5g, Sugar 13g), Sodium 57mg (47mg without coulis) (106mg with NSA chicken broth)

Recipe Notes

1 – Cut off 1–2 inches from the spear ends and remove lower 3 inches of outer skin with a vegetable peeler. (If using thin-stalked spears, this step is not necessary.) For cooking and storage info, see *Asparagus*, pg 243.

2 – Substitute chopped leeks (white and light green parts) instead of shallots (see *Leeks*, pg 249, for cleaning and storing info).

3 – Coulis (pronounced COO-lee) is a roasted red pepper purée that takes this soup from everyday to gourmet faire.

TOTAL SODIUM & FAT BY INGREDIENT

Sodium:
- 2 lb asparagus spears - 8mg
- 3 c *Chicken Broth* - 60mg
  or NSA chicken broth - 255mg
- 2 t LS chicken bouillon - 10mg
- 3 shallots - 15mg
- 2 garlic cloves - 1mg
- ⅓ c LF milk - 35mg
- ½ c LF sour cream - 60mg
- Red Pepper Coulis - 40mg

Fat (Sat Fat):
- 3 c *Chicken Broth* - 1g (0g)
  or NSA chicken broth - 0g (0g)
- 1 T NSA butter - 12g (7g)
  or NSA margarine - 9g (4g)
- 1 T olive oil - 14g (2g)
- ⅓ c LF milk - 2g (1g)
- ½ c LF sour cream - 10g (6g)
- Red Pepper Coulis - 13g (0g)

Brands used/alternatives:
- *Pacific Foods* Organic Unsalted Chicken Stock
- *Herb Ox* NSA Chicken Bouillon
- *Simple Truth* 2% Milk
- *Daisy Light* Sour Cream

CURRIED YAM & APPLE BISQUE

Sodium Per Serving – 42mg   Serves 8

Friends and family rave about this soup (another favorite from my dear friend, Sally), which I've desalted and perked up with hot curry powder and hot pepper sauce. The combination of sweetness and heat creates a delicious accompaniment to any meal.

- 1 tablespoon olive oil
- 1 tablespoon unsalted butter or margarine
- 1 yellow onion, chopped
- 2 sweet apples, chopped, such as Braeburn, Fuji, or Jazz
- 1 tablespoon hot curry powder[1]
- ½ teaspoon ground coriander
- ¼ teaspoon garlic powder
- ⅛ teaspoon ground black pepper
- 1 clove garlic, minced
- 1 cup dry sherry, Madeira, or brandy
- 7 cups *Chicken Broth (pg 208)* or unsalted chicken broth
- 1 tablespoon LS chicken bouillon
- 2 large yams or dark-skinned sweet potatoes, cubed (about 2 pounds)[2]
- 2–3 drops hot pepper sauce, such as *Tabasco*
- **Lowfat sour cream or plain yogurt**

1. Heat oil and butter in a large saucepan over medium heat; add onion, apples, curry, coriander, garlic, and pepper. Cook, stirring frequently, until onions are translucent, 3 to 4 minutes. Add garlic; cook, stirring constantly, until you smell the garlic, about 1 minute.
2. Add sherry, chicken broth, bouillon, yams, and hot pepper sauce; bring to boil. Decrease heat to low, cover, and simmer until potatoes are done, about 20 minutes. Remove from heat and cool slightly.
3. Place one-third of the apple-yam mixture in a blender or food processor and pulse until smooth; repeat with remaining mixture.
4. Return purée to pan and heat through. Serve with a dollop of sour cream or yogurt.

NUTRITIONAL INFO PER SERVING: Calories 210, Fat 6g (Sat Fat 3g), Chol 19mg, Carb 27g (Fiber 3g, Sugar 5g), Sodium 42mg (99mg with NSA chicken broth)

Recipe Notes

1 – I like a lot of heat and use hot curry powder, however, any variety of curry may be used. For additional curry info, see *Curry Powder*, pg 247.

2 – Although similar, sweet potatoes and yams are from different species. In the U.S. there are two common sweet potatoes: a pale skin and a darker orange variety. Although the latter is called a yam, to the rest of the world, it's a sweet potato.

TOTAL SODIUM & FAT BY INGREDIENT

Sodium:
- 1 onion - 4mg
- 2 apples - 4mg
- 1 garlic clove - 1mg
- 1 T curry powder - 3mg
- 1 c sherry - 22mg
- 7 c *Chicken Broth* - 140mg
  - or NSA chicken broth - 595mg
- 1 T LS chicken bouillon - 15mg
- 2 lb yams - 29mg
- 2 drops hot pepper sauce - 1mg
- 1 c LF sour cream - 120mg
  - or LF plain yogurt - 40mg

Fat (Sat Fat):
- 1 T NSA butter - 12g (7g)
  - or NSA margarine - 9g (4g)
- 1 T olive oil - 14g (2g)
- 2 apples - 1g (0g)
- 1 T curry powder - 1g (0g)
- 7 c *Chicken Broth* - 2g (1g)
  - or NSA chicken broth - 0g (0g)
- 2 lb yams - 1g (0g)
- 1 c LF sour cream - 20g (12g)
  - or LF plain yogurt - 3g (2g)

Brands used/alternatives:
Pacific Foods Organic Unsalted Chicken Stock
Herb Ox NSA Chicken Bouillon
Daisy Light Sour Cream

ARTICHOKE & LEEK SOUP

Sodium Per Serving – 74mg | Serves 4

This pleasing soup gets additional flavor from the cumin and cayenne. Using frozen artichokes instead of canned, saves 180mg sodium per serving.

- 1 tablespoon olive oil
- 1 tablespoon unsalted butter or margarine
- 3 leeks, cleaned and thinly sliced (white and light green parts)[1]
- 2 garlic cloves, finely minced
- 2 tablespoons uncooked white rice
- 1 russet potato, peeled and chopped
- 1 (9-oz) package frozen artichoke hearts, defrosted and halved[2]
- 4 cups *Chicken Broth (pg 208)* or unsalted chicken broth
- 1 teaspoon LS chicken bouillon
- 1 teaspoon Worcestershire sauce
- ½ teaspoon ground cumin
- ¼ teaspoon garlic powder
- ¼ teaspoon ground black pepper
- ¼ teaspoon dried thyme
- Pinch cayenne pepper
- 1 tablespoon lemon juice
- 1 tablespoon chopped fresh Italian parsley

1. Heat oil and butter in a large saucepan over medium heat; add leeks and garlic. Cook, stirring frequently, until leeks are soft, 3 to 4 minutes.
2. Stir in rice and cook, stirring frequently, 3 minutes. Add potato, artichokes, chicken broth, bouillon, Worcestershire, cumin, garlic powder, black pepper, thyme, and cayenne; bring to boil. Reduce heat to low, cover, and simmer until potatoes are done, about 30 minutes. Remove from heat and cool slightly.
3. Place one-half of the artichoke-leek mixture in a blender or food processor and pulse until smooth; repeat with remaining mixture. Return purée to pan, add lemon juice and heat through. Sprinkle with parsley and serve.

NUTRITIONAL INFO PER SERVING: Calories 204, Fat 7g (Sat Fat 2g), Chol 13mg, Carb 32g (Fiber 7g, Sugar 4g), Sodium 74mg (139mg with NSA chicken broth)

Recipe Notes

1 – For information on cleaning and storing leeks, see *Leeks*, pg 249.
2 – Avoid canned artichoke hearts, they average 420mg sodium per ½ cup, whereas frozen hearts have about 55mg.

TOTAL SODIUM & FAT BY INGREDIENT

Sodium:
- 3 leeks - 54mg
- 2 garlic cloves - 1mg
- 1 potato - 11mg
- 9 oz artichoke hearts - 120mg
- 4 c *Chicken Broth* - 80mg
  or NSA chicken broth - 340mg
- 1 t LS chicken bouillon - 5mg
- 1 t Worcestershire - 20mg
- ½ t cumin - 2mg
- 1 T parsley - 2mg

Fat (Sat Fat):
- 1 T olive oil - 14g (2g)
- 1 T NSA butter - 12g (7g)
  or NSA margarine - 9g (4g)
- 9 oz artichoke hearts - 1g (0g)
- 4 c *Chicken Broth* - 1g (0g)
  or NSA chicken broth - 0g (0g)

Brands used/alternatives:
Private Selection Artichoke Hearts
Pacific Foods Organic Unsalted Chicken Stock
Herb Ox NSA Chicken Bouillon

CREAMED BROCCOLI SOUP WITH MANDARIN ORANGES

Sodium Per Serving – 82mg   Serves 4

Cream soups are notoriously high in fat and salt. This luscious low-sodium soup has been lightened up using half-and-half, milk, and sour cream. In addition to its rich flavor, the mandarin oranges lend an unexpected twist.

- 1 tablespoon unsalted butter or margarine
- 3–4 small red potatoes, quartered[1]
- ½ teaspoon ground cumin
- ¼ teaspoon garlic powder
- ¼ teaspoon ground black pepper
- 1 small sweet onion, thinly sliced
- 4 cups or 1 (16-oz) package broccoli florets
- 2 cups *Chicken Broth (pg 208)* or unsalted chicken broth
- 2 teaspoons LS chicken bouillon
- ½ cup half-and-half[2]
- ½ cup lowfat milk
- 2 tablespoons lowfat sour cream
- ⅛ teaspoon ground nutmeg
- 1 (12-oz) can mandarin oranges in light syrup, drained

1. Melt butter in a large saucepan over medium heat; add potatoes, cumin, garlic powder, and pepper, stirring until potatoes are well coated. Mix in onions and broccoli; cook, stirring frequently, until onions are soft, 2 to 3 minutes.
2. Add chicken broth and bouillon; bring to a boil. Decrease heat to medium-low; cover, and simmer until vegetables are tender, 10 to 15 minutes.
3. Stir in the half-and-half, milk, and sour cream. Remove from heat and cool slightly.
4. Place one-half broccoli mixture in a blender or food processor and pulse until smooth; repeat with remaining mixture.
5. Return purée to pan, add nutmeg and mandarin oranges; heat through.

NUTRITIONAL INFO PER SERVING: Calories 270, Fat 8g (Sat Fat 5g), Chol 25mg, Carb 41g (Fiber 6g, Sugar 15g), Sodium 82mg (92mg with NSA chicken broth)

VARIATION
CHEESY BROCCOLI SOUP
1. Omit the mandarin oranges and add 2 oz shredded Cheddar cheese (about ½ cup) to the puréed soup; stir until melted.

NUTRITIONAL INFO PER SERVING: Calories 293, Fat 13g (Saturated Fat 8g), Cholesterol 39mg, Carbohydrates 34g (Fiber 5g, Sugar 8g), Sodium 167mg (199mg with NSA chicken broth)

Recipe Notes
1 – Other potato choices you can use are Yukon gold or white potatoes. For additional varieties, see *Potatoes*, pg 252.
2 – If you don't have half-and-half on hand, increase the milk to ⅔ cup and the sour cream to ½ cup. NOTE: I often use fat-free half & half without much loss of richness.

TOTAL SODIUM & FAT BY INGREDIENT
Sodium:
- 3 red potatoes - 30mg
- ½ t cumin - 2mg
- 1 sweet onion - 13mg
- 4 c broccoli - 120mg
- 2 c *Chicken Broth* - 40mg
  or NSA chicken broth - 170mg
- 2 t LS chicken bouillon - 10mg
- ½ c half-and-half - 40mg
- ½ c LF milk - 58mg
- 2 T LF sour cream - 15mg

Fat (Sat Fat):
- 1 T NSA butter - 12g (7g)
  or NSA margarine - 8g (4g)
- 3 red potatoes - 1g (0g)
- 4 c broccoli - 1g (0g)
- 2 c *Chicken Broth* - 1g (0g)
  or NSA chicken broth - 0g (0g)
- ½ c half-and-half - 14g (8g)
- ½ c LF milk - 3g (1g)
- 2 T LF sour cream - 3g (2g)

Brands used/alternatives:
Pacific Foods Organic Unsalted Chicken Stock
Herb Ox NSA Chicken Bouillon
Organic Valley Half and Half
Daisy Light Sour Cream
Simple Truth 2% Milk

Mighty Fine Borscht

Sodium Per Serving – 98mg   Serves 12

Originally from Russia, this beet soup is prepared in a variety of ways—with or without meat and with a combination of vegetables. It's usually made either thick and stew-like or light and brothy. Serve it hot or cold and always with a dollop of sour cream or yogurt on top. My borscht is very thick and the longer it cooks, the better it gets, so allow 1 to 2 hours of simmering time. For a meatless version, omit the beef without much loss of flavor.

- 8 oz round steak or other lean meat, sliced in thin strips
- ½ teaspoon garlic powder
- ⅛ teaspoon ground black pepper
- 1 tablespoon olive oil
- 1 onion, sliced
- 2 shallots, minced
- 2–3 garlic cloves, minced
- 1 (28-oz) can crushed tomatoes
- 1 (8-oz) can NSA tomato purée
- 1 (6-oz) can NSA tomato paste
- 5 cups water
- 1 tablespoon cider vinegar
- 1 tablespoon LS beef bouillon
- 1 tablespoon sugar
- 2 bay leaves
- 4–5 large beets, peeled and grated (about 8 cups)[1]
- 1 small head cabbage, finely shredded, or 1 (10-oz) package coleslaw mix
- 1 (12-oz) package frozen peas and carrots
- Lowfat sour cream or lowfat plain yogurt[2]

1. Season meat with garlic powder and pepper.
2. Heat oil in a large pot or Dutch oven over medium-high heat; add meat and brown on all sides, stirring frequently, 3 to 4 minutes. Add onions, shallots, and garlic; cook, stirring constantly, until onions are soft, 2 to 3 minutes.
3. Stir in crushed tomatoes, tomato purée, tomato paste, water, vinegar, bouillon, sugar, bay leaves, beets, and cabbage. Decrease heat to medium-low; cover, and simmer 1 to 2 hours. *NOTE: The longer this simmers, the better it tastes.*
4. Stir in peas and carrots; continue simmering 30 minutes more.
5. Remove bay leaves; serve with a dollop of sour cream.

NUTRITIONAL INFO PER SERVING: Calories 191, Fat 5g (Sat Fat 2g), Chol 24mg, Carb 26g (Fiber 6g, Sugar 14g), Sodium 98mg
WITHOUT MEAT: Calories 153, Fat 3g (Sat Fat 1g), Chol 7mg, Carb 26g (Fiber 6g, Sugar 14g), Sodium 90mg

VARIATION
Borscht with Beef Broth
1. For a lighter soup, omit the tomato purée and tomato paste; replace with 3 cups *Beef Broth (pg 208)* or canned low-salt beef broth.

NUTRITIONAL INFO PER SERVING: Calories 171, Fat 5g (Sat Fat 2g), Chol 24mg, Carb 21g (Fiber 5g, Sugar 11g), Sodium 88mg (95mg with NSA beef broth)

Recipe Notes
1 – If using a processor, grate with the finest blade.
2 – Don't omit the sour cream or yogurt, it makes it rich and creamy.

TOTAL SODIUM & FAT BY INGREDIENT

Sodium:
- 8 oz round steak - 93mg
- 1 onion - 4mg
- 2 shallots - 10mg
- 1 garlic clove - 1mg
- 28 oz crushed tomatoes - 260mg
- 1 c NSA tomato purée - 60mg
- 6 oz NSA tomato paste - 120mg
- 1 T LS beef bouillon - 15mg
- 4 beets - 308mg
- 1 sm head cabbage - 100mg
- 12 oz peas and carrots - 80mg
- 1 c LF sour cream - 120mg
  or LF plain yogurt - 40mg

Fat (Sat Fat):
- 1 T olive oil - 14g (2g)
- 8 oz round steak - 21g (8g)
- 4 beets - 1g (0g)
- 1 c LF sour cream - 20g (12g)
  or LF plain yogurt - 3g (2g)

Brands used/alternatives:
Cento Crushed Tomatoes
Cento Tomato Purée
Bionaturae NSA Tomato Paste
Herb Ox NSA Beef Bouillon
Kroger Peas & Carrots
Daisy Light Sour Cream

Mushroom Bisque with Brandy

Sodium Per Serving – 78mg   Serves 4

This rich and creamy soup is ready in less than 30 minutes. The addition of brandy enhances the subtle flavors. For added taste, stir in 1 tablespoon fresh thyme (or 1 teaspoon dried) to the mushrooms while they sauté.

- 1 tablespoon olive oil
- 1 tablespoon unsalted butter or margarine
- 1 medium onion, diced
- 1 shallot, minced
- 2 garlic cloves, finely minced
- 8 oz portobello mushrooms, stemmed and sliced[1]
- ¼ teaspoon garlic powder
- ¼ teaspoon ground white pepper
- ¼ cup brandy, dry sherry, or Madeira
- 1 small russet potato, peeled and diced
- 3 cups *Chicken Broth (pg 208)* or unsalted chicken broth
- 2 teaspoons LS chicken bouillon
- ½ cup half-and-half or light cream
- ½ cup lowfat milk
- 2 tablespoons lowfat sour cream
- 2 tablespoons chopped fresh chives (optional)

1. Heat oil and butter in large saucepan over medium heat; add onions and shallots. Cook, stirring frequently, until onions are translucent, about 3 to 4 minutes. Add mushrooms, garlic powder, and white pepper; cook, stirring occasionally, for 5 minutes.
2. Stir in brandy, potatoes, chicken broth, and bouillon; simmer until potatoes are done, about 15 minutes. Remove from heat and cool slightly.
3. Place half the mushroom mixture in a blender or food processor and pulse until smooth; repeat with remaining mixture. Return purée to pan; stir in the half-and-half, milk, and sour cream. If soup is too thick, thin with additional chicken broth or milk. Heat through and serve with chopped chives.

NUTRITIONAL INFO PER SERVING: Calories 245g, Fat 12g (Sat Fat 5g), Chol 17mg, Carb 21g (Fiber 2g, Sugar 7g), Sodium 78mg (126mg with NSA chicken broth)

Recipe Notes

1 – Portobellos are mature criminis, reaching up to 6 inches in diameter and are very flavorful and meaty. Substitute criminis or porcinis for the portobellos. See *Mushrooms*, pg 250, for varieties, preparation, and storage.

TOTAL SODIUM & FAT BY INGREDIENT

Sodium:
- 1 onion - 4mg
- 1 shallot - 5mg
- 2 garlic cloves - 1mg
- 8 oz portobellos - 112mg
- 1 russet potato - 11mg
- 3 c *Chicken Broth* - 60mg
  or NSA chicken broth - 255mg
- 2 t LS chicken bouillon - 10mg
- ½ c half-and-half - 40mg
- ½ c LF milk - 53mg
- 2 T LF sour cream - 15mg

Fat (Sat Fat):
- 1 T olive oil - 14g (2g)
- 1 T NSA butter - 12g (7g)
  or NSA margarine - 9g (4g)
- 8 oz portobellos - 1g (0g)
- 3 c *Chicken Broth* - 1g (0g)
  or NSA chicken broth - 0g (0g)
- ½ c half-and-half - 14g (8g)
- ½ c LF milk - 3g (2g)
- 2 T LF sour cream - 3g (2g)

Brands used/alternatives:
- *Pacific Foods* Organic Unsalted Chicken Stock
- *Herb Ox* NSA Chicken Bouillon
- *Organic Valley* Half and Half
- *Simple Truth* 2% Milk
- *Daisy Light* Sour Cream

Fresh Carrot Potage

Sodium Per Serving – 122mg Serves 4

This creamy soup with a hint of basil and dill is one of my favorites. Not only is it ready in 30 minutes, but it contains ingredients usually on hand.

- **1 tablespoon olive oil**
- **1 tablespoon unsalted butter or margarine**
- **1 small sweet onion, chopped**
- **1–2 garlic cloves, minced**
- **½ teaspoon garlic powder**
- **¼ teaspoon ground black pepper**
- **5 large carrots, sliced (about 3 cups)**[1]
- **2½ cups *Chicken Broth (pg 208)* or unsalted chicken broth**
- **½ cup Madeira wine or dry sherry**
- **½ cup uncooked medium-grain rice**
- **1 teaspoon LS chicken bouillon**
- **1 teaspoon dried basil**
- **¼ teaspoon dried dill weed**
- **2–3 drops hot pepper sauce, such as *Tabasco***
- **½ cup lowfat sour cream**
- **¾ cup lowfat milk**
- **Freshly grated nutmeg**
- **2 tablespoons chopped fresh Italian parsley (optional)**

1. Heat oil and butter in a large saucepan over medium heat; add onions. Cook, stirring frequently, until onions are soft, 3 to 4 minutes. Add garlic, garlic powder, and pepper; cook, stirring constantly, until you smell the garlic, about 1 minute.
2. Add carrots, chicken broth, Madeira, rice, bouillon, basil, dill, and hot pepper sauce; bring to boil. Decrease heat to low; cover, and cook, stirring occasionally, until rice is cooked, 20 to 25 minutes. Remove from heat and cool slightly.
3. Place half the carrot mixture in a blender or processor and pulse until smooth; repeat with remaining mixture.
4. Return purée to pan and bring to simmer over low heat. Stir in sour cream and milk; heat through. Top with nutmeg and parsley; serve.

NUTRITIONAL INFO PER SERVING: Calories 318, Fat 10g (Saturated Fat 5g), Cholesterol 26mg, Carbohydrates 42g (Fiber 4g, Sugar 13g), Sodium 122mg (213mg with NSA chicken broth)

VARIATION
Curried Carrot Soup
1. Instead of the basil and dill, add 1 tablespoon curry powder, ½ teaspoon dried coriander, and ¼ teaspoon dried cardamom.

NUTRITIONAL INFO PER SERVING: Calories 322, Fat 11g (Sat Fat 5g), Chol 27mg, Carb 42g (Fiber 4g, Sugar 13g), Sodium 123mg (163mg with NSA chicken broth)

Recipe Notes
1 – You can also substitute parsnips or a combination of parsnips and carrots. Parsnips have a sweetness, similar to carrots, but with much less sodium (7mg vs 50mg for a medium carrot).

TOTAL SODIUM & FAT BY INGREDIENT

Sodium:
- 1 sweet onion - 27mg
- 1 garlic clove - 1mg
- 5 carrots - 249mg
- 2½ c *Chicken Broth* - 50mg or NSA chicken broth - 213mg
- ½ c Madeira wine - 12mg
- 1 t LS chicken bouillon - 5mg
- ¼ t dill weed - 1mg
- 2 drops hot pepper sauce - 1mg
- ½ c LF sour cream - 60mg
- ¾ c LF milk - 79mg
- 2 T parsley - 4mg

Fat (Sat Fat):
- 1 T olive oil - 14g (2g)
- 1 T NSA butter - 12g (7g) or NSA margarine - 9g (4g)
- 5 carrots - 1g (0g)
- 2½ c *Chicken Broth* - 1g (0g) or NSA chicken broth - 0g (0g)
- ½ c LF sour cream - 10g (6g)
- ¾ c LF milk - 4g (3g)

Brands used/alternatives:
Pacific Foods Organic Unsalted Chicken Stock
Herb Ox NSA Chicken Bouillon
Daisy Light Sour Cream
Simple Truth 2% Milk

Cream of Leek Soup

Sodium Per Serving – 81mg   Serves 4

This mild soup gets added flavor from the caramelization of the vegetables. Make this the day before to let the flavors intensify, as it only gets better the next day.

- 1 tablespoon olive oil
- 1 tablespoon unsalted butter or margarine
- 4–5 leeks, sliced (white and light green parts)
- 1 sweet onion, chopped
- 1 celery stalk, chopped
- 2 medium red potatoes, diced
- ¼ teaspoon garlic powder
- ⅛ teaspoon celery seed
- ⅛ teaspoon ground black pepper
- 1–3 garlic cloves, minced
- ¼ cup Madeira wine or dry sherry
- 3 cups *Chicken Broth (pg 208)* or unsalted chicken broth
- 2 teaspoons LS chicken bouillon
- ¼ cup chopped fresh Italian parsley[1]
- 4–5 drops hot pepper sauce, such as Tabasco
- ½ cup lowfat milk
- ¼ cup lowfat sour cream
- Freshly grated nutmeg

1. Heat oil and butter in a large pan over medium-low heat; add leeks, onion, celery, potatoes, garlic powder, celery seed, and pepper. Cook, stirring occasionally, until potatoes are tender and golden brown, about 20 minutes.
2. Add garlic and cook, stirring frequently, until you smell the garlic, 1 to 2 minutes; stir in Madeira, chicken broth, bouillon, and parsley. Cover and simmer 1 hour. Remove from heat and cool slightly.
3. Place half the leek mixture in a blender or food processor and pulse until smooth; repeat with remaining mixture.
4. Return purée to pan and stir in hot pepper sauce, milk, and sour cream; heat through. Top with nutmeg and serve.

NUTRITIONAL INFO PER SERVING: Calories 272, Fat 9g (Sat Fat 3g), Chol 19mg, Carb 40g (Fiber 5g, Sugar 13g), Sodium 81mg (109mg with NSA chicken broth)

VARIATION
Mushroom-Leek Soup
1. For a heartier soup, add 8 oz (about 2 cups) sliced mushrooms (such as cremini, button, and/or shiitake) and increase the butter to 2 tablespoons; proceed as directed.

NUTRITIONAL INFO PER SERVING: Calories 309, Fat 12g (Sat Fat 5g), Chol 27mg, Carb 41g (Fiber 5g, Sugar 14g), Sodium 84mg (111mg with NSA chicken broth)

Recipe Notes
1 – For variety, replace half the parsley with minced fresh basil or tarragon.

TOTAL SODIUM & FAT BY INGREDIENT

Sodium:
- 4 leeks - 72mg
- 1 sweet onion - 27mg
- 1 celery stalk - 32mg
- 2 red potatoes - 20mg
- 1 garlic clove - 1mg
- ¼ c Madeira - 6mg
- 3 c *Chicken Broth* - 60mg
  or NSA chicken broth - 255mg
- 2 t LS chicken bouillon - 10mg
- ¼ c parsley - 8mg
- 4 drops hot pepper sauce - 1mg
- ½ c LF milk - 58
- ¼ c LF sour cream - 30mg

Fat (Sat Fat):
- 1 T olive oil - 14g (2g)
- 1 T NSA butter - 12g (7g)
  or NSA margarine - 9g (4g)
- 3 c *Chicken Broth* - 1g (0g)
  or NSA chicken broth - 0g (0g)
- ½ c LF milk - 3g (1g)
- ¼ c LF sour cream - 5g (3g)

Brands used/alternatives:
Pacific Foods Organic Unsalted Chicken Stock
Herb Ox NSA Chicken Bouillon
Simple Truth 2% Milk
Daisy Light Sour Cream

French Onion Soup

Sodium Per Serving – 92mg · Serves 8

My friend, Jeannette Phillips, prepared this delicious soup during a "girls only weekend." Although onion soup is normally high in sodium (about 1,053mg per cup), my low-salt adaptation is rich and creamy and, I think, just as good. The slow caramelizing of the onions and the Madeira wine adds to the taste and richness. NOTE: The amount of sodium per serving will vary depending on the bread and cheese used.

- 2 tablespoons olive oil
- 2 tablespoons unsalted butter or margarine
- 4 large yellow onions, thinly sliced[1]
- ½ teaspoon garlic powder
- ¼ teaspoon ground black pepper
- 3 cloves garlic, minced
- 1 teaspoon sugar
- 6 cups *Beef Broth (pg 208)* or unsalted beef broth
- 1 cup water
- 4 teaspoons LS beef bouillon
- 1 teaspoon onion soup base (optional)[2]
- 2 cups Madeira wine[3]
- 2 tablespoons flour, mixed with 4 tablespoons water to form a paste
- 8 slices *Everyday Multigrain Bread (pg 194)* or LS multigrain bread[4]
- 8 slices Swiss cheese

1. Heat oil and butter in a large skillet over medium heat; add onions. Cook, stirring frequently, until they start to brown, 4 to 5 minutes; sprinkle with garlic powder and pepper. Decrease heat to medium-low; cook, stirring frequently, until onions are a deep brown color and caramelized, 30 to 45 minutes.
2. Stir in garlic and sugar; add beef broth, water, bouillon, soup base, Madeira, and flour paste. Continue stirring until flour is mixed in well; cover and cook 30 minutes. Remove lid and simmer, uncovered, 15 minutes longer.
3. Ladle into oven-proof bowls; place a piece of bread on soup and top with 1 slice cheese. Broil until cheese melts and edges of bread start to brown, about 2 minutes.

NUTRITIONAL INFO PER SERVING: Calories 473, Fat 17g (Sat Fat 6g), Chol 41mg, Carb 53g (Fiber 3g, Sugar 13g), Sodium 92mg (133mg with NSA beef broth)

Recipe Notes

1 – Yellow onions are preferred, as they have less water than other onions, allowing for better caramelization. For additional info, see *Caramelizing Onions*, pg 245.

2 – I use *Vogue Cuisine* Onion Base. It takes this soup from good to outstanding!

3 – Madeira gives a rich creamy taste to the soup, but you may substitute brandy or sherry. There will be a subtle change in taste depending on which is used, but I highly recommend using Madeira. *NOTE:* Madeira is harder to find than in previous years, but is well worth it if you do.

4 – There are many LS breads, thin slice breads are a good option, as they usually are low in sodium. Look for brands with 80mg or less a slice. Visit *LowSaltFoods.com* for a list of LS brands.

TOTAL SODIUM & FAT BY INGREDIENT

Sodium:
- 4 onions - 24mg
- 3 garlic cloves - 2mg
- 6 c *Beef Broth* - 120mg
  or NSA beef broth - 450mg
- 4 t LS beef bouillon - 20mg
- 1 t onion soup base - 170mg
- 2 c Madeira wine - 48mg
- 8 sl *Everyday Bread* - 191mg
  or LS bread - 360mg
- 8 sl Swiss cheese - 160mg

Fat (Sat Fat):
- 2 T olive oil - 28g (4g)
- 2 T NSA butter - 23g (14g)
  or NSA margarine - 18g (7g)
- 4 onions - 1g (0g)
- 6 c *Beef Broth* - 1g (0g)
  or NSA beef broth - 0g (0g)
- 8 sl *Everyday Bread* - 39g (15g)
  or LS bread - 3g (0g)
- 8 sl Swiss cheese - 48g (16g)

Brands used/alternatives:
Swanson Unsalted Beef Broth
Herb Ox NSA Beef Bouillon
Vogue Cuisine Onion Soup Base
Pepperidge Farm Light 100% Whole Wheat Bread
Great Value Sliced Baby Swiss

Pumpkin Jalapeño Soup

Sodium Per Serving – 72mg   Serves 4

This deliciously light and aromatic soup recipe was given to me by my dear friend, Sally Pearce, who truly is a "soup queen." After a few low-salt substitutions, I think you'll love the sweet taste of pumpkin combined with the heat of the jalapeños, not to mention the wonderful aroma that fills the house as it's cooking.

- **2 tablespoons unsalted butter or margarine**
- **1 small onion, chopped**
- **2–4 jalapeños, seeded and chopped[1]**
- **1 russet potato, cubed**
- **1 clove garlic, minced**
- **½ teaspoon curry powder**
- **½ teaspoon garlic powder**
- **½ teaspoon ground white pepper**
- **2 carrots, chopped**
- **⅓ cup chopped fresh Italian parsley**
- **4 cups *Chicken Broth (pg 208)* or unsalted chicken broth, divided**
- **1 tablespoon LS chicken bouillon**
- **1 (15-oz) can pumpkin purée**
- **¼ cup Madeira wine or dry sherry**
- **2–3 drops hot pepper sauce, such as *Tabasco***
- **Freshly ground nutmeg**
- **½ cup lowfat sour cream (optional)**

1. Melt butter in a large pot over medium heat; add onion and jalapeños. Cook, stirring frequently, until onions are translucent, about 4 minutes. Mix in potatoes, curry, garlic, garlic powder, and white pepper; cook 1 minute longer.
2. Add carrots, parsley, 2 cups chicken broth, and bouillon; bring to boil. Decrease heat to low; cover and simmer until vegetables are cooked, about 20 minutes. Remove from heat and cool slightly.
3. Place one-half pumpkin mixture in a blender or food processor and pulse until smooth; repeat with remaining mixture.
4. Return purée to pan; add remaining 2 cups chicken broth, pumpkin, Madeira, and hot pepper sauce. Heat through and serve, topped with nutmeg and a dollop of sour cream.

NUTRITIONAL INFO PER SERVING: Calories 238, Fat 9g (Sat Fat 5g), Chol 31mg, Carb 30g (Fiber 5g, Sugar 9g), Sodium 72mg (137mg with NSA chicken broth)

Recipe Notes
1 – Two jalapeños give this soup a hint of heat, but if you like it hot… add all four! For information on handling jalapeños, see *Chile Peppers*, pg 251.

TOTAL SODIUM & FAT BY INGREDIENT

Sodium:
- 1 onion - 2mg
- 1 russet potato - 11mg
- 1 garlic clove - 1mg
- ½ t curry - 1mg
- 2 carrots - 84mg
- ⅓ c parsley - 11mg
- 4 c *Chicken Broth* - 80mg
  - or NSA chicken broth - 340mg
- 1 T LS chicken bouillon - 15mg
- 15 oz pumpkin - 18mg
- ¼ c Madeira - 6mg
- 2 drops hot pepper sauce - 1mg
- ½ c LF sour cream - 60mg

Fat (Sat Fat):
- 2 T NSA butter - 23g (14g)
  - or NSA margarine - 18g (7g)
- 4 c *Chicken Broth* - 1g (0g)
  - or NSA chicken broth - 0g (0g)
- 15 oz pumpkin - 2g (0g)
- ½ c LF sour cream - 10g (6g)

Brands used/alternatives:
- *Pacific Foods* Organic Unsalted Chicken Stock
- *Herb Ox* NSA Chicken Bouillon
- *Daisy Light* Sour Cream

Split Pea Soup

Sodium Per Serving – 41mg Serves 8

I've always been fond of split pea soup and as a young child, going to "Pea Soup Andersen's" just north of Santa Barbara, California, for a bowl of their famous pea soup was a big event. Here is an equally good version that is made without ham and is both thick and luscious.

- 1 tablespoon olive oil
- 1 small onion, chopped
- 2 celery stalks, chopped
- 2 medium carrots, chopped
- 2 garlic cloves, minced
- ¼ teaspoon dried basil
- ¼ teaspoon celery seed
- ¼ teaspoon garlic powder
- ¼ teaspoon ground black pepper
- ¼ teaspoon dried thyme
- 2 cups dried split peas, rinsed
- 1 medium russet potato, peeled and cubed, or 2 red potatoes, cubed[1]
- ½ cup barley, uncooked
- 4 cups *Chicken Broth (pg 208)* or unsalted chicken broth
- 3½ cups water
- ½ cup brandy (optional)[2]
- 1 tablespoon LS chicken bouillon
- 1 bay leaf

1. Heat oil in a large pot over medium heat; add onion, celery stalks, and carrots. Cook, stirring frequently, until onion is translucent, 4 to 5 minutes. Stir in garlic, basil, celery seed, garlic powder, pepper, and thyme; continue cooking and stirring until you smell the garlic, about 1 minute.
2. Add remaining ingredients; bring to boil. Decrease heat to low; cover and simmer, stirring occasionally, until most of the water has been absorbed and soup has thickened, 2 to 3 hours. Remove and let cool slightly.
3. Remove bay leaf and place one-third of the split pea mixture in a blender or food processor and pulse until smooth; repeat with remaining mixture. *NOTE:* If you like it chunky, skip this step.
4. Return purée to pot and heat through; serve.

NUTRITIONAL INFO PER SERVING: Calories 312, Fat 3g (Saturated Fat 0g), Cholesterol 3mg, Carbohydrates 49g (Fiber 16g, Sugar 6g), Sodium 41mg (73mg with NSA chicken broth)

VARIATION
Spicy Split Pea Soup
1. For a spicy flavor, instead of the basil and thyme, substitute 2 teaspoons NSA chili powder, 1 teaspoon ground cumin, ½ teaspoon ground coriander, ½ teaspoon ground turmeric, and ¼ teaspoon ground ginger.

NUTRITIONAL INFO PER SERVING: Calories 315, Fat 3g (Sat Fat 0g), Chol 3mg, Carb 50g (Fiber 16g, Sugar 6g), Sodium 41mg (74mg with NSA chicken broth)

Recipe Notes
1 – To add a hint of sweetness, substitute a sweet potato for the russet.
2 – If not adding brandy, increase chicken broth or water by ½ cup.

TOTAL SODIUM & FAT BY INGREDIENT
Sodium:
- 1 sweet onion - 2mg
- 2 celery - 64mg
- 2 carrots - 84mg
- 2 garlic cloves - 1mg
- ¼ t celery seed - 1mg
- 2 c dried split peas - 59mg
- 1 potato - 11mg
- ½ c barley - 9mg
- 4 c *Chicken Broth* - 80mg
  or NSA chicken broth - 340mg
- 1 T LS chicken bouillon - 15mg

Fat (Sat Fat):
- 1 T olive oil - 14g (2g)
- 2 c dried split peas - 5g (0g)
- ½ c barley - 1g (0g)
- 4 c *Chicken Broth* - 1g (0g)
  or NSA chicken broth - 0g (0g)

Brands used/alternatives:
Pacific Foods Organic Unsalted Chicken Stock
Herb Ox NSA Chicken Bouillon

MINESTRONE

Sodium Per Serving – 56mg Serves 12

My Italian grandmother made the best vegetable soup. Although I haven't captured the exact flavor, my desalted version is pretty close. It makes a load of soup and can easily be cut in half. Better yet, freeze some and save for another day. This also is a great way to clean out the refrigerator.

- 1 tablespoon olive oil
- 1 onion, diced
- 2 celery stalks, chopped
- 2 carrots, chopped
- 2 garlic cloves, minced
- ½ teaspoon garlic powder
- ½ teaspoon ground black pepper
- 4 cups *Chicken Broth (pg 208)* or unsalted chicken broth
- 2 cups *Beef Broth (pg 208)* or unsalted beef broth
- 1 (28-oz) can crushed tomatoes[1]
- 1 tablespoon LS beef or chicken bouillon
- 3 cups fresh or frozen vegetables, sliced or cut into bite-sized chunks[2]
- 1 medium potato, diced
- 1¼ cups NSA frozen peas
- 1 (15-oz) can NSA red kidney beans, undrained
- 1½ cups whole corn, fresh or frozen
- 2 cups shredded cabbage
- 4 oz uncooked pasta, such as elbow, penne, or ziti
- 1 tablespoon cider vinegar
- 1 tablespoon sugar
- ½ teaspoon dried basil
- ½ teaspoon dried oregano
- ½ teaspoon dried rosemary, crumbled

1. Heat oil in a large pot over medium heat; add onion, celery, carrots, garlic, garlic powder, and pepper. Cook, stirring frequently, until onion is translucent, 3 to 4 minutes.
2. Add remaining ingredients and bring to boil. Decrease heat to medium-low; cover, and simmer until veggies and pasta are tender, about 40 minutes. Serve with Parmesan cheese, if desired.

NUTRITIONAL INFO PER SERVING: Calories 199, Fat 2g (Sat Fat 0g), Chol 2mg, Carb 38g (Fiber 8g, Sugar 10g), Sodium 56mg (85mg with NSA chicken and NSA beef broth)

Recipe Notes
1 – Although most of the sodium in this soup comes from the crushed tomatoes, I think the added salt is necessary for a flavorful soup (look for brands with 50mg or less per ¼ cup). Visit LowSaltFoods.com for a list of brands.
2 – Use any combination of veggies that you like, such as broccoli, cauliflower, green beans, or zucchini.

TOTAL SODIUM & FAT BY INGREDIENT

Sodium:
- 1 onion - 4mg
- 2 celery - 64mg
- 2 carrots - 84mg
- 2 garlic cloves - 1mg
- 4 c *Chicken Broth* - 80mg
  or NSA chicken broth - 340mg
- 2 c *Beef Broth* - 40mg
  or NSA beef broth - 130mg
- 28 oz crushed tomatoes - 260mg
- 1 T bouillon - 15mg
- 3 c mixed veggies - 60mg
- 1 potato - 11mg
- 5 oz peas - 0mg
- 15 oz NSA kidney beans - 18mg
- 15 oz NSA whole corn - 10mg
- 2 c cabbage - 25mg
- 4 oz macaroni - 7mg

Fat (Sat Fat):
- 1 T olive oil - 14g (2g)
- 4 c *Chicken Broth* - 1g (0g)
  or NSA chicken broth - 0g (0g)
- 15 oz NSA corn - 2g (0g)
- 4 oz macaroni - 2g (0g)

Brands used/alternatives:
Pacific Foods Organic Unsalted Chicken Stock
Swanson Unsalted Beef Broth
Cento Crushed Tomatoes
Herb Ox NSA Chix or Beef Bouillon
Birds Eye C&W Ultimate Petite Mixed Veggies
Birds Eye Steamfresh Peas
Kuner's NSA Red Kidney Beans
Kroger Super Sweet Corn

Grandma's Lentil Soup

Sodium Per Serving – 85mg   Serves 6

This is one of the wonderful dishes my Italian grandmother prepared for family gatherings. Filled with many vegetables, this thick and yummy soup is one of my favorites.

- **2 tablespoons olive oil**
- **3 carrots, chopped**
- **2 celery stalks, chopped**
- **1 onion, chopped**
- **2 garlic cloves, minced**
- **1 teaspoon dried basil**
- **½ teaspoon garlic powder**
- **½ teaspoon dried oregano**
- **½ teaspoon ground black pepper**
- **½ teaspoon dried thyme**
- **5 cups *Chicken Broth (pg 208)* or unsalted chicken broth**
- **1 tablespoon LS chicken bouillon**
- **1 (14-oz) can crushed tomatoes[1]**
- **2 cups dry red lentils[2]**
- **1 potato, peeled and chopped**
- **2 bay leaves**
- **1–2 teaspoons hot pepper sauce, such as *Tabasco***
- **¼ cup chopped fresh Italian parsley**

1. Heat oil in a large pot over medium heat; add carrots, celery, and onions. Cook, stirring frequently, until onions are transparent, 4 to 5 minutes; add garlic and cook, stirring frequently, until you smell the garlic, about 1 minute.
2. Decrease heat to medium-low; stir in basil, garlic powder, oregano, pepper, and thyme. Add chicken broth, bouillon, tomatoes, lentils, potatoes, and bay leaves; cover and simmer until lentils are tender and soup has thickened, about 45 minutes to an hour. Remove from heat and cool slightly.
3. Remove bay leaves and place one-half of lentil mixture in a blender or food processor; pulse until smooth. Return purée to pot and stir in hot pepper sauce, and parsley; serve.

NUTRITIONAL INFO PER SERVING: Calories 223, Fat 5g (Sat Fat 1g), Chol 5mg, Carb 37g (Fiber 10g, Sugar 9g), Sodium 85mg (98mg with NSA chicken broth)

Recipe Notes

1 – Several manufacturers make NSA tomato products with 50mg or less sodium in a ½ cup serving (visit LowSaltFoods.com, for a list of LS brands).

2 – There are several varieties of lentils, but the red will cook up faster. See *Lentils*, pg 249, for varieties and preparation information.

TOTAL SODIUM & FAT BY INGREDIENT

Sodium:
- 3 carrots - 126mg
- 2 celery stalks - 64mg
- 1 onion - 4mg
- 2 garlic cloves - 1mg
- 5 c *Chicken Broth* - 100mg
  or NSA chicken broth - 175mg
- 3 t LS chicken bouillon - 15mg
- 15 oz NSA tomatoes - 140mg
- 2 c dried lentils - 8mg
- 1 potato - 11mg
- 1 t hot pepper sauce - 35mg
- ¼ c parsley - 8mg

Fat (Sat Fat):
- 2 c lentils - 2g (0g)
- 2 T olive oil - 28g (4g)
- 5 c *Chicken Broth* - 2g (1g)
  or NSA chicken broth - 0g (0g)

Brands used/alternatives:
- *Pacific Foods* Organic Unsalted Chicken Stock
- *Herb Ox* NSA Chicken Bouillon
- *Simple Truth Organic* Crushed Tomatoes

SEAFOOD CHOWDERS

SIMPLY WHITE CLAM CHOWDER

Sodium Per Serving – 136mg　　　　　　　　　　　　　　　　　　　　Serves 4

Clam chowder, particularly the white or New England variety, is loaded with sodium, averaging 992mg a cup. This yummy version is thick and creamy with substantially less salt. The hot pepper sauce is a must, adding a little heat and spiciness that goes perfectly with the chowder.

- 1 tablespoon olive oil
- 1 tablespoon unsalted butter or margarine
- 1 small sweet onion, chopped
- 1 carrot, chopped
- 1 celery stalk, chopped
- 1 red potato, diced (about 1 cup)
- ¼ teaspoon herbes de Provence[1]
- ¼ teaspoon garlic powder
- ¼ teaspoon dried marjoram
- ¼ teaspoon dried thyme
- ⅛ teaspoon celery seed
- ⅛ teaspoon white pepper
- 1 (15-oz) can NSA cream corn
- ½ cup *Chicken Broth (pg 208)* or unsalted chicken broth
- 1 teaspoon LS chicken bouillon
- 1 (10-oz) can baby clams, drained, minced, and juice reserved
- 1½ cups lowfat milk[2]
- 4–5 drops hot pepper sauce, such as *Tabasco*
- ⅛ teaspoon *Liquid Smoke*[3]
- 2 tablespoons cornstarch, mixed with ¼ cup water to make a paste
- Chopped fresh Italian parsley (optional)

1. Heat oil and butter in a large pan over medium heat; add onion, carrot, celery, potato, herbes de Provence, garlic powder, marjoram, thyme, celery seed, and white pepper. Cook, stirring frequently, until onion is translucent, about 4 minutes.
2. Stir in corn, chicken broth, bouillon, and reserved clam juice; decrease heat to low, cover, and simmer until vegetables are tender, 20 to 30 minutes.
3. Add clams, milk, hot pepper sauce, and *Liquid Smoke*; increase heat to medium and heat through.
4. Slowly mix in cornstarch paste, stirring constantly until thickened to desired consistency. Serve with parsley and additional hot pepper sauce.

NUTRITIONAL INFO PER SERVING: Calories 291, Fat 9g (Sat Fat 3g), Chol 56mg, Carb 44g (Fiber 3g, Sugar 12g), Sodium 136mg (145mg with NSA chicken broth)

Recipe Notes

1 – Herbes de Provence is a blend of herbs commonly used in French cooking – most often a mix of basil, chervil, fennel, lavender, marjoram, rosemary, sage, savory, and thyme. The combination and portions vary depending on the manufacturer.

2 – For a richer soup, instead of milk, use light cream or half-and-half.

3 – *Liquid Smoke* gives a smoky flavor to foods and is available in most supermarkets in the grilling sauces and marinades section.

TOTAL SODIUM & FAT BY INGREDIENT

Sodium:
- 1 sweet onion - 13mg
- 1 carrot - 42mg
- 1 celery stalk - 32mg
- 1 red potato - 10mg
- 15 oz NSA cream corn - 15mg
- ½ c *Chicken Broth* - 10mg or NSA chicken broth - 43mg
- 1 t LS chicken bouillon - 5mg
- 10 oz clams w/juice - 260mg
- 1½ c LF milk - 153mg
- 4 drops hot pepper sauce - 1mg
- 2 T parsley - 4mg

Fat (Sat Fat):
- 1 T olive oil - 14g (2g)
- 1 T NSA butter - 12g (7g) or NSA margarine - 9g (4g)
- 15 oz NSA cream corn - 2g (0g)
- 10 oz clams - 2g (0g)
- ½ c *Chicken Broth* - 10mg or NSA chicken broth - 18mg
- 1 t LS chicken bouillon - 1g (0g)
- 1½ c LF milk - 8g (3g)

Brands used/alternatives:
Del Monte NSA Cream Corn
Pacific Foods Organic Unsalted Chicken Stock
Herb Ox NSA Chicken Bouillon
Geisha Whole Baby Clams
Simple Truth 2% Milk

BEAN SOUPS & CHILI

Hearty Black Bean Soup

Sodium Per Serving – 55mg   Serves 4

This filling soup with a hint of orange goes together quickly. Use a large skillet, so the liquid cooks down quickly to a rich and tasty broth. This serves 4 as a first course or 2 as a main dish.

- 1 tablespoon olive oil
- ½ onion, chopped
- 1 carrot, diced
- 1 celery stalk, diced
- 1 garlic clove, minced
- 1 (15-oz) can NSA black beans, drained and rinsed[1]
- 4 cups *Chicken Broth (pg 208)* or unsalted chicken broth
- 1 (15-oz) can NSA whole corn, drained
- ½ (6-oz) can NSA tomato paste
- 2 teaspoons LS chicken bouillon
- 1–2 teaspoons NSA chili powder[2]
- ½ teaspoon dried cumin
- ¼ teaspoon ground black pepper
- Pinch cayenne pepper
- ½ teaspoon finely grated orange rind

Optional Garnishes:
- Lowfat sour cream
- Swiss cheese, shredded

1. Heat oil in a large skillet over medium heat; add onions, carrots, and celery. Cook, stirring frequently, until onions are translucent, 4 to 5 minutes. Add garlic; cook, stirring constantly, until you smell the garlic, 1 to 2 minutes.
2. Stir in the beans, chicken broth, corn, tomato paste, bouillon, chili powder, cumin, black pepper, cayenne, and orange rind; cook, uncovered, until vegetables are tender, 40 to 45 minutes. *NOTE:* Liquid will reduce to about 2 cups, creating a deep-colored, rich-tasting broth.
3. Serve, topped with sour cream and cheese.

NUTRITIONAL INFO PER SERVING (without garnishes): Calories 234, Fat 4g (Sat Fat 1g), Chol 6mg, Carb 35g (Fiber 11g, Sugar 8g), Sodium 55mg (152mg with NSA chicken broth)

Recipe Notes
1 – There are several brands of NSA black beans. See *Canned Beans*, pg 243, for additional info.
2 – Surprisingly, most chili powders contain sodium (26mg per tsp). Look for brands without salt listed in the ingredients.

For a spicy soup, use 2 tsp chili powder. For a less spicy version, 1 tsp is probably enough.

TOTAL SODIUM & FAT BY INGREDIENT

Sodium:
- ½ onion - 2mg
- 1 garlic clove - 1mg
- 1 carrot - 42mg
- 1 celery stalk - 32mg
- 15 oz NSA black beans - 18mg
- 4 c *Chicken Broth* - 80mg
  or NSA chicken broth - 340mg
- 2 t LS chicken bouillon - 10mg
- 15 oz NSA corn -10mg
- ½ t cumin - 2mg

Fat (Sat Fat):
- 1 T olive oil - 14g (2g)
- 4 c *Chicken Broth* - 1g (0g)
  or NSA chicken broth - 0g (0g)
- 15 oz NSA corn - 2g (0g)

Brands used/alternatives:
- *Kuner's NSA* Black Beans
- *Libby's Naturals* NSA Whole Kernel Sweet Corn
- *Bionaturae* NSA Tomato Paste
- *Pacific Foods* Organic Unsalted Chicken Stock
- *Herb Ox* NSA Chicken Bouillon

EASY 4-BEAN SOUP

Sodium Per Serving – 159mg   Serves 8

This delicious chili-like soup is ideal for spur-of-the-moment gatherings; just open a few cans, pour in a pot and heat it up. Add a tossed salad, Cornbread (pg 198), and you have a great crowd pleaser.

- 2 (15-oz) cans NSA kidney beans, undrained[1]
- 1 (15-oz) can NSA black beans, undrained[1]
- 1 (15-oz) can NSA pinto beans, undrained[1]
- 1 (15-oz) can NSA garbanzo beans, undrained[1]
- 1 (15-oz) can *Amy's Light in Sodium* Chili[2]
- 1 package *Dash* Chili Seasoning Mix
- 1 (4-oz) can diced green chiles
- 2 cups salsa[3]
- 1½ cups whole corn, fresh or frozen
- 2 tablespoons chipotle chile paste or minced chipotle peppers in adobo sauce[4]

Optional garnishes:
- 2 oz shredded Cheddar cheese (about ½ cup)
- 4 oz shredded Swiss cheese (about 1 cup)
- Chopped sweet onion or green onions (white and light green parts)
- Diced avocado

1. Combine all ingredients, except garnishes, in a pot over medium heat; cook, stirring occasionally, until heated through, 10 to 15 minutes.
2. Mix Cheddar and Swiss cheeses together. Serve soup with cheese and onions on top.

NUTRITIONAL INFO PER SERVING (without garnishes): Calories 355, Fat 4g (Saturated Fat 0g), Cholesterol 0mg, Carbohydrates 58g (Fiber 21g, Sugar 7g), Sodium 159mg

VARIATION
MEATY BEAN SOUP

1. Heat 1 tablespoon olive oil in a large pot over medium heat; brown ½ pound ground beef or turkey. Add 1 teaspoon NSA chili powder[5], ½ teaspoon spicy seasoning[6], ¼ teaspoon ground cumin, ¼ teaspoon garlic powder, ⅛ teaspoon ground black pepper, and ¼ cup salsa. Stir in beans and remaining ingredients; proceed as directed.

NUTRITIONAL INFO PER SERVING: Calories 446, Fat 11g (Sat Fat 3g), Chol 20mg, Carb 59g (Fiber 21g, Sugar 7g), Sodium 188mg

TOTAL SODIUM & FAT BY INGREDIENT

Sodium:
- 30 oz NSA kidney beans - 35mg
- 15 oz NSA black beans - 18mg
- 15 oz NSA pinto beans - 18mg
- 15 oz NSA garbanzoss - 35mg
- 15 oz *Amy's* Chili - 500mg
- 16 oz salsa - 640mg
- 2 T chipotle chile paste - 30mg
  or 2 T chipotle in adobo - 140mg

Fat (Sat Fat):
- 15 oz NSA garbanzos - 7g (0g)
- 15 oz *Amy's* Chili - 16g (2g)
- 2 T chipotle chile paste - 6g (0g)
  or 2 T chipotle in adobo - 1g (0g)

Brands used/alternatives:
- *Kuner's* NSA Red Kidney, Black, and Pinto Beans
- *Westbrae Natural* Garbanzo Beans
- *Amy's Light in Sodium* Chili
- *Frog Ranch* Salsa
- *Gran Luchito* Chipolte Chile Paste or *Herdez* Chipotle in Adobo

Recipe Notes

1 – Visit LowSaltFoods.com for a list of NSA bean brands.
2 – The NSA chili I originally used is no longer available. As a substitute, I use *Amy's Light in Sodium Chili*, which tastes even better, even though it does have more salt.
3 – Most bottled tomato salsas average 256mg sodium per 2 tbsp, bean and corn salsa has 180mg, and fresh salsa, 142mg. Look for one of many delicious LS varieties with less than 80mg.
4 – I use *Gran Luchito* Chipotle Chile Paste, available at Walmart and Amazon. It has a wonderful smoky flavor and only has 15mg sodium per tbsp (versus 70mg-130mg for chipotles in adobo sauce).
5 – Surprisingly, most chili powders contain sodium (26mg per tsp). Look for brands without salt listed in the ingredients.
6 – Use several unsalted spicy seasonings used for Cajun or barbecue rubs or no-salt dried seasoning spices in the Hispanic section of many supermarkets.

Texas-Style Turkey Chili

Sodium Per Serving – 96mg   Serves 8–10

This is a very hearty and spicy chili that goes together quickly using canned beans. Allow the chili to cook at least an hour or more. If you like it spicy, add more dried red pepper flakes and/or cayenne pepper.

- 1 tablespoon olive oil
- ½ onion, chopped
- 2 bell peppers, chopped
- 4 garlic cloves, minced
- 1½ pounds lean ground turkey
- 2 tablespoons NSA chili powder[1]
- 1½ teaspoons ground cumin
- 1 teaspoon dried basil
- 1 teaspoon dried oregano
- 1 teaspoon dried red pepper flakes or ½ teaspoon hot pepper sauce, such as *Tabasco*
- ½ teaspoon cayenne pepper
- ½ teaspoon ground cinnamon
- ½ teaspoon ground black pepper
- 2 (15-oz) cans NSA diced tomatoes[2]
- 2 (15-oz) cans NSA kidney beans, drained[3]
- 1 (15-oz) can NSA tomato purée
- 1 (4-oz) can diced green chiles

1. Heat oil in a large pot over medium heat; add onion and bell peppers. Cook, stirring frequently, until onions are translucent, 4 to 5 minutes; add garlic and cook, stirring frequently, until you smell the garlic, about 1 minute.
2. Add turkey; cook until no longer pink, stirring frequently and breaking up any large pieces, about 5 minutes. Add the chili powder, cumin, basil, oregano, red pepper flakes, cayenne, cinnamon, and black pepper; thoroughly mix.
3. Stir in undrained tomatoes, beans, tomato purée, and green chiles. Bring to a boil; decrease heat to medium-low. Cover and simmer, stirring occasionally, for 1 to 2 hours. NOTE: The longer this cooks, the more the flavors intensify and the richer the soup becomes.

NUTRITIONAL INFO PER SERVING: Calories 272, Fat 3g (Sat Fat 0g), Chol 41mg, Carb 32g (Fiber 11g, Sugar 7g), Sodium 96mg

Recipe Notes

1 – Surprisingly, chili powder contains sodium (26mg per tsp). Look for NSA brands, like *The Spice Hunter*, available at many supermarkets or from online grocers.

2 – Several manufacturers offer NSA diced tomatoes with 30mg or less sodium per ½ cup serving. Visit *LowSaltFoods.com* for a list of NSA brands.

3 – Most canned kidney beans have up to 480mg sodium in ½ cup. There are several NSA brands which have less than 40mg a serving. Also see *Canned Beans*, pg 243, for additional info.

TOTAL SODIUM & FAT BY INGREDIENT

Sodium:
- ½ onion - 4mg
- 2 bell peppers - 7mg
- 4 garlic cloves - 2mg
- 1½ lb ground turkey - 330mg
- 1½ t cumin - 6mg
- ½ t hot pepper flakes - 1mg
- 30 oz NSA tomatoes - 106mg
- 30 oz NSA kidney beans - 35mg
- 15 oz NSA tomato purée - 98mg
- 4 oz green chiles - 180mg

Fat (Sat Fat):
- 1 T olive oil - 14g (2g)
- 1½ lb ground turkey - 6g (0g)
- 2 T NSA chili powder - 2g (0g)

Brands used/alternatives:
- *Jennie-O* 99% Lean Ground Turkey
- *Simple Truth Organic* NSA Diced Tomatoes
- *Kuner's* NSA Red Kidney Beans
- *Cento* Tomato Purée
- *La Preferida* Organic Diced Green Chiles

SALADS & SALAD DRESSINGS

SIDE SALADS
- Black Bean & Pepper Salad 58
- Bean, Pepper & Chèvre Salad 58
- Bean, Pepper & Stilton Salad........... 58
- Four Bean Salad................. 59
- Pea Salad with Bacon & Cashews 60
- Roasted Beet & Walnut Salad 60
- Sweet & Sour Cole Slaw 61
- Spicy Cole Slaw 61
- Baked Potato Salad 62
- German Potato Salad 63
- Warm Potato Salad 63
- Three-Layer Molded Salad............. 64
- Fruit Salad with Vanilla Yogurt......... 65
- Grand Marnier Fruit Salad 65
- Mediterranean Pasta Salad............ 66

TOSSED SALADS
- Favorite Tossed Salad 67
- Chicken, Romaine & Stilton Salad 67
- Mâche, Pear & Toasted Walnut Salad.... 68
- Spinach, Pear & Walnut Salad 68
- Mixed Greens with Avocado & Orange.. 68
- Mesclun with Stilton & Sugared Pecans ..69
- Spinach, Dried Cranberries & Chèvre....69
- Caesar Salad........................70
- Chicken Caesar 70
  - Caesar Dressing....................70
- Spinach Salad with Warm Bacon Dressing........................71
  - Warm Bacon Dressing 71

MAIN COURSE SALADS
- Avocado, Apple, Dates & Jicama Salad....72
- Chicken, Apple & Pecan Tossed Salad....72
- Cobb Salad........................73
- Curried Chicken Waldorf 74

SALAD DRESSINGS
- Orange Vinaigrette 75
- Poppy Seed Dressing..................75
- The Best Vinaigrette 76
- French Dressing.....................76
- Raspberry Vinaigrette.................76
- Shallot Vinaigrette...................76
- Roasted Garlic Dressing...............76
- Ranch Dressing 77
- Green Goddess Dressing 77

SIDE SALADS

Black Bean & Pepper Salad
Sodium Per Serving – 16mg Serves 10–12

This salad is a personal favorite. Not only colorful, it's quick and easy to make. Perfect for a picnic or potluck – make lots as everyone will come back for more!

Salad:
- 2 (15-oz) cans NSA black beans, drained and rinsed[1]
- 2 green bell peppers, diced
- 1 red bell pepper, diced
- 1 yellow bell pepper, diced
- 1 small sweet onion, diced
- 1 (15-oz) can NSA whole kernel corn, drained[2]

Dressing:
- ¼ cup balsamic vinegar
- ¼ cup extra-virgin olive oil
- ¼ teaspoon finely minced garlic
- 1 teaspoon Dijon-style mustard
- 2 teaspoons sugar
- 2 tablespoons chopped fresh Italian parsley (optional)

1. In a large bowl, combine beans, peppers, onion, and corn.
2. *For the dressing:* Blend together the vinegar, oil, garlic, mustard, and sugar, either by whisking in a small bowl or by shaking well in a screw-top jar. Pour over bean mixture and mix thoroughly; cover and refrigerate several hours.
3. Before serving, mix in parsley and stir well.

NUTRITIONAL INFO PER SERVING: Calories 173, Fat 6g (Saturated Fat 1g), Cholesterol 0mg, Carbohydrates 23g (Fiber 8g, Sugar 6g), Sodium 16mg

---

VARIATIONS

Bean, Pepper & Chèvre Salad
1. Before serving, mix in 2 oz crumbled chèvre[3] cheese.

NUTRITIONAL INFO PER SERVING: Calories 189, Fat 7g (Sat Fat 2g), Chol 4mg, Carb 23g (Fiber 8g, Sugar 6g), Sodium 25mg

Bean, Pepper & Stilton Salad
1. Before serving, mix in 2 oz crumbled Stilton or blue cheese[4].

NUTRITIONAL INFO PER SERVING: Calories 211, Fat 9g (Sat Fat 3g), Chol 10mg, Carb 23g (Fiber 8g, Sugar 6g), Sodium 69mg

---

TOTAL SODIUM & FAT BY INGREDIENT

Sodium:
- 30 oz NSA black beans - 35mg
- 2 green bell pepper - 7mg
- 1 red bell pepper - 5mg
- 1 yellow bell pepper - 5mg
- 1 sweet onion - 35mg
- 15 oz NSA whole corn - 35mg
- ¼ c balsamic - 15mg
- ¼ c olive oil - 1mg
- 1 t Dijon mustard - 40mg
- 2 T parsley - 4mg

Fat (Sat Fat):
- 15 oz NSA whole corn - 5g (0g)
- ¼ c olive oil - 54g (7g)

Brands used/alternatives:
- Kuner's NSA Black Beans
- Libby's Naturals NSA Whole Kernel Sweet Corn
- Gold's Dijon Mustard

Recipe Notes
1 – Most canned kidney beans have up to 480mg sodium in ½ cup. There are several NSA brands which have less than 40mg a serving. See *Canned Beans*, pg 243, for additional info.
2 – Instead of canned corn, use 1½ cups fresh (about 3 ears).
3 – Goat cheese ranges from sweet and mild to tangy and sharp. The type (soft, semi-soft, etc) determines the amount of sodium, ranging from 50mg-140mg an oz. Chèvre is generally on the low side.
4 – Look for Stilton or blue cheese varieties with 260mg sodium or less.

Four Bean Salad

Sodium Per Serving – 61mg Serves 12–14

I have made this delicious salad for more than 25 years, except now I use no-salt-added beans. For the best taste, let the flavors marinate at least 6 hours ahead of time or the day before.

Salad:
- 1 (15-oz) can NSA red kidney beans, drained[1]
- 2 (15-oz) cans NSA whole green beans, drained
- 1 cup yellow (wax) beans, drained
- 1 (15-oz) can NSA garbanzo beans, drained
- 1 red or green bell pepper, chopped
- 1 small sweet onion, chopped

Dressing:
- ½ cup cider vinegar
- 8 tablespoons sugar
- 2 tablespoons extra-virgin olive oil
- ¼ teaspoon onion or garlic powder
- ¼ teaspoon ground black pepper

1. *For the salad:* In a large bowl, combine beans, bell pepper, and onion.
2. *For the dressing:* Blend together the vinegar, sugar, oil, garlic powder, and pepper, either by whisking in a small bowl or by shaking well in a screw-top jar.
3. Pour dressing over beans, mixing well. Cover and refrigerate for several hours or overnight.

NUTRITIONAL INFO PER SERVING: Calories 132, Fat 3g (Sat Fat 0g), Chol 0mg, Carb 21g (Fiber 5g, Sugar 9g), Sodium 61mg

Recipe Notes
1 – Substitute NSA pinto or black beans for the kidney beans. See *Canned Beans*, pg 243, for more info.

Variations
Other additions to cut up and add to the salad: 1 roasted red pepper, a 4-oz jar of pimentos, or 2 celery stalks.

To jazz up the dressing, add a finely minced garlic clove and 1/2 tsp of celery seed, dried basil, or dried tarragon.

TOTAL SODIUM & FAT BY INGREDIENT

Sodium:
- 15 oz NSA kidney beans - 18mg
- 30 oz NSA green beans - 70mg
- 1 c yellow beans - 580mg
- 15 oz NSA garbanzos - 35mg
- 1 red bell pepper - 5mg
- 1 sweet onion - 13mg
- ½ c vinegar - 6mg

Fat (Sat Fat):
- 15 oz NSA garbanzos - 7g (0g)
- 2 T olive oil - 28g (4g)

Brands used/alternatives:
- *Kuner's* NSA Red Kidney Beans
- *Del Monte* NSA Cut Green Beans
- *Kroger* Cut Wax Beans
- *Westbrae Natural* Garbanzo Beans

Pea Salad with Bacon & Cashews

Sodium Per Serving – 40mg   Serves 8

This simple and "crunchy" salad is perfect for a potluck or barbecue. Although bacon is very salty, using a small amount of a lower-sodium brand allows this "no-no" to fit into a low-salt diet. This salad is best if made the day before to allow the flavors to blend.

- 1 (16-oz) package frozen NSA peas, do not thaw
- 1 small sweet onion, chopped
- 2 celery stalks, chopped
- 1 (8-oz) can water chestnuts, drained and chopped
- 2/3 cup lowfat sour cream
- 1/4 teaspoon onion or garlic powder
- 1/8 teaspoon ground black pepper
- 4 slices lower-sodium turkey bacon, cooked and crumbled[1]
- 1/3 cup chopped unsalted cashews or peanuts

1. Combine peas, onion, celery, water chestnuts, sour cream, onion powder, and pepper; cover and refrigerate overnight.
2. Before serving, fold in bacon and cashews. Let stand at room temperature 30 minutes before serving.

NUTRITIONAL INFO PER SERVING: Calories 112, Fat 4g (Saturated Fat 2g), Cholesterol 9mg, Carbohydrates 12g (Fiber 3g, Sugar 5g), Sodium 40mg

Roasted Beet & Walnut Salad

Sodium Per Serving – 87mg   Serves 10

If you like beets, you'll love this wonderfully rich salad. The deep maroon color of the beets makes a beautiful presentation, especially on buffet tables. Prepare the day before, adding the nuts and cheese just before serving.

- 2 tablespoons balsamic or red wine vinegar
- 2 tablespoons extra virgin olive oil
- 1 teaspoon Dijon-style mustard
- 1-2 teaspoons sugar
- 6–8 beets, roasted and cubed (about 5–6 cups)
- 1/2 cup chopped walnuts
- 2 oz Stilton, crumbled[3]

1. Blend together vinegar, oil, mustard, and sugar either by whisking in a small bowl or by shaking well in a screw-top jar.
2. In a large bowl, combine beets and dressing: chill at least 30 minutes. Before serving, mix in walnuts and cheese.

NUTRITIONAL INFO PER SERVING: Calories 112, Fat 9g (Sat Fat 2g), Chol 6mg, Carb 6g (Fiber 2g, Sugar 4g), Sodium 87mg

Recipe Notes

1 – Use turkey bacon to keep fat down.
2 – See *Roasting Beets*, pg 253.
3 – Stilton is milder and firmer than other blue cheeses, plus it has much less sodium. Listed below are several popular blue cheese varieties and the average sodium per oz:

Stilton	220mg	Blue	395mg
Gorgonzola	350mg	Roquefort	513mg

TOTAL SODIUM & FAT BY INGREDIENT

PEA SALAD
Sodium:
- 1 sweet onion - 13mg
- 2 celery stalks - 64mg
- 2/3 c LF sour cream - 80mg
- 4 sl LS turkey bacon - 160mg

Fat (Sat Fat):
- 2/3 c LF sour cream - 13g (8g)
- 4 sl LS turkey bacon - 4g (1g)
- 1/3 c NSA cashews - 17g (3g)

Brands used/alternatives:
- *Bird's Eye C&W* Petite Peas
- *Daisy Light* Sour Cream
- *Butterball* Lower Sodium Turkey Bacon

ROASTED BEET SALAD
Sodium:
- 2 T balsamic - 7mg
- 1 t Dijon mustard - 40mg
- 6 beets - 384mg
- 1/2 c walnuts - 1mg
- 2 oz Stilton cheese - 440mg

Fat (Sat Fat):
- 1 T olive oil - 28g (4g)
- 1/2 c walnuts - 38g (4g)
- 2 oz Stilton cheese - 18g (12g)

Brands used/alternatives:
- *Gold's* Dijon Mustard
- *Clawson* Blue Stilton Cheese

Sweet & Sour Cole Slaw

Sodium Per Serving – 28mg Serves 8

This tangy, sweet slaw is a great alternative to the heavy, mayo-based salads in the supermarket. Allow several hours for the flavors to blend or make a day ahead of time.

Dressing:
- 3 tablespoons extra-virgin olive oil
- 2 tablespoons cider vinegar
- 1 tablespoon lemon or lime juice
- 1/3 cup sugar
- 1 garlic clove, minced
- 1/2 teaspoon hot pepper sauce, such as Tabasco, or 1/4 teaspoon crushed red pepper flakes
- 1/2 teaspoon garlic or onion powder
- 1/4 teaspoon ground black pepper

Salad:
- 6–8 cups (1 medium head) green cabbage, shredded, or 1 (16-oz) package coleslaw mix
- 1 small sweet onion, chopped
- 1 large carrot, grated
- 2 celery stalks, chopped

1. *For the dressing:* Blend together oil, vinegar, lemon juice, sugar, garlic, hot pepper sauce, garlic powder, and pepper, either by whisking in a small bowl or by shaking well in a screw-top jar.
2. *For the salad:* In a large bowl, combine cabbage, onion, carrot, and celery; add dressing and toss. Season with additional pepper to taste.
3. Cover and refrigerate 2 to 3 hours to allow flavors to blend. Toss before serving.

NUTRITIONAL INFO PER SERVING: Calories 92, Fat 5g (Saturated Fat 1g), Cholesterol 0mg, Carbohydrates 15g (Fiber 2g, Sugar 12g), Sodium 28mg

---

VARIATION
Spicy Cole Slaw
1. For a spicy taste, add 1/2 teaspoon ground cumin to the dressing and to the salad add 1/4 cup chopped cilantro.

NUTRITIONAL INFO PER SERVING: Calories 92, Fat 5g (Sat Fat 1g), Chol 0mg, Carb 15g (Fiber 2g, Sugar 12g), Sodium 28mg

---

TOTAL SODIUM & FAT BY INGREDIENT

Sodium:
- 2 T cider vinegar - 2mg
- 1 garlic clove - 1mg
- 1/3 c sugar - 1mg
- 1/2 t hot pepper sauce - 18mg
- 6 c cabbage - 76mg
- 1 sweet onion - 13mg
- 1 carrot - 50mg
- 2 celery stalks - 64mg

Fat (Sat Fat):
- 3 T olive oil - 42g (6g)

Baked Potato Salad

Sodium Per Serving – 74mg   Serves 10

This is a crowd favorite. The addition of mustard and pickle relish imparts enough flavor that no one misses the salt. Because potatoes are very absorbent, marinating them in pickle relish adds a lot of flavor. Allow several hours for the flavors to blend.

- **4 russet potatoes (about 2½ pounds), baked and cooled slightly**[1]
- **2 tablespoons sweet pickle relish**
- **½ cup sweet onion, chopped**
- **2 celery stalks, chopped**
- **1 oz LS black olives, chopped**
- **1 tablespoon yellow or honey mustard**[2]
- **⅓ cup mayonnaise or mayonnaise-like dressing**
- **½ teaspoon garlic or onion powder**
- **½ teaspoon ground black pepper**
- **⅛ teaspoon ground cumin (optional)**

1. While potatoes are still warm, cut into cubes and place in a large bowl. Mix in pickle relish; cover and refrigerate 15 minutes to allow the flavor of the relish to permeate the potatoes.
2. Add remaining ingredients to the potato mixture. If salad seems a little dry, add a little more mustard, mayo, or plain yogurt. Cover and refrigerate 2 to 3 hours to allow flavors to blend.

NUTRITIONAL INFO PER SERVING: Calories 83, Fat 7g (Sat Fat 1g), Chol 8mg, Carb 17g (Fiber 1g, Sugar 1g), Sodium 74mg

Recipe Notes

1 – To bake potatoes, prick in several places, wrap in aluminum foil and bake in a preheated oven at 425°F (220°C) for 60 minutes. Let cool completely before cutting into cubes. For added flavor and color, do not remove the skins.

2 – I generally use yellow mustard, but honey mustard not only reduces the sodium by 9mg a serving, but also adds a hint of sweet tartness.

TOTAL SODIUM & FAT BY INGREDIENT

Sodium:
- 4 russet potatoes - 43mg
- ½ c sweet onion - 4mg
- 2 celery stalks - 64mg
- 1 oz ripe olives - 80mg
- 2 T pickle relish - 120mg
- 1 T yellow mustard - 165mg or honey mustard - 75mg
- ⅓ c mayonnaise - 267mg
- ⅛ t cumin - 1mg

Fat (Sat Fat):
- 4 russet potatoes - 1g (0g)
- 1 oz ripe olives - 6g (2g)
- ⅓ c mayonnaise - 59g (8g)

Brands used/alternatives:
Heinz Sweet Pickle Relish
Mario LS Black Olives
French's Yellow Mustard
Great Value Honey Mustard
Chosen Foods Classic Mayo w/ Avocado Oil

German Potato Salad

Sodium Per Serving – 38mg   Serves 10

This classic is a nice alternative to mayo-based potato salads. It gets even better over time, so make it a day ahead and let the flavors blend.

- **6 slices lower-sodium turkey bacon, cooked, reserving drippings**[1]
- **6–8 large red potatoes, cooked and cubed, do not remove skins**[2]
- **½ cup chopped sweet onion**
- **½ red bell pepper, chopped**
- **2 tablespoons chopped fresh Italian parsley**

Dressing:
- **⅓ cup red wine or cider vinegar**
- **2 tablespoons sugar**
- **¼ teaspoon garlic or onion powder**
- **¼ teaspoon ground marjoram**
- **¼ teaspoon mustard powder**
- **⅛ teaspoon ground black pepper**
- **⅛ teaspoon ground thyme**

1. *For the salad:* In a large bowl, combine bacon, potatoes, onion, bell pepper, and parsley.
2. *For the dressing:* Blend together reserved bacon drippings (plus enough olive oil to equal 1 tablespoon), vinegar, sugar, garlic powder, marjoram, mustard powder, pepper, and thyme, either by whisking in a small bowl or by shaking well in a screw-top jar.
3. Pour dressing over potatoes, mixing well. Cover and refrigerate at least 2 to 3 hours or overnight to let flavors blend.

NUTRITIONAL INFO PER SERVING: Calories 116, Fat 1g (Saturated Fat 0g), Cholesterol 3mg, Carbohydrates 24g (Fiber 2g, Sugar 5g), Sodium 38mg

---

VARIATION
Warm Potato Salad

1. In skillet, add enough olive oil to bacon drippings to equal 1 tablespoon, stir in dressing ingredients (vinegar through thyme).
2. Cook over medium heat until hot; pour over potato mixture and mix carefully. Serve at once.

NUTRITIONAL INFO PER SERVING: Calories 116, Fat 1g (Sat Fat 0g), Chol 3mg, Carb 24g (Fiber 2g, Sugar 5g), Sodium 38mg

---

TOTAL SODIUM & FAT BY INGREDIENT

Sodium:
- 6 sl LS turkey bacon - 240mg
- 6 red potatoes - 126mg
- ½ c sweet onion - 4mg
- ½ red bell pepper - 2mg
- 2 T parsley - 4mg
- ⅓ c red wine vinegar - 4mg

Fat (Sat Fat):
- 6 sl LS turkey bacon - 6g (3g)
- 6 red potatoes - 2g (1g)

Brands used/alternatives:
Butterball Lower Sodium Turkey Bacon

Recipe Notes
1 – Visit *LowSaltFoods.com* for lower-salt bacon brands.
2 – Substitute Yukon gold, white, fingerling, or new potatoes or the red potatoes.

Three-Layer Molded Salad

Sodium Per Serving – 64mg
Serves 10–12

This festive red, white, and green salad is perfect during the holidays. The cream cheese layer is rich-tasting, making this an extra special salad. Allow plenty of preparation time, as each gelatin layer needs several hours of refrigeration in order to set up. Substitute other gelatin flavors for a change of pace and use berries or other fruit instead of cranberries.

- 1 package (4 servings) lime-flavored gelatin mix[1]
- 1 cup chopped celery
- ½ cup (4 oz) whipped cream cheese
- ½ cup lowfat whipped topping[2]
- ¼ cup sugar
- 1 teaspoon vanilla extract
- 1 package (4 servings) cherry or raspberry-flavored gelatin mix[1]
- 2 cups cranberries, chopped
- 1 orange, peeled and cut into bite-size pieces
- ¼ cup unsalted walnuts (optional)

1. Prepare lime gelatin per package directions; stir in celery and pour into a gelatin mold. Cover and refrigerate until gelatin has set.
2. Mix together cream cheese, whipped topping, sugar, and vanilla. Spread over the set-up lime gelatin. Cover and refrigerate until cream cheese has set.
3. Prepare cherry or raspberry gelatin per package directions; stir in cranberries, orange, and walnuts. Cover and refrigerate 30 minutes; pour onto cream cheese layer.
4. Cover and refrigerate for several hours until set; unmold and serve.

NUTRITIONAL INFO PER SERVING: Calories 100, Fat 4g (Sat Fat 2g), Chol 6mg, Carb 13g (Fiber 2g, Sugar 8g), Sodium 64mg

Recipe Notes

1 – Most gelatin mixes average between 55-98mg sodium per serving. *Kroger's Sugar Free Gelatin Desserts* have 20mg-50mg per serving.

2 – Whipped topping has little to no sodium, either frozen or pressurized.

TOTAL SODIUM & FAT BY INGREDIENT

Sodium:
- Lime gelatin (4 serv) - 80mg
- 1 c celery - 137mg
- 4 oz whip cream cheese - 340mg
- Cherry gelatin (4 serv) - 80mg
- 2 c cranberries - 4mg
- 1 orange - 1mg
- ¼ c NSA walnuts - 1mg

Fat (Sat Fat):
- 4 oz whip cr cheese - 18g (12g)
- ½ c LF whip topping - 4g (4g)
- ¼ c NSA walnuts - 20g (2g)

Brands used/alternatives:
Kroger Gelatin Dessert Sugar Free Lime and Cherry
Philadelphia Whipped Cream Cheese

Fruit Salad with Vanilla Yogurt

Sodium Per Serving – 5mg Serves 8

This is a favorite fruit salad; any mixture of fresh fruit works well. We love to eat it the next day for breakfast with warm muffins... yum!

- **2 apples, cubed**
- **1 bunch green or red seedless grapes**
- **2 plums, cut into bite-sized chunks**
- **1 pear, cubed**
- **1 cup fresh blueberries or strawberries, cut into bite-size pieces**
- **1 (10-oz) can mandarin oranges, drained**
- **½ cup lowfat or nonfat vanilla yogurt**
- **¼ cup unsalted walnuts (optional)**

1. In a large bowl, combine apples, grapes, plums, pear, blueberries, and mandarin oranges. Stir in yogurt until fruit is well coated. Add walnuts and serve.

NUTRITIONAL INFO PER SERVING: Calories 115, Fat 3g (Saturated Fat 0g), Cholesterol 0mg, Carbohydrates 22g (Fiber 3g, Sugar 17g), Sodium 5mg

---

VARIATION
Grand Marnier Fruit Salad

1. Instead of vanilla yogurt, combine 2–3 tablespoons Grand Marnier or Triple Sec, 1 tablespoon sugar, and 4 tablespoons orange juice; blend into the fruit and refrigerate an hour or more before serving.

NUTRITIONAL INFO PER SERVING: Calories 140, Fat 3g (Sat Fat 0g), Chol 0mg, Carb 28g (Fiber 4g, Sugar 22g), Sodium 2mg

---

TOTAL SODIUM & FAT BY INGREDIENT

Sodium:
- 2 apples - 4mg
- 1 c grapes - 3mg
- 1 pear - 2mg
- 1 c blueberries - 2mg
- ½ c LF vanilla yogurt - 27mg
- ¼ c walnuts - 1mg

Fat (Sat Fat):
- 2 apples - 1g (0g)
- 1 c blueberries - 1g (0g)
- ½ c LF vanilla yogurt - 1g (1g)
- ¼ c walnuts - 20g (2g)

Brands used/alternatives:
Two Good Vanilla Yogurt

Mediterranean Pasta Salad

Sodium Per Serving – 59mg   Serves 8

This is a simple but yummy pasta salad. The flavor gets even better after marinating in the dressing for several hours.

- **12 oz (about 3 cups) macaroni or penne pasta, cooked per package directions[1]**
- **1 red bell pepper, chopped**
- **½ cup oil-packed sun-dried tomatoes, drained and chopped[2]**
- **1 (15-oz) can NSA whole corn, drained[3]**
- **10 LS black olives, chopped (about 3 tablespoons)**
- **1 carrot, chopped**
- **½ sweet onion, chopped**
- **4 oz Swiss cheese, cubed**

Dressing:
- **3 tablespoons extra virgin olive oil**
- **3 tablespoons red wine vinegar**
- **2 tablespoons grated parmesan cheese**
- **2 tablespoons chopped fresh basil**
- **½ teaspoon garlic powder or onion powder**
- **½ teaspoon dried oregano**
- **¼ teaspoon ground black pepper**

1. Mix together cooked pasta with the bell pepper, tomato, corn, olives, carrot, onion and Swiss cheese.
2. Blend together dressing ingredients either by processing in a blender or shaking well in a screw-top jar. Pour over pasta and mix well. Cover and refrigerate an hour or more; serve chilled or at room temperature.

NUTRITIONAL INFO PER SERVING: Calories 332, Fat 13g (Sat Fat 4g), Chol 14mg, Carb 40g (Fiber 3g, Sugar 5g), Sodium 59mg

Recipe Notes

1 – When cooking pasta, there is no need to add salt to the water. If you want additional flavor, stir 1–2 teaspoons LS chicken bouillon into the cooking water.

2 – CAUTION: There is a vast range of sodium in sun-dried tomato brands... a 0.5 oz serving has anywhere from 5mg to 270mg.

3 – Substitute frozen corn or fresh kernels cut from 2-3 ears of corn.

TOTAL SODIUM & FAT BY INGREDIENT

Sodium:
- 12 oz macaroni - 20mg
- 1 red pepper - 5mg
- ½ c sun-dried tomato - 20mg
- 15 oz NSA whole corn - 35mg
- 2 T ripe olives - 80mg
- 1 carrot - 42mg
- ½ onion - 7mg
- 4 oz Swiss cheese - 200mg
- 3 T red wine vinegar - 2mg
- 2 T Parmesan cheese - 60mg

Fat (Sat Fat):
- 12 oz macaroni - 1g (0g)
- ½ c sun-dried tomato - 12g (1g)
- 15 oz NSA corn - 5g (0g)
- 2 T ripe olives - 3g (0g)
- 4 oz Swiss cheese - 36g (20g)
- 3 T olive oil - 42g (6g)
- 2 T Parmesan - 4g (2g)

Brands used/alternatives:
Jeff's Naturals Sun-Ripen Tomatoes
Libby's Naturals NSA Whole Kernel Sweet Corn
Mario's LS Black Olives
Great Value Swiss Cheese
365 Whole Foods 3 Cheese Blend

TOSSED SALADS

Favorite Tossed Salad

Sodium Per Serving – 63mg Serves 4

This is the tossed salad we serve most often in our family. For the dressing, I particularly like using a slightly sweet vinaigrette; any dressing of your choice will taste great, too.

- 1 head romaine lettuce, torn into bite-sized pieces, or 5 cups mixed greens
- ½ small sweet onion, thinly sliced
- ½ red bell pepper, sliced
- ½ cucumber, sliced
- ½ cup NSA whole kernel corn[1]
- 1 tomato, cut into bite-size pieces
- 1 oz Stilton cheese, crumbled (about ¼ cup) (optional)[2]
- **The Best Vinaigrette (pg 76)**

1. In a large bowl, mix together all ingredients, tossing well. Add freshly ground black pepper to taste and serve.

NUTRITIONAL INFO PER SERVING (without dressing): Calories 75, Fat 3g (Sat Fat 2g), Chol 8mg, Carb 9g (Fiber 2g, Sugar 5g), Sodium 63mg

TOTAL SODIUM & FAT BY INGREDIENT

Sodium:
- 1 head romaine - 5mg
   or 5 c mixed greens - 25mg
- ½ sweet onion - 7mg
- ½ red bell pepper - 3mg
- ½ cucumber - 3mg
- ½ c NSA corn - 10mg
- 1 tomato - 6mg
- 1 oz Stilton cheese - 220mg

Fat (Sat Fat):
- ½ c NSA corn - 1g (0g)
- 1 oz Stilton cheese - 10g (6g)

Brands used/alternatives:
- *Libby's Naturals* NSA Whole Kernel Sweet Corn
- *Clawson* Blue Stilton Cheese

VARIATION

Chicken, Romaine & Stilton Salad

1. For a main course salad for 4, add 12 oz cooked chicken (cut into bite-size pieces) and increase the romaine to 1½ heads (or about 8 cups).

NUTRITIONAL INFO PER SERVING (without dressing): Calories 185, Fat 6g (Sat Fat 3g), Chol 56mg, Carb 10g (Fiber 2g, Sugar 5g), Sodium 94mg

Recipe Notes

1 – For variety, add half of a chopped apple or red seedless grapes.

2 – Although high in sodium, the strong flavor of blue cheese allows a little to go a long way. There are many blue cheese varieties and the amount of sodium varies with the type and brand of cheese. Stilton generally has the least, averaging 220mg per oz, Gorgonzola has 350mg, Blue cheese 395mg, and Roquefort, the most at 513mg.

Mâche, Pear & Toasted Walnut Salad

Sodium Per Serving – 76mg   Serves 6

The combination of flavors in this traditional dish is lovely. If unable to find mâche, substitute mixed greens. This also makes a nice luncheon salad, serving 3 or 4.

- 1 (5-oz) package mâche or mixed greens[1]
- 2 pears (such as Anjou, Bartlett, or Bosc), cored and sliced lengthwise
- ¼ medium sweet onion, thinly sliced
- 2 oz Stilton, crumbled (about ½ cup)[2]
- ½ cup walnuts or pecans, toasted and chopped
- ½ cup *French Dressing (pg 76)*

1. Toss mâche with the onions and half the vinaigrette; place on individual plates. Equally divide pear slices and place on top; sprinkle with Stilton and walnuts. Drizzle remaining vinaigrette on top and serve.

NUTRITIONAL INFO PER SERVING (without dressing): Calories 143, Fat 10g (Saturated Fat 3g), Cholesterol 10mg, Carbohydrates 12g (Fiber 3g, Sugar 7g), Sodium 76mg

---

VARIATION
Spinach, Pear & Walnut Salad
1. Substitute 1 (6-oz) pkg baby spinach for the mâche.

NUTRITIONAL INFO PER SERVING (without dressing): Calories 145, Fat 10g (Sat Fat 3g), Chol 10mg, Carb 12g (Fiber 3g, Sugar 7g), Sodium 96mg

---

Mixed Greens with Avocado & Orange

Sodium Per Serving – 20mg   Serves 6

This colorful tossed salad with avocado, mandarin oranges, and dried cranberries is not only festive, but also very tasty.

- 1 (6-oz) package mixed greens (about 6 cups)[3]
- 1 large avocado, peeled and sliced
- ½ sweet onion, sliced
- 1 (11-oz) can mandarin oranges, drained[4]
- 2 tablespoons dried cranberries or cherries
- *Orange Vinaigrette (pg 75)*

1. In a large bowl, mix together all ingredients, tossing well. Add freshly ground black pepper to taste and serve.

NUTRITIONAL INFO PER SERVING (without dressing): Calories 105, Fat 4g (Sat Fat 0g), Chol 0mg, Carb 17g (Fiber 3g, Sugar 12g), Sodium 20mg

---

TOTAL SODIUM & FAT BY INGREDIENT

MÂCHE PEAR WALNUT SALAD
Sodium:
- 5 oz mâche - 6mg or 6 c mixed greens - 100mg
- 2 pears - 3mg
- ¼ onion - 4mg
- 2 oz Stilton - 440mg
- ½ c walnuts - 1mg

Fat (Sat Fat):
- 5 oz mâche - 1g (0g)
- 2 oz Stilton - 18g (10g)
- ½ c walnuts - 39g (4g)

Brands used/alternatives:
Clawson Blue Stilton Cheese

MIXED GREENS & AVOCADO
Sodium:
- 6 c mixed greens - 100mg
- 1 avocado - 11mg
- ½ sweet onion - 7mg
- 2 T dried cranberries - 1mg

Fat (Sat Fat):
- 1 avocado - 21g (3g)

Brands used/alternatives:
Dole Mandarins in Light Syrup

Recipe Notes
1 – Mâche (pronounced MOSH), also known as corn salad or lamb's lettuce, has a mild buttery flavor and is available in many larger supermarkets.

2 – Although high in sodium, the strong flavor of blue cheese allows a little to go a long way. There are many blue cheese varieties and the amount of sodium varies with the type and brand of cheese. Stilton has the least, averaging 220mg per oz, Gorgonzola has 350mg, Blue cheese 395mg, and Roquefort, the most at 513mg.

3 – Substitute ½ head red-leaf and ½ head green-leaf lettuce. For info on varieties, see *Lettuce/Other Salad Greens*, pg 249.

4 – Instead of canned mandarins, use several fresh satsumas, clementines, or tangerines, divided into segments.

MESCLUN WITH STILTON & SUGARED PECANS

Sodium Per Serving – 109mg   Serves 6

Mesclun is nothing more than a mixture of baby greens. By adding sugared pecans, you have a restaurant quality salad. This also is a great luncheon main course, serving 3 or 4.

- 1 (6-oz) package mesclun or mixed field greens (about 6 cups)[1]
- ¼ small sweet onion, thinly sliced
- 2 cups red, seedless grapes
- *The Best Vinaigrette (pg 76)*
- 2 ounces Stilton blue cheese, crumbled (about ½ cup)[2]
- ¼ cup sugared chopped pecans[3]

1. In a large bowl, mix together the mesclun, onion, grapes, and vinaigrette, tossing well. Divide and place on individual plates. Sprinkle with cheese and pecans; add freshly ground black pepper to taste and serve.

NUTRITIONAL INFO PER SERVING (without dressing): Calories 109, Fat 6g (Sat Fat 2g), Chol 10mg, Carb 13g (Fiber 1g, Sugar 10g), Sodium 109mg

SPINACH, DRIED CRANBERRIES & CHÈVRE

Sodium Per Serving – 42mg   Serves 6

The sweetness of the cranberries and the tart cheese go together beautifully in this tasty salad.

- 1 (6-oz) packaged baby spinach (about 6 cups)
- ¼ small sweet onion, thinly sliced
- ½ cup dried cranberries
- *Raspberry Vinaigrette (pg 76)*
- 2 oz Chèvre goat cheese (about ½ cup)[4]
- ¼ cup walnuts, chopped and toasted[3]

1. In a large bowl, mix together the spinach, onion, cranberries, and vinaigrette, tossing well. Divide and place on individual plates. Sprinkle with cheese and walnuts; add freshly ground black pepper to taste and serve.

NUTRITIONAL INFO PER SERVING (without dressing): Calories 128, Fat 5g (Sat Fat 2g), Chol 7mg, Carb 18g (Fiber 2g, Sugar 13g), Sodium 42mg

> **TOTAL SODIUM & FAT BY INGREDIENT**
> **MESCLUN STILTON & PECANS**
> *Sodium:*
>   6 c mixed greens - 100mg
>   ¼ sweet onion - 7mg
>   2 c grapes - 6mg
>   2 oz Stilton cheese - 440mg
>   ¼ c pecans - 100mg
> *Fat (Sat Fat):*
>   ¼ c pecans - 14g (0g)
>   2 oz Stilton cheese - 18g (10g)
> **Brands used/alternatives:**
>   *Clawson* Blue Stilton Cheese
>
> **SPINACH & CHÈVRE**
> *Sodium:*
>   6 c spinach - 128mg
>   ¼ sweet onion - 7mg
>   ½ c dried cranberries - 4mg
>   2 oz Chèvre cheese - 110mg
>   ¼ c walnuts - 1mg
> *Fat (Sat Fat):*
>   6 c spinach - 1g (0g)
>   2 oz Chèvre cheese - 12g (8g)
>   ¼ c walnuts - 20g (2g)
> **Brands used/alternatives:**
>   *Vermont Creamery* Herb Goat Cheese

Recipe Notes

1 – Mesclun is a mixture of baby greens. Use any lettuce combination of your choice (for varieties and other info, see *Lettuce/Other Salad Greens*, pg 249).

2 – Although high in sodium, the strong flavor of blue cheese allows a little to go a long way. There are many blue cheese varieties and the amount of sodium varies with the type and brand of cheese. Stilton has the least, averaging 220mg per oz and Roquefort, the most at 513mg.

3 – See *Toasting Nuts*, pg 250, for several ways of toasting nuts.

4 – Chèvre goat cheese has a tart flavor. It will keep up to 2 weeks in the refrigerator, after that it becomes sour. Goat cheese can range from sweet and mild to tangy and sharp and has a wide range of sodium from 50mg-140mg an oz, depending on the type (soft, semi-soft, etc). Chèvre is generally on the low side. If you're not a goat cheese fan, Stilton blue cheese also works well in this salad.

Caesar Salad

Sodium Per Serving – 40mg   Serves 6 (Serves 2 as a main dish)

This classic salad has been lightened up in both fat and sodium. Add cooked chicken or shrimp for a scrumptious main course.

- 1 head romaine, torn into bite-size pieces
- 1 cup *Herbed Garlic Croutons (pg 204)* or LS croutons
- *Caesar Dressing (recipe follows)*
- ¼ cup Parmesan cheese[1]
- Freshly ground pepper

1. Mix lettuce and *Caesar Dressing* together in a large bowl; add croutons and toss until well mixed. Divide onto six plates, sprinkle with Parmesan and top with freshly ground pepper.

NUTRITIONAL INFO PER SERVING: Calories 154, Fat 11g (Saturated Fat 2g), Cholesterol 4mg, Carbohydrates 13g (Fiber 3g, Sugar 2g), Sodium 40mg

---

VARIATION
Chicken Caesar

1. For a main course for 4, add 12 oz cooked and sliced chicken breast (such as *Fried Chicken (pg 80)*) to the above salad.

NUTRITIONAL INFO PER SERVING: Calories 336, Fat 19g (Sat Fat 4g), Chol 55mg, Carb 19g (Fiber 4g, Sugar 2g), Sodium 90mg

---

Caesar Dressing

Sodium Per Serving – 4mg   Makes ⅓ cup (6 servings)

This classic dressing is made without raw eggs and anchovies. It is delicious on most any tossed salad.

- 3 tablespoons extra-virgin olive oil
- 1 tablespoon red or white wine vinegar
- 1 tablespoon fresh lemon juice
- ½ teaspoon Dijon mustard
- Dash Worcestershire sauce[2]
- 1 garlic clove, finely minced
- 1 tablespoon finely minced shallot (optional)[3]

1. Blend together all ingredients, either by whisking in a small bowl or by shaking well in a screw-top jar. Pour over salad and toss.

NUTRITIONAL INFO PER SERVING: Calories 63, Fat 7g (Sat Fat 1g), Chol 0mg, Carb 1g (Fiber 0g, Sugar 0g), Sodium 4mg

Recipe Notes

1 – You can substitute 2 oz finely shredded Swiss cheese.

2 – Worcestershire sauce is made with anchovies and averages 55mg per tsp; reduced sodium Worcestershire is made without anchovies and has about 20-45mg, depending on the brand.

3 – Shallots look like small onions, but have a mild garlic flavor. For additional information on choosing and storing shallots, see *Shallots*, pg 253.

TOTAL SODIUM & FAT BY INGREDIENT

CAESAR SALAD
Sodium:
- 1 head romaine - 50mg
- 1 c *Herb Garlic Croutons* - 47mg
- ¼ c Parmesan - 120mg
- *Caesar Dressing* - 25mg

Fat (Sat Fat):
- 1 head romaine - 2g (0g)
- 1 c *Herb Croutons* - 13g (3g)
- ¼ c Parmesan - 8g (4g)

Brands used/alternatives:
365 Whole Foods 3 Cheese Blend

CAESAR DRESSING
Sodium:
- 1 T red wine vinegar - 1mg
- ½ t Dijon mustard - 20mg
- Dash Worcestershire - 3mg
- 1 garlic clove - 1mg
- 1 shallot - 1mg

Fat (Sat Fat):
- 3 T olive oil - 42g (6g)

Brands used/alternatives:
Gold's Dijon Mustard
Robbie's Worcestershire Sauce

Spinach Salad with Warm Bacon Dressing

Sodium Per Serving – 104mg | Serves 4

The delicious salad is ready in less than 15 minutes. Using lower-sodium bacon creates a reduced-salt dish that is a perfect starter for that special dinner.

- **1 (6-oz) package baby spinach (about 6 cups)**
- **¼ sweet onion, thinly sliced**
- **Warm Bacon Dressing (recipe follows)**
- **⅛ teaspoon ground black pepper**
- **2 medium hard-boiled eggs, chopped**

1. In a large bowl, gently toss the *Warm Bacon Dressing* with the spinach and onion until the spinach begins to wilt. Sprinkle with egg and reserved bacon; season with pepper and serve.

NUTRITIONAL INFO PER SERVING: Calories 64, Fat 3g (Saturated Fat 1g), Cholesterol 87mg, Carbohydrates 4g (Fiber 1g, Sugar 2g), Sodium 104mg

Warm Bacon Dressing

Sodium Per Serving – 41mg | Serves 4

In addition to spinach salad, serve this tasty dressing over asparagus or green beans.

- **4 slices lower-sodium turkey bacon[1]**
- **1-2 tablespoons olive oil**
- **3 tablespoons apple cider vinegar**
- **1 teaspoon sugar**

1. In a large skillet over medium-high heat, fry bacon until crisp on both sides, about 5 minutes. Remove bacon and drain on paper towels; let cool until able to handle. Crumble and set aside.
2. Add to the bacon fat in skillet enough olive oil to equal 3 tablespoons. Mix in vinegar and sugar; stirring constantly, over medium heat, scrape up any browned bits of bacon. While still warm, pour over spinach.

NUTRITIONAL INFO PER SERVING: Calories 19, Fat 1g (Sat Fat 0g), Chol 5mg, Carb 1g (Fiber 0g, Sugar 1g), Sodium 41mg

Recipe Notes

1 – There are several lower-sodium bacon brands. To keep fat to a minimum, I use turkey bacon. Visit *LowSaltFoods.com* for a list of LS brands.

TOTAL SODIUM & FAT BY INGREDIENT

SPINACH SALAD
Sodium:
- 6 oz spinach - 128mg
- ¼ sweet onion - 3mg
- 2 med eggs - 123mg
- Warm Bacon Dressing - 162mg

Fat (Sat Fat):
- 2 med eggs - 8g (3g)
- Warm Bacon Dressing - 4g (1g)

WARM BACON DRESSING
Sodium:
- 4 sl LS turkey bacon - 160mg
- 2 T cider vinegar - 2mg

Fat (Sat Fat):
- 2 sl LS turkey bacon - 4g (1g)

Brands used/alternatives:
Butterball Lower Sodium Turkey Bacon

MAIN COURSE SALADS

Avocado, Apple, Dates & Jicama Salad

Sodium Per Serving – 32mg Serves 4

My pal, Sally, loves this delicious salad. Although high in fat, the majority comes from the avocados and almonds, which contain monounsaturated fats (considered "good" fats, as they lower the bad LDL cholesterol).

- 4 avocados, cubed
- 4 apples, diced
- 2 celery stalks, sliced
- 1 medium jicama, peeled and cubed (about 2 cups)[1]
- 12 date halves, pitted and chopped
- ½ cup sliced almonds, toasted[2]
- 12 lettuce leaves, such as romaine
- Orange Vinaigrette (pg 75)

1. In a large bowl, gently mix the avocados, apples, celery, jicama, dates, and almonds; mix in *Orange Vinaigrette*.
2. Place several lettuce leaves on a plate and top with one-fourth salad.

NUTRITIONAL INFO PER SERVING (without dressing): Calories 510, Fat 30g (Sat Fat 4g), Chol 0mg, Carb 52g (Fiber 18g, Sugar 28g), Sodium 32mg

---

Chicken, Apple & Pecan Tossed Salad

Sodium Per Serving – 93mg Serves 4

Add freshly-baked Lemon Currant Scones (pg 200) and you have a delicious main course meal.

- 12 oz cooked chicken breast, cubed (about 3 cups)[3]
- 1 head romaine lettuce, torn into bite-size pieces (about 8 cups)
- 2 apples, cored and cut into bite-size pieces[4]
- ½ cup *Poppy Seed Dressing* (pg 75)
- 4 oz Swiss cheese, shredded (about 1 cup)
- ½ cup chopped pecans, toasted[2]
- Freshly ground black pepper

1. In a large bowl, combine chicken, romaine, and apples. Mix in dressing; tossing well. Divide salad onto 4 plates and sprinkle with cheese, pecans, and freshly ground black pepper; serve.

NUTRITIONAL INFO PER SERVING (without dressing): Calories 375, Fat 23g (Sat Fat 7g), Chol 74mg, Carb 20g (Fiber 7g, Sugar 12g), Sodium 93mg

---

TOTAL SODIUM & FAT BY INGREDIENT

AVOCADO APPLE DATE JICAMA
Sodium:
- 4 avocados - 44mg
- 4 apples - 7mg
- 2 celery stalks - 64mg
- 1 jicama - 5mg
- 12 date halves - 1mg
- 12 lettuce leaves - 6mg

Fat (Sat Fat):
- 4 avocados - 84g (12g)
- 4 apples - 1g (0g)
- ½ c almonds - 34g (3g)

CHICKEN APPLE SALAD
Sodium:
- 12 oz chicken breasts - 120mg
- 1 head romaine - 50mg
- 2 apples - 4mg
- 4 oz Swiss cheese - 200mg

Fat (Sat Fat):
- 12 oz chicken - 12g (5g)
- 1 head romaine - 2g (0g)
- 2 apples - 1g (0g)
- 4 oz Swiss cheese - 36g (20g)
- ½ c pecans - 40g (4g)

Brands used/alternatives:
Tyson All Natural Chicken Breast
Great Value Swiss Cheese

Recipe Notes
1 – See *Jicama*, pg 249, for info on this Mexican root vegetable.
2 – Toasting the nuts intensifies their flavor (see *Toasting Nuts*, pg 250, for toasting methods).
3 – You can also use my delicious *Fried Chicken*, pg 80.
4 – Use tart or semi-tart apples, such as Granny Smith, Braeburn, or Jazz.

Cobb Salad

Sodium Per Serving – 183mg Serves 4

The Cobb Salad, created in the 1930's by Bob Cobb, then owner of the Brown Derby in Hollywood, is arguably one of the most famous American dishes. Many chefs still abide by the original ingredients, although just about anything works. To be a true Cobb, however, it must contain several veggies (such as avocado and tomatoes), cheese, and a protein (like poultry, fish, beef, or eggs). Generally, the presentation is what makes a Cobb salad unique—all ingredients are placed in single rows on the plate (it also is quite acceptable to toss the salad and then serve it). Prepare and chill the cooked ingredients before making the salad.

- 6–8 cups mixed greens[1]
- 12 oz cooked chicken breast, cubed (about 3 cups)[2]
- 16 cherry tomatoes, cut in half, or 2 large tomatoes, chopped
- 16 cooked asparagus spears
- 1 avocado, cubed or sliced
- 4 oz Swiss cheese, cubed (about 1 cup)[3]
- 4 slices lower-salt bacon, crispy-cooked and crumbled[4]
- 2 medium hard-boiled eggs, chopped
- 2 tablespoons chopped chives or 2 green onions, chopped (green part only)
- ½ cup *The Best Vinaigrette (pg 76)* or *French Dressing (pg 76)*

1. Evenly divide all ingredients, beginning with the mixed greens. Starting in the middle, place chicken in a row on top of the greens; working out to both sides, arrange the tomato and asparagus on one side, and the avocado and cheese on the other.
2. Sprinkle each salad with bacon, eggs, and chives; drizzle with dressing (or serve the dressing on the side, so each guest can add their own.)

NUTRITIONAL INFO PER SERVING (without dressing): Calories 364, Fat 20g (Sat Fat 8g), Chol 117mg, Carb 10g (Fiber 5g, Sugar 3g), Sodium 183mg

Recipe Notes

1 – The original Cobb had a mixture of romaine, bibb lettuce, watercress, and chicory; use any combination of greens.
2 – My delicious *Fried Chicken*, pg 80. also works well.
3 – For a change, substitute a LS goat cheese, such as Chèvre or Montrachet, for the Swiss cheese.
4 – Visit *LowSaltFoods.com* for LS bacon brands.

TOTAL SODIUM & FAT BY INGREDIENT

Sodium:
 6 c mixed greens - 100mg
 12 oz chicken breast - 120mg
 16 cherry tomatoes - 13mg
 16 asparagus - 5mg
 1 avocado - 11mg
 4 oz Swiss cheese - 200mg
 4 sl LS turkey bacon - 160mg
 2 med eggs - 123mg

Fat (Sat Fat):
 12 oz chicken breast - 12g (5g)
 1 avocado - 21g (3g)
 4 oz Swiss cheese - 36g (20g)
 4 sl LS turkey bacon - 4g (1g)
 2 med eggs - 9g (3g)

Brands used/alternatives:
Tyson All Natural Chicken Breast
Great Value Swiss Cheese
Butterball Lower Sodium Turkey Bacon

SALADS & SALAD DRESSINGS - Main Course Salads

CURRIED CHICKEN WALDORF

Sodium Per Serving – 112mg   Serves 4

Here's a salad that's full of flavor and combines chicken with fruit, nuts, and curry. This also makes a delicious filling for pita sandwiches or wraps. Allow 2 hours for the flavors to intensify before serving.

Dressing:
- 2/3 cup lowfat plain Greek yogurt
- 1/4 cup mayonnaise or mayonnaise-like dressing
- 1 tablespoon curry powder
- 1 tablespoon fresh lime juice
- 1 teaspoon sugar
- 1/2 teaspoon grated gingerroot
- 1/4 teaspoon onion powder
- 1/8 teaspoon ground black pepper

Salad:
- 4 cups cubed cooked chicken breast (about 16 oz)
- 2 apples (such as Braeburn, Fuji, or Jazz), cubed
- 4–5 green onions, chopped (about 1 cup)
- 1 celery stalk, chopped
- 1/2 cup raisins
- 1/2 cup almonds, toasted and chopped[1]
- Lettuce leaves

1. *For the dressing:* Mix together yogurt, mayonnaise, curry, lime juice, sugar, gingerroot, onion powder, and black pepper.
2. *For the salad:* In a large bowl, mix together chicken, apples, onions, celery, and raisins; pour dressing over and mix well. Cover and refrigerate 2 hours or overnight.
3. Place one-fourth salad on lettuce leaves, sprinkle with almonds, and serve.

NUTRITIONAL INFO PER SERVING: Calories 448, Fat 25g (Sat Fat 4g), Chol 81mg, Carb 36g (Fiber 6g, Sugar 23g), Sodium 112mg

Recipe Notes
1 – Toasting brings out the flavor of the nuts (see *Toasting Nuts*, pg 250, for toasting methods).

TOTAL SODIUM & FAT BY INGREDIENT

Sodium:
- 2/3 c LF Greek yogurt - 27mg
- 1/4 c mayonnaise - 200mg
- 1 T curry - 3mg
- 4 c chicken breast - 160mg
- 2 apples - 4mg
- 1 c green onions - 10mg
- 1 celery stalk - 32mg
- 1/2 c raisins - 9mg
- 4 romaine leaves - 6mg

Fat (Sat Fat):
- 2/3 c LF Greek yogurt - 2g (1g)
- 1/4 c mayo - 44g (6g)
- 1 T curry - 1g (0g)
- 4 c chicken breast - 16g (6g)
- 2 apples - 1g (0g)
- 1/2 c almonds - 34g (3g)

Brands used/alternatives:
- *Two Good* Plain Yogurt
- *Chosen Foods* Classic Mayo w/ Avocado Oil
- *Tyson* All Natural Chicken Breast

SALAD DRESSINGS

ORANGE VINAIGRETTE

Sodium Per Serving – 6mg Makes about ½ cup

This tangy dressing is a wonderful accompaniment to any salad.

- ¼ cup extra-virgin olive oil
- 2 tablespoons orange juice
- 2 teaspoons sugar
- 1 tablespoon lemon or lime juice
- ½ teaspoon Dijon-style mustard
- ½ teaspoon curry powder[1]
- ¼ teaspoon paprika
- 1–2 garlic cloves, finely minced, or 1 teaspoon finely minced shallot

1. Mix together all ingredients, either by whisking in a small bowl or by shaking well in a screw-top jar. Will keep for up to a week in a covered container in the refrigerator.

NUTRITIONAL INFO PER 2 TABLESPOONS: Calories 134, Fat 14g (Saturated Fat 2g), Cholesterol 0mg, Carbohydrates 4g (Fiber 0g, Sugar 3g), Sodium 6mg

POPPY SEED DRESSING

Sodium Per Serving – 1mg Makes about 3/4 cup

This sweet dressing is delicious on most salads or mixed with fresh fruit.

- ⅓ cup sugar
- 3 tablespoons apple cider or red wine vinegar
- 1 tablespoon lemon juice
- 1 teaspoon mustard powder
- ¼ teaspoon garlic powder
- 2 tablespoons finely minced onion
- ½ cup extra-virgin olive oil
- 1½ teaspoons poppy seeds

1. Place sugar, vinegar, lemon juice, mustard powder, garlic powder, and onion in a blender. With blender running, slowly add oil until well mixed; stir in poppy seeds. (If mixing by hand, either whisk together ingredients in a small bowl or shake well in a screw-top jar.) Will keep for up to a week in a covered container in the refrigerator.

NUTRITIONAL INFO PER 2 TABLESPOONS: Calories 159, Fat 14g (Sat Fat 2g), Chol 0mg, Carb 9g (Fiber 0g, Sugar 9g), Sodium 1mg

---

TOTAL SODIUM & FAT BY INGREDIENT

ORANGE VINAIGRETTE
Sodium:
- ¼ c oil - 1mg
- ½ t Dijon mustard - 20mg
- ½ t curry - 1mg
- 1 garlic clove - 1mg

Fat (Sat Fat):
- 2 T olive oil - 54g (7g)

Brands used/alternatives:
- Gold's Dijon Mustard

POPPY SEED DRESSING
Sodium:
- ⅓ c sugar - 1mg
- 2 t onion - 2mg
- 1½ t poppy seeds - 2mg
- ½ c olive oil - 2mg

Fat (Sat Fat):
- 1 t dry mustard - 1g (0g)
- 1½ t poppy seeds - 2g (0g)
- ½ c olive oil - 108g (14g)

Recipe Notes

1 – I like to vary this salad by sometimes adding either hot or sweet curry powder (see *Curry Powder*, pg 247, for varieties and other info).

THE BEST VINAIGRETTE

Sodium Per Serving – 8mg Serves 6

Everyone loves this easy-to-make dressing. The addition of garlic is the secret ingredient. You can use it on just about any tossed salad.

- **2 tablespoons white balsamic or red wine vinegar[1]**
- **2 tablespoons extra-virgin olive oil**
- **1 teaspoon Dijon-style mustard[2]**
- **1 teaspoon sugar**
- **1 garlic clove, finely minced (about ½ teaspoon)**
- **⅛ teaspoon dried basil or tarragon**

1. Blend together all ingredients, either by whisking in a small bowl or by shaking well in a screw-top jar. Pour over salad and toss.

NUTRITIONAL INFO PER 2 TABLESPOONS: Calories 48, Fat 5g (Saturated Fat 1g), Cholesterol 0mg, Carbohydrates 2g (Fiber 0g, Sugar 1g), Sodium 8mg

---

VARIATIONS

FRENCH DRESSING
1. Omit the sugar and increase the Dijon-style mustard to 1½ teaspoons.

NUTRITIONAL INFO PER 2 TABLESPOONS: Calories 46, Fat 5g (Saturated Fat 1g), Cholesterol 0mg, Carbohydrates 1g (Fiber 0g, Sugar 1g), Sodium 11mg

RASPBERRY VINAIGRETTE
1. Substitute 2 tablespoons raspberry vinegar for the balsamic and ½ teaspoon finely grated orange peel for the garlic; reduce sugar to ½ teaspoon.

NUTRITIONAL INFO PER 2 TABLESPOONS: Calories 44, Fat 5g (Saturated Fat 1g), Cholesterol 0mg, Carbohydrates 1g (Fiber 0g, Sugar 0g), Sodium 7mg

SHALLOT VINAIGRETTE
1. Omit the garlic and sugar, add 2 tablespoons finely minced shallots.

NUTRITIONAL INFO PER 2 TABLESPOONS: Calories 48, Fat 5g (Saturated Fat 1g), Cholesterol 0mg, Carbohydrates 2g (Fiber 0g, Sugar 1g), Sodium 8mg

ROASTED GARLIC DRESSING
1. Add 1 tablespoon roasted garlic *(see Roasting Garlic, pg 249)*.

NUTRITIONAL INFO PER 2 TABLESPOONS: Calories 48, Fat 5g (Saturated Fat 1g), Cholesterol 0mg, Carbohydrates 1g (Fiber 0g, Sugar 1g), Sodium 8mg

---

Recipe Notes
1 – White balsamic vinegar is made from white grapes and is combined with white wine vinegar. Although milder and sweeter, it also is not as overpowering in salads as the darker balsamic vinegar.

2 – Dijon mustard averages 120mg sodium per tsp. There are several brands with less than 70mg per tsp. Visit LowSaltFoods.com for a list of LS brands.

TOTAL SODIUM & FAT BY INGREDIENT

Sodium:
- 2 T balsamic - 7mg
- 1 t Dijon mustard - 40mg
- ½ t roasted garlic - 1mg

Fat (Sat Fat):
- 2 T olive oil - 28g (4g)

Brands used/alternatives:
Gold's Dijon Mustard

RANCH DRESSING

Sodium Per Serving – 51mg Makes about 1 cup

Once you try this low-fat dressing, you won't use the bottled variety again. Keep refrigerated in a covered container for up to a week. This also makes a great addition to wraps.

- ⅔ cup lowfat buttermilk
- 2 tablespoons mayonnaise
- 2 tablespoons lowfat sour cream
- 1 tablespoon finely chopped fresh Italian parsley[1]
- 1 tablespoon finely chopped basil or 1 teaspoon dried[1]
- 1 teaspoon finely minced garlic
- 1 teaspoon mustard powder
- ½ teaspoon onion powder
- ⅛ teaspoon celery seed
- ⅛ teaspoon ground black pepper
- Dash dried thyme or dill weed

1. Blend together all ingredients by whisking in a small bowl. Pour desired amount of dressing over salad and toss.

NUTRITIONAL INFO PER 2 TBSP: Calories 86, Fat 7g (Sat Fat 2g), Chol 13mg, Carb 3g (Fiber 0g, Sugar 2g), Sodium 51mg

GREEN GODDESS DRESSING

Sodium Per Serving – 33mg Makes about 1 cup

This is my low-salt version of this classic dressing. Usually made with anchovies, I substitute Dijon mustard instead and add an avocado for creaminess.

- 1 ripe avocado, peeled, pitted, and quartered
- ½ cup lowfat sour cream
- 2 garlic cloves, chopped
- 1 green onion, chopped
- 1 tablespoon fresh tarragon or ½ teaspoon dried
- 2 tablespoons olive oil
- 1 tablespoon lemon juice or white balsamic vinegar[2]
- 1 teaspoon Dijon-style mustard
- ½ teaspoon Worcestershire sauce
- ¼ teaspoon hot pepper sauce, such as *Tabasco*
- ½ teaspoon garlic powder
- ⅛ teaspoon ground black pepper

1. Place all ingredients in a blender or food processor and purée until smooth. Let sit 30 minutes in the refrigerator before serving. Will keep up to 3 days in a covered container in the refrigerator.

NUTRITIONAL INFO PER 2 TABLESPOONS: Calories 170, Fat 15g (Sat Fat 3g), Chol 10mg, Carb 6g (Fiber 2g, Sugar 1g), Sodium 33mg

Recipe Notes
1 – For a change of pace, use fresh dill in place of the parsley and basil.
2 – White balsamic vinegar is made from white grapes and is combined with white wine vinegar. Although milder and sweeter, it also is not as overpowering in salads as the darker balsamic vinegar. You can also substitute white wine vinegar for the lemon juice or white balsamic.

TOTAL SODIUM & FAT BY INGREDIENT

RANCH DRESSING
Sodium:
- ⅔ c LF buttermilk - 83mg
- 2 T mayonnaise - 100mg
- 2 T LF sour cream - 15mg
- 1 T parsley - 2mg
- 1 t garlic - 1mg
- ½ t onion powder - 1mg

Fat (Sat Fat):
- ⅔ c LF buttermilk - 3g (2g)
- 2 T mayonnaise - 22g (3g)
- 2 T LF sour cream - 3g (2g)
- 1 t mustard powder - 1g (0g)

Brands used/alternatives:
- *Friendship* Light Buttermilk
- *Chosen Foods* Classic Mayo w/ Avocado Oil
- *Daisy Light* Sour Cream

GREEN GODDESS DRESSING
Sodium:
- 1 avocado - 11mg
- ½ c LF sour cream - 60mg
- 2 garlic cloves - 1mg
- 1 green onion - 2mg
- 1 t Dijon mustard - 40mg
- ½ t Worcestershire - 10mg
- ¼ t hot pepper sauce - 9mg

Fat (Sat Fat):
- 1 avocado - 21g (3g)
- ½ c LF sour cream - 10g (6g)
- 2 T olive oil - 28g (4g)

Brands used/alternatives:
- *Daisy Light* Sour Cream
- *Gold's* Dijon Mustard
- *Robbie's* Worcestershire Sauce

MAIN COURSES

POULTRY

Fried Chicken 80
Oven-Baked Chicken 80
Fried Chicken with Country Gravy 81
Chicken Diane. 82
Chicken Piccata 83
Herbed Goat Cheese Stuffed Chicken 84
    Herbed Goat Cheese. 84
Feta-Stuffed Chicken 85
Creamy Cheesy Chicken 85
Sun-Dried Tomato Chicken. 86
Chicken Paprika with Tomato Cream
    Sauce. 87
Mushroom Chicken Paprikash 87
Marsala Chicken .88
Chicken in Mushroom-Asparagus-
    Tarragon Sauce 89
Chicken Breasts with Shallot Sauce 90
    Shallot Sauce 90
Chicken Breasts in Mushroom-Shallot
    Sauce. 91
Creamy Artichokes, Mushrooms, Peas
    & Chicken 91
Chicken Piri Piri .92
    Piri Piri Sauce .92
Asparagus Chicken with Cream Sauce. . . .93
Chicken Sausage with Artichokes. 94
Chicken Stroganoff 95
Rich & Creamy Chicken Stroganoff 95
Tuscan Chicken Stew 96
Chicken Tagine with Eggplant 97
Chicken Pot Pie 98
Coq Au Vin 99
Sweet & Sour Turkey Meatloaf 100
Beef, Pork & Veal Meatloaf 100
Herb Roasted Game Hens 101
Roasted Game Hens with Orange-Herb
    Sauce. 101

BEEF, VEAL, LAMB & PORK

Pan-Seared Steaks with Tarragon
    Shallot Sauce 102
Rib-Eye Steak with Brandied
    Mushrooms 103
Top Sirloin with Mustard Sauce 104
Steaks with Wild Mushroom-Mustard
    Sauce. 104
Pot Roast. 105
Beef Stroganoff 106
Veal Marsala. 107
Roast Leg of Lamb with Mustard
    Rosemary Crust 108
Pork Chops with Raspberry Sauce 109
Fruit Stuffed Pork Tenderloin 110

FISH & SEAFOOD

Red Snapper Beurre Meunière 111
Orange Roughy in Creamy Leek Sauce . 112
Broiled Salmon with Pesto. 112
Horseradish Grilled Salmon 113
The Best Grilled Salmon. 113

Salmon Cakes 114
   Orange Butter Sauce 115
   Lemon Butter Sauce 115
Shrimp in Garlic Butter 115
Shrimp Curry 116
Tuna in Marsala Sauce 117
Grilled Mahi Mahi Almondine 118
Crab Quiche 119
Scallops with Beurre Blanc Sauce 120
   Beurre Blanc Sauce 120

MEATLESS DISHES

Veggies in Cream Cheese Sauce 121
Onion, Mushroom & Chèvre Tart 122
Vegetable Strudel with Red Pepper
   Coulis 123
   Red Pepper Coulis 124
   Chipotle Pepper Sauce 124
Creamy Polenta with Mushroom Sauce   125
   Mushroom Sauce 125
Veggie Burgers 126
Vegetable Crepes with Cheese Sauce . . . 127
   Cheese Sauce 128
Crustless Spinach–Mushroom Quiche . 129
Stuffed Baked Potatoes 130
Stroganoff Stuffed Potatoes 130
Creamy Mushroom Stuffed Potatoes . . . 130
Chili Stuffed Potatoes 130
Creamy Cheesy Chicken Stuffed
   Potatoes 130

PASTA DISHES & PIZZA

15-Minute Spaghetti 131
Meatballs with Marinara Sauce 132
Sicilian Meatballs 132
   Marinara Sauce 133
Creamy Mushroom Pasta 134
Turkey Sausage & Edamame Pasta 135
Quick Pesto 136
Sun-Dried Tomato Pesto 136
Linguine with Clam Sauce 137
Lasagna with a Cinnamon Twist 138
Vegetable Lasagna 138
Chicken, Spinach & Sun-Dried
   Tomato Pizza 139
Pesto, Tomato & Fresh Mozzarella Pizza 139

ASIAN ENTREES

Moo Goo Gai Pan 140
Sweet & Sour Pork 141

HISPANIC DISHES

Easy Fiesta Casserole 142
Quick Fajitas 143
Chicken Burritos with Tomatillo Sauce . 144
   Tomatillo Sauce 145
Beef Quesadillas 146
Stuffed Quesadillas 147
Yummy Turkey Tacos 148
Grilled Fish Tacos 149
Tostadas with Chicken & Guacamole . . 150

POULTRY

Fried Chicken

Sodium Per Serving – 40mg   Serves 4

The secret to this delicious chicken is the combination of spices, which I often use as a basic seasoning in many of my recipes.

- 2 tablespoons all-purpose flour
- ½ teaspoon dried basil
- ½ teaspoon garlic powder
- ¼ teaspoon ground black pepper
- ¼ teaspoon dried rosemary, crushed
- ¼ teaspoon dried tarragon
- ¼ teaspoon dried thyme
- 4 boneless, skinless chicken breasts or thighs (about 1 pound)[1]
- 1–2 tablespoons olive oil

1. Mix together flour, basil, garlic powder, pepper, rosemary, tarragon, and thyme; dredge chicken in flour mixture, shaking off any excess.
2. Heat oil in a large skillet over medium-high heat; add chicken. Cook until brown on one side, 4 to 5 minutes; turn. Decrease heat to medium-low; cover and cook until chicken is no longer pink, but still moist inside, 15 to 20 minutes.

NUTRITIONAL INFO PER SERVING: Calories 186, Fat 8g (Saturated Fat 2g), Cholesterol 65mg, Carbohydrates 3g (Fiber 0g, Sugar 0g), Sodium 40mg

---

VARIATION
Oven-Baked Chicken

1. Beat together 2 eggs and place in a dish or shallow bowl. Substitute ½ cup panko or LS bread crumbs[2] for the flour and mix with the spices. Dip chicken in eggs, then coat with bread crumb mixture.
2. Bake in a preheated oven at 350ºF (180ºC) for about 20 minutes, or until chicken is no longer pink, but still moist inside.

NUTRITIONAL INFO PER SERVING: Calories 230, Fat 8g (Sat Fat 2g), Chol 65mg, Carb 11g (Fiber 2g, Sugar 1g), Sodium 67mg

---

TOTAL SODIUM AND FAT BY INGREDIENT

Sodium:
 1 lb chicken breasts - 160mg
  or chicken thighs - 300mg

Fat (Sat Fat):
 1 lb chicken breasts - 4g (0g)
  or chicken thighs - 40g (12g)
 1 T olive oil - 14g (2g)

Brands used/alternatives:
 Tyson All Natural Chicken Breasts or Thighs

Recipe Notes
1 – Breast meat has less fat and sodium than thigh meat, thighs are juicier and more flavorful.
2 – Panko or "Japanese bread crumbs" are lighter than regular crumbs, and don't pack together, resulting in a crispier crust. Plus, they don't have fat and are very low in sodium (45mg vs 270mg an oz). See *Bread Crumbs*, pg 244. for more info.

FRIED CHICKEN WITH COUNTRY GRAVY
Sodium Per Serving – 45mg   Serves 4

This yummy gravy gets its richness and flavor from sake. Make extra gravy and serve over Herbed Buttermilk Biscuits *(pg 199).*

- **4 servings** *Fried Chicken* **(pg 80)**
- **1–2 tablespoons all-purpose flour**
- **½ cup sake or fortified wine, such as a dry sherry or Madeira**[1]
- **1 teaspoon LS chicken bouillon**
- **½ cup water**
- **2 tablespoons lowfat milk**
- **2–3 drops** *Kitchen Bouquet* **(optional)**[2]

Optional spices:
- **⅛ teaspoon dried basil**
- **⅛ teaspoon garlic powder**
- **Pinch ground black pepper**
- **Pinch dried rosemary, crumbled**
- **Pinch dried tarragon**
- **Pinch dried thyme**

1. Cook *Fried Chicken* according to directions, reserve any excess flour for the gravy.
2. In a small bowl, combine reserved flour and enough additional flour to equal 2 tablespoons. (If there is less than a tablespoon of reserved flour, add the optional spices to the combined flours; mix with the sake, stirring until smooth.
3. In same skillet chicken was cooked, increase heat to medium-high; stir in sake/flour mixture, scraping up any browned bits of chicken.
4. Mix in bouillon and water; cook, stirring constantly, until sauce thickens to a gravy consistency, 2 to 3 minutes. Stir in 2 tablespoons milk and Kitchen Bouquet; serve over chicken.

NUTRITIONAL INFO PER SERVING (without gravy): Calories 239, Fat 8g (Saturated Fat 2g), Cholesterol 66mg, Carbohydrates 8g (Fiber 0g, Sugar 2g), Sodium 45mg
GRAVY ONLY NUTRITIONAL INFO: Calories 53, Fat 0g (Saturated Fat 0g), Cholesterol 1mg, Carbohydrates 5g (Fiber 0g, Sugar 2g), Sodium 5mg

Recipe Notes
1 – Sake adds a light, rich flavor to this gravy (inexpensive sake is found in most supermarkets). You can also use a fortified wine (see *Fortified Wines, pg 14*) or dry white wine. What you use adds a subtle difference in flavor to the gravy.

2 – *Kitchen Bouquet* is a browning and seasoning sauce that was popular in the 1960s and 70s. It is used to lightly brown gravies and add a little punch to bland or mellow sauces. A drop or two goes a long way. It is found with the steak sauces in most supermarkets.

TOTAL SODIUM AND FAT BY INGREDIENT
Sodium:
  4 *Fried Chicken* - 160mg
  ½ c sake - 2mg
    or sherry - 11mg
  1 t LS chicken bouillon - 5mg
  2 T LF milk - 13mg
Fat (Sat Fat):
  4 *Fried Chicken* - 30g (8g)
  2 T LF milk - 1g (0g)
Brands used/alternatives:
  Herb Ox NSA Chiicken Bouillon
  Simple Truth 2% Milk

Chicken Diane

Sodium Per Serving – 65mg Serves 4

This is my poultry version of Steak Diane, an elegant dish usually served table side in finer restaurants. It's so quick and easy, you'll want to serve it often, not just on special occasions.

- **4 boneless, skinless chicken breasts (about 1 pound), flattened to ¼-inch thick**[1]
- **½ teaspoon garlic or onion powder**
- **¼ teaspoon ground black pepper**
- **1 tablespoon olive oil**

Sauce:
- **1 tablespoon unsalted butter or margarine**
- **2 garlic cloves, minced**
- **1 large shallot, finely chopped**[2]
- **4 oz sliced mushrooms (about 1 cup)**
- **1 teaspoon LS chicken bouillon**
- **¼ cup dry white wine**[3]
- **2 tablespoons brandy**
- **1 tablespoon lemon juice**
- **2 teaspoons Dijon-style mustard**
- **2–3 drops hot pepper sauce, such as *Tabasco***
- **¼ teaspoon Worcestershire sauce**
- **1 tablespoon chopped fresh Italian parsley (optional)**

1. Season chicken with garlic powder and pepper.
2. Heat oil in a large skillet over medium-high heat; add chicken. Cook until lightly browned on both sides, 3 to 4 minutes per side. (Chicken is done when it is no longer pink, but still moist inside.)
3. Transfer chicken to a platter and keep warm while preparing the sauce.
4. *For the sauce:* In the same skillet, melt butter; decrease heat to medium and add garlic and shallots. Cook, stirring constantly, until you smell the garlic, about 1 minute. Add mushrooms and cook, stirring frequently, until mushrooms soften, 4 to 5 minutes. Stir in bouillon, wine, brandy, lemon juice, mustard, hot pepper sauce, and Worcestershire; bring to boil. Cook, stirring frequently, until liquid is reduced to a gravy consistency, 3 to 4 minutes.
5. Serve chicken with sauce on top; sprinkle with parsley.

NUTRITIONAL INFO PER SERVING: Calories 242, Fat 10g (Sat Fat 4g), Chol 73mg, Carb 4g (Fiber 1g, Sugar 2g), Sodium 65mg

Recipe Notes

1 – To flatten: Place chicken, smooth side down, between two sheets of waxed paper, plastic wrap, or aluminum foil; pound gently with a meat mallet, rolling pin, or rubber hammer until flattened to desired thickness.

2 – Shallots look like small onions and have a mild flavor, somewhere between an onion and garlic (see *Shallots*, pg 253, for additional info). If shallots are unavailable, substitute 2 finely chopped green onions.

3 – Use a sherry or Madeira instead of white wine.

TOTAL SODIUM AND FAT BY INGREDIENT

Sodium:
- 1 lb chicken breasts - 160mg
- 2 garlic cloves - 1mg
- 1 shallot - 5mg
- 4 oz mushrooms - 2mg
- 1 t LS chicken bouillon - 5mg
- ¼ c white wine - 3mg
- 2 t Dijon mustard - 80mg
- 2 drops hot pepper sauce - 1mg
- ¼ t Worcestershire - 5mg

Fat (Sat Fat):
- 1 lb chicken breasts - 16g (6g)
- 1 T olive oil - 14g (2g)
- 1 T NSA butter - 12g (7g)
  or NSA margarine - 9g (4g)

Brands used/alternatives:
Tyson All Natural Chicken Breast
Herb Ox NSA Chicken Bouillon
Gold's Dijon Mustard
Robbie's Worcestershire Sauce

CHICKEN PICCATA

Sodium Per Serving – 50mg Serves 4

You won't believe how easy it is to make this delicious dish, which is served in many upscale restaurants. Although chicken piccata is often prepared with capers (which are high in sodium), this version, without the capers, is just as tasty. This is an impressive dinner party entrée and takes less than 15 minutes to prepare, so have everything ready before cooking the chicken. Serve with Caramelized Shallots & Asparagus (pg 152) and Basic Steamed Rice (pg 172).

- 2 tablespoons all-purpose flour
- 1 teaspoon dried tarragon
- ½ teaspoon dried basil
- ½ teaspoon garlic powder
- ½ teaspoon dried rosemary, crushed
- ½ teaspoon dried thyme
- ¼ teaspoon ground black pepper
- 4 boneless, skinless chicken breasts (about 1 pound), flattened to ¼-inch thick[1]
- 1 tablespoon olive oil

Sauce:
- 1 tablespoon unsalted butter or margarine
- 1 large shallot, minced[2]
- 2–3 tablespoons lemon juice
- ½ cup Madeira or dry white wine
- ¼ teaspoon Worcestershire sauce
- 4–5 drops hot pepper sauce, such as *Tabasco*
- 2–3 tablespoons lowfat milk[3]
- 1 tablespoon chopped fresh Italian parsley (optional)

1. Mix flour, tarragon, basil, garlic powder, rosemary, thyme, and pepper together; dredge chicken in flour mixture, shaking off any excess.
2. Heat oil in a large skillet over medium-high heat; add chicken. Cook until lightly browned on both sides, 3 to 4 minutes per side. (Chicken is done when it is no longer pink, but still moist inside.)
3. Transfer chicken to a platter and keep warm while preparing the sauce.
4. For the sauce: In the same skillet, melt butter; add shallots. Cook, stirring frequently, until shallots are soft, 1 to 2 minutes. Add lemon juice, Madeira, Worcestershire, and hot pepper sauce; cook, stirring frequently, for 2 minutes. Mix one tablespoon of the pan sauce into the milk (to prevent milk from curdling); stir into shallot mixture. Cook, stirring constantly, until sauce has thickened to a gravy consistency, 2 to 3 minutes.
5. Pour sauce over chicken and serve with parsley sprinkled on top.

NUTRITIONAL INFO PER SERVING: Calories 271, Fat 11g (Sat Fat 4g), Chol 73mg, Carb 11g (Fiber 1g, Sugar 4g), Sodium 50mg

Recipe Notes
1 – To flatten: Place chicken, smooth side down, between two sheets of waxed paper, plastic wrap, or aluminum foil; pound gently with a meat mallet, rolling pin, or rubber hammer until flattened to desired thickness.
2 – For information on selecting and storing shallots, see *Shallots*, pg 253.
3 – For a creamier sauce, use a light cream or half-and-half.

TOTAL SODIUM AND FAT BY INGREDIENT

Sodium:
- 1 lb chicken breasts - 160mg
- 1 shallot - 5mg
- ½ cup Madeira wine - 12mg
- ¼ t Worcestershire - 5mg
- 4 drops red pepper sauce - 1mg
- 2 T LF milk - 13mg
- 1 T parsley - 2mg

Fat (Sat Fat):
- 1 lb chicken breasts - 16g (6g)
- 1 T olive oil - 14g (2g)
- 1 T NSA butter - 12g (7g) or NSA margarine - 9g (4g)
- 2 T LF milk - 1g (0g)

Brands used/alternatives:
Tyson All Natural Chicken Breast
Robbie's Worcestershire Sauce
Simple Truth 2% Milk

Herbed Goat Cheese Stuffed Chicken

Sodium Per Serving – 64mg Serves 4

Don't be fooled by the simplicity of this delightful dish. Filled with sun-dried tomato and herb goat cheese, it's elegant enough for company.

- 4 boneless, skinless chicken breasts (about 1 pound), flattened to ¼-inch thick[1]
- 2 tablespoons all-purpose flour
- ½ teaspoon dried basil
- ½ teaspoon garlic powder
- ¼ teaspoon ground black pepper
- ¼ teaspoon dried rosemary, crushed
- ¼ teaspoon dried tarragon
- ¼ teaspoon dried thyme
- 1–2 tablespoons olive oil
- *Herbed Goat Cheese (recipe follows)*

1. Place one-fourth of the *Herbed Goat Cheese* in the center of each breast and roll up; secure with a toothpick, if necessary, to hold together.
2. Mix flour, basil, garlic powder, pepper, rosemary, tarragon, and thyme together; dredge chicken rolls in flour mixture, shaking off any excess.
3. Heat oil in a large skillet over medium-high heat; add chicken. Cook until lightly browned on one side, 4 to 5 minutes; turn. Decrease heat to medium-low; cover and cook until chicken is no longer pink, but still moist inside, about 15 minutes.

NUTRITIONAL INFO PER SERVING: Calories 228, Fat 11g (Saturated Fat 3g), Cholesterol 73mg, Carbohydrates 5g (Fiber 0g, Sugar 1g), Sodium 64mg

Herbed Goat Cheese

Sodium Per Serving – 24mg Serves 4

This cheese mixture is also good as a spread on crackers and served as an appetizer.

- 2 oz goat (Chèvre) cheese[2]
- 1 tablespoon oil-packed sun-dried tomatoes, drained and minced[3]
- 1 tablespoon chopped fresh Italian parsley
- 1½ teaspoons chopped fresh basil or ½ teaspoon dried
- ½ teaspoon finely minced garlic
- ¼ teaspoon onion powder
- ⅛ teaspoon black pepper

1. Mix together goat cheese, tomatoes, parsley, basil, garlic, and onion powder. Refrigerate until ready to use.

NUTRITIONAL INFO PER SERVING: Calories 43, Fat 4g (Sat Fat 1g), Chol 8mg, Carb 2g (Fiber 0g, Sugar 1g), Sodium 24mg

Recipe Notes

1 – To flatten: Place chicken, smooth side down, between two sheets of waxed paper, plastic wrap, or aluminum foil; pound gently with a meat mallet, rolling pin, or rubber hammer until flattened to desired thickness.

2 – Most goat cheese is low sodium and ranges from sweet and mild to tangy and sharp. A popular variety is Chèvre. It usually has the least sodium, averaging 50mg an ounce.

3 – Sun-dried tomatoes come bottled in olive oil or dried in bags. Generally, bottled tomatoes have less sodium than packaged, but read labels carefully, some brands have added sodium. Either are okay to use, but the latter must be reconstituted in warm water for 30 minutes before using.

TOTAL SODIUM AND FAT BY INGREDIENT

HERB GOAT CHEESE CHICKEN
Sodium:
  1 lb chicken breasts - 160mg
  Herbed Goat Cheese - 97mg
Fat (Sat Fat):
  1 lb chicken breasts - 16g (6g)
  1 T olive oil - 14g (2g)
  Herbed Goat Cheese - 15g (3g)
Brands used/alternatives:
  Tyson All Natural Chicken Breast

HERBED GOAT CHEESE
Sodium:
  2 oz goat cheese - 90mg
  1 T sun-dried tomatoes - 5mg
  1 T parsley - 2mg
Fat (Sat Fat):
  2 oz goat cheese - 12g (3g)
  1 T sun-dried tomatoes - 3g (0g)
Brands used/alternatives:
  Vermont Creamery Herb Chèvre
  Jeff's Naturals Sun-dried Tomatoes

> **VARIATION**
> ### FETA-STUFFED CHICKEN
> 1. Instead of *Herbed Goat Cheese*, use 2 oz Mediterranean herb flavored feta.
>
> NUTRITIONAL INFO PER SERVING: Calories 220, Fat 10g (Saturated Fat 4g), Cholesterol 75mg, Carbohydrates 4g (Fiber 1g, Sugar 0g), Sodium 150mg

CREAMY CHEESY CHICKEN

Sodium Per Serving – 223mg   Serves 6

This is a quick and delicious way to prepare chicken. Similar to the previous dish except some of the cheese oozes out and creates a yummy cheese sauce. Serve over a bed of pasta or rice and garnish with chopped green onions.

- 6 boneless, skinless chicken breasts (about 1½ pounds), flattened to ¼-inch thick[1]
- 1 (6.5-oz) container garlic and herbs spreadable cheese[2]
- 2 tablespoons all-purpose flour
- ½ teaspoon dried basil
- ½ teaspoon garlic powder
- ¼ teaspoon ground black pepper
- ¼ teaspoon dried rosemary, crushed
- ¼ teaspoon dried tarragon
- ¼ teaspoon dried thyme
- 1 tablespoon olive oil
- ½ cup dry white wine
- 6 oz sliced mushrooms (about 2½ cups)[3]
- 1 teaspoon LS chicken bouillon
- 1 tablespoon cornstarch, mixed with 2 tablespoons water to form a paste
- Chopped green onions (optional)

1. Spread 2 tablespoons cheese over the top of each breast and roll up, jelly-roll style.
2. Mix flour, basil, garlic powder, pepper, rosemary, tarragon, and thyme together; dredge chicken rolls in flour mixture, shaking off any excess.
3. Heat oil in a large skillet over medium-high heat; add chicken. Cook until lightly browned on one side, 4 to 5 minutes; turn. Decrease heat to medium-low; add wine, mushrooms, and bouillon. Cover and cook until chicken is no longer pink, but still moist inside, about 15 minutes. Transfer chicken to a platter and keep warm.
4. Stir remaining cheese spread into sauce until heated. If sauce is not thick and creamy, increase heat to medium and slowly add cornstarch paste, stirring constantly, until thickened to a gravy consistency. Serve over chicken and top with green onions, if desired.

NUTRITIONAL INFO PER SERVING: Calories 303, Fat 17g (Sat Fat 8g), Chol 98mg, Carb 8g (Fiber 1g, Sugar 1g), Sodium 223mg

Recipe Notes

1 – To flatten: Place chicken, smooth side down, between two sheets of waxed paper, plastic wrap, or aluminum foil; pound gently with a meat mallet, rolling pin, or rubber hammer until flattened to desired thickness.

2 – I use *Alouette's Garlic & Herbs* spreadable cheese. Unfortunately, over the years the sodium has increased from 60mg per 2 tbsp, to 3 times that! Nevertheless, I still prefer it in this dish.

3 – Use any variety or combination of mushrooms. For info on mushroom varieties, see *Mushrooms*, pg 250.

> **TOTAL SODIUM AND FAT BY INGREDIENT**
>
> Sodium:
> 1½ lbs chicken breasts - 240mg
> 6.5 oz spread cheese - 1,080mg
> ½ c white wine - 6mg
> 6 oz mushrooms - 8mg
> 1 t LS chicken bouillon - 5mg
> Fat (Sat Fat):
> 1½ lbs chicken - 24g (9g)
> 6.5 oz cheese - 64g (36g)
> 1 T olive oil - 14g (2g)
> 6 oz mushrooms - 1g (0g)
> **Brands used/alternatives:**
> *Tyson All* Natural Chicken Breast
> *Alouette* Garlic & Herbs Spread
> *Herb Ox* NSA Chicken Bouillon

Sun-Dried Tomato Chicken

Sodium Per Serving – 89mg Serves 4

So quick and so-o-o good. The sun-dried tomatoes lend an intense, tangy flavor. Serve over a bed of rice and garnish with chopped chives.

- **4 boneless, skinless chicken breasts (about 1 pound)**
- **2 tablespoons all-purpose flour**
- **½ teaspoon garlic powder**
- **½ teaspoon ground black pepper**
- **⅛ teaspoon cayenne pepper**
- **1 tablespoon olive oil**

Sauce:
- **1 tablespoon unsalted butter or margarine**
- **1 onion, chopped**[1]
- **2 garlic cloves, minced**
- **¼ cup oil-packed sun-dried tomatoes, drained and chopped**[2]
- **2 tablespoons chopped ripe olives (optional)**[3]
- **½ teaspoon dried basil**
- **1 cup dry white wine**
- **⅔ cup lowfat sour cream**

1. Place chicken, smooth side down, between two sheets of waxed paper or aluminum foil; pound gently with a meat mallet, rolling pin, or hammer until flattened to ¼-inch thick.
2. Mix flour with garlic powder, black pepper, and cayenne; dredge chicken in flour mixture, shaking off any excess.
3. Heat oil in a large skillet over medium-high heat; add chicken. Cook until lightly browned on both sides, 3 to 4 minutes per side. (Chicken is done when it is no longer pink, but still moist inside.)
4. Transfer chicken to a platter and keep warm while preparing the sauce.
5. *For the sauce:* Melt butter in the same skillet chicken was cooked; add onion and garlic. Cook, stirring frequently, until onions are translucent, 2 to 3 minutes. Decrease heat to medium; stir in tomatoes, olives, basil, wine, and sour cream. Cook, uncovered, until sauce thickens and is reduced by one-half, 3 to 5 minutes. Return chicken to the skillet; simmer until chicken is heated through, 2 to 3 minutes.

NUTRITIONAL INFO PER SERVING: Calories 368, Fat 18g (Sat Fat 6g), Chol 86mg, Carb 12g (Fiber 1g, Sugar 5g), Sodium 89mg

Recipe Notes
1 – Instead of onion, substitute 3 chopped shallots.
2 – Generally, bottled sun-dried tomatoes have less sodium than packaged, but read labels carefully, some brands have added sodium.
3 – The olives add a bit of saltiness; if omitting, decrease sodium to 69mg a serving.

TOTAL SODIUM AND FAT BY INGREDIENT

Sodium:
1 lb chicken breasts - 160mg
1 onion - 4mg
2 garlic cloves - 1mg
¼ c sun-dried tomatoes - 20mg
2 T ripe olives - 80mg
1 cup white wine - 12mg
⅔ c LF sour cream - 80mg

Fat (Sat Fat):
1 lb chicken breasts - 16g 6g)
1 T olive oil - 14g (2g)
1 T NSA butter - 12g (7g)
  or NSA margarine - 9g (4g)
¼ c dried tomatoes - 12g (0g)
2 T ripe olives - 6g (2g)
⅔ c LF sour cream - 13g (8g)

Brands used/alternatives:
*Tyson All N*atural Chicken Breast
Jeff's Naturals Sun-Dried Tomatoes
Mario's LS Black Olives
Daisy Light Sour Cream

Chicken Paprika with Tomato Cream Sauce

Sodium Per Serving – 57mg   Serves 6

This creamy paprika-flavored chicken is served in Hungary for Christmas dinner, but you don't have to wait until then to try this classic. Serve over noodles or rice.

- 2 tablespoons all-purpose flour
- 1 tablespoon paprika[1]
- ½ teaspoon garlic powder
- ¼ teaspoon ground black pepper
- 6 boneless, skinless chicken breasts (about 1½ pounds)
- 1 tablespoon olive oil
- 1 tablespoon unsalted butter or margarine
- 1 onion, sliced
- 1 garlic clove, minced
- 1 green bell pepper, seeded and chopped
- 1 cup water
- ½ cup dry white wine[2]
- 2 large tomatoes, chopped (about 2 cups)
- 1 teaspoon LS chicken bouillon
- 1 teaspoon mustard powder
- ¼ teaspoon cayenne pepper
- 2 tablespoons cornstarch, mixed with ¼ cup water to make a paste
- ½ cup lowfat sour cream
- Cooked noodles or rice (optional)

1. Place flour, paprika, garlic powder, and black pepper in a small paper bag; add chicken one piece at a time and shake until well coated. Set aside.
2. Heat oil and butter in a large skillet over medium heat; add onions, garlic, and bell pepper. Cook, stirring frequently, until onions are translucent, 3 to 4 minutes. Transfer onion mixture to a bowl, reserve.
3. Add floured chicken to same skillet; increase heat to medium-high and cook chicken until lightly browned on both sides, 3 to 4 minutes per side. Stir in a few tablespoons of water, scraping up any browned bits of chicken. Add remaining water, wine, tomatoes, bouillon, mustard, cayenne, and reserved onion mixture; stir well. Decrease heat to medium-low; cover and cook until chicken is no longer pink, but still moist inside, about 20 minutes.
4. Just before serving, slowly add cornstarch paste, stirring until sauce has thickened to a gravy consistency. Mix in sour cream and serve over noodles or rice, if desired.

NUTRITIONAL INFO PER SERVING: Calories 262, Fat 10g (Sat Fat 4g), Chol 77mg, Carb 12g (Fiber 2g, Sugar 4g), Sodium 57mg

---

VARIATION
Mushroom Chicken Paprikash

1. Cook 1 cup sliced mushrooms with the onions and peppers; proceed as directed.

NUTRITIONAL INFO PER SERVING: Calories 265, Fat 10g (Sat Fat 4g), Chol 77mg, Carb 12g (Fiber 2g, Sugar 4g), Sodium 58mg

---

Recipe Notes
1 – Paprika comes in sweet or hot varieties. Most American paprika is sweet, while Hungarian paprika is more pungent. If using a hot paprika, omit the cayenne pepper.
2 – Substitute a dry sherry, Madeira, or Marsala for the white wine.

TOTAL SODIUM AND FAT BY INGREDIENT

Sodium:
- 1 tbsp paprika - 5mg
- 1½ lbs chicken breasts - 240mg
- 1 onion - 4mg
- 1 garlic clove - 1mg
- 1 bell pepper - 4mg
- ½ c white wine - 6mg
- 2 tomatoes - 18mg
- 1 t LS chicken bouillon - 5mg
- 1 T cornstarch - 1mg
- ½ c LF sour cream - 60mg

Fat (Sat Fat):
- 1 tbsp paprika - 1g (0g)
- 1½ lbs chicken - 24g (9g)
- 1 T olive oil - 14g (2g)
- 1 T NSA butter - 12g (7g) or NSA margarine - 9g (4g)
- 2 tomatoes - 1g (0g)
- 1 T mustard powder - 1g (0g)
- ½ c LF sour cream - 10g (6g)

Brands used/alternatives:
Tyson All Natural Chicken Breast
Herb Ox NSA Chicken Bouillon
Daisy Light Sour Cream

Marsala Chicken

Sodium Per Serving – 49mg   Serves 4

This classic Italian dish is so quick and easy to make, yet elegant enough to serve when company comes.

- 4 boneless, skinless chicken breasts, flattened to ¼-inch thick[1]
- 2 tablespoons all-purpose flour
- ½ teaspoon garlic or onion powder
- ½ teaspoon Tuscan spice blend[2]
- ¼ teaspoon ground black pepper
- 1 tablespoon olive oil

Sauce:
- 1 tablespoon olive oil
- 1 shallot, minced[3]
- 2–3 garlic cloves, minced
- 8 oz sliced mushrooms[4]
- ½ cup Marsala wine[5]
- ¼ cup dry sherry
- 1 teaspoon LS chicken bouillon
- ½ teaspoon sugar
- 1 tablespoon unsalted butter or margarine
- 2 tablespoons chopped fresh Italian parsley (optional)

1. Mix flour with garlic powder, Tuscan spice blend, and pepper; dredge chicken in flour mixture, shaking off any excess.
2. Heat oil in a large skillet over medium-high heat; add chicken. Cook until lightly browned on both sides, 3 to 4 minutes per side. (Chicken is done when it is no longer pink, but still moist inside.)
3. Transfer chicken to a platter and keep warm while preparing the sauce.
4. *For the sauce:* Heat oil in the same skillet over medium heat; add shallots and garlic. Cook, stirring frequently, until you smell the garlic, 2 to 3 minutes. Add mushrooms and cook, stirring frequently, until the mushrooms soften, 2 to 3 minutes. Stir in Marsala, sherry, bouillon, and sugar; reduce heat to medium-low, cover and simmer 10 to 15 minutes. The sauce should be the consistency of gravy; if not, raise heat to medium-high and cook a few minutes longer until reduced. Stir in butter.
5. Return chicken to skillet; simmer, covered, until chicken is heated through, 2 to 3 minutes. Serve chicken with mushroom sauce on top; sprinkle with parsley.

NUTRITIONAL INFO PER SERVING: Calories 299, Fat 14g (Sat Fat 4g), Chol 73mg, Carb 11g (Fiber 1g, Sugar 3g), Sodium 49mg

Recipe Notes

1 – To flatten: Place chicken, smooth side down, between two sheets of waxed paper, plastic wrap, or aluminum foil; pound gently with a meat mallet, rolling pin, or rubber hammer until flattened to desired thickness.

2 – Tuscan spice blends are found in most supermarkets. To make your own, use equal amounts of dried rosemary, sage, thyme, and basil.

3 – For shallot selection and storage, see *Shallots, pg 253*. If shallots are unavailable, substitute 2 tablespoons minced onion or leek.

4 – For a richer flavor, soak 2 oz dried porcini mushrooms in 1 cup warm water for 30 minutes. Pat dry with paper towel and coarsely chop; proceed as directed in Step 4.

5 – Use Marsala wine, not cooking wine, which has too much sodium (183mg an oz).

VARIATION

For a tangy sauce, stir in the juice of half a lemon (about 1 tbsp) before serving.

TOTAL SODIUM AND FAT BY INGREDIENT

Sodium:
- 4 chicken breasts - 160mg
- 1 shallot - 5mg
- 2 garlic cloves - 1mg
- 8 oz mushrooms - 11mg
- ½ c Marsala wine - 3mg
- ¼ c sherry - 5mg
- 1 t LS chicken bouillon - 5mg
- 2 T parsley - 4mg

Fat (Sat Fat):
- 4 chicken breasts - 16g (6g)
- 2 T olive oil - 28g (4g)
- 8 oz mushrooms - 1g (0g)
- 1 T NSA butter - 12g (7g) or NSA margarine - 9g (4g)

Brands used/alternatives:
Tyson All Natural Chicken Breast
Herb Ox NSA Chicken Bouillon

Chicken in Mushroom-Asparagus-Tarragon Sauce

Sodium Per Serving – 53mg   Serves 4

This pleasing dish has a rich, creamy sauce. The caramelized onions and mushrooms add a bit of sweetness, while the asparagus adds another element of flavor.

- 2 tablespoons olive oil, divided
- 1 tablespoon unsalted butter or margarine
- 1 medium onion, sliced
- 1 shallot, chopped
- 1 teaspoon sugar
- 2 tablespoons all-purpose flour
- 1 teaspoon dried tarragon
- ½ teaspoon garlic powder
- ½ teaspoon dried rosemary, crushed
- ½ teaspoon dried thyme
- 4 boneless, skinless chicken breasts, flattened to ¼-inch thick[1]

Sauce:
- 4 oz mushrooms, sliced (about 1 cup)[2]
- ½ cup dry white wine[3]
- 1 cup asparagus pieces (about 6 spears, cut in 1-inch pieces)
- 1 teaspoon LS chicken bouillon, mixed with ½ cup water
- ¼ cup half-and-half or light cream
- ¼ teaspoon ground black pepper
- 3 tablespoons chopped fresh tarragon or 1 tablespoon dried

1. Heat 1 tablespoon oil and butter in a large skillet over medium heat; add onions and shallots. Cook, stirring frequently, until onions are translucent, 3 to 4 minutes. Decrease heat to medium-low; cook, uncovered, stirring frequently, until onions are a deep golden brown, about 20 minutes. Stir in sugar and set aside.
2. Meanwhile, mix flour with dried tarragon, garlic powder, rosemary, and thyme; dredge chicken in flour mixture, shake off any excess.
3. Heat remaining 1 tablespoon oil in another skillet over medium-high heat; add chicken. Cook until lightly browned on both sides, 3 to 5 minutes on each side; add mushrooms and cook, stirring occasionally, until mushrooms have softened, 3 to 5 minutes.
4. Stir in wine, asparagus, and bouillon; reduce heat to medium. Cover and simmer until chicken is no longer pink, but still moist inside, about 10 minutes. Transfer chicken to a platter and keep warm while preparing the sauce.
5. *Sauce:* Add caramelized onion mixture, half-and-half, pepper, and fresh tarragon to the mushrooms; stir until well mixed and slightly thickened. *NOTE:* If sauce is not thick enough, mix together 1 tablespoon cornstarch with 1 tablespoon water; gradually add to sauce, stirring constantly, until desired consistency.
6. Slice chicken on the diagonal and serve with sauce on top.

NUTRITIONAL INFO PER SERVING: Calories 320, Fat 16g (Sat Fat 5g), Chol 78mg, Carb 13g (Fiber 2g, Sugar 5g), Sodium 53mg

Recipe Notes

1 – To flatten: Place chicken, smooth side down, between two sheets of waxed paper, plastic wrap, or aluminum foil; pound gently with a meat mallet, rolling pin, or rubber hammer until flattened to desired thickness.

2 – Use any variety or combination of mushrooms. I often use several varieties of wild mushrooms, both dried and fresh. (If using dried mushrooms, reconstitute in water, wine, or chicken broth for 30 minutes.) For info on mushroom varieties, see *Mushrooms*, pg 250.

3 – Use a dry sherry or Madeira instead of white wine.

TOTAL SODIUM AND FAT BY INGREDIENT

Sodium:
- 1 onion - 4mg
- 1 shallot - 5mg
- 4 chicken breasts - 160mg
- 1 c mushrooms - 6mg
- ½ c white wine - 6mg
- 6 asparagus spears - 2mg
- 1 t LS chicken bouillon - 5mg
- ¼ c half-and-half - 20mg
  or light cream - 40mg
- 3 tbsp fresh tarragon - 3mg

Fat (Sat Fat):
- 2 T olive oil - 28g (4g)
- 1 T NSA butter - 12g (7g)
  or NSA margarine - 9g (4g)
- 4 chicken breasts - 16g (6g)
- ¼ c half-and-half - 7g (4g)
  or light cream - 18g (11g)

Brands used/alternatives:
Tyson All Natural Chicken Breast
Herb Ox NSA Chicken Bouillon
Organic Valley Half and Half

Chicken Breasts with Shallot Sauce

Sodium Per Serving – 49mg   Serves 4

Rosemary and chicken blend together nicely in this simple yet flavorful dish. Serve over a bed of rice to soak up the savory sauce.

- **4 boneless, skinless chicken breasts (about 1 pound), flattened to ¼-inch thick**[1]
- **1 tablespoon olive oil**
- **1 tablespoon lemon juice**[2]
- **¼ teaspoon garlic or onion powder**
- **¼ teaspoon ground black pepper**
- **1 tablespoon fresh rosemary, minced, or 1 teaspoon dried**
- **Shallot Sauce (recipe follows)**
- **4 cups cooked rice (see *Basic Steamed Rice*, pg 172)**
- **1 tablespoon chopped fresh Italian parsley (optional)**

1. Place chicken in a baking dish. Mix oil, lemon juice, garlic powder, pepper, and rosemary together and rub into chicken, coating both sides. Cover and let marinate 30 minutes or more in refrigerator, turning chicken a couple of times.
2. Bake in a preheated oven at 350ºF (180ºC) for 30 to 35 minutes, until chicken is no longer pink, but still moist inside.
3. Slice chicken on the diagonal and place on a bed of rice; pour *Shallot Sauce* over the chicken and top with chopped parsley.

NUTRITIONAL INFO PER SERVING: Calories 452, Fat 13g (Saturated Fat 4g), Cholesterol 73mg, Carbohydrates 52g (Fiber 1g, Sugar 4g), Sodium 49mg

Shallot Sauce

Sodium Per Serving – 7mg   Serves 4

This sauce is also good on burgers or mashed potatoes.

- **2 teaspoons olive oil**
- **1 shallot, minced**[3]
- **1 teaspoon fresh rosemary, minced, or ¼ teaspoon dried**
- **1 teaspoon LS chicken bouillon**
- **½ cup water**
- **½ cup Madeira wine or dry sherry**
- **4–5 drops hot pepper sauce, such as *Tabasco***
- **¼ teaspoon Worcestershire sauce**
- **1 tablespoon unsalted butter or margarine**

1. Heat 2 teaspoons oil in a skillet over medium heat; add shallots and rosemary. Cook, stirring frequently, until shallots are translucent, 4 to 5 minutes. Add bouillon, water, wine, hot pepper sauce, and Worcestershire; cook until liquid is slightly thickened, 4 to 5 minutes. Stir in butter before serving. *(also see Variation, pg 91)*

NUTRITIONAL INFO PER SERVING: Calories 103, Fat 5g (Sat Fat 2g), Chol 8mg, Carb 6g (Fiber 0g, Sugar 3g), Sodium 7mg

Recipe Notes

1 – To flatten: Place chicken, smooth side down, between two sheets of waxed paper, plastic wrap, or aluminum foil; pound gently with a meat mallet, rolling pin, or rubber hammer until flattened to desired thickness.

2 – For a stronger lemon flavor, add ½ teaspoon finely grated lemon zest to the marinade.

3 – Shallots look like small onions and have a mild garlic flavor. For additional information, see *Shallots*, pg 253.

TOTAL SODIUM AND FAT BY INGREDIENT

CHICKEN WITH SHALLOTS
Sodium:
- 1 lb chicken breasts - 160mg
- Shallot Sauce - 29mg
- 4 c cooked rice - 6mg
- 1 T parsley - 2mg

Fat (Sat Fat):
- 1 lb chicken breasts - 16g (6g)
- 1 T olive oil - 14g (2g)
- Shallot Sauce - 22g (9g)
- 4 c cooked rice - 2g (1g)

Brands used/alternatives:
Tyson All Natural Chicken Breast

SHALLOT SAUCE
Sodium:
- 1 shallot - 5mg
- 1 t LS chicken bouillon - 5mg
- ½ c Madeira wine - 12mg
- 4 drops hot pepper sauce - 1mg
- ¼ t Worcestershire - 5mg

Fat (Sat Fat):
- 1 T NSA butter - 12g (7g) or NSA margarine - 9g (4g)
- 2 t olive oil - 10g (2g)

Brands used/alternatives:
Tyson All Natural Chicken Breast
Herb Ox NSA Chicken Bouillon
Robbie's Worcestershire Sauce

> **VARIATION**
> ### CHICKEN BREASTS IN MUSHROOM-SHALLOT SAUCE
> 1. Cook 1 cup thinly sliced cremini mushrooms with the shallots; proceed as directed.
>
> NUTRITIONAL INFO PER SERVING: Calories 107, Fat 5g (Saturated Fat 2g), Cholesterol 8mg, Carbohydrates 7g (Fiber 1g, Sugar 4g), Sodium 8mg

CREAMY ARTICHOKES, MUSHROOMS, PEAS & CHICKEN

Sodium Per Serving – 101mg   Serves 4

Another quick and delicious way to prepare leftover turkey or chicken. Serve over noodles or rice and enjoy this family favorite.

- **1 tablespoon olive oil**
- **1 onion, chopped**
- **1 garlic clove, minced**
- **8 oz sliced mushrooms (about 2 cups)**
- **½ cup Madeira wine**
- **1 teaspoon LS chicken bouillon**
- **1 cup water**
- **2–3 drops hot pepper sauce, such as Tabasco**
- **¼ teaspoon Worcestershire sauce**
- **1 tablespoon fresh lemon juice**
- **1 (10-oz) package frozen peas**
- **1 (12-oz) package frozen artichoke hearts, thawed and halved[1]**
- **2 cups cooked chicken breast, cubed[2]**
- **½ cup lowfat sour cream**
- **1 tablespoon cornstarch, mixed with 2 tablespoons water to make a paste**
- **4 cups cooked rice (see *Basic Steamed Rice*, pg 172), noodles, or pasta**

1. Heat oil in a large skillet over medium-high heat; add onions. Cook, stirring frequently, until onions are translucent, 2 to 3 minutes; add garlic. Cook, stirring constantly, until you smell the garlic, about 1 minute; add mushrooms and cook until softened, 3 to 4 minutes.
2. Mix in Madeira, bouillon, water, hot pepper sauce, Worcestershire, lemon juice, peas, artichoke hearts, and chicken. Reduce heat to medium-low; cover and simmer 10 minutes, until peas and artichoke hearts are cooked.
3. Stir in sour cream. The sauce should be thick and creamy, if not, slowly stir in cornstarch paste until thickened. Serve over rice.

NUTRITIONAL INFO PER SERVING (with rice): Calories 548, Fat 10g (Sat Fat 1g), Chol 59mg, Carb 73g (Fiber 9g, Sugar 11g), Sodium 101mg

Recipe Notes
1 – Avoid bottled, marinated artichoke hearts. They average 440mg sodium per ½ cup, compared to frozen hearts with about 50mg.
2 – Avoid packaged chicken that has been precooked, it is loaded with sodium. For a delicious cooked chicken, see *Fried Chicken, pg 80*. If using oven roasted chicken, remove the skin to lessen the amount of fat and sodium.

> **TOTAL SODIUM AND FAT BY INGREDIENT**
>
> *Sodium:*
> 1 onion - 4mg
> 1 garlic clove - 1mg
> 8 oz mushrooms - 11mg
> ½ c Madeira wine - 12mg
> 1 t LS chicken bouillon - 5mg
> 2 drops hot pepper sauce - 1mg
> ¼ t Worcestershire - 5mg
> 12 oz frozen artichokes - 180mg
> 2 c cooked chicken - 120mg
> ½ c LF sour cream - 60mg
> 1 T cornstarch - 1mg
> 4 c cooked rice - 6mg
> *Fat (Sat Fat):*
> 1 T olive oil - 14g (2g)
> 8 oz mushrooms - 1g (0g)
> 2 c cooked chicken - 12g (5g)
> ½ c LF sour cream - 10g (6g)
> 4 c cooked rice - 2g (1g)
> **Brands used/alternatives:**
> *Herb Ox* NSA Chicken Bouillon
> *Robbie's* Worcestershire Sauce
> *Bird's Eye C&W* Petite Peas
> *Private Selection* Artichoke Hearts
> *Tyson All* Natural Chicken Breast
> *Daisy Light* Sour Cream

Chicken Piri Piri

Sodium Per Serving – 45mg | Serves 6

This hot and spicy dish (beef version shown on the cover) is Portuguese in origin with links to Africa (piri piri is Swahili for the fiery hot peppers of Africa). Make the sauce several days before to allow the peppers to intensify.

- 1½ pounds boneless, skinless chicken breasts, cut into 2-inch pieces
- **Piri Piri Sauce (recipe follows)**, divided
- 1 tablespoon olive oil
- ½ sweet onion, diced
- 1 red bell pepper, thinly sliced
- 2–3 garlic cloves, finely minced
- ½ cup brandy, dry sherry, or chicken broth
- 1 (12-oz) package frozen pearl onions

1. Place chicken in a baking dish and spread all but ½ cup *Piri Piri Sauce* over the chicken; cover with foil or plastic wrap and marinate in the refrigerator for 3 hours.
2. Preheat oven to 350°F (180°C); bake chicken with marinade for 20 to 25 minutes, until chicken is no longer pink, but still moist inside.
3. Meanwhile, heat oil in a large skillet over medium heat; add diced onions and bell pepper. Cook, stirring frequently, until onions are translucent, 3 to 4 minutes; add garlic. Cook, stirring constantly, until you smell the garlic, about 1 minute.
4. Add brandy, pearl onions, and reserved *Piri Piri Sauce*. Cook, stirring frequently, until sauce has thickened to a gravy consistency, about 5 minutes; add baked chicken and serve.

NUTRITIONAL INFO PER SERVING: Calories 498, Fat 35g (Saturated Fat 6g), Cholesterol 65mg, Carbohydrates 13g (Fiber 2g, Sugar 6g), Sodium 45mg

Piri Piri Sauce

Sodium Per Serving – 2mg | Makes about 1½ cups

Traditionally this sauce steeps for a week before using, but this version is ready in 24 hours (however, the longer this sits, the hotter it gets). The sauce will keep for a month and is great on grilled chicken and fish.

- ¾ cup olive oil
- ¼ cup fresh lemon juice or red wine vinegar
- 2–4 jalapeno or serrano peppers, stems removed[1]
- 2 garlic cloves
- 1 red bell pepper, quartered
- 1 teaspoon crushed red pepper flakes
- ½ teaspoon dried cumin
- ½ teaspoon dried oregano
- ½ teaspoon paprika
- ½ teaspoon black pepper
- ½ teaspoon dried thyme
- ½ teaspoon garlic powder
- ½ teaspoon onion powder

1. Place all ingredients in a saucepan and simmer over medium-low heat for 10 minutes; remove and let cool completely.
2. Place in a blender or food processor and pulse until smooth. Place purée in a covered container and let sit at room temperature for 24 hours or longer to allow peppers to intensify.

NUTRITIONAL INFO PER ¼ CUP: Calories 252, Fat 28g (Sat Fat 4g), Chol 0mg, Carb 4g (Fiber 1g, Sugar 1g), Sodium 2mg

Recipe Notes
1 – Two peppers may be enough heat. If you like it hot... add all 4! See *Chile Peppers*, pg 251, for pepper heat ratings.

TOTAL SODIUM AND FAT BY INGREDIENT

CHICKEN PIRI PIRI
Sodium:
1½ lb chicken - 240mg
Piri Piri Sauce - 11mg
½ sweet onion - 13mg
1 red bell pepper - 5mg
2 garlic cloves - 1mg
Fat (Sat Fat):
1½ lb chicken - 24g (9g)
Piri Piri Sauce - 169g (23g)
1 T olive oil - 14g (2g)
Brands used/alternatives:
Tyson All Natural Chicken Breast
Great Value Pearl Onions

PIRI PIRI SAUCE
Sodium:
¾ c olive oil - 3mg
1 t crushed chili flakes - 1mg
1 red bell pepper - 5mg
2 garlic cloves - 1mg
½ t cumin - 2mg
Fat (Sat Fat):
¾ c olive oil - 168g (23g)

Asparagus Chicken with Cream Sauce

Sodium Per Serving – 187mg   Serves 4

This is a great dish for leftover chicken or turkey. Mix in a few items from the pantry and serve this thick and creamy delight over rice or pasta. Although high in fat, much of it comes from the almonds which have monounsaturated fats (considered "good" fats, as they lower LDLs, the "bad" cholesterol).

- 1 tablespoon olive oil
- 1 small sweet onion, chopped
- 2 cloves garlic, minced
- 4 oz sliced mushrooms (about 1 cup)
- 2 cups asparagus, cut in 2-inch lengths
- 1 (8-oz) can sliced water chestnuts, drained
- 2 cups cooked chicken breast, cubed
- 2 teaspoons LS chicken bouillon
- ½ cup water
- ¼ cup dry sherry
- 1 tablespoon lemon juice
- ½ teaspoon onion or garlic powder
- ½ teaspoon ground black pepper
- ½ teaspoon herbes de Provence[1]
- ⅓ cup sliced unsalted almonds, toasted[2]
- ½ of 6.5 oz garlic and herbs spreadable cheese or ½ cup lowfat cream cheese[3]
- 4 cups cooked rice (see *Basic Steamed Rice*, pg 172) or pasta

1. Heat oil in a large skillet over medium-high heat; add onions. Cook, stirring frequently, until onions are translucent, 2 to 3 minutes; add garlic and cook, stirring constantly, until you smell the garlic, about 1 minute.
2. Stir in mushrooms, asparagus, water chestnuts, chicken, bouillon, water, sherry, lemon juice, onion powder, pepper, and herbes de Provence; cook until asparagus is fork tender, about 5 minutes.
3. Stir in almonds and cheese spread; mix until cheese is melted, forming a thick sauce. Serve over rice or pasta.

NUTRITIONAL INFO PER SERVING: Calories 589, Fat 21g (Sat Fat 7g), Chol 78mg, Carb 61g (Fiber 3g, Sugar 6g), Sodium 187mg

Recipe Notes

1 – Herbes de Provence is a blend of herbs commonly used in French cooking, most often a mix of basil, chervil, fennel, lavender, marjoram, rosemary, sage, savory, and thyme. The combination and portions vary depending on the manufacturer.

2 – To toast almonds, spread nuts in a dry skillet. Cook over medium-low heat, stirring or shaking frequently, until they start to turn golden, 5 to 7 minutes. See *Toasting Nuts*, pg 250, for additional toasting methods.

3 – I use *Alouette's Garlic & Herbs* spreadable cheese. Unfortunately, over the years the sodium has increased from 60mg per 2 tbsp, to 3 times that! Nevertheless, I still prefer it in this dish.

TOTAL SODIUM AND FAT BY INGREDIENT

Sodium:
- 1 sweet onion - 13mg
- 2 garlic cloves - 1mg
- 4 oz mushrooms - 6mg
- 2 c asparagus - 4mg
- 1½ c cooked chicken - 160mg
- 2 t LS chicken bouillon - 10mg
- ¼ c sherry - 5mg
- ¼ t onion powder - 1mg
- 3.2 oz cheese spread - 540mg
  or ½ c LF cr cheese - 420mg
- 4 c cooked rice - 6mg

Fat (Sat Fat):
- 1 T olive oil - 14g (2g)
- 1½ c cooked chicken - 16g (6g)
- ⅓ c NSA almonds - 23g (2g)
- 4 oz cheese spread - 32g (18g)
  or ½ c LF cr cheese - 24g (14g)
- 4 c cooked rice - 2g (1g)

Brands used/alternatives:
Kroger Water Chestnuts
Tyson All Natural Chicken Breast
Herb Ox NSA Chicken Bouillon
Alouette Garlic & Herb Cheese
Great Value Neufchâtel Cheese

Chicken Sausage with Artichokes

Sodium Per Serving – 257mg   Serves 4

This dish shows that you can have high-sodium foods, like sausage, and still remain within sodium guidelines, particularly if you add low-salt side dishes.

- **1 tablespoon olive oil**
- **2 sweet chicken sausage links (about 6 oz)[1]**
- **½ sweet onion, chopped**
- **3 garlic cloves, minced**
- **½ teaspoon herbes de Provence[2]**
- **¼ teaspoon garlic powder**
- **¼ teaspoon ground black pepper**
- **1 (12-oz) package frozen artichoke hearts, thawed and halved[3]**
- **2 large tomatoes, chopped (about 2 cups)**
- **½ cup dry white wine**
- **1 teaspoon LS chicken bouillon**
- **1 tablespoon unsalted butter or margarine**
- **4 cups cooked pasta, noodles, or rice**
- **2 tablespoons chopped fresh Italian parsley (optional)**

1. Heat oil in a large skillet over medium-high heat; add sausage. Cook until slightly browned on all sides, about 5 minutes. Remove sausage and let cool slightly; slice into bite-sized pieces. Set aside.
2. In same skillet, cook onion, stirring frequently, until translucent; add garlic. Cook, stirring constantly, until you smell the garlic, 1 to 2 minutes; mix in herbes de Provence, garlic powder, pepper, and sliced sausage. Add artichokes, tomatoes, wine, and bouillon; decrease heat to medium-low. Cover and cook until artichokes are soft, 10 to 15 minutes.
3. Stir in butter and heat through. Serve over pasta and top with parsley.

NUTRITIONAL INFO PER SERVING: Calories 395, Fat 10g (Sat Fat 3g), Chol 35mg, Carb 56g (Fiber 8g, Sugar 10g), Sodium 257mg

Recipe Notes

1 – Most sausages have way too much sodium. A few manufacturers, such as *Al Fresca, Shelton's,* and *Bilinski's,* offer lower sodium chicken sausages. Generally, links have less salt than patties, and sweet sausages are lower in sodium.

2 – Herbes de Provence is a blend of herbs commonly used in French cooking, most often a mix of basil, chervil, fennel, lavender, marjoram, rosemary, sage, savory and/or thyme. The combination and portions vary depending on the manufacturer.

3 – Instead of frozen artichokes, cook 5 fresh artichokes; remove and cut up the hearts. Add to the tomato-wine mixture during the last 5 minutes, stirring frequently, until heated through; proceed as directed.

TOTAL SODIUM AND FAT BY INGREDIENT

Sodium:
- 6 oz chicken sausage - 800mg
- ½ sweet onion - 7mg
- 3 garlic cloves - 2mg
- 12 oz artichoke hearts - 180mg
- 2 tomatoes - 18mg
- ½ c white wine - 6mg
- 1 t LS chicken bouillon - 5mg
- 4 c cooked pasta - 5mg
- 2 T parsley - 4mg

Fat (Sat Fat):
- 1 T olive oil - 14g (2g)
- 6 oz chicken sausage - 9g (3g)
- 2 tomatoes - 1g (0g)
- 1 T NSA butter - 12g (7g)
  or NSA margarine - 9g (4g)
- 4 c cooked pasta - 5g (1g)

Brands used/alternatives:
Al Fresco Sweet Apple Chicken Sausage
Private Selection Artichoke Hearts
Herb Ox NSA Chicken Bouillon

CHICKEN STROGANOFF

Sodium Per Serving – 99mg Serves 4

This is another yummy variation of the classic Stroganoff. I'm sure your family will love it as much as mine.

- 12 oz cooked chicken breast, cubed
- 1 tablespoon olive oil
- 1 sweet onion, sliced
- 2 garlic cloves, minced
- 4 oz sliced mushrooms (about 1 cup)
- ½ teaspoon herbes de Provence[1]
- ¼ teaspoon ground black pepper
- 1 cup broccoli florets
- 1 cup snap peas, broken in half
- 1 cup *Chicken Broth (pg 208)* or unsalted chicken broth
- 1 teaspoon LS chicken bouillon
- ¼ cup brandy[2]
- 6 oz (¾ cup) lowfat sour cream
- ¼ cup slivered almonds, toasted (optional)[3]
- 4 cups cooked pasta, noodles, or rice

1. Heat oil in a large skillet over medium heat; add onions. Cook, stirring frequently, until onions are translucent, 3 to 4 minutes; add garlic. Cook, stirring constantly, until you smell the garlic, 1 to 2 minutes.
2. Add mushrooms, herbes de Provence, and pepper; cook, stirring frequently, until mushrooms soften, about 3 minutes. Stir in chicken, broccoli, peas, chicken broth, bouillon, and brandy; cover and cook until veggies are soft, 10 to 15 minutes.
3. Stir in sour cream and almonds; heat through. Serve over pasta.

NUTRITIONAL INFO PER SERVING: Calories 496, Fat 14g (Saturated Fat 3g), Cholesterol 58mg, Carbohydrates 50g (Fiber 5g, Sugar 7g), Sodium 99mg (103mg with NSA chicken broth)

VARIATION
RICH & CREAMY CHICKEN STROGANOFF

1. For a richer and creamier version, instead of ¾ cup sour cream, use ¼ cup lowfat cream cheese, ¼ cup lowfat milk, and ¼ cup lowfat sour cream.

NUTRITIONAL INFO PER SERVING: Calories 504, Fat 15g (Sat Fat 4g), Chol 59mg, Carb 50g (Fiber 5g, Sugar 7g), Sodium 138 mg (142mg with NSA chicken broth)

Recipe Notes

1 – Herbes de Provence is a blend of herbs commonly used in French cooking, most often a mix of basil, chervil, fennel, lavender, marjoram, rosemary, sage, savory, and/or thyme. The combination and portions vary depending on the manufacturer.

2 – Substitute a dry sherry or Madeira wine for the brandy.

3 – To toast almonds, spread nuts in a dry skillet. Cook over medium-low heat, stirring or shaking frequently, until they start to turn golden, 5 to 7 minutes. See *Toasting Nuts*, pg 250, for additional toasting methods.

TOTAL SODIUM AND FAT BY INGREDIENT

Sodium:
- 12 oz cooked chicken - 225mg
- 1 sweet onion - 13mg
- 2 garlic cloves - 1mg
- 4 oz mushrooms - 6mg
- 1 c broccoli - 30mg
- 1 c snap peas - 6mg
- 1 c *Chicken Broth* - 20mg
  or NSA chicken broth - 85mg
- 1 t LS chicken bouillon - 5mg
- 6 oz LF sour cream - 90mg
- 4 c cooked pasta - 5mg

Fat (Sat Fat):
- 12 oz cooked chicken - 5g (0g)
- 1 T olive oil - 14g (2g)
- 6 oz LF sour cream - 15g (9g)
- ¼ c NSA almonds - 17g (2g)
- 4 c cooked pasta - 5g (1g)

Brands used/alternatives:
Tyson All Natural Chicken Breast
Kroger Sugar Snap Peas
Pacific Foods Organic Unsalted Chicken Stock
Herb Ox NSA Chicken Bouillon
Daisy Light Sour Cream

Tuscan Chicken Stew

Sodium Per Serving – 138mg   Serves 4

This excellent one-pot meal is ready in less than one hour. Serve as is or over a bed of rice or pasta.

- 3 tablespoons all-purpose flour, divided
- 1 teaspoon garlic powder
- 1 teaspoon dried rosemary, crumbled
- ½ teaspoon ground black pepper
- ½ teaspoon dried thyme
- 4 boneless, skinless chicken breasts and/or thighs (about 1 pound)[1]
- 1 tablespoon olive oil
- 1 small sweet onion, sliced
- 1 red bell pepper, sliced
- 4 garlic cloves, minced
- 4 small red potatoes, quartered
- 2 carrots, sliced
- 4 oz sliced mushrooms (about 1 cup)
- 2 teaspoons LS chicken bouillon
- ½ cup Madeira wine or dry sherry
- 2 tablespoons chopped ripe olives (optional)
- 1 tablespoon cornstarch, mixed with 2 tablespoons water to make a paste

1. Mix 2 tablespoons flour with garlic powder, rosemary, pepper, and thyme; dredge chicken in flour mixture, shaking off excess.
2. Heat oil in a large skillet or pot over medium heat; add chicken. Lightly brown on each side, about 5 minutes per side; remove chicken.
3. In same skillet, add onion and bell pepper; cook, stirring frequently, until onions are translucent, about 5 minutes. Add garlic; cook, stirring constantly, until you smell the garlic, about 1 minute.
4. Return chicken to skillet. Add potatoes, carrots, mushrooms, bouillon, and Madeira; bring to boil. Decrease heat to medium-low, cover, and simmer until potatoes are tender, about 30 minutes.
5. Mix in olives; increase heat to medium. Gradually add cornstarch paste, stirring constantly, until sauce has thickened to a gravy consistency.

NUTRITIONAL INFO PER SERVING: Calories 397, Fat 7g (Sat Fat 1g), Chol 80mg, Carb 50g (Fiber 6g, Sugar 10g), Sodium 138mg

Recipe Notes

1 – Different chicken parts have a varying amount of fat and sodium. For example, a 4 oz breast with skin averages 10g fat, 3g sat fat, and 71mg sodium; without skin it's 3g fat, 1g sat fat, and 51mg sodium. See *Chicken and Turkey*, pg 246, for a comparison of fat and sodium.

TOTAL SODIUM AND FAT BY INGREDIENT

Sodium:
- 1 lb chicken breasts - 300mg or chicken thighs - 300mg
- 1 sm sweet onion - 13mg
- 1 bell pepper - 5mg
- 4 garlic cloves - 2mg
- 4 sm red potatoes - 40mg
- 2 carrots - 84mg
- 4 oz mushrooms - 6mg
- 2 t LS chicken bouillon - 10mg
- ½ c Madeira wine - 12mg
- 2 T ripe olives - 80mg
- 1 T cornstarch - 1mg

Fat (Sat Fat):
- 1 lb chicken breasts - 4g (0g) or chicken thighs - 40g (12g)
- 1 T olive oil - 14g (2g)
- 4 sm red potatoes - 1g (0g)
- 2 T ripe olives - 6g (2g)

Brands used/alternatives:
- Tyson All Natural Chicken Breasts or Thighs
- Herb Ox NSA Chicken Bouillon
- Mario LS Black Olives

Chicken Tagine with Eggplant

Sodium Per Serving – 100mg Serves 10

Tagine (pronounced ta-zheen) is from Morocco and refers both to a slow-cooked stew or the conical-shaped pot used to cook the stew. This throw-it-in-the-pot-and-forget-about it dish uses a variety of intense spices and flavors. It is my adaptation of a recipe from Bon Appetit and is both delicious and colorful. The longer this cooks the better it is; allow 2 to 3 hours cooking time. This recipe makes a lot of sauce; freeze leftovers and use again later.

- ¼ cup all-purpose flour
- 1½ tablespoons paprika
- 1½ teaspoons ground black pepper, divided
- 1 teaspoon garlic powder
- 1½ pounds chicken breast and 1 pound thighs, bone in, skin removed
- 3 tablespoons olive oil, divided
- 1 large sweet onion, sliced
- 6 garlic cloves, minced
- 1½ tablespoons ground coriander
- 1½ tablespoons ground fennel seeds
- 1½ tablespoons turmeric
- 1½ teaspoons ground cumin
- 1½ teaspoons ground ginger
- 2 (15-oz) cans NSA diced tomatoes, drained
- 4 cups *Chicken Broth (pg 208)* or 2 (15-oz) cans unsalted chicken broth
- 2 teaspoons LS chicken bouillon
- 2 tablespoons lemon juice
- 1 large eggplant, unpeeled and cubed[1]
- 1½ teaspoons dried marjoram
- Chopped cilantro (optional)
- Slivered almonds (optional)

1. Place flour, paprika, pepper, and garlic powder in a small paper bag; add chicken, a few pieces at a time, and shake until well coated.
2. Heat 1 tablespoon oil in a large heavy pot over medium-high heat; add chicken. Cook until lightly browned on all sides, 4 to 5 minutes.
3. Add 1 tablespoon oil to same pot; add onions. Cook, stirring frequently, until onions are translucent, 4 to 5 minutes; add garlic. Cook, stirring constantly, until you smell the garlic, 1 to 2 minutes.
4. Mix in coriander, fennel, turmeric, cumin, ginger, tomatoes, chicken broth, bouillon, and lemon juice; bring to boil. Decrease heat to medium-low; cover and simmer, stirring occasionally, until chicken is tender and falls away from the bone, about 2 hours.
5. Meanwhile, preheat oven to 400ºF (200ºC); coat a baking sheet with nonstick cooking spray. In a bowl, mix eggplant and remaining 1 tablespoon oil until coated thoroughly. Place on baking sheet and bake until soft and brown, 20 to 25 minutes.
6. Ten minutes before serving, stir eggplant and marjoram into the stew; simmer uncovered 10 minutes. Serve topped with cilantro and/or almonds.

NUTRITIONAL INFO PER SERVING: Calories 256, Fat 10g (Sat Fat 2g), Chol 86mg, Carb 21g (Fiber 5g, Sugar 6g), Sodium 100mg

Recipe Notes
1 – See *Eggplant*, pg 248, for info on choosing eggplants.

TOTAL SODIUM AND FAT BY INGREDIENT

Sodium:
- ¼ c flour - 1mg
- 1½ T paprika - 7mg
- 2½ lb chicken - 750mg
- 1 sweet onion - 13mg
- 6 garlic cloves - 3mg
- 1½ T coriander - 3mg
- 1½ t cumin - 5mg
- 1½ T fennel - 8mg
- 1½ T turmeric - 4mg
- 30 oz NSA diced tomatoes - 105mg
- 4 c *Chicken Broth* - 80mg or NSA chicken broth - 340mg
- 1 t LS chicken bouillon - 10mg
- 1 eggplant - 7mg

Fat (Sat Fat):
- ¼ c flour - 1g (0g)
- 1½ T paprika - 1g (0g)
- 2½ lb chicken - 46g (12g)
- 3 T olive oil - 42g (6g)
- 1½ T coriander - 1g (0g)
- 1½ t cumin - 1g (0g)
- 1½ T fennel - 1g (0g)
- 1½ T turmeric - 1g (0g)
- 4 c *Chicken Broth* - 1g (0g) or NSA chicken broth - 0g (0g)
- 1 eggplant - 2g (0g)

Brands used/alternatives:
- *Tyson* All Natural Chicken Breas and Thighs
- *Simple Truth Organic* NSA Diced Tomatoes
- *Pacific Foods* Organic Unsalted Chicken Stock
- *Herb Ox* NSA Chicken Bouillon

Chicken Pot Pie

Sodium Per Serving – 70mg

Makes 2 pies, serves 12

This one-crust pie is the ultimate in comfort food. It may look time-consuming, but it takes less than 30 minutes to prepare and 45 minutes to bake.

- 2 tablespoons unsalted butter or margarine
- 1 sweet onion, chopped
- ½ teaspoon dried basil
- ½ teaspoon dried rosemary, crushed
- ½ teaspoon dried tarragon
- ½ teaspoon dried thyme
- ¼ teaspoon garlic powder
- ¼ teaspoon black pepper
- 2 med red potatoes, diced
- 2 carrots, diced
- 1 celery stalk, diced
- 2 garlic cloves, minced
- ½ cup all-purpose flour
- 2 cups *Chicken Broth (pg 208)* or unsalted chicken broth
- ½ cup white wine
- 1 tablespoon LS chicken bouillon
- 1 teaspoon mustard powder
- ½ cup lowfat sour cream
- 1 tablespoon coarse-grain mustard
- 4 (4-oz) cooked boneless, skinless chicken breasts, cubed
- 4 oz cremini mushrooms, thickly sliced
- 10-oz frozen NSA peas
- 10-oz frozen pearl onions
- 2 tablespoons chopped fresh flat-leaf parsley (optional)
- 2 *Basic Pie Crusts (pg 205)* or LS pie crusts

> **TOTAL SODIUM AND FAT BY INGREDIENT**
>
> *Sodium:*
> 1 sweet onion - 13mg
> 2 red potatoes - 42mg
> 2 carrots - 84mg
> 1 celery stalk - 32mg
> 2 garlic cloves - 1mg
> ½ c flour - 3mg
> 2 c *Chicken Broth* - 40mg
>   or NSA chicken broth - 170mg
> 1 T LS chicken bouillon - 15mg
> ½ c white wine - 6mg
> ½ c LF sour cream - 60mg
> 1 T mustard - 75mg
> 1 lb chicken breasts - 160mg
> 4 oz mushrooms - 6mg
> 2 T parsley - 4mg
> 2 *Basic Pie Crusts* - 299mg
>   or LS pie crust - 800mg
>
> *Fat (Sat Fat):*
> 2 T NSA butter - 24g (14g)
>   or NSA margarine - 18g (7g)
> 2 red potatoes - 1g (0g)
> ½ c flour - 1g (0g)
> 2 c *Chicken Broth* - 1g (0g)
>   or NSA chicken broth - 0g (0g)
> 1 t mustard powder - 3g (0g)
> ½ c LF sour cream - 10g (6g)
> 1 lb chicken breasts - 16g (6g)
> 2 *Basic Pie Crusts* - 148g (56g)
>   or LS pie crust - 128g (56g)
>
> **Brands used/alternatives:**
> *Pacific Foods* Organic Unsalted Chicken Stock
> *Herb Ox* NSA Chicken Bouillon
> *Daisy Light* Sour Cream
> *Gold's* LS New York Deli Mustard
> *Tyson* All Natural Chicken Breast
> *Great Value* Pearl Onions
> *Marie Callender's* Pie Shell

1. Preheat oven to 350°F (180°C). Coat two 9-inch round, 2-inch deep pans or casserole dishes with nonstick cooking spray.
2. Melt butter in a large pot over medium heat; add onions, basil, rosemary, tarragon, thyme, garlic powder, and pepper. Cook, stirring frequently, until onions are translucent, about 5 minutes. Add potatoes, carrots, celery, and garlic; cook, stirring frequently, 2 to 3 minutes.
3. Mix flour and ½ cup chicken broth together; add to veggies and cook, stirring constantly, for 2 minutes.
4. Stir in remaining 1½ cups broth, wine, bouillon, and mustard powder; increase heat to medium-high and bring to a boil. Decrease heat to medium and continue cooking, stirring frequently, until sauce is thick enough to coat the back of a spoon.
5. Mix sour cream with mustard and add to broth mixture; stir in chicken, mushrooms, peas, pearl onions, and parsley.
6. Divide chicken mixture equally and pour into prepared pans; top each with a pie crust. Trim any dough overhang and tuck edges inside the pan; cut several slits in the crust for steam to escape.
7. Place pies on a baking sheet (to catch any juices) and bake in a preheated oven for 45 minutes, or until crust is golden brown. *NOTE: You can make the filling the day before, cover and refrigerate until ready to bake.*

NUTRITIONAL INFO PER SERVING: Calories 408, Fat 17g (Saturated Fat 7g), Cholesterol 31mg, Carbohydrates 49g (Fiber 3g, Sugar 7g), Sodium 70mg (112mg with LS pie crust)

Coq Au Vin

Sodium Per Serving – 81mg Serves 4

Coq Au Vin is a classic French dish that is usually made with chicken, vegetables, bacon, and red wine. My quick and easy version is without bacon and uses white wine.

- 4 boneless, skinless chicken breasts
- ¼ teaspoon garlic powder
- ⅛ teaspoon ground black pepper
- 1 tablespoon olive oil
- 1 small sweet onion, sliced
- 2 carrots, sliced
- 8 oz mushrooms, sliced (about 2 cups)
- 2 medium red potatoes, cubed
- 1–2 garlic cloves, minced
- ½ cup white wine
- 1 teaspoon LS chicken bouillon
- 1 teaspoon dried Tuscan spice blend[1]
- 1 tablespoon cornstarch, mixed with 2 tablespoons water to make a paste
- 1 tablespoon chopped fresh Italian parsley

1. Season chicken with garlic powder and pepper. Heat oil in a large skillet over medium-high heat; add chicken. Cook until lightly browned on both sides, 3 to 4 minutes per side; decrease heat to medium-low.
2. Add onions, carrots, mushrooms, potatoes, garlic, wine, bouillon, and Tuscan herbs; cover and simmer 30 minutes or until vegetables are cooked.
3. Increase heat to medium, slowly add cornstarch paste, stirring constantly, until sauce has thickened to the consistency of gravy. Sprinkle with parsley and serve.

NUTRITIONAL INFO PER SERVING: Calories 330, Fat 8g (Sat Fat 2g), Chol 65mg, Carb 28g (Fiber 4g, Sugar 6g), Sodium 81mg

Recipe Notes

1 – Tuscan spice blends are found in most supermarkets. To make your own, mix together equal amounts of dried rosemary, sage, thyme, and basil.

TOTAL SODIUM AND FAT BY INGREDIENT

Sodium:
- 1 lb chicken breasts - 160mg
- 1 sm sweet onion - 13mg
- 2 carrots - 84mg
- 2 c mushrooms - 11mg
- 2 red potatoes - 42mg
- 1 garlic clove - 1mg
- ½ c white wine - 6mg
- 1 t LS chicken bouillon - 5mg
- 1 T cornstarch - 1mg
- 1 T parsley - 2mg

Fat (Sat Fat):
- 1 lb chicken breasts - 16g (6g)
- 1 T olive oil - 14g (2g)
- 2 c mushrooms - 1g (0g)
- 2 red potatoes - 1g (0g)

Brands used/alternatives:
Tyson All Natural Chicken Breast
Herb Ox NSA Chicken Bouillon

Sweet & Sour Turkey Meatloaf

Sodium Per Serving – 112mg   Serves 6

This spicy meatloaf is balanced with a tangy sweet and sour sauce. If you think meatloafs are bland, this will change your mind. Everyone loves this one! Plus, there's plenty left over for meatloaf sandwiches ... yum!

- 1½ pounds ground lean turkey or chicken or a combination of turkey and chicken
- ¾ cup LS plain bread crumbs[1]
- 1 bell pepper, diced
- ½ sweet onion, diced
- 2–3 tablespoons chopped fresh Italian parsley
- ½ teaspoon dried basil
- ½ teaspoon garlic powder
- ½ teaspoon dried rosemary, crumbled
- ½ teaspoon dried thyme
- ¼ teaspoon ground black pepper
- 2 eggs, lightly beaten[2]
- ⅓ cup lowfat milk

Sweet and Sour Sauce:
- ½ cup NSA ketchup
- 1 tablespoon cider vinegar
- 1 teaspoon LS coarse-grain mustard
- 1 teaspoon sugar

1. Preheat oven to 350ºF (180ºC). Coat a 9x5x3-inch baking dish or loaf pan with nonstick cooking spray.
2. In a large bowl, combine turkey, bread crumbs, bell pepper, onions, parsley, basil, garlic powder, rosemary, thyme, and black pepper. Add eggs and milk; mix well and form into a loaf. Place in prepared baking dish and bake, uncovered, in preheated oven for 30 minutes.
3. Meanwhile, mix together ketchup, vinegar, mustard, and sugar; pour over meatloaf. Continue baking for 30 to 45 minutes longer, until no longer pink in the center and internal temperature registers 160ºF (71ºC).

NUTRITIONAL INFO PER SERVING: Calories 248, Fat 4g (Saturated Fat 1g), Cholesterol 126mg, Carbohydrates 25g (Fiber 2g, Sugar 8g), Sodium 112mg

---

VARIATION
Beef, Pork & Veal Meatloaf

1. Instead of turkey or chicken, substitute 12 oz lean ground beef, 6 oz ground pork, and 6 oz ground veal; proceed as directed.

NUTRITIONAL INFO PER SERVING: Calories 344, Fat 18g (Sat Fat 6g), Chol 137mg, Carb 23g (Fiber 2g, Sugar 8g), Sodium 121mg

Recipe Notes
1 – To make fresh bread crumbs, see *Bread Crumbs*, pg 244.
2 – To keep fat to a minimum, use an egg substitute. See *Eggs and Egg Substitutes*, pg 23, for a comparison of fat and sodium in eggs and egg substitutes.

VARIATION
For a delicious change, instead of sweet and sour sauce, pour a LS barbecue sauce on top of the meatloaf.

TOTAL SODIUM AND FAT BY INGREDIENT

Sodium:
- 1½ lb ground turkey - 420mg or ground chicken - 450mg
- ½ c sweet onion - 7mg
- 1 bell pepper - 4mg
- 2 T parsley - 4mg
- 2 eggs - 140mg
- ⅓ c LF milk - 35mg
- ½ c ketchup - 40mg
- 1 t mustard - 25mg

Fat (Sat Fat):
- 1½ lb turkey - 9g (3g)
- ¾ c NSA crumbs - 3g (0g)
- 2 eggs - 10g (3g)
- ⅓ c LF milk - 2g (1g)

Brands used/alternatives:
Jennie-O 99% Lean Ground Turkey
Perdue 98% Lean Ground Chicken Breast
4C Salt Free Bread Crumbs
Simple Truth 2% Milk
Heinz NSA Ketchup
Gold's LS New York Deli Mustard

Herb Roasted Game Hens

Sodium Per Serving – 105mg   Serves 4

This is an elegant meal that takes very little time to prepare. For added flavor, refrigerate the hens overnight in the herbal marinade. The perfect accompaniment is Rice Stuffing with Almonds & Olives (pg 175).

- **2 Cornish game hens (about 1½ pounds each), defrosted and halved lengthwise[1]**

Marinade:
- **¼ cup dry sherry**
- **1 tablespoon olive oil**
- **6 garlic cloves, minced**
- **2 tablespoons chopped fresh basil or 2 teaspoons dried[2]**
- **2 tablespoons chopped fresh rosemary or 2 teaspoons dried[2]**
- **2 tablespoons chopped fresh tarragon or 2 teaspoons dried[2]**

1. *For the marinade:* Mix together the sherry, oil, garlic, basil, rosemary, and tarragon.
2. Place hens in a plastic bag; add marinade and refrigerate at least 4 hours or overnight, turning bag several times.
   - *If using fresh herbs:* Strain marinade, reserve liquid. Place the strained solids (herbs and garlic) and 1–2 tablespoons reserved liquid in a blender, pulse until a smooth paste (add more reserved liquid, if necessary).
   - *If using dried herbs:* Measure 2 tablespoons marinade and set aside; reserve remaining marinade.
3. Preheat oven to 350ºF (180ºC). Position rack in bottom third of the oven.
4. Gently slide fingertips under the skin of the game hen to loosen; rub one-fourth of the herb paste (or marinade) onto each hen. Place skin side up in a roasting pan; drizzle reserved marinade over hens. Bake in preheated oven for 30 minutes, or until golden brown and juices run clear when pierced with a fork. Baste with pan juices every 10 minutes.
5. Serve with rice stuffing.

> **TOTAL SODIUM AND FAT BY INGREDIENT**
> *Sodium:*
> 2 game hens w/o skin - 410mg
> ¼ c sherry - 5mg
> 6 garlic cloves - 3mg
> 2 T tarragon - 2mg
> *Fat (Sat Fat):*
> 2 game hens w/o skin - 19g (5g)
> 1 T olive oil - 14g (2g)
> **Brands used/alternatives:**
> *Tyson* All Natural Game Hens

NUTRITIONAL INFO PER SERVING (WITHOUT THE SKIN): Calories 231, Fat 8g (Saturated Fat 2g), Cholesterol 132mg, Carbohydrates 4g (Fiber 0g, Sugar 0g), Sodium 105mg

---

VARIATION
Roasted Game Hens with Orange-Herb Sauce

1. Add 1 tablespoon finely grated orange peel to the marinade; proceed as directed in Step 1 above. Once cooked, transfer hens to a platter and keep warm.
2. *For the sauce:* Place roasting pan (with juices) on stove over medium-high heat; stir in ½ cup orange juice, ½ cup *Chicken Broth (pg 208)* or NSA chicken broth, and ½ teaspoon LS chicken bouillon, scraping up any browned bits.
3. Bring to a boil; continue cooking until reduced to a gravy consistency, 2 to 3 minutes. Spoon sauce over hens and serve.

NUTRITIONAL INFO PER SERVING: Calories 249, Fat 8g (Saturated Fat 2g), Cholesterol 132mg, Carbohydrates 8g (Fiber 0g, Sugar 3g), Sodium 108mg

---

Recipe Notes
1 – Game hens are usually purchased frozen. Once defrosted, remove the giblets and rinse the hen cavity with water before cutting in half.
2 – Use fresh herbs if possible, the flavor is far superior to dried.

BEEF, VEAL, LAMB & PORK

Pan-Seared Steaks with Tarragon Shallot Sauce

Sodium Per Serving – 73mg Serves 4

This outstanding dish could not be any simpler and is an excellent entrée for entertaining. The tarragon sauce makes this a "restaurant quality" steak.

- **4 (¾-inch thick) top loin or New York strip steaks (about 1 pound)[1]**
- **¼ teaspoon garlic powder**
- **¼ teaspoon ground black pepper**

Tarragon Shallot Sauce:
- **2 shallots, finely chopped**
- **2 tablespoons balsamic vinegar**
- **2 tablespoons white wine vinegar or a dry white wine[2]**
- **⅔ cup *Beef Broth (pg 208)* or unsalted beef broth**
- **½ teaspoon LS beef bouillon**
- **2 tablespoons unsalted butter or margarine**
- **½ teaspoon dried tarragon**
- **1 tablespoon chopped fresh Italian parsley (optional)**

1. Sprinkle steaks with garlic powder and pepper.
2. To cook steaks:
   - *Stove-top:* Place a large skillet on medium-high heat; when hot, cook steaks for 4 to 5 minutes on each side (medium rare), or until desired doneness. Transfer to a platter and keep warm while preparing sauce.
   - *Oven:* Preheat oven to 400ºF (200ºC). Place an oven-proof skillet over medium-high heat; when hot, quickly brown steaks on all sides. Add 2 tablespoons beef broth; place skillet with steaks in the oven for 10 minutes (medium rare), or until desired doneness. Transfer steaks to a platter and keep warm while preparing the sauce.
3. *For the sauce:* Place the skillet where the steaks were cooked on medium-high heat; add shallots and cook, stirring constantly, for 1 minute. Stir in balsamic and white wine vinegars, beef broth, bouillon, butter, and tarragon, scraping up any browned bits. Bring to a boil; cook, stirring frequently, until sauce has thickened to a gravy consistency. Spoon over steaks and top with parsley.

CAUTION: I can't tell you the number of times I've forgotten that the skillet used in the oven is extremely hot. Place a pot holder over the handle to remind you not to touch the bare metal.

NUTRITIONAL INFO PER SERVING: Calories 230, Fat 11g (Saturated Fat 6g), Cholesterol 68mg, Carbohydrates 6g (Fiber 1g, Sugar 3g), Sodium 73mg (80mg with NSA beef broth)

Recipe Notes

1 – Use loin cuts for this dish; they are the most tender and flavorful and are best for pan-searing or broiling (see *Beef, Cuts of Beef,* pg 244, for varieties).

2 – Substitute red wine vinegar, a dry sherry, or Marsala wine for the white wine vinegar.

TOTAL SODIUM AND FAT BY INGREDIENT

Sodium:
- 1 lb top loin - 256mg
- 2 shallot - 10mg
- 2 tbsp balsamic vinegar - 7mg
- ⅔ c *Beef Broth* - 13mg
  - or NSA beef broth - 50mg
- ½ t LS beef bouillon - 3mg
- 1 T parsley - 2mg

Fat (Sat Fat):
- 1 lb top loin - 21g (8g)
- 2 T NSA butter - 23g (14g)
  - or NSA margarine - 18g (7g)

Brands used/alternatives:
Swanson Unsalted Beef Broth
Herb Ox NSA Beef Bouillon

Rib-Eye Steak with Brandied Mushrooms

Sodium Per Serving – 60mg | Serves 4

Another excellent and easy-to-prepare dish that will win raves from family and friends.

- 1 pound rib-eye (or Delmonico), club, or strip steak, cut into 4 pieces[1]
- ¼ teaspoon garlic or onion powder
- ⅛ teaspoon ground black pepper
- 1 tablespoon olive oil
- ¼ cup sliced sweet onion
- 2 oz sliced mushrooms (about ½ cup)
- 2–3 garlic cloves, minced
- 2 tablespoons chopped fresh Italian parsley
- ½ cup *Beef Broth (pg 208)* or unsalted beef broth
- ½ teaspoon LS beef bouillon
- 2 tablespoons brandy
- 1 tablespoon unsalted butter or margarine

1. Season meat with garlic powder and pepper.
2. Heat oil in a heavy skillet over medium-high heat; add meat and brown on both sides, 4 to 5 minutes a side (medium rare), or until desired doneness. Transfer steaks to a platter and keep warm while preparing sauce.
3. *For the sauce:* Decrease heat to medium; add onion, mushrooms, garlic, and parsley. Cook, stirring frequently, until onions and mushrooms are soft, 3 to 4 minutes. Add beef broth, bouillon, and brandy; bring to boil and cook, uncovered, until sauce is reduced to a thick, gravy consistency, about 5 minutes. Stir in butter and serve over steaks. Top with additional chopped parsley.

NUTRITIONAL INFO PER SERVING: Calories 373, Fat 29g (Sat Fat 11g), Chol 98mg, Carb 2g (Fiber 0g, Sugar 1g), Sodium 60mg (64mg with NSA beef broth)

Recipe Notes

1 – Rib cuts are very tender and flavorful and are best for pan searing or broiling. You can also substitute other less expensive cuts, such as round steak and top sirloin.

TOTAL SODIUM AND FAT BY INGREDIENT

Sodium:
- 1 lb rib-eye steaks - 220mg
- ¼ c sweet onion - 2mg
- 2 garlic cloves - 1mg
- 2 oz mushrooms - 3mg
- 2 T parsley - 4mg
- ½ cup *Beef Broth* - 10mg
  or NSA beef broth - 38mg
- ½ t LS beef bouillon - 3mg

Fat (Sat Fat):
- 1 lb rib-eye steaks - 92g (36g)
- 1 T olive oil - 14g (2g)
- 1 T NSA butter - 12g (7g)
  or NSA margarine - 9g (4g)

Brands used/alternatives:
Swanson Unsalted Beef Broth
Herb Ox NSA Beef Bouillon

Top Sirloin with Mustard Sauce

Sodium Per Serving – 107mg   Serves 4

This dish is simple to prepare, just pan fry the steaks, add a sauce, and "wow" everyone with a restaurant-quality meal.

- **1 pound top sirloin, cut into 4 pieces**[1]
- **½ teaspoon garlic or onion powder**
- **¼ teaspoon ground black pepper**
- **1 teaspoon olive oil**

Mustard Sauce:
- **3 tablespoons brandy**
- **1 cup** *Beef Broth (pg 208)* **or unsalted beef broth**
- **½ teaspoon LS beef bouillon**
- **2 tablespoons coarse-grain mustard**[2]
- **1 tablespoon unsalted butter or margarine**

1. Season meat with garlic powder and pepper.
2. Heat oil in a large skillet over medium-high heat; add meat and brown on both sides, 4 to 5 minutes per side (medium rare), or until desired doneness. Transfer steaks to a platter and keep warm while preparing sauce.
3. *For the Mustard Sauce:* Decrease heat to medium; stir in brandy and deglaze by scraping up any brown bits of meat. Add beef broth and bouillon; bring to a boil and cook, uncovered, until the sauce is reduced to about ½ cup and has thickened to a gravy consistency. Stir in mustard.
4. Pour sauce on top of steaks and serve.

NUTRITIONAL INFO PER SERVING: Calories 235, Fat 9g (Saturated Fat 4g), Cholesterol 60mg, Carbohydrates 1g (Fiber 0g, Sugar 0g), Sodium 107mg

---

VARIATION
Steaks with Wild Mushroom-Mustard Sauce

1. After deglazing the pan (Step 3 above), add 1 minced shallot and 1 cup sliced wild mushrooms (such as oyster and shiitake). Cook, stirring frequently, until shallots are translucent, 2 to 3 minutes.
2. When you add the beef broth and bouillon, also add 1 tablespoon chopped fresh tarragon (or 1 teaspoon dried) and ½ cup white wine; proceed are directed. Before serving, stir in ¼ cup lowfat milk, half-and-half, or light cream. (It will be richer-tasting with half-and-half or light cream.)

NUTRITIONAL INFO PER SERVING: Calories 277, Fat 10g (Sat Fat 4g), Chol 62mg, Carb 5g (Fiber 1g, Sugar 2g), Sodium 117mg

TOTAL SODIUM AND FAT BY INGREDIENT

Sodium:
- 1 lb top sirloin - 256mg
- 1 c *Beef Broth* - 20mg
  or NSA beef broth - 75mg
- ½ t bouillon - 3mg
- 2 tbsp mustard - 150mg

Fat (Sat Fat):
- 1 lb top sirloin - 21g (8g)
- 1 t olive oil - 5g (1g)
- 1 T NSA butter - 12g (7g)
  or NSA margarine - 9g (4g)

Brands used/alternatives:
Swanson Unsalted Beef Broth
Herb Ox NSA Beef Bouillon
Gold's LS New York Deli Mustard

Recipe Notes
1 – Substitute any lean and flavorful cut of your choice, like Porterhouse, rib-eye, beef tenderloin, or filet mignon.
2 – Most coarse-grained mustard has 60mg sodium per tsp, look for NSA brands with 30mg or less (visit *LowSaltFoods.com* for a list of LS brands).

POT ROAST

Sodium Per Serving – 161mg Serves 8–10

The secret to a tender and succulent pot roast is the long, slow cooking (about 3 hours).

- 3½ pounds chuck roast
- 1 teaspoon garlic powder
- 1 teaspoon sweet paprika
- 1 teaspoon dried rosemary, crushed
- 1 teaspoon dried thyme
- 1 teaspoon ground black pepper
- 1 tablespoon olive oil
- ¾ cup *Beef Broth (pg 208)* or unsalted beef broth
- 1 teaspoon LS beef bouillon
- 2 yellow onions, cut into wedges
- 4 garlic cloves, minced
- 3 large carrots, cut in 1" pieces
- 3 large red potatoes, cut in 1" pieces
- ½ cup red wine
- 2 tablespoons cornstarch, mixed with 2 tablespoons water to make a paste

1. Preheat oven to 350°F (180°C).
2. Combine garlic powder, paprika, pepper, rosemary, thyme, and pepper; rub onto roast.
3. Heat oil in a large oven-proof pan over medium-high heat; brown roast on all sides. Remove and set aside.
4. Stir in beef broth and deglaze by scraping up any browned bits of meat; mix in bouillon. Return roast to pan; arrange onions and garlic on top; cover and bake in a preheated oven for 2 hours. Remove from oven.
5. Lift out roast and place onions underneath; add carrots, potatoes, and enough liquid (broth and/or water) to nearly cover veggies. Place roast on top of veggies (roast should be out of the liquid). Cook, covered, for 1 hour more; remove roast and let sit 10 minutes before slicing.
6. Remove vegetables to a platter and keep warm while preparing the gravy.
7. *For the gravy:* Place roasting pan (with juices) over medium-high heat; add wine, scraping up any browned bits of meat. Bring to a boil; gradually add cornstarch paste, stirring constantly, until thickened to a gravy consistency.
8. Slice meat and place on a platter with vegetables; serve with gravy poured on top.

TOTAL SODIUM AND FAT BY INGREDIENT

Sodium:
- 3½ lb chuck roast - 1,050mg
- ¾ c Beef Broth - 15mg
   or NSA beef broth - 56mg
- 1 t LS beef bouillon - 5mg
- 2 onions - 9mg
- 4 garlic cloves - 2mg
- 3 carrots - 149mg
- 3 red potatoes - 50mg
- ½ c red wine - 6mg
- 1 T cornstarch - 1mg

Fat (Sat Fat):
- 3½ lb chuck roast - 350g (140g)
- 1 T olive oil - 14g (2g)
- ¾ c Beef Broth - 1g (0g)
   or NSA beef broth - 0g (0g)

Brands used/alternatives:
Swanson Unsalted Beef Broth
Herb Ox NSA Beef Bouillon

NUTRITIONAL INFO PER SERVING: Calories 603, Fat 46g (Saturated Fat 18g), Cholesterol 140mg, Carbohydrates 9g (Fiber 2g, Sugar 3g), Sodium 161mg (162mg with NSA beef broth)

Beef Stroganoff

Sodium Per Serving – 135mg   Serves 4

Beef, mushrooms, and brandy simmered in a thick sour cream sauce that is laced with dill. Serve this family favorite over pasta.

- **1 tablespoon all-purpose flour**
- **½ teaspoon garlic or onion powder**
- **½ teaspoon ground black pepper**
- **⅛ teaspoon paprika**[1]
- **1 pound top sirloin, cut into strips**[2]
- **1 tablespoon olive oil**
- **1 large sweet onion, sliced**
- **2 garlic cloves, minced**
- **16 oz cremini mushrooms, sliced (about 4 cups)**[3]
- **¼ cup brandy**[4]
- **2 cups *Beef Broth (pg 208)* or unsalted beef broth**
- **2 teaspoons LS beef bouillon**
- **1 teaspoon Worcestershire sauce**
- **1½ tablespoons prepared horseradish**
- **1-2 sprigs fresh dill, snipped (optional)**[5]
- **½ cup lowfat sour cream**
- **8 oz pasta, such as penne**

1. Mix together the flour, garlic powder, pepper, and paprika; place in a paper bag. Add meat and shake until well coated.
2. Heat oil in a large skillet over medium-high heat; add meat. Cook, stirring frequently, until browned on all sides, 2 to 3 minutes; remove meat and set aside.
3. Add onions and cook, stirring frequently, until onions are translucent, 2 to 3 minutes; add garlic and mushrooms and cook, stirring frequently, until the mushrooms soften, 3 to 4 minutes.
4. Stir in 2 tablespoons brandy and deglaze skillet by scraping up any browned bits. Add broth, bouillon, Worcestershire, and remaining 2 tablespoons brandy; decrease heat to medium-low and simmer, uncovered, until liquid is reduced by half, about 10 minutes. Stir in meat, horseradish, dill, and sour cream; cook until meat is heated through, about 3 minutes. Serve over cooked linguine or pasta; sprinkle with paprika.

NUTRITIONAL INFO PER SERVING: Calories 548, Fat 13g (Sat Fat 4g), Chol 63mg, Carb 59g (Fiber 4g, Sugar 10g), Sodium 135mg (150mg with NSA beef broth)

Recipe Notes

1 – I like a little zip in this dish, so I add Hungarian hot paprika, but sweet paprika works well, too. If you use sweet paprika, and want a little heat, add a pinch of cayenne pepper or dash of hot pepper sauce before serving.

2 – Because the meat is not cooked for very long, the more tender the beef, the better it will be. Other comparable cuts to use, include beef tenderloin (or filet mignon) and Porterhouse steaks.

3 – Criminis are similar to button mushrooms, but have more flavor. Use criminis, buttons, or a combination of both. For other mushroom varieties, see *Mushrooms*, pg 250.

4 – Substitute Marsala or red wine for the brandy.

5 – Use kitchen shears to snip the dill into small pieces.

TOTAL SODIUM AND FAT BY INGREDIENT

Sodium:
- 1 lb top sirloin - 256mg
- 1 sweet onion - 27mg
- 2 garlic cloves - 1mg
- 1 lb mushrooms - 22mg
- 2 c *Beef Broth* - 40mg
  or NSA beef broth - 150mg
- 2 t LS beef bouillon - 10mg
- 1 t Worcestershire - 20mg
- 1½ T horseradish - 90mg
- ½ c LF sour cream - 60mg
- 8 oz pasta - 14mg

Fat (Sat Fat):
- 1 lb top sirloin - 21g (8g)
- 1 T olive oil - 14g (2g)
- 1 lb mushrooms - 2g (0g)
- 1½ T horseradish - 2g (0g)
- ½ c LF sour cream - 10g (6g)
- 8 oz pasta - 3g (1g)

Brands used/alternatives:
Swanson Unsalted Beef Broth
Herb Ox NSA Beef Bouillon
Robbie's Worcestershire Sauce
Beaver Cream Horseradish
Daisy Light Sour Cream
Kroger Penne Rigate Pasta

Veal Marsala

Sodium Per Serving – 100mg   Serves 4

This classic Italian dish is sure to impress any guest, especially if you use a nice cut of veal. (Although veal is a bit pricey, it's well worth the extra cost.) Veal Marsala is often made with demi-glace, a rich brown concentrate that is the basis for many delicious sauces. Even though making demi-glace is very time consuming, bottled demi-glace is available in many supermarkets. Unfortunately, it is very high in sodium. This version does not use demi-glace, but achieves a similar taste and richness (and without the salt) by cooking down the liquids to a syrup consistency. NOTE: Do not overcook, meat becomes tough if cooked to long.

- **1 pound sliced veal cutlets**
- **2 tablespoons all-purpose flour**
- **¼ teaspoon garlic powder**
- **¼ teaspoon dried oregano**
- **¼ teaspoon dried thyme**
- **⅛ teaspoon ground black pepper**
- **1 tablespoon olive oil**

Sauce:
- **2 tablespoons unsalted butter or margarine, divided**
- **6 oz sliced mushrooms, such as cremini or button (about 3 cups)[1]**
- **1 garlic clove, minced**
- **½ cup Marsala wine**
- **½ cup *Beef Broth (pg 208)* or unsalted beef broth**
- **1 teaspoon LS beef bouillon**
- **Parsley (optional)**

1. Mix flour with garlic powder, oregano, thyme, and pepper; dredge veal in flour mixture, shaking off any excess.
2. Heat oil in skillet over medium-high heat; add veal and brown on both sides, 2 to 3 minutes a side. Transfer veal to a platter and keep warm while making the sauce.
3. *For the sauce:* Decrease heat to medium; melt 1 tablespoon butter in the same skillet. Add mushrooms and cook, stirring frequently, until soft, 3 to 4 minutes; add garlic and cook, stirring constantly, until you smell the garlic, about 1 minute. Stir in Marsala and deglaze the pan by scraping up any brown bits; add beef broth and bring to a boil. Continue cooking until sauce thickens to a syrup consistency; stir in remaining 1 tablespoon butter.
4. Return veal to skillet and heat through. Transfer veal to a platter, pour sauce over meat and serve with parsley sprinkled on top.

NUTRITIONAL INFO PER SERVING: Calories 280, Fat 13g (Sat Fat 5g), Chol 105mg, Carb 10g (Fiber 1g, Sugar 4g), Sodium 100mg (103mg with NSA beef broth)

Recipe Notes
1 – Criminis are similar to button mushrooms, but have more flavor. Use any mushroom or combination of mushrooms (see *Mushrooms*, pg 250, for varieties).

TOTAL SODIUM AND FAT BY INGREDIENT

Sodium:
- 1 lb veal - 360mg
- 1 garlic clove - 1mg
- 8 oz mushrooms - 11mg
- ½ cup Marsala wine - 12mg
- ½ cup *Beef Broth* - 10mg
  - or NSA beef broth - 38mg
- 1 t LS beef bouillon - 5mg

Fat (Sat Fat):
- 1 lb veal - 12g (4g)
- 1 T olive oil - 14g (2g)
- 2 T NSA butter - 24g (14g)
  - or NSA margarine -18g (8g)
- 8 oz mushrooms - 1g (0g)

Brands used/alternatives:
Swanson Unsalted Beef Broth
Herb Ox NSA Beef Bouillon

Roast Leg of Lamb with Mustard-Rosemary Crust

Sodium Per Serving – 142mg   Serves 8

This lamb is so delicious and easy to prepare. To help keep the juices inside, it is covered with a garlic, rosemary, and mustard crust. Use a food processor, or pestle and mortar, to make the paste that is rubbed on the lamb. (Do not use a blender, as the paste is too thick for a blender to process.)

- 1 (3-pound) boneless leg of lamb, excess fat trimmed, and lamb tied
- 4 garlic cloves, finely minced
- 2 tablespoons chopped fresh rosemary or 2 teaspoons dried
- 1 tablespoon mustard
- ¼ teaspoon garlic powder
- ¼ teaspoon ground black pepper
- ½ cup red wine
- ½ cup *Beef Broth (pg 208)* or unsalted beef broth
- 1 teaspoon LS beef bouillon
- 1–2 teaspoons cornstarch, mixed with 1–2 tablespoons water to make a paste
- 1–2 tablespoons unsalted butter or margarine

1. Preheat oven to 350°F (180°C). Adjust shelf to middle of the oven.
2. Place lamb in a shallow roasting pan. Using a food processor or pestle and mortar, make a paste with the garlic, rosemary, mustard, garlic powder, and pepper; rub over the lamb.
3. Roast lamb, uncovered, in a preheated oven until thermometer reaches 140°F (60°C), about 1½ hours. Transfer lamb to a cutting board and let stand for 15 to 20 minutes. *NOTE:* Roast will continue cooking as it sits; internal temperature will rise to about 150°F (65°C) for medium doneness. For medium-rare, remove roast when the thermometer reaches 130°F (55°C). Keep warm while preparing gravy.
4. *For the gravy:* Pour off all but 1 tablespoon fat from roasting pan and place pan over medium-high heat. Add wine; stirring constantly, deglaze pan by scraping up any brown bits of lamb. Add beef broth and bouillon; cook, stirring frequently, until sauce has thickened to a gravy consistency, 2 to 3 minutes (if necessary, slowly add cornstarch paste, stirring constantly, until thickened to desired consistency). Just before serving, remove from heat and stir in butter.
5. Slice lamb and serve with gravy.

NUTRITIONAL INFO PER SERVING: Calories 236, Fat 5g (Sat Fat 1g), Chol 104mg, Carb 1g (Fiber 0g, Sugar 0g), Sodium 142mg (144 with NSA beef broth)

TOTAL SODIUM AND FAT BY INGREDIENT

Sodium:
- 3 lb leg of lamb - 960mg
- 4 garlic cloves - 2mg
- 2 T mustard - 150mg
- ½ c red wine - 6mg
- ½ c Beef Broth - 10mg
  or NSA beef broth - 38mg
- 1 t LS beef bouillon - 5mg

Fat (Sat Fat):
- 3 lb leg of lamb - 32g (16g)
- 1 T NSA butter - 12g (7g)
  or NSA margarine - 9g (4g)

Brands used/alternatives:
Gold's LS New York Deli Mustard
Swanson Unsalted Beef Broth
Herb Ox NSA Beef Bouillon

Pork Chops with Raspberry Sauce

Sodium Per Serving – 56mg Serves 4

This is so simple to prepare and absolutely divine! The sweet-tart taste of the raspberry sauce is the perfect compliment to the pork chops.

- 4 (4-oz) boneless pork loin chops
- ½ teaspoon dried sage
- ½ teaspoon dried thyme
- ¼ teaspoon garlic or onion powder
- ⅛ teaspoon ground black pepper
- 1 tablespoon olive oil

Raspberry Sauce:
- ⅓ cup fruit sweetened raspberry jam[1]
- 2 tablespoons orange juice
- 1 tablespoon raspberry or balsamic vinegar
- 2 tablespoons dry sherry
- 2–3 drops hot pepper sauce, such as *Tabasco* (optional)
- 1 tablespoon unsalted butter or margarine

1. Combine sage, thyme, garlic powder, and pepper; rub over pork chops.
2. Heat oil in a large skillet over medium-high heat; add chops. Lightly brown on both sides, 4 to 5 minutes a side. Transfer chops to a platter and keep warm while preparing sauce.
3. *For the Raspberry Sauce:* In same skillet, stir in jam, orange juice, vinegar, sherry, and hot pepper sauce; bring to a boil. Cook, stirring constantly, until sauce has thickened to a gravy consistency, 2 to 3 minutes; stir in butter. Serve over pork chops.

NUTRITIONAL INFO PER SERVING: Calories 302, Fat 18g (Sat Fat 5g), Chol 83mg, Carb 17g (Fiber 0g, Sugar 11g), Sodium 56mg

Recipe Notes
1 – I prefer a fruit-sweetened jam rather than a sugar-sweetened one. If you want a smooth sauce, use seedless jam.

TOTAL SODIUM AND FAT BY INGREDIENT

Sodium:
- 1 lb pork chops - 220mg
- 2 T sherry - 3mg
- 2 drops hot pepper sauce - 1mg

Fat (Sat Fat):
- 1 lb pork chops - 48g (10g)
- 1 T olive oil - 14g (2g)
- 1 T NSA butter - 12g (7g)
  or NSA margarine - 9g (4g)

Brands used/alternatives:
Smucker's Simply Fruit Raspberry

Fruit Stuffed Pork Tenderloin

Sodium Per Serving – 71mg   Serves 6

This is a family favorite at Easter and other special occasions. The colorful stuffing makes a beautiful presentation and the apple-brandy flavored gravy is a delicious accompaniment.

- 1½ pound boneless pork loin tenderloin[1]
- 1 tablespoon fresh rosemary, crumbled, or 1 teaspoon dried
- ¼ teaspoon garlic powder
- ⅛ teaspoon ground black pepper
- 2 teaspoons roasted garlic, minced[2]
- 5–6 dried apricots, chopped
- ¼ cup dried cranberries[3]
- 2 tablespoons chopped fresh Italian parsley
- 1–2 tablespoons prepared horseradish[4]

Gravy:
- ¼ cup brandy[5]
- 1 cup *Chicken Broth (pg 208)* or unsalted chicken broth
- ⅓ cup apple juice or cider
- 1 teaspoon LS chicken bouillon
- 1–2 teaspoons cornstarch, mixed with 1–2 tablespoons water to make a paste

1. Preheat oven to 350°F (180°C).
2. Slit pork lengthwise, but not quite all the way through, to form a deep pocket. Sprinkle the inside with rosemary, garlic powder, pepper, and garlic. Stuff with apricots, cranberries, and parsley. Roll up and tie with heavy string, securing at 1-inch intervals. Rub horseradish over the outside of the roast.
3. Heat oil in a large skillet over medium-high heat; brown roast on all sides. Remove roast and insert a thermometer; place in a shallow roasting pan. Bake in a preheated oven until the internal temperature registers 160°F (71°C), about 1½ hours. Transfer roast to a cutting board and let stand 10 minutes while preparing gravy.
4. *For the gravy:* Place roasting pan (with juices) over medium-high heat; stir in brandy and deglaze pan by scraping up any browned bits of pork. Add chicken broth, apple juice, and bouillon; bring to a boil. Cook, stirring frequently, until sauce begins to thicken. If needed, gradually add cornstarch paste, stirring constantly, until it thickens to a gravy consistency.
5. Slice the pork and serve with gravy on the side.

NUTRITIONAL INFO PER SERVING: Calories 232, Fat 6g (Sat Fat 2g), Chol 76mg, Carb 16g (Fiber 1g, Sugar 9g), Sodium 71mg

Recipe Notes
1 – Many pork loins are packaged in brine; look for tenderloins packaged without brine.
2 – I like to make extra roasted garlic (see *Garlic, Roasting, pg 249*) and keep it on hand to use in different dishes. You can also use fresh or bottled garlic, although I think the flavor of roasted garlic tastes better.
3 – Substitute raisins or currants for the cranberries.
4 – Rubbing horseradish onto the roast helps lock in the juices and keeps moisture from escaping during the cooking process.
5 – Use Madeira, Marsala, or a dry red wine instead of brandy.

TOTAL SODIUM AND FAT BY INGREDIENT

Sodium:
- 1½ lb pork tenderloin - 330mg
- 2 t garlic cloves - 1mg
- 5 dried apricots - 2mg
- ¼ c dried cranberries - 2mg
- 2 T parsley - 4mg
- 1 T horseradish - 60mg
- 1 t LS chicken bouillon - 5mg
- ⅓ c apple juice - 3mg
- 1 c *Chicken Broth* - 20mg
  or NSA chicken broth - 85mg

Fat (Sat Fat):
- 1½ lb pork loin - 36g (12g)
- 1 T horseradish - 2g (0g)

Brands used/alternatives:
- *Beaver* Cream Horseradish
- *Pacific Foods* Organic Unsalted Chicken Stock
- *Herb Ox* NSA Chicken Bouillon

FISH & SEAFOOD

Red Snapper Beurre Meunière

Sodium Per Serving – 112mg   Serves 4

Beurre Meunière simply means the fish is coated in flour, then sautéed, and served in a lemony butter sauce with a hint of tarragon. This elegant dish takes less than 10 minutes from start to finish and will win rave reviews from any fish lover.

- 4 red snapper filets (about 1 pound)[1]
- 2 tablespoons all-purpose flour
- ¼ teaspoon garlic or onion powder
- ⅛ teaspoon ground black pepper
- 1 tablespoon olive oil
- 3 tablespoons unsalted butter or margarine, divided
- 1 shallot, finely minced
- ¼ cup sake or vermouth[2]
- 1 garlic clove, finely minced
- 1 tablespoon fresh lemon juice
- 1 tablespoon chopped fresh tarragon or 1½ teaspoons dried
- 2–3 drops hot pepper sauce, such as *Tabasco*

Garnishes:
- **Lemon slices**
- **Fresh parsley**

1. Combine flour, garlic powder, and pepper; dredge snapper in flour, shaking off any excess.
2. Heat oil in a large skillet over medium heat; add snapper. Cook fish until golden brown, 2 to 3 minutes; turn and cook until fish flakes easily with a fork, 2 to 3 minutes. Transfer to a platter and keep warm while preparing sauce.
3. *For the sauce:* In another skillet, melt 1 tablespoon butter over medium heat; add shallots and garlic. Cook, stirring constantly, until shallots are soft, about 2 minutes; add sake, lemon juice, and tarragon. Cook, stirring constantly, until reduced slightly.
4. Remove skillet from heat and stir in remaining 2 tablespoons butter; mix in hot pepper sauce. Spoon sauce over fish and garnish with lemon slices and fresh parsley, if desired.

NUTRITIONAL INFO PER SERVING: Calories 260, Fat 15g (Sat Fat 6g), Chol 88mg, Carb 7g (Fiber 1g, Sugar 1g), Sodium 112mg

Recipe Notes
1 – Substitute sea bass, cod, tilapia, rockfish, or monkfish for the red snapper.
2 – Instead of sake or vermouth, use a dry white wine, like Chardonnay.

TOTAL SODIUM AND FAT BY INGREDIENT

Sodium:
- 1 lb red snapper - 440mg
- 1 shallot - 5mg
- 1 garlic clove - 1mg
- ¼ c sake - 1mg
- 1 T tarragon - 1mg
- 2 drops hot pepper sauce - 1mg

Fat (Sat Fat):
- 1 lb red snapper - 8g (0g)
- 2 T olive oil - 14g (2g)
- 3 T NSA butter - 38g (21g)
  or NSA margarine - 27g (11g)

Brands used/alternatives:
Great Value Wild Red Snapper

Orange Roughy in Creamy Leek Sauce

Sodium Per Serving – 139mg   Serves 4

Orange Roughy is a mild-tasting fish that comes from New Zealand and is low in both fat and sodium (18mg per oz). I'm not sure where this recipe came from, but I use sake, which has a subtle flavor, and the addition of leeks, compliments the fish very well. Use the sauce on other mild-tasting fish, like sole, cod, and flounder.

- 2 tablespoons unsalted butter or margarine
- 2 leeks, sliced (white and lite green parts)[1]
- 1/2 teaspoon dried thyme
- 4 Orange Roughy fillets (about 1 1/2 pound)[2]
- 1/4 teaspoon onion powder
- 1/8 teaspoon ground black pepper
- 1/2 cup half-and-half or whipping cream
- 1/4 cup sake[3]
- 2 tablespoons chopped fresh chives or green onions (green part only)

1. Melt butter in a large skillet over medium heat; add leeks and thyme. Cook, stirring frequently, until leeks start to soften, about 5 minutes. Decrease heat to low; cover and cook, stirring occasionally, until leeks are soft, 10 minutes.
2. Season fish with onion powder and pepper; arrange fish on top of leeks. Add half-and-half and sake; cover and cook until fish is opaque, about 8 minutes. Remove fish and transfer to a platter; keep warm while preparing sauce.
3. Raise heat to medium-high and bring leeks and sauce to a boil; continue cooking, stirring frequently, until slightly thickened, about 3 minutes. Pour over fish and garnish with chives.

NUTRITIONAL INFO PER SERVING: Calories 268, Fat 11g (Sat Fat 6g), Chol 125mg, Carb 9g (Fiber 1g, Sugar 3g), Sodium 139mg

Broiled Salmon with Pesto

Sodium Per Serving – 111mg   Serves 4

Another simple and delicious way to prepare salmon.

- 1–1 1/2 pounds salmon filet
- 1/4 teaspoon garlic powder
- 1/8 teaspoon black pepper
- 2 tablespoons unsalted butter or margarine, melted
- Juice of 1/2 lemon (about 1 tablespoon)
- 1/4–1/2 cup *Quick Pesto (pg 136)* or ready-to-use basil pesto[4]

1. Season salmon with garlic powder and pepper. Place skin-side down in a baking pan. Mix together butter and lemon juice; pour over the salmon.
2. Broil about 5 inches from the heat source until fish flakes easily with a fork, 8 to 10 minutes. Transfer salmon to a platter; spread 1–2 tablespoons pesto on top of fish and serve.

NUTRITIONAL INFO PER SERVING: Calories 319, Fat 23g (Sat Fat 6g), Chol 78mg, Carb 8g (Fiber 1g, Sugar 0g), Sodium 111mg

Recipe Notes

1 – See *Leeks*, pg 249 for additional info on cleaning and storing.
2 – Cod, flounder, sole, or haddock also works well in this recipe.
3 – Instead of sake, substitute vermouth or white wine.
4 – Most ready-to-use pesto has over 600mg sodium in 1/4 cup. There are several low-salt varieties (visit LowSaltFoods.com for a current list of products).

TOTAL SODIUM AND FAT BY INGREDIENT

ORANGE ROUGHY IN SAUCE
Sodium:
- 2 leeks - 36mg
- 1 lb orange roughy - 480mg
- 1/2 c half-and-half - 40mg
  or whipping cream - 40mg
- 1/4 c sake - 1mg

Fat (Sat Fat):
- 2 leeks - 1g (0g)
- 2 T NSA butter - 24g (14g)
  or NSA margarine - 18g (8g)
- 1 lb orange roughy - 4g (0g)
- 1/2 c half-and-half - 14g (8g)
  or whipping cream - 40g (28g)

Brands used/alternatives:
Kroger Wild Orange Roughy
Organic Valley Half & Half

BROILED SALMON WITH PESTO
Sodium:
- 1 lb salmon - 360mg
- 1/2 c *Quick Pesto* - 85mg
  or ready-to-eat - 760mg

Fat (Sat Fat):
- 1 lb salmon - 20g (2g)
- 2 T NSA butter - 24g (14g)
  or NSA margarine - 18g (7g)
- 1/2 c *Quick Pesto* - 49g (9g)
  or ready-to-eat - 88g (8g)

Brands used/alternatives:
Wild Alaskan Sockeye Salmon

Horseradish Grilled Salmon

Sodium Per Serving – 113mg   Serves 6

Salmon is a part of every Northwesterner's diet and during the summer months it is not uncommon to have salmon several nights a week. This is a great way of grilling salmon on the barbecue, as it comes out moist and succulent every time.

- **1½–2 pounds salmon filet, cut into 3 or 4 large pieces**[1]
- **¼ teaspoon garlic powder**
- **⅛ teaspoon ground white pepper**
- **¼ cup lowfat sour cream**
- **1 heaping tablespoon prepared horseradish**
- **1 tablespoon lite mayonnaise or mayonnaise-type dressing**
- **Lemon wedges**

1. Preheat barbecue or gas grill to 400°F (204°C).
2. Check the salmon for any small pin bones that run the length of the filet. Remove with a tweezer or needle-nose plier.
3. Sprinkle with garlic powder and pepper. Mix together sour cream, horseradish, and mayonnaise; coat all sides of the salmon.
4. Place fish, skin-side down, on a preheated grill coated with cooking spray. Grill 5 to 6 minutes; turn fish over and continue cooking until fish flakes easily with a fork, about 3 minutes. Transfer fish to a platter and serve with lemon wedges.

NOTE: If barbecuing over coals, you can also push the coals to the outside of the grill and "bake" the salmon for 9 to 14 minutes (depending on the fire's heat). If you do this, it's not necessary to turn the salmon.

NUTRITIONAL INFO PER SERVING: Calories 184, Fat 8g (Sat Fat 1g), Chol 66mg, Carb 7g (Fiber 0g, Sugar 0g), Sodium 113mg

---

TOTAL SODIUM AND FAT BY INGREDIENT

Sodium:
1½ lb salmon - 540mg
¼ c LF sour cream - 30mg
1 T horseradish - 60mg
1 T lite mayonnaise - 50mg

Fat (Sat Fat):
1½ lb salmon - 30g (3g)
¼24 c LF sour cream - 5g (3g)
1 T horseradish - 2g (0g)
1 T lite mayonnaise - 11g (2g)

Brands used/alternatives:
Wild Alaskan Sockeye Salmon
Daisy Light Sour Cream
Beaver Cream Horseradish
Chosen Foods Classic Mayo w/ Avocado Oil

VARIATION
The Best Grilled Salmon

1. Preheat barbecue or gas grill to 400°F (204°C).
2. Prepare baste in the following proportions: ¼ cup white wine, ¼ cups Worcestershire sauce, and ¼ cup butter, melted.
3. Brush meat side of salmon with olive oil and season with garlic powder. Cook meat side down for 2-4 minutes to lightly brown, baste continuously. Spray skin side with nonstick cooking spray, turn and cook skin side down, 4-5 minutes, or until desired doneness, continue basting.

NUTRITIONAL INFO PER SERVING: Calories 277, Fat 10g (Sat Fat 4g), Chol 62mg, Carb 5g (Fiber 1g, Sugar 2g), Sodium 117mg

Recipe Notes
1 – The variety of salmon determines the amount of sodium per serving. See *Fish and Seafood*, pg 248, for a comparison.

Salmon Cakes

Sodium Per Serving – 84mg | Makes 8 cakes

Although crab cakes are a favorite for many people, they usually have too much sodium for a low-salt diet (a 3 oz cake averages 366mg). If you're a fan of crab cakes, you'll love this version made with salmon. Serve it plain or with a light butter sauce.

- 1 pound salmon filet, cubed[1]
- 2 green onions, chopped (white and lite green parts)
- 2 shallots, chopped[2]
- 3 tablespoons lemon juice
- 2 tablespoons mayonnaise or mayonnaise-like dressing
- 1 tablespoon prepared horseradish
- 1 teaspoon grated lemon peel
- ¼ teaspoon garlic or onion powder
- ⅛ teaspoon ground black pepper
- ½ teaspoon sugar
- 2½ cups LS bread or panko crumbs[3]
- 2 eggs, lightly beaten[4]
- *Orange or Lemon Butter Sauce (pg 115)*

1. Combine salmon, green onions, shallots, lemon juice, mayonnaise, horseradish, lemon peel, garlic powder, pepper, and sugar in a food processor; pulse until coarsely chopped. Transfer to a bowl; mix in bread crumbs and eggs. Form into 8 patties.
2. *To oven bake:* Place cakes on a baking sheet and bake in a preheated oven at 475ºF (240ºC) for 15 to 18 minutes, or until golden brown.
3. *To pan fry:* Heat 1 tablespoon oil in a large skillet over medium-high heat; cook cakes until lightly browned on each side, about 4 minutes per side. Remove and drain on paper towels. NOTE: Salmon cakes are also good when grilled until lightly browned on each side.
4. Serve with *Orange or Lemon Butter Sauce*.

NUTRITIONAL INFO PER CAKE: Calories 267, Fat 9g (Sat Fat 1g), Chol 88mg, Carb 34g (Fiber 5g, Sugar 3g), Sodium 84mg

Recipe Notes

1 – Use cooked or canned NSA salmon (visit *LowSaltFoods.com* for LS brands).
   CAUTION: If using fresh salmon, there might be some small pin bones that run the length of the filet. Before cooking, remove with tweezers or needle-nose pliers.

2 – See *Shallots*, pg 253, for shallot information.

3 – Panko or "Japanese bread crumbs" are lighter than regular crumbs, and don't pack together, resulting in a crispier crust. Plus, they don't have fat and are very low in sodium (45mg vs 270mg an oz). See *Bread Crumbs*, pg 244, for more info.

4 – To keep fat to a minimum, use an egg substitute. See *Eggs and Egg Substitutes*, pg 23, for a comparison of fat and sodium in eggs and egg substitutes.

TOTAL SODIUM AND FAT BY INGREDIENT

Sodium:
- 1 lb salmon - 360mg
- 2 green onions - 5mg
- 2 shallots - 20mg
- 2 T lite mayonnaise - 100mg
- 1 T horseradish - 50mg
- 2½ c LS bread crumbs - 0mg or panko crumbs - 88mg
- 2 eggs - 140mg

Fat (Sat Fat):
- 1 lb salmon - 20g (2g)
- 2 T lite mayonnaise - 22g (3g)
- 1 T horseradish - 11g (2g)
- 2½ c LS crumbs - 10g (0g) or panko crumbs - 0g (0g)
- 2 eggs - 10g (3g)

Brands used/alternatives:
Wild Alaskan Sockeye Salmon
Chosen Foods Classic Mayo w/ Avocado Oil
Beaver Cream Horseradish
4C Salt Free Bread Crumbs or
Kikkoman Japanese Panko Bread Crumbs

ORANGE BUTTER SAUCE

Sodium Per Serving – 1mg Makes about ¾ cup

This butter sauce is also good on most mild-tasting or grilled fish.

- ⅓ cup unsalted butter or margarine, divided
- ¼ cup orange juice concentrate
- 1 shallot, finely minced
- 1 teaspoon white wine vinegar or white balsamic vinegar

1. Melt 1 tablespoon butter in a sauce pan over medium heat; stir in orange juice, shallots, and vinegar. Add remaining butter, 1 tablespoon at a time, stirring until melted before adding next piece. Serve over fish or salmon cakes.

NUTRITIONAL INFO PER SERVING: Calories 150, Fat 16g (Saturated Fat 9g), Cholesterol 40mg, Carbohydrates 3g (Fiber 0g, Sugar 2g), Sodium 1mg

---

VARIATION
LEMON BUTTER SAUCE

1. Instead of orange juice and vinegar, substitute 1½ tablespoons lemon juice and 2 tablespoons white wine; proceed as directed.

NUTRITIONAL INFO PER SERVING: Calories 149, Fat 16g (Saturated Fat 9g), Cholesterol 40mg, Carbohydrates 2g (Fiber 0g, Sugar 1g), Sodium 2mg

---

SHRIMP IN GARLIC BUTTER

Sodium Per Serving – 117mg Serves 4

This is for all you garlic lovers!

- 1 pound large shrimp, peeled and deveined
- 1 tablespoon olive oil
- 2 tablespoons unsalted butter or margarine
- 2–3 garlic cloves, crushed
- ¼ teaspoon garlic powder
- ⅛ teaspoon ground white pepper
- 3 tablespoons dry vermouth or white wine
- 3 tablespoons lemon juice (about 1 large lemon)
- 1 tablespoon chopped fresh Italian parsley (optional)

1. Heat oil in a large skillet over medium-high heat; add shrimp. Cook, stirring frequently, until shrimp begins to turn pink; decrease heat to medium-low.
2. Stir in butter, garlic, garlic powder, and pepper; add vermouth and lemon juice. Cook, stirring constantly, for 1 minute; serve immediately with parsley sprinkled on top.

NUTRITIONAL INFO PER SERVING: Calories 184, Fat 11g (Sat Fat 4g), Chol 160mg, Carb 4g (Fiber 0g, Sugar 1g), Sodium 117mg

---

TOTAL SODIUM AND FAT BY INGREDIENT

ORANGE BUTTER SAUCE
Sodium:
¼ c OJ concentrate - 1mg
1 shallot - 5mg
Fat (Sat Fat):
⅓ c NSA butter - 64g (37g)
 or NSA margarine - 48g (21g)

SHRIMP IN GARLIC BUTTER
Sodium:
1 lb shrimp - 460mg
1 garlic clove - 1mg
3 T vermouth - 4mg
1 T parsley - 2mg
Fat (Sat Fat):
1 lb shrimp - 4g (0g)
1 T olive oil - 14g (2g)
2 T NSA butter - 24g (14g)
 or NSA margarine - 18g (7g)
Brands used/alternatives:
Simple Truth Raw Shrimp

Shrimp Curry

Sodium Per Serving – 198mg   Serves 4

This recipe was developed while living in Hawaii. The original called for Lipton's Onion Soup Mix, which has way too much sodium for a low-salt lifestyle. I've come up with an alternative that tastes very much like the original. Serve with a variety of condiments, so that each person can add whatever they like.

- 1/3 cup unsalted butter or margarine
- 1/4 cup dried minced onion
- 2–3 tablespoons curry powder[1]
- 1 tablespoon LS beef bouillon
- 1 teaspoon onion or garlic powder
- 1 teaspoon dried parsley flakes
- 1/2 teaspoon sugar
- 1/2 teaspoon celery seed
- 1/4 teaspoon ground ginger
- 1/8 teaspoon ground black pepper
- 1 pound small or salad shrimp, cooked[2]
- 2 cups unsweetened applesauce
- 3/4 cup lowfat sour cream
- 1/2 cup lowfat milk
- 6 cups cooked rice

Condiments:
- Raisins
- Chopped green onions (white and light green parts)
- Diced pineapple
- Chopped hard boiled egg
- Shredded coconut
- Unsalted peanuts
- LS chutney[3]

1. In a saucepan over medium heat, combine all ingredients, except rice and condiments; cook, stirring occasionally, until heated through, 5 to 10 minutes.
2. Serve over rice and top with condiments of your choice.

NUTRITIONAL INFO PER SERVING (without condiments): Calories 485, Fat 16g (Sat Fat 8g), Chol 200mg, Carb 62g (Fiber 2g, Sugar 12g), Sodium 198mg

Recipe Notes

1 – I like a lot of heat and use a hot curry powder, but you can use any variety of curry may be used (see *Curry Powder*, pg 247, for more info).

2 – You can use canned shrimp, although it averages 5 times more sodium than fresh (550mg vs 101mg per 3 oz).

3 – Mango chutney goes well with shrimp, unfortunately many brands have 170mg sodium or more per tbsp. For LS varieties, visit *LowSaltFoods.com*.

TOTAL SODIUM AND FAT BY INGREDIENT

Sodium:
- 1/4 c dried onion - 4mg
- 2 T curry - 9mg
- 1 T LS beef bouillon - 15mg
- 1 t onion powder - 2mg
- 1 t parsley flakes - 2mg
- 1/2 t celery seed - 2mg
- 1 lb shrimp - 1,000mg
- 3/4 c LF sour cream - 90mg
- 1/2 c LF milk - 53mg
- 6 c cooked rice - 10mg

Fat (Sat Fat):
- 1/3 c NSA butter - 64g (37g) or NSA margarine - 48g (19g)
- 2 T curry - 1g (0g)
- 1 lb shrimp - 8g (2g)
- 3/4 c LF sour cream - 15g (9g)
- 1/2 c LF milk - 3g (2g)
- 6 c cooked rice - 3g (1g)

Brands used/alternatives:
- *Herb Ox* NSA Beef Bouillon
- *Kroger* Wild Caught Salad Shrimp
- *Motts* Unsweetened Applesauce
- *Daisy Light* Sour Cream
- *Simple Truth* 2% Milk
- *Stonewall Kitchen* Mango Chutney

Tuna in Marsala Sauce

Sodium Per Serving – 56mg Serves 4

While vacationing on Maui, my friend, Margaret Napora, prepared this dish for a spur-of-the-moment dinner. It is so simple and absolutely divine—fresh fish is a must!

- **4 yellowfin or albacore tuna steaks (about 1 pound)[1]**
- **¼ teaspoon garlic powder**
- **⅛ teaspoon ground black pepper**
- **1 tablespoon olive oil**
- **4 tablespoons unsalted butter or margarine**
- **1 shallot, minced**
- **1 garlic clove, finely minced**
- **½ cup Marsala or Madeira wine[2]**
- **Juice of 1 lemon (about 2 tablespoons)**
- **1 tablespoon minced fresh herbs, such as chives, tarragon, or Italian parsley**

1. Season tuna with garlic powder and pepper.
2. Heat oil in skillet over medium-high heat; cook steaks for 3 to 4 minutes per side (medium-rare). Transfer tuna to a platter and keep warm while preparing sauce.
3. *For the sauce:* In same skillet, decrease heat to medium and melt butter; add shallots and garlic. Cook, stirring constantly, for 2 minutes; add wine, scraping up any browned bits. Bring to boil; cook, stirring frequently, until sauce is reduced by about half, 2 to 3 minutes. Stir in lemon juice and fresh herbs. Spoon over the tuna and serve.

NUTRITIONAL INFO PER SERVING: Calories 313, Fat 16g (Sat Fat 8g), Chol 75mg, Car 7g (Fiber 0g, Sugar 3g), Sodium 56mg

Recipe Notes

1 – Substitute halibut or swordfish for the tuna.
2 – Use Madeira or red wine instead of Marsala wine.

TOTAL SODIUM AND FAT BY INGREDIENT

Sodium:
- 1 lb tuna - 208mg
- 1 shallot - 5mg
- 1 garlic clove - 1mg
- ½ c Marsala wine - 12mg

Fat (Sat Fat):
- 1 lb tuna - 2g (1g)
- 1 T olive oil - 14g (2g)
- ¼ c NSA butter - 46g (29g)
  or NSA margarine - 36g (14g)

Grilled Mahi Mahi Almondine

Sodium Per Serving – 101mg   Serves 4

This grilled dish brings back memories of my days in Hawaii. It's simple enough for everyday faire, but also is an elegant dinner party entrée.

4 mahi mahi filets (about 1 pound)[1]
¼ teaspoon garlic powder
⅛ teaspoon ground black pepper
1 garlic clove, finely minced
2½ teaspoons lemon juice, divided
¼ cup olive oil
3 tablespoons unsalted butter or margarine
⅓ cup sliced almonds
1 tablespoon chopped fresh Italian parsley

1. Season mahi mahi with garlic powder and pepper; place in a shallow pan.
2. Mix together garlic, 2 teaspoons lemon juice, and oil; pour over fish and marinate 30 minutes or more, turning fish several times. Remove fish from marinade and place skin-side down on a preheated grill coated with nonstick cooking spray; grill mahi mahi, brushing frequently with marinade, until it flakes easily, 4 or 5 minutes on each side; transfer fish to a platter.
3. Meanwhile, melt butter in a skillet over medium-high heat; add almonds. Cook, stirring frequently, until almonds are a light, golden brown, 2 to 3 minutes; add reserved ½ teaspoon lemon juice and pour over fish. Garnish with parsley and serve.

NUTRITIONAL INFO PER SERVING: Calories 354, Fat 30g (Sat Fat 8g), Chol 106mg, Carb 2g (Fiber 1g, Sugar 0g), Sodium 101mg

Recipe Notes

1 – Substitute swordfish for the mahi mahi. Other alternatives are monkfish and tuna, but they won't be as sweet as the mahi mahi.

TOTAL SODIUM AND FAT BY INGREDIENT

Sodium:
  1 lb mahi mahi - 400mg
  1 garlic clove - 1mg
  1 T parsley - 2mg
Fat (Sat Fat):
  1 lb mahi mahi - 4g (1g)
  ¼ c olive oil - 56g (8g)
  3 T NSA butter - 36g (21g)
    or NSA margarine - 27g (11g)
  ⅓ c sliced almonds - 23g (2g)

CRAB QUICHE
Sodium Per Serving – 153mg Serves 6

Crab lovers, beware! Alaskan king crab is very high in sodium (237mg an oz), but other crab varieties, like blue or Dungeness are much less (83mg an oz).

- **2 tablespoons unsalted butter or margarine**
- **1 shallot, minced**
- **1 tablespoon flour**
- **2 (6-oz) cans lump crab meat**[1]
- **3 eggs**[2]
- **¾ cup lowfat milk**
- **¼ cup lowfat sour cream**
- **2 tablespoons dry white wine or sherry**
- **¼ teaspoon garlic powder**
- **⅛ teaspoon ground white pepper**
- **2–3 drops hot pepper sauce, such as Tabasco**
- **4 oz Swiss cheese, shredded (about 1 cup)**
- **1 *Basic Pie Crust (pg 205)* or LS pie crust**
- **⅛ teaspoon hot paprika or cayenne pepper**[3]

1. Preheat oven to 350ºF (180ºC).
2. Melt butter in a skillet over medium heat; add shallots. Cook, stirring frequently, until shallots soften, about 2 minutes; stir in flour and crab meat. Set aside.
3. In a large bowl, beat together eggs, milk, sour cream, wine, garlic powder, white pepper, and hot pepper sauce; stir in crab mixture.
4. Sprinkle half the cheese in the pie crust, pour in crab mixture; top with remaining cheese. Sprinkle with paprika and bake in a preheated oven for 40 to 45 minutes, or until eggs are set and knife inserted in center comes out clean. Allow quiche to cool slightly at room temperature, 5 to 10 minutes, before serving.

NUTRITIONAL INFO PER SERVING: Calories 438, Fat 27g (Sat Fat 12g), Chol 177mg, Carb 30g (Fiber 1g, Sugar 5g), Sodium 153mg (194mg with LS pie crust)

Recipe Notes
1 – Crab ranges from 40mg to 238mg per oz (see *Fish and Seafood Comparison*, pg 248, for more info on sodium and fat in crab varieties).
2 – To keep fat to a minimum, use an egg substitute. See *Eggs and Egg Substitutes*, pg 23, for a comparison of fat and sodium in eggs and egg substitutes.
3 – Most paprika sold is sweet. Hungarian paprika, available in some gourmet stores and supermarkets, is hot. I prefer a little heat in this dish and use the Hungarian. If unable to find, use regular paprika and add a dash of cayenne pepper.

TOTAL SODIUM AND FAT BY INGREDIENT

Sodium:
- 1 shallot - 5mg
- 12 oz crab - 240mg
- 3 eggs - 210mg
- ¾ c LF milk - 79mg
- ¼ c LF sour cream - 30mg
- 2 T white wine - 2mg
- 2 drops hot pepper sauce - 1mg
- 4 oz NSA Swiss cheese - 200mg
- 1 *Basic Pie Crust* - 150mg
  or LS pie crust - 400mg

Fat (Sat Fat):
- 2 T NSA butter - 24g (14g)
  or NSA margarine - 18g (7g)
- 12 oz crab - 2g (0g)
- 3 eggs - 15g (5g)
- ¾ c LF milk - 4g (2g)
- ¼ c LF sour cream - 5g (3g)
- 4 oz NSA Swiss - 36g (20g)
- 1 *Basic Pie Crust* - 74g (28g)
  or LS pie crust - 64g (28g)

Brands used/alternatives:
Kroger Premium Lump Crab
Simple Truth 2% Milk
Daisy Light Sour Cream
Great Value Swiss Cheese
Marie Callender's Pie Shell

SCALLOPS WITH BEURRE BLANC SAUCE

Sodium Per Serving – 166mg   Serves 6

This is an outstanding way to serve scallops. Once you try this butter sauce, you'll never eat scallops any other way!

- 1½–2 pounds large scallops (about 4–6 per person)
- ¼ teaspoon garlic powder
- ⅛ teaspoon ground white pepper
- 2 tablespoons all-purpose flour
- 2 tablespoons olive oil
- *Beurre Blanc Sauce (recipe follows)*
- 1 tablespoon chopped fresh Italian parsley

1. Prepare *Beurre Blanc Sauce* and keep warm while cooking scallops.
2. Pat scallops dry and sprinkle with garlic powder and pepper; dredge in flour, shaking off any excess.
3. Heat oil in a large skillet over medium-high heat; add scallops. Cook, turning once, until golden brown and opaque in center, about 3 minutes per side. Do not overcook. Remove from skillet and serve with sauce on top. Garnish with parsley.

NUTRITIONAL INFO PER SERVING (with sauce): Calories 322, Fat 25g (Saturated Fat 13g), Cholesterol 78mg, Carbohydrates 8g (Fiber 1g, Sugar 3g), Sodium 166mg

BEURRE BLANC SAUCE

Sodium Per Serving – 5mg   Makes about ¾ cup

This classic French sauce is usually made with butter. To cut the saturated fat and cholesterol, use half butter and half margarine. This sauce is also delicious on vegetables and other seafood.

- ¾ cup water
- 3 tablespoons white balsamic vinegar[1]
- 3 tablespoons tarragon vinegar[1]
- 2 shallots, finely minced
- 2 tablespoons half-and-half or whipping cream
- 10 tablespoons unsalted butter or margarine or combination of both

1. In a saucepan over medium-high heat; boil the water, balsamic and tarragon vinegars, and shallots until 2 tablespoons liquid remains, about 10 minutes. Stir in the half-and-half; decrease heat to low. Add butter, 1 tablespoon at a time, stirring constantly until melted.
2. Strain sauce through a fine-mesh sieve, pressing with the back of a spoon to remove as much liquid as possible; return strained sauce to pan and keep warm until ready to serve.

NUTRITIONAL INFO PER SERVING: Calories 192, Fat 20g (Sat Fat 12g), Chol 53mg, Carb 4g (Fiber 0g, Sugar 3g), Sodium 5mg

Recipe Notes

1 – I like to use two kinds of vinegar, one of which is usually an herbal variety. Instead of white balsamic, use white wine vinegar.

TOTAL SODIUM AND FAT BY INGREDIENT

SCALLOPS
Sodium:
- 1½ lb scallops - 960mg
- Beurre Blanc Sauce - 31mg
- 1 T parsley - 2mg

Fat (Sat Fat):
- 1½ lbs scallops - 3g (0g)
- 2 T olive oil - 28g (4g)
- Beurre Blanc Sauce - 119g (74g)

Brands used/alternatives:
Simple Truth Wild Caught Jumbo Sea Scallops

BEURRE BLANC SAUCE
Sodium:
- 3 T balsamic vinegar - 11mg
- 2 shallots - 10mg
- 2 T half-and-half - 10mg
  or whipping cream - 10mg

Fat (Sat Fat):
- 2 T half-and-half - 3g (2g)
  or whipping cream - 10g (7g)
- 10 T NSA butter - 115g (72g)
  or NSA margarine - 90g (35g)

Brands used/alternatives:
Organic Valley Half & Half

MEATLESS DISHES

Veggies in Cream Cheese Sauce

Sodium Per Serving – 125mg Serves 4

This creamy and delicious stroganoff is ready in less than 15 minutes and is very versatile. Use any variety of veggies you like and serve it over rice or pasta.

- 1 tablespoon olive oil
- ½ sweet onion, sliced
- 2 cups broccoli florets
- 2 cups snow peas, pinch off tips and remove strings
- 5 oz mushrooms, sliced (about 2 cups)[1]
- 1 garlic clove, minced
- ¼ cup water
- 1 teaspoon lemon juice
- ½ teaspoon LS chicken bouillon
- ¼ teaspoon herbes de Provence[2]
- ⅛ teaspoon ground black pepper
- ½ cup lowfat sour cream
- 4 oz (½ cup) whipped cream cheese
- 4 cups cooked rice or pasta

1. Heat oil in a large skillet over medium-high heat; add onions, broccoli, peas, and mushrooms. Cook, stirring frequently, until onions are translucent, about 4 minutes.
2. Add garlic, water, lemon juice, bouillon, herbes de Provence, and pepper; cook, stirring occasionally, until veggies are tender, about 5 minutes.
3. Stir in sour cream and cream cheese; heat through and pour over rice or pasta.

NUTRITIONAL INFO PER SERVING: Calories 377, Fat 11g (Sat Fat 5g), Chol 25mg, Carb 59g (Fiber 4g, Sugar 7g), Sodium 125mg

Recipe Notes
1 – Use any variety or combination of mushrooms (see *Mushrooms*, pg 250, for varieties).
2 – Herbes de Provence is a blend of herbs used in French cooking; most often a mix of basil, chervil, fennel, lavender, marjoram, rosemary, sage, savory, and/or thyme. The combination and portions vary depending on the manufacturer.

TOTAL SODIUM AND FAT BY INGREDIENT

Sodium:
- ½ sweet onion - 13mg
- 2 c broccoli - 60mg
- 2 c snow peas - 8mg
- 5 oz mushrooms - 7mg
- 1 garlic clove - 1mg
- ½ t LS chicken bouillon - 3mg
- ½ c LF sour cream - 60mg
- 4 oz whipped cheese - 340mg
- 4 c cooked rice - 7mg
  or pasta - 5mg

Fat (Sat Fat):
- 1 T olive oil - 14g (2g)
- 2 c broccoli - 1g (0g)
- 5 oz mushrooms - 1g (0g)
- ½ c LF sour cream - 10g (6g)
- 4 oz whip cr cheese - 18g (12g)
- 4 c cooked rice - 2g (1g)
  or pasta - 5g (1g)

Brands used/alternatives:
Herb Ox NSA Chicken Bouillon
Daisy Light Sour Cream
Philadelphia Whip Cream Cheese

Onion, Mushroom & Chèvre Tart

Sodium Per Serving – 102mg   Serves 6–8

The filling for this yummy tart is also great in strudel or baked in small tart cups and served as an appetizer.

- 1 *Basic Pie Crust (pg 205)* or LS pie crust
- 1 tablespoon olive oil
- 1 tablespoon unsalted butter or margarine
- ½ sweet onion, thinly sliced
- 1 shallot, finely minced
- 1 pound mushrooms, sliced (about 6½ cups, use a combination, such as shiitake, button, or cremini)[1]
- 1 tablespoon roasted garlic, minced[2]
- ¼ teaspoon garlic powder
- ⅛ teaspoon ground black pepper
- 4 oz Chèvre cheese, softened
- ½ cup lowfat sour cream
- 2 tablespoons lowfat milk or half-and-half
- 2 eggs[3]
- 1 teaspoon chopped fresh thyme or ¼ teaspoon dried

1. Preheat oven to 350ºF (180ºC).
2. Prick crust with a fork; line bottom of shell with aluminum foil. Pour pie weights into the pie crust to hold its shape while baking (see *Pie Weights*, pg 252). Bake for 10 minutes in a preheated oven; remove weights and bake 5 minutes more. Remove from oven and let cool slightly. *NOTE: If using a refrigerated or frozen pie crust, this step is not necessary.*
3. Meanwhile, heat oil and butter in a skillet over medium heat; add onions and shallots. Cook, stirring frequently, until the onions are translucent, 3 to 4 minutes. Add mushrooms, garlic, garlic powder, and pepper; cook, stirring frequently, until mushrooms are soft and most of the liquid is absorbed, about 10 minutes. Let cool slightly.
4. In a bowl, mix together the Chèvre, sour cream, and half-and-half; beat in eggs, one at a time. Set aside.
5. Spread mushroom mixture on the bottom of the precooked crust; pour egg mixture over the onions. Sprinkle with thyme and bake in a preheated oven for 20 minutes, or until golden brown.

NUTRITIONAL INFO PER SERVING: Calories 390, Fat 24g (Sat Fat 10g), Chol 96mg, Carb 32g (Fiber 1g, Sugar 6g), Sodium 102mg (143mg with LS pie crust)

Recipe Notes

1 – See *Mushrooms*, pg 250, for info on mushroom varieties.

2 – I like to make extra roasted garlic (see *Garlic, Roasting, pg 249*) and keep it on hand to use in different dishes. You can also use fresh or bottled garlic, although I think the flavor of roasted garlic tastes better.

3 – To keep fat to a minimum, use an egg substitute. See *Eggs and Egg Substitutes*, pg 23, for a comparison of fat and sodium in eggs and egg substitutes.

Variation

Instead of a flour crust, thinly slice 1-2 sweet potatoes and cover the bottom of the pie dish. There's no need to pre-bake; prepare filling and proceed and directed.

TOTAL SODIUM AND FAT BY INGREDIENT

Sodium:
- 1 *Basic Pie Crust* - 150mg or LS pie crust - 400mg
- ½ sweet onion - 13mg
- 1 shallot - 5mg
- 12 oz mushrooms - 7mg
- 1 T garlic - 2mg
- 4 oz Chèvre - 220mg
- ½ c LF sour cream - 60mg
- 2 T LF milk - 13mg or half-and-half - 14mg
- 2 eggs - 140mg

Fat (Sat Fat):
- 1 *Basic Pie Crust* - 74g (28g) or LS pie crust - 64g (28g)
- 1 T olive oil - 14g (2g)
- 1 T NSA butter - 12g (7g) or NSA margarine - 9g (4g)
- 4 oz Chèvre - 24g (16g)
- ½ c LF sour cream - 10g (6g)
- 2 eggs - 10g (3g)

Brands used/alternatives:
Vermont Creamery Herb Chèvre
Daisy Light Sour Cream
Simple Truth 2% Milk
Marie Callender's Pie Shell

VEGETABLE STRUDEL WITH RED PEPPER COULIS

Sodium Per Serving – 128mg   Serves 6

Not only is this colorful strudel full of flavor, but it also is surprisingly easy to make. To shorten preparation time, make the filling and Red Pepper Coulis in advance and refrigerate until ready to use.

- 1 tablespoon olive oil
- 1 tablespoon unsalted butter or margarine
- 1 leek, chopped (white and some green parts), or ½ cup chopped sweet onion
- 1 shallot, chopped
- 1 garlic clove, minced
- 1 portobello mushroom, chopped
- 1 cup chopped mushrooms[1]
- ¾ teaspoon dried tarragon
- ½ teaspoon dried thyme
- ¼ teaspoon garlic powder
- ⅛ teaspoon ground black pepper
- 1 zucchini, shredded
- ½ cup broccoli, chopped
- ½ cup oil-packed sun-dried tomatoes, drained and chopped
- ¼ cup water chestnuts, chopped
- ½ cup lowfat sour cream
- 2 teaspoons Dijon-style mustard
- 4 oz shredded Swiss cheese (about 1 cup)
- 8 (13 x 9-inch) sheets phyllo (fillo) dough[2]
- Butter-flavor cooking spray or melted butter[3]
- ***Red Pepper Coulis (pg 124)***

1. Preheat oven to 350ºF (180ºC).
2. Heat oil and butter in a skillet over medium heat; add leeks. Cook, stirring constantly, until leeks are translucent, about 3 to 4 minutes. Add shallots and garlic, cook stirring constantly, until you smell the garlic, 1 to 2 minutes.
3. Add mushrooms, tarragon, thyme, garlic powder, and pepper; cook until mushrooms soften, about 5 minutes. Stir in zucchini, broccoli, tomatoes, and water chestnuts; cover and simmer, stirring occasionally, until veggies are tender, about 5 minutes.
4. Mix together sour cream and mustard; stir into mushroom mixture. Add cheese and mix thoroughly; remove from heat; cool slightly.
5. *To prepare strudel:* Place 1 sheet of phyllo dough on a flat surface; spray with butter-flavored spray. Place another sheet on top of the dough and spray with butter spray; repeat until there is a total of 4 sheets. Place half the mushroom mixture in the center of the dough; roll into a log, folding in both ends about an inch. Repeat with remaining sheets of phyllo and mushroom mixture.
6. Place strudels on a baking sheet and spray tops with butter-flavored spray; cut several diagonal slits in the top about 1-inch apart. Bake in a preheated oven for 30 minutes or until golden brown. Remove and let stand 5 minutes before slicing into serving pieces. Top with *Red Pepper Coulis* and serve.

NUTRITIONAL INFO PER SERVING (with coulis): Calories 326, Fat 19g (Sat Fat 6g), Chol 28mg, Carb 27g (Fiber 3g, Sugar 9g), Sodium 128mg

Recipe Notes

1 – Use any combination of mushrooms, see *Mushrooms*, pg 250, for varieties.
2 – To keep the phyllo from drying out, work quickly and cover unused sheets with a damp towel.
3 – To keep fat to a minimum, use butter-flavored cooking spray; butter results in a flakier strudel.

TOTAL SODIUM AND FAT BY INGREDIENT

Sodium:
- 1 leek - 18mg
- 1 shallot - 5mg
- 1 garlic clove - 1mg
- 1 portobello mushroom - 6mg
- 1 c mushrooms - 4mg
- 1 zucchini - 20mg
- ½ c broccoli - 15mg
- ½ c sun-dried tomatoes - 40mg
- ½ c LF sour cream - 60mg
- 2 t Dijon mustard - 80mg
- 4 oz NSA Swiss cheese - 200mg
- 5 butter sprays - 5mg
- 8 phyllo sheets - 272mg
- Red Pepper Coulis - 40mg

Fat (Sat Fat):
- 1 T olive oil - 14g (2g)
- 1 T NSA butter - 12g (7g) or NSA margarine - 9g (4g)
- ½ c dried tomatoes - 24g (0g)
- ½ c LF sour cream - 10g (6g)
- 4 oz NSA Swiss - 36g (20g)
- 8 phyllo sheets - 2g (0g)
- 5 butter sprays - 1g (0g)
- Red Pepper Coulis - 13g 0g)

Brands used/alternatives:
- *Jeff's Naturals* Sun-Dried Tomatoes
- *Kroger* Water Chestnuts
- *Daisy Light* Sour Cream
- *Gold's* Dijon Mustard
- *Great Value* Swiss Cheese
- *Athens* Phyllo Dough

Red Pepper Coulis

Sodium Per Serving – 10mg — Serves 4

Coulis (koo-LEE) is a puréed sauce, usually made from fruits or vegetables. The fresh flavor of the roasted red peppers in this coulis is delicious. Serve over burgers, pastas, on pizzas, or add a dollop to a creamy vegetable soup.

- **2 red bell peppers, roasted[1]**
- **¼ cup oil-packed sun-dried tomatoes, drained and chopped[2]**
- **¾ cup water**
- **1 tablespoon dry sherry**
- **1 tablespoon white balsamic vinegar[3]**
- **1 teaspoon LS chicken bouillon**
- **¼ teaspoon garlic powder**
- **⅛ teaspoon ground black pepper**

1. Place all ingredients in a blender or food processor and pulse until the consistency of a thick spaghetti sauce. *NOTE: If too thick, stir in additional water.* Pour purée into a saucepan and place over medium heat; cook, stirring frequently, until heated through, about 3 to 4 minutes. Pour over entrée and serve.

NUTRITIONAL INFO PER SERVING: Calories 76, Fat 3g (Saturated Fat 0g), Cholesterol 0mg, Carbohydrates 9g (Fiber 1g, Sugar 5g), Sodium 10mg

---

VARIATION

Chipotle Pepper Sauce

1. For a smoky, spicy sauce, add 1–2 teaspoons minced chipotle chilies in adobo sauce.[4] (NOTE: Adobo is a spicy tomato sauce with a smoked flavor. You can find chipotle chiles in the Hispanic section of most large supermarkets.)

NUTRITIONAL INFO PER SERVING: Calories 77, Fat 3g (Saturated Fat 0g), Cholesterol 0mg, Carbohydrates 9g (Fiber 1g, Sugar 5g), Sodium 17mg

---

Recipe Notes

1 – Roasting peppers brings out their sweetness. There are several ways to roast peppers, see *Roasting Peppers*, pg 251. To save time, use bottled peppers, but I think the flavor of fresh roasted peppers tastes better.

2 – Sun-dried tomatoes come bottled in olive oil or dried in bags. Generally, bottled tomatoes have less sodium than packaged, but read labels carefully, some brands have added sodium. Either are okay to use, but the latter must be reconstituted in warm water for 30 minutes before using. Drain tomatoes before chopping.

3 – White balsamic vinegar is made from white grapes and is combined with white wine vinegar. Although milder and sweeter, it also is not as overpowering in salads as the darker balsamic vinegar.

4 – You can also use *Gran Luchito* Chipotle Chile Paste, available at Walmart and Amazon. It has a wonderful smoky flavor and only has 15mg sodium per tbsp (versus 70mg-130mg for chipotles in adobo sauce).

TOTAL SODIUM AND FAT BY INGREDIENT

Sodium:
- 2 red bell peppers - 10mg
- ¼ c sun-dried tomatoes - 20mg
- 1 T dry sherry - 2mg
- 1 T balsamic vinegar - 4mg
- 1 t LS chicken bouillon - 5mg

Fat (Sat Fat):
- 2 red bell peppers - 1g (0g)
- ¼ c dried tomatoes - 6g (1g)

Brands used/alternatives:
Jeff's Naturals Sun-Dried Tomatoes
Herb Ox NSA Chicken Bouillon

CREAMY POLENTA WITH MUSHROOM SAUCE

Sodium Per Serving – 54mg   Serves 4

Polenta is a mainstay of Italy and is prepared in a variety of ways, using cheese and/or vegetables. Serve it as a main entrée or side dish.

- **4 cups water**
- **1 teaspoon LS chicken bouillon**
- **1 cup yellow cornmeal**
- **2 tablespoons unsalted butter or margarine**
- **¼ cup Parmesan cheese, freshly grated**
- ***Mushroom Sauce (recipe follows)***

1. In a large saucepan over medium-high heat, bring water and bouillon to a boil; add cornmeal, stirring constantly, a little at a time. Decrease heat to low; cook, stirring occasionally, until cornmeal has thickened to an oatmeal consistency, about 30 minutes. Stir in butter and Parmesan; serve in bowls topped with mushroom sauce.

NUTRITIONAL INFO PER SERVING: Calories 608, Fat 20g (Sat Fat 7g), Chol 31mg, Carb 45g (Fiber 5g, Sugar 8g), Sodium 54mg

MUSHROOM SAUCE

Sodium Per Serving – 22mg   Serves 4

This delicious sauce is good on top of steaks, chicken, pasta, or rice.

- **2 tablespoons olive oil**
- **½ sweet onion, chopped**
- **1 shallot, minced²**
- **2 garlic cloves, minced**
- **½ cup Madeira or Marsala wine**
- **½ cup dry white wine**
- **8 oz sliced mushrooms (about 3½ cups), such as cremini, portobello, oyster, or dried porcinis³**
- **¼ teaspoon dried thyme or rosemary**
- **¼ teaspoon garlic powder**
- **⅛ teaspoon black pepper**
- **2 cups *Chicken Broth (pg 208)* or unsalted chicken broth**
- **1 tablespoon unsalted butter or margarine, melted**
- **1 tablespoon cornstarch**

1. Heat oil in a large saucepan over medium-high heat; add onions and shallots. Cook, stirring frequently, until onions are translucent, 13 to 4 minutes. Add garlic and cook, stirring constantly, until you smell the garlic, 1 to 2 minutes.
2. Add Madeira and white wine; bring to a boil and continue cooking until liquid nearly evaporates, about 10 minutes.
3. Add mushrooms, garlic powder, thyme, pepper, and chicken broth; bring to a boil. Decrease heat to medium-low and simmer, uncovered, for 10 minutes.
4. Mix together butter and cornstarch; add to mushroom mixture. Cook, stirring frequently, until sauce thickens slightly, about 2 to 3 minutes.

NUTRITIONAL INFO PER SERVING: Calories 216, Fat 10g (Sat Fat 3g), Chol 10mg, Carb 14g (Fiber 2g, Sugar 7g), Sodium 22mg (55mg with NSA chicken broth)

TOTAL SODIUM AND FAT BY INGREDIENT

CREAMY POLENTA
Sodium:
- 1 t LS chicken bouillon - 5mg
- Mushroom Sauce - 89mg
- ¼ c Parmesan - 200mg

Fat (Sat Fat):
- 1 c cornmeal - 6g (0g)
- 2 T NSA butter - 23g (14g)
  or NSA margarine - 16g (3g)
- ¼ c Parmesan - 6g (4g)
- Mushroom Sauce - 41g (11g)

Brands used/alternatives:
Herb Ox NSA Chicken Bouillon
365 Whole Foods 3 Cheese Blend

MUSHROOM SAUCE
Sodium:
- ½ sweet onion - 13mg
- 1 shallot - 5mg
- 2 garlic cloves - 1mg
- ½ c Madeira - 12mg
- ½ c white wine - 6mg
- 8 oz mushrooms - 11mg
- 2 c *Chicken Broth* - 40mg
  or NSA chicken broth - 170mg
- 1 T cornstarch - 1mg

Fat (Sat Fat):
- 2 T olive oil - 28g (4g)
- 8 oz mushrooms - 1g (0g)
- 2 c *Chicken Broth* - 1g (0g)
  or NSA chicken broth - 0g (0g)
- 1 T NSA butter - 12g (7g)
  or NSA margarine - 9g (4g)

Brands used/alternatives:
Pacific Foods Organic Unsalted Chicken Stock

Recipe Notes

1 – Use fresh parmesan, not the canned variety.
2 – Shallots look like small onions and have a mild garlic flavor (see *Shallots*, pg 253, for more info).
3 – Use any variety or combination of mushrooms (for mushroom varieties, see *Mushrooms*, pg 250).

Veggie Burgers

Sodium Per Serving – 115mg Serves 4

These burgers go together quickly using a food processor. Even guests who love their meat, enjoy this tasty delight.

- **1 cup uncooked bulgur or couscous**
- **1 carrot, shredded**
- **1 celery stalk, minced**
- **½ cup sweet onion, minced**
- **½ green bell pepper, minced**
- **1 garlic clove, finely minced**
- **1 cup NSA kidney or black beans, rinsed and drained**
- **1 cup LS vegetable juice**
- **1 egg, lightly beaten[1]**
- **4–5 drops hot pepper sauce, such as *Tabasco***
- **2 tablespoons chopped fresh Italian parsley**
- **½ teaspoon dried basil**
- **¼ teaspoon garlic powder**
- **⅛ teaspoon ground black pepper**
- **1 cup LS bread crumbs[2]**
- **4 *Hamburger Buns (pg 196)* or LS buns**
- **4 slices Swiss cheese (optional)**
- **Sliced onion**
- **Sliced tomato**
- **Lettuce leaves**

1. Preheat broiler.
2. In a food processor, add bulgur, carrot, celery, onion, bell pepper, garlic, beans, vegetable juice, egg, hot pepper sauce, parsley, basil, garlic powder, and pepper; pulse until a paste-like consistency. Transfer to a large bowl, mix in bread crumbs and shape into patties.
3. Broil, turning once, until lightly browned and crisp on both sides, about 4 minutes per side. Serve on buns; top with cheese, onion, tomato, lettuce, and other condiments of your choice.

NUTRITIONAL INFO PER BURGER (without cheese and condiments): Calories 378, Fat 6g (Sat Fat 2g), Chol 73mg, Carb 78g (Fiber 20g, Sugar 15g), Sodium 180mg (150mg with cheese) (180mg with LS bun) (215mg with cheese and LS bun)

Recipe Notes

1 – To keep fat to a minimum, use an egg substitute. See *Eggs and Egg Substitutes*, pg 23, for a comparison of fat and sodium in eggs and egg substitutes.

2 – To make fresh bread crumbs, see *Bread Crumbs*, pg 244.

TOTAL SODIUM AND FAT BY INGREDIENT

Sodium:
- 1 c bulgur - 9mg
- 1 carrot - 42mg
- 1 celery stalk - 32mg
- ½ c onion - 4mg
- ½ bell pepper - 2mg
- 1 garlic clove - 1mg
- 1 c NSA kidney beans - 9mg
- 1 c LS vegetable juice - 45mg
- 1 egg - 70mg
- 4 drops hot pepper sauce - 1mg
- 2 T parsley - 4mg
- 4 *Hamburger Buns* - 241mg or LS bun - 500mg

Fat (Sat Fat):
- 1 egg - 5g (2g)
- 1 c NSA bread crumbs - 4g (0g)
- 4 *Hamburger Buns* - 35g (13g) or LS bun - 15g (8g)

Brands used/alternatives:
Kuner's Kidney Beans
RW Knudsen Very Veggie LS Juice
4C Salt Free Bread Crumbs
King's Hawaiian Hamburger Buns
Great Value Swiss Cheese

VEGETABLE CREPES WITH CHEESE SAUCE

Sodium Per Serving – 191mg   Serves 4

This is a great recipe for using leftover vegetables from the refrigerator. This goes together quickly using tortillas, and the mild cheese sauce is a perfect topping.

- **1 tablespoon olive oil**
- **½ sweet onion, thinly sliced, or 1 leek, sliced (white and lite green parts)**
- **1 garlic clove, minced**
- **16 oz bag mixed veggies or 4 cups sliced, shredded, or cubed veggies (such as red bell pepper, mushrooms, broccoli, snow peas, zucchini, and carrots)**
- **¼ cup water chestnuts, chopped[1]**
- **¼ cup dry sherry**
- **¼ teaspoon garlic powder**
- **⅛ teaspoon ground black pepper**
- **1 teaspoon seasoning combination[2]**
- **4 large (8"-10") LS flour tortillas[3]**
- **1½ cups *Cheese Sauce (pg 128)***
- **2 tablespoons chopped fresh Italian parsley or cilantro (optional)**

1. Heat oil in a skillet over medium heat; add onion. Cook, stirring frequently, until onions are translucent, 2 to 3 minutes; add garlic and cook, stirring constantly, until you smell the garlic, 1 to 2 minutes. Add mixed veggies, water chestnuts, sherry, garlic powder, pepper, and seasoning combination; cook 10 minutes until veggies are tender and liquid is absorbed.
2. Warm tortillas before filling with veggies:

   Microwave – Warm tortillas for 30 seconds on high. *NOTE: Warm just before preparing, as they stiffen as they cool.*

   Oven – Preheat oven to 150ºF (75ºC), wrap tortillas in aluminum foil and place in oven until heated through, about 5 minutes.

   Stove top – Place a skillet on medium-high heat and coat with vegetable spray; quickly warm each tortilla, turning once, 15 to 20 seconds per side.
3. Place one-fourth of the filling on each warm tortilla and roll up; continue with remaining filling and tortillas. *NOTE: For a crisper crepe, cook in 2 tablespoons oil or butter until golden brown and crisp on both sides, 3 to 4 minutes.*
4. Pour cheese sauce on top of crepes and sprinkle with chopped parsley (or cilantro, if using the spicy seasoning combination)

NUTRITIONAL INFO PER SERVING (with cheese sauce): Calories 522, Fat 23g (Sat Fat 11g), Chol 44mg, Carb 55g (Fiber 8g, Sugar 6g), Sodium 191mg

Recipe Notes

1 – Water chestnuts add crunch to the crepes. You can also use toasted almonds, walnuts, or pecans.

2 – Different combinations of spices will give a unique flavor to the filling:

   Spicy: ½ tsp NSA chili powder, ½ tsp ground cumin, and dash of hot pepper sauce (such as *Tabasco*).

   Herbal: ½ tsp herbes de Provence (or ¼ tsp dried thyme, ⅛ tsp dried rosemary, and ⅛ tsp dried sage).

3 – Most 8-inch flour tortillas average 364mg sodium, but a few manufacturers, offer LS shells (visit LowSaltFoods.com for a current list). You can also use 2 large corn tortillas instead of 1 flour tortilla, although they will taste more like tacos than crepes.

TOTAL SODIUM AND FAT BY INGREDIENT

Sodium:
½ sweet onion - 13mg
1 garlic clove - 1mg
¼ c sherry - 5mg
1 t spice mix - 1mg
4 c mixed veggies - 90mg
4 LS flour tortillas - 340mg
1½ c *Cheese Sauce* - 309mg
2 T parsley - 4mg

Fat (Sat Fat):
1 T olive oil - 14g (2g)
4 LS flour tortillas - 14g (6g)
1½ c *Cheese Sauce* - 63g (36g)

Brands used/alternatives:
Birds Eye C&W Ultimate Petite Mixed Veggies
La Banderia LS Flour Tortillas

MAIN COURSES - Meatless Dishes

Cheese Sauce

Sodium Per Serving – 77mg   Makes about 1½ cups

This easy-to-prepare cheese sauce has a mild flavor. It also goes well with vegetables, burgers, and biscuits.

- 2 tablespoons unsalted butter or margarine
- 2 tablespoons all-purpose flour
- 1 teaspoon LS chicken bouillon
- ⅔ cup water[1]
- ⅔ cup lowfat milk
- ½ cup dry sherry or white wine
- ½ teaspoon Dijon-style mustard
- ½ teaspoon mustard powder
- 2–3 drops hot pepper sauce, such as *Tabasco*
- 4 oz Swiss cheese, shredded (about 1 cup)
- ⅛ teaspoon ground black pepper
- Freshly grated nutmeg or paprika
- 1–2 tablespoons chopped fresh Italian parsley (optional)

1. Melt butter in a saucepan over medium-high heat; add flour. Cook, stirring constantly, until flour paste begins to brown, 1 to 2 minutes; decrease heat to medium.
2. Mix in bouillon, water, and milk; bring to a boil. Decrease heat to medium-low; cook, stirring frequently, until thickened to a gravy consistency, 4 to 5 minutes.
3. Add Dijon, mustard powder, hot pepper sauce, and cheese; cook, stirring constantly, until cheese has melted, about 2 minutes. Season with pepper and nutmeg; garnish with parsley and serve.

NUTRITIONAL INFO PER SERVING: Calories 245, Fat 16g (Sat Fat 9g), Chol 44mg, Carb 10g (Fiber 0g, Sugar 3g), Sodium 77mg

Recipe Notes
1 – For a richer-tasting sauce, use *Chicken Broth*, pg 208, or unsalted chicken broth instead of water.

TOTAL SODIUM AND FAT BY INGREDIENT

Sodium:
- 1 t LS chicken bouillon - 5mg
- ⅔ c LF milk - 70mg
- ½ c sherry - 11mg
- ½ t Dijon mustard - 20mg
- 2 drops hot pepper sauce - 1mg
- 4 oz NSA Swiss cheese - 200mg
- 1 T parsley - 2mg

Fat (Sat Fat):
- 2 T NSA butter - 23g (14g) or NSA margarine - 18g (7g)
- ⅔ c LF milk - 3g (2g)
- ½ t mustard powder - 1g (0g)
- 4 oz NSA Swiss - 36g (20g)

Brands used/alternatives:
- *Herb Ox* NSA Chicken Bouillon
- *Simple Truth* 2% Milk
- *Gold's* Dijon Mustard
- *Great Value* Swiss Cheese

CRUSTLESS SPINACH–MUSHROOM QUICHE

Sodium Per Serving – 210mg entrée (105mg side dish)   Serves 6 as an entrée, 8 as a side dish

This recipe was given to me by a vegetarian friend. It is so good and no one will ever know it contains tofu...unless you tell them! This also makes a nice side dish to serve with poultry or beef.

- 1 tablespoon olive oil
- 1 tablespoon unsalted butter or margarine
- ½ sweet onion, diced
- 2 shallots, chopped[1]
- 4 oz mushrooms, chopped (about 1½ cups)[2]
- 1 garlic clove, minced
- ¼ teaspoon dried basil
- ¼ teaspoon garlic or onion powder
- ¼ teaspoon dried tarragon
- ¼ teaspoon dried thyme
- ⅛ teaspoon ground black pepper
- 3 eggs, beaten[3]
- 8 oz firm tofu
- ½ cup part-skim ricotta cheese
- 2 oz Swiss cheese, shredded (about ½ cup)
- ¼ cup lowfat milk
- 1 (16-oz) package frozen chopped spinach, thawed and moisture squeezed out
- ⅛ teaspoon freshly grated nutmeg[4]

1. Preheat oven to 350ºF (180ºC). Coat a 9-inch quiche or pie dish with nonstick cooking spray.
2. Heat oil and butter in a skillet over medium heat; add onions, shallots and mushrooms. Cook, stirring frequently, until onions are translucent, 3 to 4 minutes; add garlic, basil, garlic powder, tarragon, thyme, and pepper. Cook, stirring constantly, until you smell the garlic, 1 to 2 minutes; remove from heat and let cool slightly.
3. Mix together eggs, tofu, ricotta, Swiss cheese, milk, and spinach; add to onion mixture. Pour into prepared quiche dish and sprinkle with nutmeg.
4. Bake in a preheated oven for 30 minutes, or until custard has set and top is lightly browned. Let cool slightly, cut into wedges and serve.

NUTRITIONAL INFO PER SERVING (ENTRÉE): Calories 325, Fat 19g (Sat Fat 7g), Chol 192mg, Carb 17g (Fiber 6g, Sugar 11g), Sodium 210 mg
SIDE DISH: Calories 163, Fat 10g (Sat Fat 4g), Chol 96mg, Carb 9g (Fiber 3g, Sugar 6g), Sodium 105mg

Recipe Notes
1 – See *Shallots*, pg 253, for additional info.
2 – Use any type or combination of mushrooms, (for varieties, see *Mushrooms*, pg 250).
3 – To keep fat to a minimum, use an egg substitute. See *Eggs and Egg Substitutes*, pg 23, for a comparison of fat and sodium in eggs and egg substitutes.
4 – I think freshly ground nutmeg tastes better than the pre-ground, but you can use ¼ teaspoon of the pre-ground.

Variation
If you prefer a crust, thinly slice 1-2 sweet potatoes and cover the bottom of the pie dish. Prepare filling as directed and pour over sweet potatoes. Add 10-15 minutes to baking time until potatoes are done.

TOTAL SODIUM AND FAT BY INGREDIENT

Sodium:
- ½ sweet onion - 13mg
- 2 shallots - 10mg
- 4 oz mushrooms - 6mg
- 1 garlic clove - 1mg
- 3 eggs - 210mg
- 8 oz tofu - 14mg
- ½ c part skim ricotta - 100mg
- 2 oz Swiss cheese - 100mg
- ¼ c LF milk - 26mg
- 10 oz spinach - 360mg

Fat (Sat Fat):
- 1 T olive oil - 14g (2g)
- 1 T NSA butter - 12g (7g)
  or NSA margarine - 9g (4g)
- 3 eggs - 15g (5g)
- 8 oz tofu - 10g (1g)
- ½ c part skim ricotta - 7g (4g)
- 2 oz Swiss cheese - 18g (10g)
- ¼ c LF milk - 1g (1g)

Brands used/alternatives:
Azumaya Firm Tofu
Kroger Part Skim Ricotta Cheese
Great Value Swiss Cheese
Simple Truth 2% Milk
Birds Eye C&W Chop Baby Spinach

STUFFED BAKED POTATOES

Serves 4

Potatoes are very low in sodium (18mg for a large russet) and are great as a main course meal. Toppings you can use are endless. Here are a few of our favorites.

4 large russet potatoes, scrubbed and rubbed with vegetable oil

2-3 cups filling/topping of your choice *(see Fillings/Toppings below)*

1. Preheat oven to 425ºF (220ºC). Arrange oven rack in middle of the oven.
2. Wrap potatoes in foil and pierce several times with a fork. Place potatoes on oven rack and bake for 50-60 minutes, or until tender and cooked through. Split lengthwise and top with filling of your choice.

NUTRITIONAL INFO PER SERVING: Varies depending on filling or topping (see below).

FILLINGS/TOPPINGS

STROGANOFF STUFFED POTATOES
1. Evenly divide the *Veggies in Cream Cheese Sauce, pg 121,* (without the rice) and pour over potatoes.

NUTRITIONAL INFO PER POTATO: Calories 494, Fat 15g (Saturated Fat 6g), Cholesterol 25mg, Carbohydrates 81g (Fiber 8g, Sugar 9g), Sodium 141mg

CREAMY MUSHROOM STUFFED POTATOES
1. Evenly divide 2-3 cups *Creamy Mushroom Pasta (omit pasta noodles), pg 134.* Pour over potatoes.

NUTRITIONAL INFO PER POTATO: Calories 537, Fat 11g (Saturated Fat 2g), Cholesterol 16mg, Carbohydrates 88g (Fiber 8g, Sugar 4g), Sodium 73mg

NOTE: The following variations contain some chicken or turkey:

CHILI STUFFED POTATOES
1. Evenly divide 2-3 cups *Texas-Style Turkey Chili, pg 56,* and pour over potatoes. Top with sour cream, shredded Swiss cheese, and chopped green onions.

NUTRITIONAL INFO PER POTATO: Calories 594, Fat 7g (Saturated Fat 1g), Cholesterol 41mg, Carbohydrates 100g (Fiber 17g, Sugar 10g), Sodium 127mg

CREAMY CHEESY CHICKEN STUFFED POTATOES
1. Evenly divide 2-3 cups *Creamy Cheesy Chicken, pg 85,* and pour over potatoes. *NOTE:* Cut large chunks of chicken into bite-size pieces.

NUTRITIONAL INFO PER POTATO: Calories 593, Fat 18g (Saturated Fat 7g), Cholesterol 112mg, Carbohydrates 74g (Fiber 5g, Sugar 3g), Sodium 261mg

PASTA DISHES & PIZZA

15-Minute Spaghetti

Sodium Per Serving – 46mg　　　　　　　　　　　　　　　　　　　　　　　　　　Serves 6

This spur-of-the-moment dish uses ingredients you usually have on hand and is a great way to jazz up a store-bought pasta sauce.

- 1 tablespoon olive oil
- ½ cup chopped sweet onion or 1 leek, sliced (white and light green parts)
- 1 shallot, minced
- 1 garlic clove, minced
- 2 cups mixed vegetables, chopped, such as zucchini, mushrooms, and broccoli
- ¼ teaspoon dried basil
- ¼ teaspoon dried oregano
- ¼ teaspoon dried thyme
- 1 (24-oz) jar LS pasta sauce[1]
- 12 oz spaghetti noodles, cooked[2]

1. Heat oil in a skillet over medium-high heat; add onions and shallots. Cook, stirring frequently, until onions are translucent, 2 to 3 minutes; add garlic and cook, stirring constantly, until you smell the garlic, 1 to 2 minutes.
2. Stir in vegetables, basil, oregano, and thyme; cook, stirring frequently, until vegetables are nearly tender, 4 to 5 minutes. Add pasta sauce and cook until heated through, about 5 minutes.
3. Combine sauce and cooked spaghetti; mixing well. Serve with Parmesan, if desired.

NUTRITIONAL INFO PER SERVING: Calories 316, Fat 4g (Sat Fat 0g), Chol 0mg, Carb 59mg (Fiber 6g, Sugar 7g), Sodium 46mg

Recipe Notes

1 – Most supermarkets carry lower salt pasta sauces, averaging about 360mg sodium per ½ cup. There are other good sauces with less than 140mg sodium (visit *LowSaltFoods.com* for a current list of products).

2 – When cooking pasta, it is not necessary to add salt to the water. If you want additional flavor, stir in 1–2 teaspoons LS chicken bouillon to the water before cooking the pasta.

TOTAL SODIUM AND FAT BY INGREDIENT

Sodium:
- ½ c sweet onion - 4mg
- 1 shallot - 5mg
- 1 garlic clove - 1mg
- 2 c mixed vegetables - 45mg
- 24 oz LS pasta sauce - 210mg
- 12 oz spaghetti - 20mg

Fat (Sat Fat):
- 1 T olive oil - 14g (2g)
- 24 oz LS pasta sauce - 12g (0g)
- 12 oz spaghetti - 5g (1g)

Brands used/alternatives:
Francesca Rinaldi NSA Pasta Sauce

Meatballs with Marinara Sauce

Sodium Per Serving – 92mg   Serves 6

This is a great family meal that my northern Italian grandmother taught me as a child. Either bake the moist and flavorful meatballs in the oven or cook them on the stove-top. Serve these meatballs with just the Marinara Sauce or on top of cooked noodles.

½ pound each ground sirloin and pork[1]
½ cup LS seasoned bread crumbs[2]
½ cup minced onion
3 tablespoons chopped fresh Italian parsley
1 garlic clove, finely minced
¼ cup lowfat milk
1 egg, beaten

2 tablespoons Parmesan cheese, freshly grated
1 teaspoon Italian seasoning[3]
½ teaspoon crushed red pepper flakes or cayenne pepper (optional)
¼ teaspoon onion or garlic powder
¼ teaspoon ground black pepper
Marinara Sauce (pg 133) or 1 (24-oz) jar LS marinara sauce
Garnish with Parmesan cheese (optional)

1. In a large bowl, mix sirloin and pork with bread crumbs, onion, parsley, garlic, milk, egg, Parmesan, Italian seasoning, red pepper flakes, onion powder, and pepper. Shape into 1¼-inch balls.
2. Cook in one of the following ways:
   - *By frying:* Heat 2 tablespoons olive oil in a nonstick skillet over medium heat; add meatballs. Cook, turning several times, until browned on all sides and cooked through, 10 to 15 minutes; add to *Marinara Sauce*.
   - *In the oven:* Preheat oven to 375ºF (190ºC). Coat a large baking dish with nonstick cooking spray. Place meatballs in prepared dish and bake until light brown and cooked through, 20 to 25 minutes; add to *Marinara Sauce*.
3. Serve with additional Parmesan, if desired.

NUTRITIONAL INFO PER SERVING: Calories 350, Fat 19g (Sat Fat 6g), Chol 90mg, Carb 24g (Fiber 6g, Sugar 10g), Sodium 92mg

---

VARIATION
Sicilian Meatballs
1. Add ½ cup dried currants, raisins, or dried cranberries to the meatball mixture; proceed as directed.

NUTRITIONAL INFO PER APPETIZER: Calories 403, Fat 19g (Sat Fat 6g), Chol 90mg, Carb 38g (Fiber 8g, Sugar 21g), Sodium 94mg

---

Recipe Notes
1 – Instead of beef and pork, use a combination of turkey or chicken (although lower in fat, the meatballs aren't as moist).
2 – To make fresh bread crumbs, see *Bread Crumbs*, pg 244. If using unseasoned crumbs, double the Italian spice blend to 2 tsp.
3 – If you don't have Italian seasoning, use ¼ tsp dried basil, ¼ tsp dried oregano, ¼ tsp dried rosemary, and ¼ tsp dried thyme.

TOTAL SODIUM AND FAT BY INGREDIENT

Sodium:
  8 oz beef - 150mg
  8 oz pork - 100mg
  ½ c onion - 3mg
  3 T parsley - 1mg
  1 garlic clove - 1mg
  ¼ c LF milk - 26mg
  1 egg - 70mg
  3 T Parmesan - 90mg
  1 t Italian seasoning - 1mg
  ½ t red pepper flakes - 2mg
  Marinara Sauce - 113mg
    or 24-oz LS pasta sauce - 200mg

Fat (Sat Fat):
  8 oz beef - 46g (17g)
  8 oz pork - 34g (12g)
  ½ c LS bread crumbs - 2g (0g)
  ¼ c LF milk - 1g (1g)
  1 egg - 5g (2g)
  3 T Parmesan - 6g (3g)
  Marinara Sauce - 21g (3g) or
    24-oz LS pasta sauce - 5g (0g)

Brands used/alternatives:
4C Salt Free Seasoned Bread Crumbs
Simple Truth 2% Milk
365 Whole Foods 3 Cheese Blend
Francesca Rinaldi NSA Pasta Sauce

MARINARA SAUCE

Sodium Per Serving – 19mg Makes about 4 cups

This fresh sauce is rich and spicy and doesn't take long to cook. For a richer, more concentrated flavor, simmer over low heat for several hours or all day.

- 1½ tablespoons olive oil
- 1 onion, chopped
- 2 garlic cloves, finely minced
- 2 (16-oz) cans NSA diced tomatoes, undrained[1]
- 1 (6-oz) can NSA tomato paste[1]
- ¼ cup red wine
- 1 teaspoon dried oregano
- ½ teaspoon dried basil
- ¼ teaspoon garlic powder
- ⅛ teaspoon ground black pepper
- ½ teaspoon salt substitute (optional)
- 2 bay leaves

1. Heat oil in a skillet over medium-high heat; cook onions, stirring frequently, until they are translucent, about 3 to 4 minutes. Add garlic and cook, stirring constantly, until you smell the garlic, 1 to 2 minutes.
2. Stir in diced tomatoes, tomato paste, wine, oregano, bay leaves, and pepper. Decrease heat to medium-low and simmer 15 to 30 minutes (the less the sauce cooks, the fresher it tastes). *NOTE:* For a more concentrated flavor, cover and simmer over low heat for several hours or all day.

NUTRITIONAL INFO PER SERVING: Calories 106, Fat 4g (Saturated Fat 1g), Cholesterol 0mg, Carbohydrates 10g (Fiber 3g, Sugar 5g), Sodium 19mg

Recipe Notes

1 – Several manufacturers make NSA tomato products with 50mg or less sodium per ½ cup serving. Visit *LowSaltFoods.com* for a current list of LS tomato products.

TOTAL SODIUM AND FAT BY INGREDIENT

Sodium:
- 1 onion - 4mg
- 2 garlic cloves - 1mg
- 32 oz NSA diced tomatoes - 105mg
- ¼ c red wine - 3mg

Fat (Sat Fat):
- 1½ T olive oil - 21g (3g)

Brands used/alternatives:
- *Simple Truth Organic* NSA Diced Tomatoes
- *Bionaturae* NSA Tomato Paste

Creamy Mushroom Pasta

Sodium Per Serving – 28mg   Serves 4-6

This delicious pasta goes together quickly and uses ingredients you usually have on hand.

- **1 tablespoon olive oil**
- **2 tablespoons unsalted butter or margarine**
- **1 pound mushrooms, sliced (about 6 cups)[1]**
- **2 shallots, chopped**
- **2 garlic cloves, minced**
- **¼ teaspoon garlic powder**
- **⅛ teaspoon ground black pepper**
- **¾ cup *Chicken Broth (pg 208)* or unsalted chicken broth**
- **1 teaspoon LS chicken bouillon**
- **1 cup fresh or frozen peas**
- **1 tablespoon fresh chopped thyme or 1 teaspoon dried**
- **½ cup lowfat sour cream**
- **8 oz linguine noodles, cooked[2]**

1. Heat oil and butter in a large skillet over medium heat; add mushrooms and shallots. Cook, stirring frequently, until onions are translucent, 3 to 5 minutes; add garlic, garlic powder, and pepper. Cook, stirring constantly, until you smell the garlic, 1 to 2 minutes.
2. Stir in chicken broth, bouillon, peas, and thyme; bring to a boil. Decrease heat to medium-low and simmer, covered, until peas are tender, about 4 minutes.
3. Remove from heat and stir in sour cream; mix with linguine.

NUTRITIONAL INFO PER SERVING: Calories 402, Fat 13g (Sat Fat 6g), Chol 26mg, Carb 58g (Fiber 6g, Sugar 8g), Sodium 28mg (40mg with NSA chicken broth)

Recipe Notes

1 – Use any type or combination of mushrooms. For additional info on mushroom varieties, see *Mushrooms*, pg 250.
2 – When cooking pasta, it is not necessary to add salt to the water. If you want additional flavor, stir in 1–2 tsp LS chicken bouillon to the cooking water before adding the pasta.

TOTAL SODIUM AND FAT BY INGREDIENT

Sodium:
- 1 lb mushrooms - 7mg
- 2 shallots - 10mg
- 2 garlic cloves - 1mg
- ¾ c *Chicken Broth* - 15mg
  or NSA chicken broth - 64mg
- 1 t LS chicken bouillon - 5mg
- ½ c LF sour cream - 60mg
- 8 oz linguine - 14mg

Fat (Sat Fat):
- 1 T olive oil - 14g (2g)
- 2 T NSA butter - 23g (14g)
  or NSA margarine - 18g (7g)
- ¾ c *Chicken Broth* - 1g (0g)
  or NSA chicken broth - 0g (0g)
- ½ c LF sour cream - 10g (6g)
- 8 oz linguine - 3g (1g)

Brands used/alternatives:
Pacific Foods Organic Unsalted Chicken Stock
Herb Ox NSA Chicken Bouillon
Bird's Eye C&W Petite Peas
Daisy Light Sour Cream

Turkey Sausage & Edamame Pasta

Sodium Per Serving – 271mgServes 4

This recipe came about when trying to find more uses for edamame beans. The results were pleasantly surprising... hope you enjoy!

- **1 tablespoon olive oil**
- **2 sweet Italian turkey sausages (about 7 oz)**[1]
- **1 tablespoon unsalted butter or margarine**
- **1 small sweet onion, chopped**
- **8 oz sliced mushrooms (about 3 cups)**
- **1 tablespoon roasted garlic, minced**[2]
- **2 cups *Chicken Broth (pg 208)* or unsalted chicken broth**
- **1 tablespoon LS chicken bouillon**
- **¼ cup dry sherry**
- **1 cup broccoli florets**
- **1 cup edamame beans**[3]
- **1 (15-oz) can NSA diced tomatoes, drained**[4]
- **¼ teaspoon dried basil**
- **¼ teaspoon garlic or onion powder**
- **¼ teaspoon ground black pepper**
- **¼ teaspoon crushed red pepper flakes**
- **1 teaspoon sugar**
- **1 tablespoon lemon juice**
- **8 oz linguine or spaghetti noodles, broken in half**
- **Garnish with Parmesan cheese (optional)**

1. Heat oil in a large pot or skillet over medium heat; brown sausage on all sides. Remove and slice into small, bite-size pieces; return to skillet and add butter. Once melted, add onions and mushrooms; cook, stirring frequently, until onions are translucent, 4 to 5 minutes. Add garlic; cook, stirring frequently, until you smell the garlic, 1 to 2 minutes.
2. Stir in chicken broth and remaining ingredients, including noodles; bring to a boil. Decrease heat to medium-low; cover and simmer, stirring occasionally, until pasta is nearly cooked, about 15 minutes. Uncover and cook another 5 minutes to reduce liquid. Serve with Parmesan on top, if desired.

NUTRITIONAL INFO PER SERVING: Calories 491, Fat 15g (Sat Fat 4g), Chol 45mg, Carb 63g (Fiber 7g, Sugar 10g), Sodium 271mg (304mg with NSA chicken broth)

Recipe Notes

1 – Although sausage is high in sodium, a small amount will give you plenty of spicy flavor.

2 – I like to make extra roasted garlic (see *Garlic, Roasting, pg 249*) and keep it on hand to use in different dishes. You can also use fresh or bottled garlic, although I think the flavor of roasted garlic tastes better.

3 – Edamame (pronounced e-duh-MA-may) are soy beans that are low in sodium and high in vitamins. They have a sweet, nutty flavor and are found in the frozen food section of most supermarkets.

4 – Several manufacturers make NSA tomato products with 50mg or less sodium per ½ cup serving. Visit LowSaltFoods.com for a list of LS tomato products.

TOTAL SODIUM AND FAT BY INGREDIENT

Sodium:
- 2 Italian sausage - 900mg
- 1 sm sweet onion - 13mg
- 8 oz mushrooms - 4mg
- 1 T roasted garlic - 2mg
- 2 c *Chicken Broth* - 40mg
  or NSA chicken broth - 170mg
- 1 T LS chicken bouillon - 15mg
- ¼ c sherry - 5mg
- 1 c broccoli - 30mg
- 1 c edamame - 9mg
- 16 oz NSA tomatoes - 53mg
- 8 oz spaghetti - 14mg

Fat (Sat Fat):
- 1 T olive oil - 14g (2g)
- 2 Italian sausage - 20g (6g)
- 1 T NSA butter - 12g (7g)
  or NSA margarine - 9g (4g)
- 1 c edamame - 8g (1g)
- 2 c *Chicken Broth* - 1g (0g)
  or NSA chicken broth - 0g (0g)
- 8 oz spaghetti - 3g (1g)

Brands used/alternatives:
Jennie-O Sweet Italian Sausage
Pacific Foods Organic Unsalted Chicken Stock
Herb Ox NSA Chicken Bouillon
Simple Truth Organic NSA Diced Tomatoes

Quick Pesto

Sodium Per Serving – 34mg   Serves 4

This delicious pesto, with less oil than most, is very versatile. Toss with pasta, use on pizza, sandwiches, grilled fish, and steaks, or mix with cream cheese for a delicious dip or spread. This makes about 1 cup pesto and can be made up to two weeks ahead of time (keep in a covered container in the refrigerator).

- ¼ cup chopped fresh basil
- ¼ cup chopped fresh Italian parsley
- ¼ cup unsalted pine nuts, walnuts, or almonds
- ¼ cup Parmesan cheese, freshly grated
- 2 garlic cloves, smashed and coarsely chopped
- ¼ teaspoon garlic powder
- ¼ teaspoon ground black pepper
- ¼ cup olive oil

1. Place basil, parsley, pine nuts, Parmesan, garlic, garlic powder, and pepper in a blender or food processor. With machine running, gradually add oil; process until a smooth paste. Mix with warm pasta noodles and serve.

NUTRITIONAL INFO PER SERVING: Calories 188, Fat 20g (Saturated Fat 3g), Cholesterol 4mg, Carbohydrates 3g (Fiber 1g, Sugar 0g), Sodium 34mg

---

VARIATION
Sun-Dried Tomato Pesto

1. Add 1½ cups oil-packed sun-dried tomatoes, increase the Parmesan cheese to ½ cup and the garlic to 3 cloves. Add to the ingredients in the blender or food processor; proceed as directed. Makes about 2 cups.

NUTRITIONAL INFO PER SERVING: Calories 526, Fat 27g (Sat Fat 5g), Chol 10mg, Carb 22g (Fiber 2g, Sugar 12g), Sodium 102mg

---

TOTAL SODIUM AND FAT BY INGREDIENT

Sodium:
- ¼ c parsley - 8mg
- ¼ c pine nuts - 40mg
- ¼ c Parmesan - 120mg
- 2 garlic cloves - 1mg

Fat (Sat Fat):
- ¼ c pine nuts - 34g (5g)
- ¼ c Parmesan - 8g (4g)
- ¼ c olive oil - 56g (8g)

Brands used/alternatives:
365 Whole Foods 3 Cheese Blend

Linguine with Clam Sauce

Sodium Per Serving – 122mg Serves 6

Many clam sauce recipes use bottled clam juice, which is high in sodium (240mg per ¼ cup). This tasty dish lowers the sodium by using the juice from canned clams. Adding a few fresh clams on top takes this from everyday faire to an elegant dinner entrée.

- 1 tablespoon olive oil
- 1 tablespoon unsalted butter or margarine
- 2 shallots, chopped
- 4 garlic cloves, finely minced
- 2 (10-oz) can baby clams, drained, reserve liquid from 1 can
- ½ cup chopped Italian parsley[1]
- ½ cup half-and-half or light cream
- ¼ cup white wine
- ½ teaspoon garlic powder
- ¼ teaspoon ground black pepper
- ¼ teaspoon crushed red pepper flakes[2]
- 1 (16-oz) linguine, freshly cooked[3]
- ¼ cup Parmesan cheese, freshly grated

1. Heat oil and butter in a large skillet over medium heat; add shallots. Cook, stirring frequently, until shallots soften, 2 to 3 minutes; add garlic and continue stirring until you smell the garlic, 1 to 2 minutes.
2. Stir in reserved clam juice, parsley, half-and-half, wine, garlic powder, black pepper, and red pepper flakes. Decrease heat to medium-low and simmer until liquid has thickened to a thin sauce consistency, 10 to 12 minutes. *NOTE: This is the final consistency of the sauce, if it is still too thin, continue to cook until the desired consistency.*
3. Stir in clams and heat through; pour over cooked linguine and toss well. *NOTE: Do not hurry this process, as you want the linguine to absorb as much of the clam sauce as possible. Add more ground black pepper, if desired, and serve with Parmesan cheese.*

NUTRITIONAL INFO PER SERVING: Calories 353, Fat 9g (Sat Fat 4g), Chol 68mg, Carb 49g (Fiber 3g, Sugar 4g), Sodium 122mg

Recipe Notes
1 – For variety, substitute fresh basil instead of the parsley.
2 – Add more pepper flakes for a hotter, spicier flavor.
3 – If linguine is slightly undercooked it will absorb more of the clam sauce.

TOTAL SODIUM AND FAT BY INGREDIENT
Sodium:
- 2 shallots - 10mg
- 4 garlic cloves - 2mg
- 20 oz clams - 520mg
- ½ c parsley - 16mg
- ½ c half-and-half - 40mg or light cream - 48mg
- ¼ c white wine - 3mg
- 12 oz linguine - 20mg
- ¼ c Parmesan - 120mg

Fat (Sat Fat):
- 1 T olive oil - 14g (2g)
- 1 T NSA butter - 12g (7g) or margarine - 9g (4g)
- 20 oz clams - 4g (0g)
- ½ c half-and-half - 14g (8g) or light cream - 24g (16g)
- 16 oz linguine - 5g (1g)
- ¼ c Parmesan - 8g (4g)

Brands used/alternatives:
Geisha Whole Baby Clams
Organic Valley Half & Half
365 Whole Foods 3 Cheese Blend

Lasagna with a Cinnamon Twist

Sodium Per Serving – 260mg   Serves 6

This lasagna is different than most with its unique cinnamon flavor. It goes together quickly if you use premade pasta sauce.

- **Marinara Sauce (pg 133)** or 1 (24-oz) LS pasta sauce, divided[1]
- 9 lasagna noodles, cooked per package directions
- 16 oz lowfat ricotta cheese
- 8 oz shredded Swiss cheese (about 3 cups)
- 2 eggs, beaten[2]
- ¼ cup chopped walnuts
- 2 oz sliced ripe olives, drained (optional)[3]
- 1 tablespoon cinnamon powder
- 1 tablespoon sugar
- 4 oz fresh mozzarella, sliced, chopped, or grated[4]
- 2 oz Parmesan cheese, freshly grated (about ¼ cup)

1. Preheat oven to 350°F (180°C).
2. Spread ½ cup spaghetti sauce in bottom of a large rectangular baking dish. Place 3 lasagna noodles on top of the sauce, covering the bottom of the dish.
3. In a large bowl, mix together ricotta, Swiss cheese, eggs, walnuts, olives, cinnamon, sugar, and ½ cup spaghetti sauce; spread half the cheese mixture over the lasagne noodles.
4. Top with 1½ cups pasta sauce. Layer with 3 more lasagna noodles, spread remaining cheese mixture and pasta sauce on top; cover with the last 3 noodles.
5. Top with mozzarella and Parmesan cheeses. Cover with aluminum foil and bake in a preheated oven for 1 hour. Remove and let sit for at least 10 minutes to let it set up before serving.

NUTRITIONAL INFO PER SERVING: Calories 629, Fat 33g (Sat Fat 15g), Chol 149mg, Carb 52g (Fiber 7g, Sugar 16g), Sodium 260mg (274mg with LS pasta sauce)

VARIATION
Vegetable Lasagna
1. Follow steps 1-3 above. Add 2–3 cups sliced or chopped vegetables, such as mushrooms, broccoli, and zucchini, to the Marinara Sauce. Proceed with steps 4 and 5.

NUTRITIONAL INFO PER SERVING: Calories 643, Fat 33g (Sat Fat 15g), Chol 149mg, Carb 53g (Fiber 7g, Sugar 17g), Sodium 265mg (279mg with LS pasta sauce)

Recipe Notes
1 – There are many LS pasta sauces available, choose varieties with less than 250mg per ½ cup serving. Visit *LowSaltFoods.com* for a current list of LS brands.
2 – To keep fat to a minimum, use an egg substitute. See *Eggs and Egg Substitutes*, pg 23, for a comparison of fat and sodium in eggs and egg substitutes.
3 – Omitting the olives reduces the sodium per serving to 233mg.
4 – Fresh mozzarella usually comes packaged in water and is low in sodium (85mg per oz). Read labels carefully, as some brands are packaged in brine, which increases the sodium.

TOTAL SODIUM AND FAT BY INGREDIENT
Sodium:
- 3 c *Marinara Sauce* - 113mg
  or LS pasta sauce - 200mg
- 9 lasagna noodles - 5mg
- 1 lb LF ricotta - 400mg
- 8 oz NSA Swiss - 400mg
- 2 eggs - 140mg
- 2 oz ripe olives - 160mg
- ¼ c walnuts - 1mg
- 1 T cinnamon - 1mg
- 4 oz fresh mozzarella - 220mg
- 2 oz Parmesan - 120mg

Fat (Sat Fat):
- 4½ c *Marinara Sauce* - 21g (3g)
  or LS pasta sauce - 5g (0g)
- 9 lasagna noodles - 5g (1g)
- 1 lb LF ricotta - 28g (16g)
- 8 oz NSA Swiss - 72g (40g)
- 2 eggs - 10g (3g)
- ¼ c walnuts - 20g (2g)
- 2 oz ripe olives - 12g (4g)
- 4 oz mozzarella - 24g (16g)
- 2 oz Parmesan - 8g (4g)

Brands used/alternatives:
Francesca Rinaldi NSA Pasta Sauce
Kroger Part-Skim Ricotta
Great Value Swiss Cheese
Mario LS Black Olives
Whole Foods Fresh Mozzarella
365 Whole Foods 3 Cheese Blend

CHICKEN, SPINACH & SUN-DRIED TOMATO PIZZA

Sodium Per Serving – 230mg   Makes 4 individual pizzas

An easy, yummy pizza that uses leftover chicken.

- **½ recipe Quick Herbal Flatbread & Pizza Dough (pg 195) or 4 LS flatbreads[1]**
- **Sun-Dried Tomato Pesto (pg 136) or prepared pesto[2]**
- **12–16 spinach leaves[3]**
- **8-oz cooked chicken breasts, cubed**
- **½ small sweet onion, thinly sliced[4]**
- **4 oz fresh mozzarella, chopped or sliced[5]**

1. Preheat oven to 350ºF (180ºC). Arrange oven rack to lowest level.
2. Place 2 flatbreads on a pizza stone or baking sheet; spread with pesto. Layer with spinach, chicken, onion, and mozzarella. Repeat with remaining 2 flatbreads.
3. Bake pizza in a preheated oven on the lowest rack for 20 minutes, or until crust is lightly browned and cheese has melted.

NUTRITIONAL INFO PER SERVING: Calories 982, Fat 42g (Sat Fat 13g), Chol 97mg, Carb 79g (Fiber 4g, Sugar 15g), Sodium 230mg (323mg with LS flatbread)

PESTO, TOMATO & FRESH MOZZARELLA PIZZA

Sodium Per Serving – 128mg   Makes 4 individual pizzas

Two slices of a 12-inch cheese pizza averages 500mg sodium or more. This lower-salt favorite is especially good in the summer when there is an abundance of fresh basil and tomatoes.

- **½ recipe Quick Herbal Flatbread & Pizza Dough (pg 195) or 4 LS flatbreads[1]**
- **Quick Pesto (pg 136) or prepared pesto[2]**
- **2 garlic cloves, minced**
- **6 basil leaves, thinly sliced**
- **2 tomatoes, sliced**
- **½ cup pine nuts**
- **4 oz fresh mozzarella, chopped or sliced[5]**

1. Preheat oven to 350ºF (180ºC). Arrange oven rack to lowest level.
2. Place 2 flatbreads on a pizza stone or baking sheet; spread with pesto. Sprinkle with garlic and basil; place tomato slices on top and sprinkle with pine nuts and mozzarella. Repeat with remaining flatbreads. *NOTE: For a fresher tomato taste, add the tomatoes after the pizza has baked.*
3. Bake pizza in a preheated oven on the lowest rack for 20 minutes, or until crust is lightly browned and cheese has melted.

NUTRITIONAL INFO PER PIZZA: Calories 724, Fat 48g (Sat Fat 11g), Chol 59mg, Carb 64g (Fiber 5g, Sugar 4g), Sodium 128mg (231mg with LS flatbread)

TOTAL SODIUM AND FAT BY INGREDIENT

CHICKEN SPINACH PIZZA
Sodium:
- ½ Quick Herbal Flatbread - 109mg or 4 flatbreads - 920mg
- Tomato Pesto - 570mg
- 12 spinach leaves - 95mg
- 2 chicken breasts - 150mg
- ½ sm sweet onion - 7mg
- 4 oz fresh mozzarella - 180mg

Fat (Sat Fat):
- ½ Quick Flatbread - 32g (10g) or 4 flatbreads - 2g (0g)
- Tomato Pesto - 102g (21g)
- 2 chicken breasts - 2g (0g)
- 4 oz mozzarella - 20g (15g)

Brands used/alternatives:
Tyson All Natural Chicken Breast
Whole Foods Fresh Mozzarella
Tumaro's Ancient Grain Wraps

PESTO TOMATO PIZZA
Sodium:
- ½ Quick Herbal Flatbread - 109mg or 4 flatbreads - 920mg
- Quick Pesto - 169mg
- 2 garlic cloves - 1mg
- 2 tomatoes - 12mg
- 4 oz fresh mozzarella - 220mg

Fat (Sat Fat):
- ½ Quick Flatbread - 32g (10g) or 4 flatbreads - 8g (0g)
- Quick Pesto - 96g (17g)
- 2 tomatoes - 1g (0g)
- ½ c pine nuts - 39g (3g)
- 4 oz mozzarella - 24g (16g)

Brands used/alternatives:
Whole Foods Fresh Mozzarella
Tumaro's Ancient Grain Wraps

Recipe Notes

1 – Substitute LS pita bread, lavash, or flour tortillas/wraps.
2 – Prepared pesto averages over 700mg sodium per ¼ cup, but there are a few lower salt varieties (visit *LowSaltFoods.com* for brands).
3 – For variety, use fresh basil leaves instead of spinach; and add some chopped garlic... yum!
4 – Caramelized onions are also delicious (see *Caramelizing Onions*, pg 245).
5 – Fresh mozzarella usually comes packaged in water and is low in sodium (85mg per oz). Read labels carefully, as some brands are packaged in brine, which increases the sodium.

ASIAN ENTRÉES

Moo Goo Gai Pan

Sodium Per Serving – 120mgServes 4

While living in Hawaii, I picked up several delicious recipes, this is one of my favorites. Moo Goo Gai Pan is nothing more than chicken and sliced mushrooms. This version also includes carrots, snow peas, and water chestnuts. While many Asian dishes are high in sodium, because of MSG (monosodium glutamate) and soy sauce, this lower-salt dish uses lite soy sauce and no MSG.

- **8-oz boneless, skinless chicken breasts, sliced in thin strips**
- **1½ tablespoons lite soy sauce[1]**
- **2 tablespoons dry sherry or natural rice wine vinegar[2]**
- **1 tablespoon cornstarch**
- **1 tablespoon olive oil**
- **8 oz sliced mushrooms (about 3 cups)**
- **2 carrots, sliced on the diagonal**
- **2–3 green onions, chopped**
- **3 garlic cloves, minced**
- **2 cups snow peas**
- **½ cup *Chicken Broth (pg 208)* or unsalted chicken broth**
- **½ teaspoon LS chicken bouillon**
- **2 tablespoons sugar**
- **1 (8-oz) can sliced water chestnuts, drained**
- **½ cup bamboo shoots[3]**
- **4 cups cooked rice**

1. Mix together soy sauce, sherry, cornstarch, and oil; add chicken strips and marinate for 20 minutes.
2. In a large skillet or pot over medium-high heat; add chicken and marinade. Cook, stirring frequently, until chicken begins to brown, 2 to 3 minutes. Stir in mushrooms, and carrots; cook stirring frequently, until mushrooms soften, about 3 minutes. Add green onions and garlic; cook, stirring constantly, until you smell the garlic, about 1 minute.
3. Stir in peas, chicken broth, bouillon, sugar, water chestnuts, and bamboo shoots; decrease heat to medium-low. Cook, stirring occasionally, until carrots are done, about 5 minutes; serve over rice.

NUTRITIONAL INFO PER SERVING: Calories 399, Fat 6g (Sat Fat 1g), Chol 33mg, Carb 58g (Fiber 7g, Sugar 12g), Sodium 120mg (128mg with NSA chicken broth)

Recipe Notes

1 – Soy sauce has 878mg sodium in a tbsp; several brands have less than 400mg. Visit *LowSaltFoods.com* for a current LS brand names.

2 – If using rice wine vinegar, be aware that some brands have added sodium. Those that say "natural" do not.

3 – Most bamboo shoots don't have added salt, but check the label, as a few brands do.

TOTAL SODIUM AND FAT BY INGREDIENT

Sodium:
- 8 oz chicken breast - 80mg
- 1½ T lite soy sauce - 270mg
- 2 T sherry - 3mg
- 1 T cornstarch - 1mg
- 8 oz mushrooms - 11mg
- 2 carrots - 84mg
- 2 green onions - 5mg
- 3 garlic cloves - 2mg
- 2 c snow peas - 8mg
- ½ c *Chicken Broth* - 10mg
  or NSA chicken broth - 65mg
- ½ t LS chicken bouillon - 3mg
- ½ c NSA bamboo shoots - 5mg

Fat (Sat Fat):
- 8 oz chicken breast - 8g (3g)
- 1 T olive oil - 14g (2g)
- 8 oz mushrooms - 1g (0g)

Brands used/alternatives:
Tyson All Natural Chicken Breast
Mrs Taste Less Sodium Soy Sauce
Pacific Foods Organic Unsalted Chicken Stock
Herb Ox NSA Chicken Bouillon

SWEET & SOUR PORK

Sodium Per Serving – 113mg Serves 4

This is a simple, yet delicious preparation of this traditional Chinese dish. Serve with steamed rice.

- **1 pound boneless pork loin, cut into 1-inch cubes**[1]
- **2 tablespoons all-purpose flour**
- **1 tablespoon cornstarch**
- **¼ teaspoon onion powder**
- **2 tablespoons olive oil**
- **2 celery stalks, sliced horizontally into ½ inch pieces**
- **1 red bell pepper, cut into thin strips**
- **½ sweet onion, thinly sliced**
- **1 (8-oz) can pineapple tidbits in its own juice**[2]
- **⅓ cup NSA ketchup**
- **1 tablespoon prepared mustard**
- **1 teaspoon cider vinegar**
- **½ teaspoon Worcestershire sauce**

1. Place pork, flour, cornstarch, and onion powder in a paper bag and shake until all pieces are coated.
2. Heat oil in a large skillet over medium-high heat; add pork. Fry, turning frequently, until brown and crispy on all sides, 8 to 10 minutes. Remove pork and keep warm.
3. In same skillet, add celery, bell pepper, onion, and pineapple (including juice); decrease heat to medium and cook, stirring frequently, until vegetables begin to soften, about 5 minutes.
4. Stir in ketchup, mustard, vinegar, and Worcestershire; cook, stirring frequently, for 2 minutes. Mix in pork and heat through; serve with rice.

NUTRITIONAL INFO PER SERVING: Calories 341, Fat 12g (Sat Fat 2g), Chol 83mg, Carb 21g (Fiber 5g, Sugar 13g), Sodium 113mg

Recipe Notes

1 – Many pork loins are packaged in brine; look for tenderloins packaged without brine.
2 – Tidbits are a good size for this dish. If using larger chunks, cut them in half.

TOTAL SODIUM AND FAT BY INGREDIENT

Sodium:
1 lb pork loin - 256mg
1 T cornstarch - 1mg
2 T olive oil - 1 mg
2 celery stalks - 64mg
1 bell pepper - 4mg
½ sweet onion - 13mg
⅓ c NSA ketchup - 27mg
1 T mustard - 75mg
½ t Worcestershire - 10mg

Fat (Sat Fat):
1 lb pork loin - 18g (6g)
2 T olive oil - 28g (4g)

Brands used/alternatives:
Dole No Sugar Pineapple Tidbits
Gold's LS New York Deli Mustard
Robbie's Worcestershire Sauce

HISPANIC DISHES

Easy Fiesta Casserole

Sodium Per Serving – 242mg   Serves 6

This yummy casserole is made with ingredients I always have on hand.

- ½ pound ground lean turkey or beef
- ½ sweet onion, chopped
- 1 (15-oz) NSA black or kidney beans, rinsed and drained[1]
- 1 cup LS tomato-based salsa[2]
- ¼ teaspoon NSA chili powder[3]
- ¼ teaspoon garlic powder
- ¼ teaspoon NSA taco or spicy seasoning[4]
- ⅛ teaspoon ground cumin
- ⅛ teaspoon dried oregano[5]
- ⅛ teaspoon ground black pepper
- 2 cups crushed unsalted tortilla chips
- 1 cup lowfat sour cream
- 2 tablespoons (about 9 small) chopped ripe olives (optional)[6]
- 1 (4-oz) can diced green chiles
- 1 (15-oz) can NSA whole corn, drained
- 1–2 tomatoes, chopped
- 4 oz Swiss cheese, shredded (about 1 cup)
- 2 oz Cheddar cheese, shredded (about ½ cup)

1. Preheat oven to 350°F (180°C). Coat a large rectangular baking dish with nonstick cooking spray.
2. In a skillet over medium heat; cook meat 4 to 5 minutes, stirring frequently and breaking up into small chunks. Add onion, beans, salsa, chili powder, garlic powder, taco seasoning, cumin, oregano, and black pepper; reduce heat to medium-low and cover. Cook, stirring occasionally, until meat is no longer pink, 5 to 10 minutes.
3. Spread crushed tortilla chips over bottom of prepared baking dish, layer turkey mixture on top, followed by sour cream, olives, green chiles, corn, tomatoes, and shredded cheeses. Cover with foil and bake for 20 to 30 minutes, until cheese is bubbly and lightly browned. Serve with additional salsa.

NUTRITIONAL INFO PER SERVING: Calories 433, Fat 18g (Sat Fat 8g), Chol 57mg, Carb 39g (Fiber 10g, Sugar 9g), Sodium 242mg

Recipe Notes

1 – See *Canned Beans*, pg 243, for info on NSA beans.

2 – Most bottled tomato salsas average 256mg sodium per 2 tbsp, bean and corn salsa has 180mg, and fresh salsa, 142mg. Look for one of many delicious LS varieties with less than 80mg (visit *LowSaltFoods.com*, for LS products).

3 – Surprisingly, chili powder contains sodium (26mg per teaspoon). Look for brands without salt listed in the ingredients.

4 – You can use one of several unsalted spicy seasonings used for Cajun or barbecue rubs. If your market has a Hispanic section, check the dried spices in bags for a no-salt taco seasoning.

5 – Look for Mexican oregano in the Hispanic section of the supermarket. It's flavor is stronger than regular oregano.

6 – Omitting the olives reduces the sodium to 229mg a serving.

TOTAL SODIUM AND FAT BY INGREDIENT

Sodium:
- ½ lb ground turkey - 140mg or ½ lb ground beef - 198mg
- ½ sweet onion - 13mg
- 15 oz NSA black beans - 18mg
- 1 c LS salsa - 320mg
- 1 c LF sour cream - 120mg
- 2 T ripe olives - 80mg
- 4 oz green chiles - 180mg
- 15 oz NSA corn - 35mg
- 1 tomato - 6mg
- 4 oz NSA Swiss cheese - 200mg
- 2 oz LF Cheddar cheese - 340mg

Fat (Sat Fat):
- 1 lb ground turkey - 3g (1g) or ½ lb ground beef - 9g (3g)
- 3 oz LS tortilla chips - 24g (4g)
- 1 c LF sour cream - 20g (12g)
- 2 T ripe olives - 3g (0g)
- 15 oz NSA corn - 5g (0g)
- 4 oz NSA Swiss - 36g (20g)
- 2 oz Cheddar - 18g (12g)

Brands used/alternatives:
- *Jennie-O* 99% Lean Ground Turkey
- *Kuner's* NSA Black Beans
- *Frog Ranch* Salsa
- *Xochitl* NS Corn Chips
- *Daisy* Light Sour Cream
- *Mario* LS Black Olives
- *La Preferida* Organic Diced Green Chiles
- *Libby's Naturals* NSA Whole Kernel Sweet Corn
- *Great Value* Swiss Cheese
- *Kraft* Shredded Cheddar Cheese

Quick Fajitas

Sodium Per Serving – 126mg | Serves 4

This is another recipe that has been passed on to me from sources unknown. We particularly like the combination of the peppers and cumin with the lime and orange juices.

- 8 oz flank steak or skinless, boneless chicken breasts, sliced into thin strips[1]
- 1 tablespoon olive oil
- 1 red bell pepper, sliced
- 1 green bell pepper, sliced
- ½ sweet onion, sliced
- 1 teaspoon NSA chili powder[2]
- 1 teaspoon ground cumin
- ½ teaspoon dried oregano
- ¼ teaspoon garlic powder
- ¼ teaspoon ground black pepper
- 3 tablespoons lime juice
- 2 tablespoons orange juice
- 4 (10 or 12-inch) LS whole wheat tortillas or 8 (6 or 7-inch) corn tortillas[3]

Optional Condiments:
- **Shredded Swiss and lowfat Cheddar cheese**
- **Chopped fresh cilantro**
- **Chopped tomatoes**
- **Shredded lettuce**
- **LS salsa**[4]

1. Heat oil in a skillet over medium heat; add beef. Cook, stirring frequently, until no longer pink, about 2 minutes; add red and green peppers and onions. Cook, stirring frequently, until onions and peppers begin to soften, 3 to 4 minutes. Stir in chili powder, cumin, oregano, garlic powder, pepper, lime juice, and orange juice; cook, stirring frequently, for 2 minutes.
2. Fill warmed tortillas with chicken mixture; add optional condiments as desired.

NUTRITIONAL INFO PER BEEF FAJITA (without condiments): Calories 325, Fat 12g (Saturated Fat 4g), Cholesterol 45mg, Carbohydrates 34g (Fiber 5g, Sugar 8g), Sodium 126mg (51mg with corn tortillas)

NUTRITIONAL INFO PER CHICKEN FAJITA (without condiments): Calories 272, Fat 8g (Saturated Fat 2g), Cholesterol 40mg, Carbohydrates 34g (Fiber 5g, Sugar 8g), Sodium 131mg (56mg with corn tortillas)

Recipe Notes

1 – These are best made with beef, but chicken is a close second.

2 – Surprisingly, chili powder contains sodium (26mg per teaspoon). Look for brands without salt listed in the ingredients.

3 – Most 10-inch flour tortillas average 364mg sodium, but a few manufacturers, offer LS ones (visit *LowSaltFoods.com* for brands). Corn tortillas average 11mg sodium per tortilla (shelf-stable shells have 80mg).

4 – Most bottled tomato salsas average 256mg sodium per 2 tbsp, bean and corn salsa has 180mg, and fresh salsa, 142mg. Look for one of many delicious LS varieties with less than 80mg (visit *LowSaltFoods. com*, for LS products).

TOTAL SODIUM AND FAT BY INGREDIENT

Sodium:
- 8 oz lean beef - 128mg or chicken breast - 102mg
- 1 red bell pepper - 10mg
- 1 green bell pepper - 7mg
- ½ sweet onion - 13mg
- 1 t ground cumin - 4mg
- 4 LS flour tortillas - 340mg or 8 corn tortillas - 40mg

Fat (Sat Fat):
- 8 oz lean beef - 19g (8g) or chicken breast - 2g (0g)
- 1 red bell pepper - 1g (0g)
- 1 T olive oil - 14g (2g)
- 4 LS flour tortillas - 14g (6g) or 8 corn tortillas - 6g (0g)

Brands used/alternatives:
La Banderita LS Flour Tortillas

Chicken Burritos with Tomatillo Sauce

Sodium Per Serving – 193mg Serves 6

These delicious burritos, covered in a yummy tomatillo sauce, are ready in less than 30 minutes.

- ¼ cup dry sherry
- 2 boneless, skinless chicken breasts (about 8 oz), cooked and cut into thin strips[1]
- 1 cup mixed vegetables, fresh or frozen chopped (such as zucchini, broccoli, mushrooms, corn, and carrots)
- 1 cup NSA black or kidney beans
- 6 (10 to 12-inch) LS flour tortillas[2]
- *Tomatillo Sauce (pg 145)*
- 3 oz shredded Swiss cheese (about ¾ cup)
- 1 oz shredded Cheddar cheese (about ¼ cup)

1. Combine sherry, chicken, veggies, and beans in a saucepan over medium heat; cover and cook, stirring occasionally, until veggies are tender, about 5 minutes.
2. Equally divide mixture and place in tortillas; roll up and pour *Tomatillo Sauce* over burritos. Top with cheese and serve.

NUTRITIONAL INFO PER SERVING: Calories 393, Fat 14g (Sat Fat 6g), Chol 40mg, Carb 45g (Fiber 6g, Sugar 12g), Sodium 193mg

Recipe Notes

1 – Use leftover chicken or cook by any preferred method, such as poached mix chicken with ¼ cup salsa and cook in 1 tablespoon olive oil.

2 – Most 10-inch flour tortillas average 335mg sodium, but a few manufacturers, offer LS ones (visit LowSaltFoods.com for a list of LS brands).

TOTAL SODIUM AND FAT BY INGREDIENT

Sodium:
- ¼ c sherry - 5mg
- 8 oz chicken breast - 80mg
- 1 c mixed veggies - 20mg
- 1 c NSA black beans - 9mg
- 6 LS flour tortillas - 510mg
- Tomatillo Sauce - 213mg
- 3 oz Swiss cheese - 150mg
- 1 oz Cheddar cheese - 170mg

Fat (Sat Fat):
- 8 oz chicken breast - 8g (3g)
- 1 c mixed veggies - 1g (0g)
- 6 LS flour tortillas - 21g (9g)
- Tomatillo Sauce - 15g (2g)
- 3 oz Swiss - 27g (15g)
- 1 oz Cheddar - 10g (5g)

Brands used/alternatives:
- *Tyson All Natural* Chicken Breast
- *Birds Eye C&W* Ultimate Petite Mixed Vegetables
- *Kuner's* NSA Black Beans
- *La Banderita* LS Flour Tortillas
- *Great Value* Swiss Cheese
- *Kraft* Cheddar Cheese

Tomatillo Sauce

Sodium Per Serving – 53mg Serves 4

This is a mild sauce, if you omit the hot peppers, but if you like it hot, you can add degrees of heat by the number and type of peppers used and whether or not you include the seeds. Ready in less than 30 minutes, it is also good with grilled halibut or other firm fish. Canned tomatillos are found in the Hispanic section (fresh ones in the produce section) of many supermarkets.

- 1 tablespoon olive oil
- 1 small onion, chopped (about ½ cup)
- 2 garlic cloves, minced
- 1 (4-oz) can diced green chiles
- 1 (28-oz) can crushed tomatillos, drained[1]
- 1 cup *Chicken Broth (pg 208)* or unsalted chicken broth
- 2 tablespoons fresh lime juice
- 1 teaspoon LS chicken bouillon
- 1 teaspoon ground cumin
- 1 teaspoon dried oregano[2]
- 1 teaspoon sugar
- 2 jalapeño or serrano peppers (optional)[3]
- ¼ cup chopped fresh cilantro

1. Heat oil in a skillet over medium-high heat; add onions. Cook, stirring frequently, until onions are soft, 3 to 4 minutes; add garlic. Cook, stirring constantly, until you smell the garlic, 1 to 2 minutes; stir in green chiles, tomatillos, chicken broth, lime juice, bouillon, cumin, oregano, sugar, and jalapeños. Decrease heat to low and simmer, uncovered, until the tomatillos are mushy, about 25 minutes.
2. Remove sauce from heat and stir in cilantro; let cool slightly. Pour into a blender or food processor and pulse until smooth; return to saucepan and reheat. Serve over burritos, enchiladas, or grilled fish. Top with more cilantro, if desired.

NUTRITIONAL INFO PER SERVING: Calories 124, Fat 4g (Saturated Fat 1g), Cholesterol 1mg, Carbohydrates 19g (Fiber 1g, Sugar 15g), Sodium 53mg (70 with NSA chicken broth)

Recipe Notes

1 – Canned crushed tomatillos are hard to find. Generally, crushed tomatoes don't have added salt, but whole canned tomatillos are loaded with sodium (800mg per ½ cup). Use fresh tomatillos (24 tomatillos or about 4 cups is equivalent to 28 oz of canned), see *Tomatillos*, pg 254, for cooking instructions.

2 – Mexican oregano is stronger and stronger than other dried oregano and is available in the Hispanic foods section of many supermarkets.

3 – On a scale of 1 to 5, jalapeños are a 3, with most of the heat contained in the seeds and veins. See *Chile Peppers*, pg 251, for a listing of peppers and the amount of heat in each.

CAUTION: When handling hot chiles, wear rubber gloves, as the oils of the pepper are very potent. A piece of plastic wrap or a sandwich bag also works to hold the pepper. If you touch the pepper with your bare fingers, wash your hands thoroughly and be sure to keep your fingers away from your eyes or you'll be in sheer agony!

TOTAL SODIUM AND FAT BY INGREDIENT

Sodium:
- 1 sm onion - 2mg
- 2 garlic cloves - 1mg
- 4 oz green chiles - 180mg
- 1 c *Chicken Broth* - 20mg
  or NSA chicken broth - 35mg
- 1 t LS chicken bouillon - 5mg
- 1 t cumin - 4mg
- ¼ c cilantro - 2mg

Fat (Sat Fat):
- 1 T olive oil - 14g (2g)

Brands used/alternatives:
La Preferida Organic Diced Green Chiles
Las Palmas Crushed Tomatillos
Pacific Foods Organic Unsalted Chicken Stock
Herb Ox NSA Chicken Bouillon

Beef Quesadillas

Sodium Per Serving – 278mg Serves 4

Quesadillas are like Mexican pizzas—put just about anything you want between two corn or flour tortillas and fry. Serve with lettuce, tomato, Guacamole (pg 28), sour cream, and salsa, if desired.

- **2 cups cooked beef, sliced, shredded, or cubed**[1]
- **½ small sweet onion, thinly sliced**
- **1–2 tomatoes, diced**
- **1 (4-oz) can diced green chiles (optional)**
- **2 tablespoons chopped ripe olives (optional)**
- **2 tablespoons chopped fresh cilantro**
- **4 oz shredded Swiss cheese (about 1 cup)**
- **2 oz shredded Cheddar cheese (about ½ cup)**
- **8 (6-inch) corn or LS flour tortillas**[2]
- **Vegetable or canola oil for frying (about ¼ cup)**
- **Toppings, such as lettuce, tomato, avocado (or guacamole), sour cream, jalapeños, and salsa**

1. Evenly divide beef and place on 4 tortillas; layer with onions, tomatoes, green chiles, olives, cilantro, and cheeses. Top with a tortilla, making a sandwich.
2. Heat oil in a skillet over medium-high heat; fry tortilla sandwich, carefully turning, until golden brown and crisp on both sides, about 3 minutes per side. Cut each quesadilla into quarters and serve with desired condiments.

NUTRITIONAL INFO PER SERVING (without toppings and oil for frying): Calories 568, Fat 35g (Sat Fat 10g), Chol 142mg, Carb 26g (Fiber 4g, Sugar 4g), Sodium 278mg

Recipe Notes

1 – Cooked chicken instead of the beef is also good in this dish.
2 – Most 10-inch flour tortillas average 364mg sodium, but a few manufacturers, offer LS varieties with less than 125mg (visit *LowSaltFoods.com* for brands). Corn tortillas average 11mg sodium per tortilla (shelf-stable shells have 80mg).

TOTAL SODIUM AND FAT BY INGREDIENT

Sodium:
- 2 c lean beef - 256mg
- ½ sweet onion - 7mg
- 1 tomato - 6mg
- 4 oz green chiles - 180mg
- 2 T ripe olives - 80mg
- 2 T cilantro - 1mg
- 8 corn tortillas - 40mg
  or 4 LS flour tortillas - 340mg
- 4 oz Swiss cheese - 20mg
- 2 oz cheddar cheese - 340mg

Fat (Sat Fat):
- 2 c lean beef - 64g (6g)
- 2 T ripe olives - 3g (0g)
- 8 corn tortillas - 6g (0g
  or 4 LS flour tortillas - 14g (6g)
- 4 oz Swiss - 36g (20g)
- 2 oz Cheddar - 18g (12g)
- 1 T olive oil - 14g (2g)

Brands used/alternatives:
- *La Preferida* Organic Diced Green Chiles
- *Mario* LS Black Olives
- *Great Value* Swiss Cheese
- *Kraft* Cheddar Cheese

Stuffed Quesadillas

Sodium Per Serving – 99mg Serves 6

This is one our most favorite put-together-quickly meals. It takes about 15 minutes and is very yummy. Set out the condiments in bowls and let each person select the toppings of their choice.

- ¼ cup dry sherry[1]
- 1 medium red potato, cubed
- 1 cup fresh or frozen broccoli, chopped
- 1 cup fresh or frozen cauliflower, chopped
- 1 cup fresh or frozen mixed vegetables (such as carrots, mushrooms, and corn)
- 1 cup NSA black or kidney beans[2]
- 6 LS large flour tortillas[3]
- 2-4 tablespoons unsalted butter or margarine

Optional Toppings:
- **Chopped onion**
- **Chopped tomato**
- **Shredded lettuce**
- **Sliced avocado**
- **Shredded Swiss and/or Cheddar cheese**
- **Lowfat sour cream or plain yogurt**
- **LS salsa**
- **Chopped cilantro**

1. In a saucepan over medium heat, add sherry, potatoes, broccoli, cauliflower, mixed vegetables, and beans. Cook, covered, until potatoes are done, about 6 to 8 minutes. *NOTE: Do not let liquid boil dry, if necessary, add more sherry or water to keep vegetables from burning.*
2. Evenly divide vegetable mixture and place in the center of each tortilla, fold in half.
3. Melt 1-2 tablespoons butter in a skillet over medium heat; fry filled tortillas until golden brown on both sides, 2 to 3 minutes per side. Repeat with remaining tortillas; add more butter as needed.
4. Serve with optional toppings.

NUTRITIONAL INFO PER QUESADILLA (without toppings): Calories 267, Fat 8g (Saturated Fat 4g), Cholesterol 10mg, Carbohydrates 41g (Fiber 7g, Sugar 3g), Sodium 99mg

Recipe Notes

1 – You can substitute white wine, water, or chicken broth for the sherry, but the sherry flavored vegetables is what makes this dish special.

2 – Instead of beans, increase the amount of other vegetables by 1 cup.

3 – Most flour tortillas are high in sodium (364mg per 10-inch tortilla), however, several low-carb varieties have less than 125mg per tortilla (visit *LowSaltFoods.com* for current LS products).

TOTAL SODIUM AND FAT BY INGREDIENT

Sodium:
- ¼ c sherry - 5mg
- 1 red potato - 21mg
- 1 c broccoli - 30mg
- 1 c cauliflower - 20mg
- 1 c NSA black beans - 9mg
- 6 LS flour tortillas - 510mg

Fat (Sat Fat):
- 1 c mixed Veg - 1g (0g)
- 6 LS flour tortillas - 21g (9g)
- 2 T NSA butter - 23g (14g)
  or NSA margarine - 18g (7g)

Brands used/alternatives:
Birds Eye C&W Ultimate Southwest Blend
Kuner's NSA Black Beans
La Banderita LS Flour Tortillas

Yummy Turkey Tacos

Sodium Per Serving – 65mg   Serves 4

We have these turkey tacos as often as possible and the best part... they're ready in about 15 minutes.

- **1 tablespoon olive oil**
- **8 oz ground lean turkey breast**
- **¼ teaspoon NSA chili powder[1]**
- **¼ teaspoon NSA taco seasoning[2]**
- **¼ teaspoon garlic powder**
- **⅛ teaspoon cumin**
- **⅛ teaspoon ground black pepper**
- **¼ cup LS tomato-based salsa[3]**
- **8 (6-inch) corn tortillas or 4 (10-inch) LS flour tortillas[4]**
- **Vegetable or canola oil for frying (about ¼ cup)**

Optional Toppings:
- **Chopped tomatoes**
- **Sliced avocado, sliced**
- **Chopped sweet onion**
- **Shredded lettuce**
- **Shredded Swiss and/or Cheddar cheese[5]**
- **Chopped fresh cilantro**
- **LS salsa**

1. Heat oil in a skillet over medium heat; add turkey, chili powder, hot chili spices, garlic powder, cumin, and pepper. Brown meat, stirring frequently and breaking up any chunks, until no longer pink, about 5 minutes. Stir in salsa; decrease heat to low and keep warm while frying tortillas.
2. Heat vegetable oil in another skillet over medium high heat; place one tortilla in hot oil and fry until golden and slightly crisp, turn, fold in half, and continue to fry each side until slightly crisp. Remove and drain on paper towels; repeat with remaining tortillas. Fill with meat mixture and desired condiments.

NUTRITIONAL INFO PER SERVING (without optional toppings and oil for frying): Calories 197, Fat 6g (Saturated Fat 1g), Cholesterol 28mg, Carbohydrates 23g (Fiber 4g, Sugar 3g), Sodium 65mg (140mg with LS flour tortillas).

Recipe Notes

1 – Surprisingly, chili powder contains sodium (26mg per teaspoon). Look for brands without salt listed in the ingredients.

2 – Look for NSA taco seasoning, such as *Dash Salt-Free*. If not available, check the Hispanic section for NSA dried spices in bags.

3 – Most bottled tomato salsas average 256mg sodium per 2 tbsp, bean and corn salsa has 180mg, and fresh salsa, 142mg. Look for one of many delicious LS varieties with less than 80mg (visit *LowSaltFoods.com*, for LS products).

4 – Most 10-inch flour tortillas average 364mg sodium, but a few manufacturers, offer LS varieties with less than 125mg. Corn tortillas average 11mg sodium per tortilla (shelf-stable shells have 80mg).

5 – Cheddar averages about 185mg sodium an oz vs 65mg for Swiss. Mixing a little Cheddar with the Swiss adds flavor, while keeping salt to a minimum.

TOTAL SODIUM AND FAT BY INGREDIENT

Sodium:
- 8 oz ground turkey - 140mg
- ¼ c LS salsa - 80mg
- 8 corn tortillas - 40mg
- or 6 LS flour tortillas - 340mg

Fat (Sat Fat):
- 1 T olive oil - 14g (2g)
- 8 oz ground turkey - 3g (1g)
- 8 corn tortillas - 6g (0g)
- or 4 LS flour - 14g (6g)

Brands used/alternatives:
- *Jennie-O* 99% Lean Ground Turkey
- *Dash* Salt-Free Taco Seasoning
- *Frog Ranch* Salsa
- *La Banderita* LS Flour Tortillas

Grilled Fish Tacos

Sodium Per Serving – 150mg Makes 6 tacos

If you've never had fish tacos, you're in for a treat. Grill marinated fish, add fresh corn salsa, and you've got a delicious, but simple meal. Serve with a side of Quick Refried Beans (pg 169) and a tossed salad.

- **1 pound halibut, cut into bite-size pieces[1]**
- **2 tablespoons lime juice**
- **¼ cup dry white wine**
- **2 tablespoons olive oil, divided**
- **1½ cups *Fresh Corn Relish* (pg 210)**
- **12 corn or 6 LS flour tortillas, grilled[2]**
- **4 oz Swiss cheese, shredded (about 1 cup)[3]**
- **2 oz Cheddar cheese, shredded (about ½ cup)[3]**
- **¼ cup chopped fresh cilantro**

1. Combine lime juice, wine, and 2 tablespoons olive oil; pour over halibut and marinate for 30 minutes.
2. Grill fish until done (meat will be opaque and still moist inside), about 5 minutes.
3. Mix grilled fish with *Fresh Corn Relish*; evenly divide and fill tortillas. Mix Swiss and Cheddar cheeses together and add to tacos; top with cilantro and salsa, if desired.

NUTRITIONAL INFO PER TACO: Calories 365, Fat 17g (Sat Fat 6g), Chol 60mg, Carb 31g (Fiber 4g, Sugar 5g), Sodium 150mg (301mg with LS flour tortillas)

Recipe Notes

1 – Use any firm fish, such as tuna or salmon.
2 – Grill tortillas for 1 minute on each side until they start to brown. Corn tortillas average 11mg sodium per tortilla, however shelf-stable shells have 80mg). Most 8-inch flour tortillas average 364mg sodium, but a few manufacturers offer LS ones (visit *LowSaltFoods.com* for LS brands).
3 – Cheddar averages 185mg sodium per ounce versus 60mg for Swiss. Mixing a little Cheddar with the Swiss adds flavor, while keeping salt to a minimum.

TOTAL SODIUM AND FAT BY INGREDIENT

Sodium:
- 1 lb halibut - 289mg
- ¼ c white wine - 3mg
- 1½ c *Corn Relish* - 27mg
- 8 corn tortillas - 40mg
 or 4 LS flour tortillas - 340mg
- 4 oz Swiss cheese - 200mg
- 2 oz cheddar cheese - 340mg
- ¼ c cilantro - 2mg

Fat (Sat Fat):
- 1 lb halibut - 6g (1g)
- 2 T olive oil - 28g (4g)
- 1½ c Corn Relish - 9g (1g)
- 8 corn tortillas - 6g (0g)
 or 4 LS flour tortillas - 14g (6g)
- 4 oz Swiss - 36g (20g)
- 2 oz Cheddar - 18g (12g)

Brands used/alternatives:
- *Great Value* Swiss Cheese
- *Kraft* Cheddar Cheese
- *Great Value* White Corn Tortillas
- *La Banderita* LS Flour Tortillas

Tostadas with Chicken & Guacamole

Sodium Per Serving – 168mg
Serves 4

A tostada is nothing more than a salad on a tortilla shell. You won't believe how easy this is to put together, the only thing you have to cook is the tortilla shell. Oh, and did I mention that these are absolutely delicious!

Guacamole (pg 28)
- 1 tablespoon lime juice, divided
- 1 cup NSA black or kidney beans, drained[1]
- 2 green onions (white and light green parts), chopped
- 1 tablespoon LS tomato-based salsa[2]
- 2 (4-oz) boneless, skinless chicken breast halves, cooked and shredded (about 2 cups)
- 1–2 tomatoes, chopped
- 2 tablespoons chopped fresh cilantro
- 1 teaspoon ground cumin
- ¼ teaspoon garlic powder
- ⅛ teaspoon ground black pepper
- 4–6 (6-inch) corn tortillas[3]
- Vegetable oil for frying (about ¼ cup)
- 2 cups shredded lettuce
- 3 oz Swiss cheese, shredded (about ¾ cup)
- 1 ounce Cheddar cheese, shredded (about ¼ cup)
- ½ cup LS salsa[2]

1. Mix together *Guacamole*, 1 teaspoon lime juice, beans, and green onions; set aside.
2. In another bowl, combine chicken, tomato, remaining 2 teaspoons lime juice, cilantro, cumin, garlic powder, and pepper; set aside.
3. Heat oil in a skillet over medium-high heat; fry tortillas, one at a time, until crisp and golden on both sides.
4. Evenly divide chicken and spread on each tortilla; top with guacamole and lettuce. Sprinkle with cheese and top with salsa.

NUTRITIONAL INFO PER SERVING (without oil for frying): Calories 376, Fat 17g (Sat Fat 6g), Chol 59mg, Carb 29g (Fiber 10g, Sugar 4g), Sodium 168mg

Recipe Notes

1 – Canned black beans average 380mg sodium per ½ cup, reduced salt varieties have 210mg, and NSA brands, 10mg.

2 – Most bottled tomato salsas average 256mg sodium per 2 tbsp, bean and corn salsa has 180mg, and fresh salsa, 142mg. Look for one of many delicious LS varieties with less than 80mg (visit LowSaltFoods.com, for LS products).

3 – Corn tortillas average 11mg sodium per tortilla and shelf-stable shells have 80mg.

TOTAL SODIUM AND FAT BY INGREDIENT

Sodium:
- 1 c Guacamole - 25mg
- 1 c NSA black beans - 9mg
- 2 green onions - 5mg
- ½ c + 1 T LS salsa - 165mg
- 8 oz chicken breast - 80mg
- 1 tomato - 6mg
- 2 T cilantro - 1mg
- 1 t cumin - 4mg
- 4 corn tortillas - 20mg
- 2 c lettuce - 21mg
- 3 oz Swiss cheese - 150mg
- 1 oz Cheddar cheese - 170mg

Fat (Sat Fat):
- 1 c Guacamole - 21g (3g)
- 8 oz chicken breast - 8g (3g)
- 4 corn tortillas - 3g (0g)
- 3 oz NSA Swiss - 27g (15g)
- 1 oz Cheddar - 10g (5g)

Brands used/alternatives:
Tyson All Natural Chicken Breast
Kuner's NSA Black Beans
Frog Ranch Salsa
Great Value White Corn Tortillas
Great Value Swiss Cheese
Kraft Cheddar Cheese

SIDE DISHES

VEGETABLES & LEGUMES

Caramelized Shallots & Asparagus 152
Succotash 152
Broccoli in Lemon-Shallot Butter 153
Roasted Vegetables 153
Carrots & Sugar Snap Peas in Thyme Sauce 154
Gingered Peas & Carrots 154
Baked Spicy French Fried Wedges 154
Spicy Carrots with Currants 155
Corn, Leek & Snap Pea Sauté 155
Green Beans Supreme 156
Herb Seasoned Green Bean Casserole 156
Green Beans & Leeks in Tarragon Sauce 157
Creamy Tarragon Green Beans 157
Green Beans in Shallot Sauce 157
Wild Mushrooms in Madeira Sauce 158
Wild Mushroom & Walnut Sauté 158
Caramelized Onion Tart 159
Caramelized Onion Tart with Parmesan 159
Onion Casserole 160
Peas & Onions au Gratin 161
Pan-Roasted Potatoes 161
Baked Idahoes with Caramelized Shallots 162
Perfect Mashed Potatoes 163
Roasted Garlic Mashed Potatoes 163
Fried Potato Patties 163
Scalloped Potatoes with Sun-Dried Tomato Pesto 165
Asparagus with Tarragon Vinaigrette 165
Souffled Sweets 165
Creamed Spinach 166
Squash & Apple Gratin 167
Tomato, Onion & Goat Cheese Tart 168
Tomato, Leek & Cheese Tart 168
Quick Refried Beans 169
Refried Black Beans 169
Killer Cowboy Beans 170

GRAINS & RICE

Herbed Couscous 171
Sun-Dried Tomato-Basil Couscous 171
Couscous with Dried Apricots & Pine Nuts 171
Risotto 172
Lemon Risotto 172
Basic Steamed Rice 172
Rice Pilaf with Pecans & Currants 173
Wild Rice & Cranberry Pilaf 173

STUFFINGS

Dried Fruit & Curry Rice Dressing 174
Rice Stuffing with Almonds & Olives 175
Herbed Bread Stuffing with Dried Cranberries 176

VEGETABLES & LEGUMES

CARAMELIZED SHALLOTS & ASPARAGUS

Sodium Per Serving – 14mg — Serves 4

This is by far our most favorite asparagus preparation and one of the most requested of my recipes. Incredibly simple and absolutely scrumptious!

- **1 tablespoon olive oil**
- **1 tablespoon unsalted butter or margarine**
- **2 shallots, minced**
- **1 teaspoon sugar**
- **20–24 asparagus spears, trimmed**

1. Heat oil and butter in a large skillet over medium-low heat, add shallots. Cook, stirring occasionally, until shallots are lightly browned and caramelized, 15 to 20 minutes; mix in sweetener.
2. Meanwhile, cook asparagus by any method desired (see *Asparagus*, pg 243, for preparation methods) until crisp tender. Add asparagus to shallots, tossing to coat; transfer asparagus to a bowl and top with excess shallots. Serve immediately.

NUTRITIONAL INFO PER SERVING: Calories 88, Fat 7g (Saturated Fat 2g), Cholesterol 8mg, Carbohydrates 10g (Fiber 2g, Sugar 3g), Sodium 14mg

SUCCOTASH

Sodium Per Serving – 15mg — Serves 8

This has been a family staple for years. For non-lima bean fans, substitute edamame (soy beans).

- **¼ cup unsalted butter or margarine**
- **½ sweet onion, chopped**
- **2 cups frozen lima beans or edamame[1]**
- **2 cups fresh or frozen corn**
- **¼ cup sherry**
- **⅛ teaspoon ground black pepper**
- **⅛ teaspoon onion powder**
- **2 tomatoes, chopped**
- **2 teaspoons chopped fresh basil or ½ teaspoon dried[2]**
- **1 teaspoon sugar**
- **2 tablespoons chopped chives or green onions (green part only)**

1. Melt butter in a large skillet over medium heat; cook onion, stirring frequently, until translucent, about 4 minutes. Add lima beans, corn, sherry, pepper, and onion powder; decrease heat to low, cover, and simmer until vegetables are tender, 15 to 20 minutes.
2. Stir in tomatoes, basil, and sugar; heat through. Sprinkle with chives and serve.

NUTRITIONAL INFO PER SERVING: Calories 388, Fat 12g (Sat Fat 7g), Chol 31mg, Carb 65g (Fiber 17g, Sugar 12g), Sodium 15mg

Recipe Notes

1 – Edamame (pronounced eh-duh-mah-may) are immature soybeans and a good substitute for lima beans. They have little sodium, a sweet, nutty flavor, and are available in the frozen food section of most supermarkets.

2 – Oregano also is a nice seasoning instead of the basil.

TOTAL SODIUM AND FAT BY INGREDIENT

CARAMELIZED SHALLOTS
Sodium:
  2 shallots - 10mg
  20 asparagus - 44mg
Fat (Sat Fat):
  1 T olive oil - 14g (2g)
  1 T NSA butter - 12g (7g)
  `or NSA margarine - 9g (4g)

SUCCOTASH
Sodium:
  2 c lima beans - 40mg or edamame - 40mg
  ½ sweet onion - 7mg
  2 tomatoes - 12mg
Fat (Sat Fat):
  ¼ c NSA butter - 46g (29g) or NSA margarine - 36g (14g)
  2 c lima beans - 0g (0g) or edamame - 8g (0g)
  2 c corn - 2g (0g)
  2 tomatoes - 1g (0g)

Brands used/alternatives:
Great Value Baby Lima Beans
Seapoint Farms Shelled Edamame
Bird's Eye C&W Petite Corn

BROCCOLI IN LEMON-SHALLOT BUTTER

Sodium Per Serving – 48mg — Serves 4

I love shallots; they add an extra depth to dishes, and I use them whenever possible. I think you'll like this simple yet delicious way of preparing broccoli.

- 1 broccoli head (about 1½ pounds), cut into florets
- 2 tablespoons unsalted butter or margarine
- 1 shallot, chopped
- 2 teaspoons lemon juice
- ¼ teaspoon garlic or onion powder
- ⅛ teaspoon ground black pepper
- 1 tablespoon grated Parmesan cheese

1. Cook broccoli by any method desired (see *Broccoli*, pg 245, for preparation methods) until bright green and crisp tender.
2. Meanwhile, melt butter in a skillet over medium heat; add shallots. Cook, stirring frequently, until shallots are translucent, about 3 minutes. Stir in lemon juice, garlic powder, and pepper; tossing with broccoli until well coated. Sprinkle with Parmesan and serve.

NUTRITIONAL INFO PER SERVING: Calories 96, Fat 7g (Saturated Fat 4g), Cholesterol 17mg, Carbohydrates 9g (Fiber 3g, Sugar 2g), Sodium 48mg

ROASTED VEGETABLES

Sodium Per Serving – 37mg — Serves 8

Roasting brings out the sweetness of vegetables, giving them a wonderful rich flavor. Cut into equal sizes so they are done at the same time.

- 3 carrots, sliced in 1½-inch chunks[1]
- 2 cups Brussels sprouts (about ½ pound), cut in half lengthwise
- 8 small red potatoes, quartered
- 1 medium yam or sweet potato, cut into 1½-inch cubes[2]
- 2–3 tablespoons olive oil
- 2 teaspoons dried basil
- 2 teaspoons dried rosemary, crumbled
- 1 teaspoon dried oregano
- 1 teaspoon dried thyme
- ½ teaspoon garlic powder
- ½ teaspoon ground black pepper

1. Preheat oven to 350ºF (180ºC).
2. Place vegetables on a rimmed baking sheet. Mix oil and remaining ingredients and spread over vegetables; stir until well coated. Roast in a preheated oven until vegetables are tender and golden brown, about 40 minutes.

NUTRITIONAL INFO PER SERVING: Calories 202, Fat 4g (Sat Fat 1g), Chol 0mg, Carb 38g (Fiber 5g, Sugar 3g), Sodium 37mg

Recipe Notes

1 – For variety, use sliced almonds instead of Parmesan. This decreases the sodium to 41mg a serving.
2 – Instead of carrots, use parsnips, which are similar in taste, but have less sodium (1 medium carrot has 27mg, 1 medium parsnip 10mg).
3 – A medium yam averages 9mg sodium, a medium sweet potato, 41mg.

TOTAL SODIUM AND FAT BY INGREDIENT

BROCCOLI IN LEMON BUTTER
Sodium:
1 head broccoli - 152mg
1 shallot - 5mg
2 t lemon juice - 2mg
¼ t garlic powder - 1mg
1 T Parmesan - 30mg
Fat (Sat Fat):
1 head broccoli - 2g (0g)
2 T NSA butter - 23g (14g)
  or NSA margarine - 18g (7g)
1 T Parmesan - 2g (1g)
Brands used/alternatives:
365 Whole Foods 3 Cheese Blend

ROASTED VEGETABLES
Sodium:
3 carrots - 80mg
2 c Brussels sprouts - 64mg
8 sm red potatoes - 136mg
1 yam - 14mg
2 t basil - 1mg
1 t thyme - 1mg
½ t garlic powder - 1mg
Fat (Sat Fat):
2 T olive oil - 28g (4g)
2 c Brussels sprouts - 2g (0g)
8 sm red potatoes - 2g (0g)

SIDE DISHES - *Vegetables & Legumes*

Carrots & Sugar Snap Peas in Thyme Sauce

Sodium Per Serving – 18mg Serves 4

This colorful side dish is quick and delicious... guaranteed to please.

- **1 tablespoon unsalted butter or margarine**
- **2 medium carrots, peeled and cut on the diagonal, or 12-16 baby carrots**
- **2 tablespoons chopped onion or shallot**
- **1 garlic clove, minced**
- **¼ teaspoon garlic or onion powder**
- **¼ teaspoon dried thyme**
- **⅛ teaspoon ground black pepper**
- **⅓ cup *Chicken Broth (pg 208)* or unsalted chicken broth**
- **½ teaspoon LS chicken bouillon**
- **1 cup sugar snap peas or snow peas**
- **1 teaspoon cornstarch**

1. Melt butter in a large skillet over medium heat; add carrots, onions, and garlic. Cook, stirring frequently, until onions are translucent, 2 to 3 minutes; add garlic powder, thyme, and pepper.
2. Stir in half the chicken broth and cook 2 to 3 minutes; add the bouillon and peas. Cook until peas are tender, about 2 minutes longer.
3. Mix remaining broth and cornstarch together; gradually add to peas, stirring constantly, until sauce thickens to a gravy consistency, 1 to 2 minutes.

NUTRITIONAL INFO PER SERVING: Calories 53, Fat 3g (Saturated Fat 2g), Cholesterol 8mg, Carbohydrates 5g (Fiber 2g, Sugar 2g), Sodium 18mg

---

VARIATION
Gingered Peas & Carrots

1. This variation adds a hint of sweetness. Instead of thyme, add 2 thin slices of fresh ginger (or ¼ teaspoon ground) and ½ teaspoon sugar; proceed as directed. *NOTE: Before serving, remove the fresh ginger.*

NUTRITIONAL INFO PER SERVING: Calories 74, Fat 3g (Sat Fat 2g), Chol 8mg, Carb 10g (Fiber 2g, Sugar 3g), Sodium 21mg

---

Baked Spicy French Fried Wedges

Sodium Per Serving – 19mg Serves 4

These spicy, lowfat "JoJos" are baked in the oven.

- **1 tablespoon olive oil**
- **½ teaspoon chili powder**
- **½ teaspoon garlic powder**
- **½ teaspoon hot paprika[1]**
- **¼ teaspoon onion powder**
- **⅛ teaspoon black pepper**
- **4 russet potatoes, unpeeled, cut each into 6-8 wedges**

1. Preheat oven to 400ºF (200ºC).
2. Mix olive oil, garlic powder, chili powder, paprika, onion powder, and pepper together. Mix with potatoes, coating all sides.
3. Place potatoes in a single layer on a baking sheet. Bake in a preheated oven, turning every 10-15 minutes until tender and evenly browned, about 30-40 minutes.

NUTRITIONAL INFO PER SERVING: Calories 325, Fat 4g (Saturated Fat 1g), Cholesterol 0mg, Carbohydrates 67g (Fiber 5g, Sugar 2g), Sodium 19mg

---

TOTAL SODIUM AND FAT BY INGREDIENT

CARROTS & PEAS IN THYME
Sodium:
- 2 carrots - 53mg
- 2 T onion - 2mg
- 1 garlic clove - 1mg
- ¼ t garlic powder - 1mg
- ⅓ c *Chicken Broth* - 7mg
  or NSA chicken broth - 13mg
- ½ t LS chicken bouillon - 3mg
- 1 c snap peas - 4mg

Fat (Sat Fat):
- 1 T NSA butter - 12g (7g)
  or NSA margarine - 8g (2g)

Brands used/alternatives:
Pacific Foods Organic Unsalted Chicken Stock
Herb Ox NSA Chicken Bouillon

BAKED SPICY FRIED WEDGES
Sodium:
- 2 lb russet potatoes - 74mg
- ½ t garlic powder - 1mg

Fat (Sat Fat):
- 2 lb russet potatoes - 1g (0g)
- 1 T olive oil - 14g (2g)

Spicy Carrots with Currants

Sodium Per Serving – 30mg   Serves 6

This sweet and spicy combination is a perfect accompaniment to blander dishes.

- 1 tablespoon olive oil
- 6 medium carrots, sliced on the diagonal, or baby carrots (about 1 pound)
- 1/4 teaspoon garlic powder
- 1/8 teaspoon cayenne pepper or to taste
- 1/8 teaspoon ground cumin
- 1/8 teaspoon ground black pepper
- 1/2 cup *Chicken Broth (pg 208)* or unsalted chicken broth
- 1/2 teaspoon LS chicken bouillon
- 1 tablespoon unsalted butter or margarine
- 1 tablespoon sugar
- 1/4 teaspoon ground cinnamon
- 1/4 cup currants or raisins[1]

1. Heat oil in a skillet over medium heat; add carrots, garlic powder, cayenne pepper, cumin, and black pepper. Cook, stirring frequently, until carrots begin to soften, 3 to 4 minutes.
2. Add chicken broth and bouillon; bring to a boil. Decrease heat to low, cover; simmer until carrots are crisp-tender, about 5 minutes.
3. Add butter, sugar, and cinnamon; cook, stirring frequently, until liquid has evaporated and carrots are glazed, 2 to 3 minutes. Stir in currants and serve.

NUTRITIONAL INFO PER SERVING: Calories 90, Fat 4g (Sat Fat 2g), Chol 6mg, Carb 13g (Fiber 3g, Sugar 10g), Sodium 30mg

Corn, Leek & Snap Pea Sauté

Sodium Per Serving – 10mg   Serves 8

Colorful, simple and very tasty... what more can you ask?

- 2 tablespoons unsalted butter or margarine
- 3 leeks, chopped (white and light green parts)
- 1 red bell pepper, thinly sliced
- 1 garlic clove, finely minced
- 1 teaspoon dried thyme
- 1/4 teaspoon garlic powder
- 1/8 teaspoon black pepper
- 1 (10-oz) pkg frozen corn, thawed (about 2 cups)
- 1/2 cup *Chicken Broth (pg 208)* or NSA chicken broth
- 1/2 teaspoon LS chicken bouillon
- 2 cups fresh or frozen snow peas or sugar snap peas

1. Melt butter in a large skillet over medium heat; add leeks, bell pepper, garlic, thyme, garlic powder, and pepper. Cook, stirring frequently, until leeks are soft, 8 to 10 minutes.
2. Add corn, chicken broth, and bouillon; cook, uncovered, until liquid is reduced by half, about 5 minutes.
3. Stir in peas; cook, uncovered, until heated through, 1 to 2 minutes, and serve.

NUTRITIONAL INFO PER SERVING: Calories 92, Fat 4g (Sat Fat 2g), Chol 8mg, Carb 13g (Fiber 4g, Sugar 5g), Sodium 10mg

Recipe Notes

1 – Currants are sometimes hard to find; use raisins instead.

TOTAL SODIUM AND FAT BY INGREDIENT

SPICY CARROTS & CURRANTS
Sodium:
- 6 carrots - 160mg
- 1/4 t garlic powder - 1mg
- 1/8 t cumin - 1mg
- 1/2 c *Chicken Broth* - 10mg
  or NSA chicken broth - 18mg
- 1/2 t LS chicken bouillon - 3mg
- 1/4 c currants - 3mg

Fat (Sat Fat):
- 1 T olive oil - 14g (2g)
- 6 carrots - 1g (0g)
- 1/2 c *Chicken Broth* - 1g (0g)
  or NSA chicken broth - 0g (0g)
- 1 T NSA butter - 12g (7g)
  or NSA margarine - 9g (4g)

Brands used/alternatives:
Pacific Foods Organic Unsalted Chicken Stock
Herb Ox NSA Chicken Bouillon

CORN, LEEK & SNAP PEA SAUTÉ
Sodium:
- 3 leeks - 54mg
- 1 red bell pepper - 5mg
- 1 garlic clove - 1mg
- 1 t thyme - 1mg
- 1/4 t garlic powder - 1mg
- 1/2 c *Chicken Broth* - 10mg
  or NSA chicken broth - 18mg
- 1/2 t LS chicken bouillon - 3mg
- 2 c snow peas - 8mg

Fat (Sat Fat):
- 2 T NSA butter - 23g (14g)
  or NSA margarine - 18g (7g)
- 10 oz corn - 3g (0g)
- 3 leeks - 1g (0g)
- 2 c snow peas - 1g (0g)

Brands used/alternatives:
Pacific Foods Organic Unsalted Chicken Stock
Herb Ox NSA Chicken Bouillon
Birds Eye Steamfresh Super Sweet Corn

Green Beans Supreme

Sodium Per Serving – 83mg   Serves 6

This creamy casserole is a take-off on an old family holiday favorite.

- **2 tablespoons unsalted butter or margarine**
- **1 medium onion, chopped**
- **2 tablespoons all-purpose flour, mixed with 2 tablespoons water to make a paste**
- **½ teaspoon finely grated lemon peel**
- **¼ teaspoon garlic powder**
- **¼ teaspoon ground black pepper**
- **2 (10-oz) packages frozen French-cut green beans, thawed**
- **3 tablespoons chopped fresh Italian parsley**
- **1 (15-oz) can LS cream of mushroom soup or 1 cup lowfat sour cream[1]**
- **2 oz Cheddar cheese, shredded**

Topping:
- **2 oz Swiss cheese, shredded**
- **½ cup LS bread crumbs[2]**

1. Preheat oven to 350°F (180°C). Coat a 2-quart baking dish with vegetable cooking spray.
2. Melt butter in a skillet over medium heat; cook onion, stirring frequently, until onions are translucent, 3 to 4 minutes. Gradually stir in flour paste, lemon peel, garlic powder, and pepper; cook, stirring constantly, until flour begins to brown, about 3 minutes. Add beans, parsley, mushroom soup, and Cheddar cheese; mix well.
3. Place mixture in prepared baking dish; sprinkle with Swiss cheese and bread crumbs. Bake, uncovered, in a preheated oven until topping is golden brown, about 30 minutes.

NUTRITIONAL INFO PER SERVING: Calories 223, Fat 12g (Saturated Fat 7g), Cholesterol 29mg, Carbohydrates 21g (Fiber 4g, Sugar 4g), Sodium 83mg

---

VARIATION
Herb Seasoned Green Bean Casserole

1. For an herbal flavor, mix together the bread crumbs with ½ teaspoon dried basil, ½ teaspoon dried parsley, ¼ teaspoon dried oregano, ⅛ teaspoon garlic powder, ⅛ teaspoon ground black pepper, and ⅛ teaspoon dried thyme; proceed as directed.

NUTRITIONAL INFO PER SERVING: Calories 224, Fat 12g (Sat Fat 7g), Chol 29mg, Carb 21g (Fiber 4g, Sugar 4g), Sodium 83mg

---

TOTAL SODIUM AND FAT BY INGREDIENT

Sodium:
- 1 onion - 4mg
- ¼ t garlic powder - 1mg
- 3 T parsley - 6mg
- 15 oz LS soup - 45mg
- 2 oz LF Cheddar cheese - 340mg
- 2 oz NSA Swiss cheese - 100mg

Fat (Sat Fat):
- 2 T NSA butter - 23g (14g) or NSA margarine - 18g (7g)
- 15 oz NSA soup - 13g (4g)
- 2 oz LF Cheddar - 18g (12g)
- 2 oz NSA Swiss - 18g (10g)
- ½ c NSA bread crumbs - 2g (0g)

Brands used/alternatives:
- *Birds Eye* Steamfresh Green Beans
- *Campbell's* LS Cream of Mushroom Soup
- *Kraft* Cheddar Cheese
- *Great Value* Swiss Cheese
- *4C* Salt Free Bread Crumbs

Recipe Notes
1 – The mushroom soup adds a richness that you don't get with sour cream.
2 – To make fresh bread crumbs, see *Bread Crumbs*, pg 244.

Green Beans & Leeks in Tarragon Sauce

Sodium Per Serving – 8mg   Serves 4

This is a simple, yet elegant way to prepare green beans. I love the combination of tarragon, leeks, and green beans with Madeira wine.

- **1 pound green beans, trimmed (about 3 cups)**
- **1 teaspoon olive oil**
- **1 tablespoon unsalted butter or margarine**
- **1 leek, sliced (white and light green parts)[1]**
- **¼ teaspoon dried tarragon**
- **¼ teaspoon garlic powder**
- **⅛ teaspoon ground black pepper**
- **1 teaspoon LS chicken bouillon**
- **½ cup Madeira wine[2]**

1. Bring a large pan of water to a boil over high heat; add green beans. Cook, covered, until crisp tender, 4 to 5 minutes; drain.
2. Meanwhile, heat oil and butter in a skillet over medium heat; add leeks, tarragon, garlic powder, and pepper. Cook, stirring frequently, for 8 to 10 minutes, until leeks are soft. Stir in bouillon and Madeira; add cooked beans and toss until well-coated.

NUTRITIONAL INFO PER SERVING: Calories 135, Fat 4g (Saturated Fat 2g), Cholesterol 8mg, Carbohydrates 16g (Fiber 4g, Sugar 7g), Sodium 8mg

---

VARIATION

Creamy Tarragon Green Beans

1. For a creamy sauce, stir into the beans, 1 tablespoon lowfat milk and 1 tablespoon lowfat sour cream before serving.

NUTRITIONAL INFO PER SERVING: Calories 141, Fat 5g (Sat Fat 2g), Chol 9mg, Carb 16g (Fiber 4g, Sugar 8g), Sodium 12mg

Green Beans in Shallot Sauce

1. Use 1 large chopped shallot instead of the leek and substitute sake for the Madeira; proceed as directed.

NUTRITIONAL INFO PER SERVING: Calories 125, Fat 4g (Sat Fat 2g), Chol 8mg, Carb 13g (Fiber 4g, Sugar 5g), Sodium 4mg

---

TOTAL SODIUM AND FAT BY INGREDIENT

Sodium:
- 1 lb green beans - 5mg
- 1 leek - 12mg
- ¼ t garlic powder - 1mg
- 1 t LS chicken bouillon - 5mg
- ½ c Madeira - 10mg

Fat (Sat Fat):
- 1 lb green beans - 1g (0g)
- 1 t olive oil - 5g (0g)
- 1 T NSA butter - 12g (7g)
  or NSA margarine - 9g (4g)

Brands used/alternatives:
Herb Ox NSA Chicken Bouillon

Recipe Notes

1 – For additional information on cleaning and storing leeks, see *Leeks*, pg 249.
2 – The creamy flavor of Madeira compliments the veggies in this dish. If you don't have Madeira, use sherry or red wine.

Wild Mushrooms in Madeira Sauce

Sodium Per Serving – 4mg   Serves 4

Wild mushrooms are much more flavorful than button mushrooms. Any combination of wild mushrooms works well in this dish.

- 1 tablespoon olive oil
- 1 tablespoon unsalted butter or margarine
- 2 green onions, chopped (white and green parts)
- 1 garlic clove, minced
- 5 oz sliced wild mushrooms, such as oyster, shiitake, or chanterelle (about 2 cups)[1]
- 1 teaspoon LS chicken bouillon
- ¼ cup Madeira[2]
- ½ teaspoon dried thyme
- ¼ teaspoon garlic powder
- ⅛ teaspoon ground black pepper

1. Heat oil and butter in a skillet over medium heat; add onions and garlic, cook, stirring frequently, until onions soften, 1 to 2 minutes. Add mushrooms; cook, stirring frequently, until mushrooms soften, 4 to 5 minutes.
2. Stir in bouillon, Madeira, thyme, garlic powder and pepper; simmer, uncovered, until liquid is nearly gone, about 5 minutes.

NUTRITIONAL INFO PER SERVING: Calories 98, Fat 6g (Saturated Fat 2g), Cholesterol 8mg, Carbohydrates 6g (Fiber 1g, Sugar 2g), Sodium 4mg

---

VARIATION
Wild Mushroom & Walnut Sauté
1. Add ½ teaspoon dried sage or rosemary (or 1 tablespoon fresh) to the mushrooms; proceed as directed. Top with chopped walnuts before serving.

NUTRITIONAL INFO PER SERVING: Calories 147, Fat 11g (Sat Fat 3g), Chol 10mg, Carb 7g (Fiber 2g, Sugar 2g), Sodium 5mg

Recipe Notes
1 – For additional information on choosing and preparing mushrooms, see *Mushrooms*, pg 250.
2 – The creamy flavor of Madeira makes this dish; if you don't have Madeira, use sherry or red wine.

TOTAL SODIUM AND FAT BY INGREDIENT
Sodium:
- 2 green onions - 5mg
- 1 garlic clove - 1mg
- 2 c mushrooms - 1mg
- 1 t LS chicken bouillon - 5mg
- ¼ c Madeira - 5mg
- ¼ t garlic powder - 1mg

Fat (Sat Fat):
- 1 T olive oil - 14g (2g)
- 1 T NSA butter - 12g (7g)
- or NSA margarine - 9g (4g)

Brands used/alternatives:
Herb Ox NSA Chicken Bouillon

CARAMELIZED ONION TART
Sodium Per Serving – 45mg   Serves 8

This deliciously mild onion tart is so versatile—serve it as a first course, side dish, or even a main entrée.

- **1 *Basic Pie Crust* (pg 205) or LS pie crust**
- **2 tablespoons olive oil**
- **2 tablespoons unsalted butter or margarine**
- **3 large yellow onions, sliced[1]**
- **¼ teaspoon garlic powder**
- **⅛ teaspoon white pepper[2]**
- **2 eggs, beaten[3]**
- **¼ cup lowfat sour cream**
- **¼ teaspoon freshly grated or ground nutmeg**

1. Preheat oven to 425ºF (220ºC). Arrange oven rack on lowest position.
2. Prick crust with a fork; line bottom of shell with aluminum foil. Pour pie weights into the pie crust to hold its shape while baking (for info on pie weights, see *Pie Weights*, pg 252). Bake in preheated oven for 5 minutes; remove weights. Return to oven and bake for 5 minutes more; remove shell from oven and let cool slightly. *NOTE: If using a refrigerated or frozen pie crust, this step is not necessary.*
3. Heat oil and butter in a large skillet over medium heat; cook onions, stirring frequently, until they begin to brown, about 5 minutes. Decrease heat to medium-low; stir in garlic powder and pepper. Cook, stirring occasionally, until onions are dark brown and caramelized, 20 to 30 minutes; remove from heat and let cool slightly.
4. Add eggs and sour cream to onions, mixing well; pour into prepared pie crust, and sprinkle nutmeg over the top. Bake in a preheated oven until filling is set, 35 to 40 minutes; let stand for 5 minutes before removing from oven. Cut into wedges and serve.

NUTRITIONAL INFO PER SERVING: Calories 284, Fat 18g (Saturated Fat 7g), Cholesterol 64mg, Carbohydrates 25g (Fiber 1g, Sugar 5g), Sodium 45mg (76mg with purchased shell)

VARIATION
CARAMELIZED ONION TART WITH PARMESAN
1. The addition of parmesan kicks this up a notch. Sprinkle 2 tablespoons freshly grated parmesan cheese on top of the tart before baking.

NUTRITIONAL INFO PER SERVING: Calories 284, Fat 18g (Sat Fat 7g), Chol 64mg, Carb 25g (Fiber 1g, Sugar 5g), Sodium 58mg (89mg with LS pie crust)

TOTAL SODIUM AND FAT BY INGREDIENT

Sodium:
- 1 *Basic Pie Crust* - 150mg
  or LS pie crust - 400mg
- 3 yellow onions - 18mg
- ¼ t garlic powder - 1mg
- 2 eggs - 142mg
- ¼ LF sour cream - 50mg

Fat (Sat Fat):
- 1 *Basic Pie Crust* - 74g (28g)
  or LS pie crust - 64g (28g)
- 2 T olive oil - 28g (4g)
- 2 T NSA butter - 23g (14g)
  or NSA margarine - 18g (7g)
- 2 eggs - 10g (3g)
- ¼ LF sour cream - 5g (4g)

Brands used/alternatives:
Daisy Light Sour Cream
Marie Callender's Pie Shell

Recipe Notes
1 – Yellow onions caramelize best, as they have less water than other onions. For additional info on caramelizing, see *Caramelizing Onions*, pg 245.
2 – White pepper is for aesthetic reasons only, using freshly ground black pepper is okay to use.
3 – To keep fat to a minimum, use an egg substitute. See *Eggs and Egg Substitutes*, pg 23, for a comparison of fat and sodium in eggs and egg substitutes.

VARIATION
To make crustless, place thinly sliced sweet potatoes in the bottom of the pan. Pour the pie mixture over the potatoes, sprinkle with nutmeg and bake as directed. This reduces the sodium in a serving by 7mg.

ONION CASSEROLE

Sodium Per Serving – 87mg Serves 8

My mother-in-law asked me to reduce the fat and salt in this favorite of hers. Although I haven't tasted the original, this version tasted so good, I had to share it with you.

- **2 tablespoons olive oil**
- **5 tablespoons unsalted butter or margarine, divided**
- **2 large onions, sliced**
- **¼ teaspoon garlic powder**
- **⅛ teaspoon ground cumin**
- **⅛ teaspoon paprika**
- **⅛ teaspoon ground black pepper**
- **25 LS crackers, crumbled**
- **3 oz Swiss cheese, shredded (about ¾ cup)**
- **1 oz Cheddar cheese, shredded (about ¼ cup)**
- **2 large eggs[1]**
- **⅔ cup lowfat milk**

1. Preheat oven to 350ºF (180ºC). Coat a 2-quart casserole dish with nonstick cooking spray.
2. Heat oil and 1 tablespoon butter in a skillet over medium heat; add onions, garlic powder, cumin, paprika, and pepper. Cook, stirring frequently, until onions are translucent and start to brown, about 5 minutes.
3. Melt remaining 4 tablespoons butter and mix with crackers; cover the bottom of a prepared baking dish with three-fourths of the crumbs, reserving one-fourth to use on top. Arrange onions over the crumbs and cover with the Swiss and Cheddar cheeses.
4. In a small bowl, mix eggs and milk together; pour over onions. Top with remaining crumbs. Bake, uncovered, in a preheated oven for 40 to 45 minutes, until top is lightly browned.

NUTRITIONAL INFO PER SERVING: Calories 241, Fat 19g (Sat Fat 9g), Chol 86mg, Carb 11g (Fiber 1g, Sugar 3g), Sodium 87mg

Recipe Notes

1 – To keep fat to a minimum, use an egg substitute. See *Eggs and Egg Substitutes*, pg 23, for a comparison of fat and sodium in eggs and egg substitutes.

TOTAL SODIUM AND FAT BY INGREDIENT

Sodium:
 2 onions - 12mg
 25 LS crackers - 150mg
 3 oz Swiss cheese - 150mg
 1 oz Cheddar cheese - 170mg
 2 eggs - 142mg
 ⅔ c LF milk - 70mg

Fat (Sat Fat):
 2 T olive oil - 28g (4g)
 5 T NSA butter - 58g (36g)
  or NSA margarine - 45g (18g)
 25 LS crackers - 20g (5g)
 3 oz Swiss - 27g (15g)
 1 oz Cheddar - 9g (6g)
 2 eggs - 10g (3g)
 ⅔ c LF milk - 3g (1g)

Brands used/alternatives:
 Ritz Hint of Salt Crackers
 Great Value Swiss Cheese
 Kraft Cheddar Cheese
 Simple Truth 2% Milk

Peas & Onions au Gratin

Sodium Per Serving – 44mg   Serves 4

This is an old stand-by and goes together quickly when you use the microwave.

- **1 (8-oz) pkg frozen NSA peas, thawed**
- **1 (6-oz) pkg frozen pearl onions, thawed**
- **2 tablespoons water**
- **2 oz (¼ cup) cream cheese[1]**
- **2 tablespoons nonfat or lowfat milk**
- **1 garlic clove, minced**
- **¼ teaspoon ground black pepper**
- **½ cup *Herbed Garlic Croutons (pg 204)* or LS seasoned croutons (about 2 oz)[2]**

1. Cooking options:
   - *Microwave:* Place peas, onions, and water in a microwave-proof dish and microwave on high until tender, 3 to 4 minutes; drain. Stir in cream cheese, milk, garlic, and pepper; microwave 2 minutes until heated through.
   - *Stove-top:* Place peas, onions, and water in a saucepan over medium-high heat; cover and cook until tender, 4 to 5 minutes. Stir in cream cheese, milk, garlic, and pepper; cook until heated through and cheese has melted, about 4 minutes.
2. Sprinkle with croutons and serve.

NUTRITIONAL INFO PER SERVING: Calories 134, Fat 6g (Saturated Fat 3g), Cholesterol 16mg, Carbohydrates 17g (Fiber 4g, Sugar 6g), Sodium 44mg

Pan-Roasted Potatoes

Sodium Per Serving – 37mg   Serves 4–6

This easy-to-prepare family favorite is great with eggs or as a side dish with grilled poultry or meat.

- **1 tablespoon olive oil**
- **5–6 small red or Yukon Gold potatoes, cubed (about 2 pounds)**
- **¼ teaspoon dried basil**
- **¼ teaspoon garlic or onion powder**
- **⅛ teaspoon ground black pepper**
- **½ cup chopped sweet onion**
- **½ cup chopped red bell pepper**
- **1 cup chopped mushrooms**

1. Heat oil in a large skillet over medium heat; add potatoes, basil, garlic powder, and pepper. Cook, stirring frequently, until potatoes begin to brown, 4 to 5 minutes.
2. Stir in onion, bell pepper, and mushrooms; decrease heat to medium-low. Cover, and continue cooking until potatoes are done, about 10 minutes.

NUTRITIONAL INFO PER SERVING: Calories 246, Fat 4g (Sat Fat 1g), Chol 0mg, Carb 48g (Fiber 5g, Sugar 5g), Sodium 37mg

Recipe Notes

1 – For a comparison of sodium and fat within cream cheese varieties, see *Cream Cheese Comparison*, pg 247.
2 – There are several LS croutons available, look for those with 35mg sodium or less in a 0.5-oz serving.

TOTAL SODIUM AND FAT BY INGREDIENT

PEAS & ONIONS AU GRATIN
Sodium:
- ¼ c cream cheese - 150mg
- 2 T LF milk - 13mg
- 1 garlic clove - 1mg
- ½ c *Herbed Croutons* - 12mg or LS croutons - 400mg

Fat (Sat Fat):
- ¼ c cream cheese - 20g (12g)
- 2 T LF milk - 1g (0g)
- ½ c *Herbed Croutons* - 3g (1g) or LS croutons - 12g (0g)

Brands used/alternatives:
Bird's Eye C&W Petite Peas
Great Value Pearl Onions
Green Valley Lactose-Free Cream Cheese
Simple Truth 2% Milk

PAN-ROASTED POTATOES
Sodium:
- 2 lb red potatoes - 105mg
- ½ c sweet onion - 36mg
- ½ red bell pepper - 1mg
- 1 c mushrooms - 4mg

Fat (Sat Fat):
- 1 T olive oil - 14g (2g)
- 2 lb red potatoes - 2g (1g)

Baked Idahoes with Caramelized Shallots

Sodium Per Serving – 52mg | Serves 8

Caramelized shallots add elegance to these cheesy potatoes. Prepare the potatoes several hours ahead of time and reheat before serving.

4 large russet potatoes (about 3 pounds)
1 teaspoon olive oil
2 tablespoons unsalted butter or margarine
½ cup lowfat sour cream
⅓ cup lowfat milk
¼ teaspoon garlic or onion powder
⅛ teaspoon white pepper
4 oz Swiss cheese, shredded (about 1 cup)
Pinch hot paprika or cayenne pepper

Shallot Topping:
1 tablespoon olive oil
1 tablespoon unsalted butter or margarine
8 shallots, thinly sliced[1]
½ teaspoon sugar
2 tablespoons chopped Italian parsley (optional)

1. Preheat oven to 400ºF (200ºC).
2. Rub potatoes with olive oil and pierce in several places with a fork. Bake until tender, about 1 hour; transfer to a wire rack and cool slightly.
3. Slice potatoes lengthwise; using a spoon, scoop out the flesh, leaving a ¼-inch thick shell, and place potato flesh in a bowl. Mash with 2 tablespoons butter, sour cream, and milk; add garlic powder and pepper. (If needed, add 1–2 tablespoons more milk until potatoes are a creamy consistency.) Stir in the Swiss cheese; divide evenly and spoon into potato shells. Sprinkle tops with paprika.
4. *For the Shallot Topping:* Meanwhile, heat 1 tablespoon oil and 1 tablespoon butter in a skillet over medium heat; add shallots. Cook, stirring frequently, until shallots are translucent, 3 to 4 minutes; decrease heat to low and continue cooking for 15 to 20 minutes, until shallots are dark brown and have caramelized. Stir in sugar; divide evenly and spoon on top of potatoes.
5. Bake potatoes in a preheated oven at 350ºF (180ºC) until heated through, 15 to 20 minutes; sprinkle with parsley and serve.

NUTRITIONAL INFO PER SERVING: Calories 314, Fat 13g (Sat Fat 6g), Chol 30mg, Carb 42g (Fiber 4g, Sugar 34g), Sodium 52mg

Recipe Notes
1 – Shallots look like small onions and have a mild garlic flavor. For additional information on preparation and storage of shallots, see *Shallots*, pg 253.

TOTAL SODIUM AND FAT BY INGREDIENT

Sodium:
4 russet potatoes - 74mg
½ c LF sour cream - 60mg
⅓ c LF milk - 35mg
¼ t garlic powder - 1mg
4 oz Swiss cheese - 200mg
8 shallots - 41mg
2 T parsley - 4mg

Fat (Sat Fat):
4 russet potatoes - 1g (0g)
1 T + 1 t olive oil - 19g (2g)
3 T NSA butter - 35g (21g)
  or NSA margarine - 27g (11g)
½ c LF sour cream - 10g (6g)
⅓ c LF milk - 2g (1g)
4 oz Swiss cheese - 36g (20g)

Brands used/alternatives:
Great Value Swiss Cheese
Daisy Light Sour Cream
Simple Truth 2% Milk

PERFECT MASHED POTATOES

Sodium Per Serving – 22mg   Serves 6

The secret to delicious mashed potatoes is leaving the skins on and cooking them whole. Potatoes are very porous and absorb liquids easily, by leaving the potatoes whole and unpeeled, the flavor is not "diluted" by the water. The same principle applies when mashing the potatoes, the first ingredient added will be absorbed by the potatoes. To get a rich, creamy flavor, butter or margarine is added first, followed by the milk and other additions.

- 6 small Yukon gold, red, or russet potatoes (about 2 pounds)[1]
- 2 teaspoons LS chicken bouillon
- ¼ cup unsalted butter or margarine, melted
- ½ cup lowfat milk
- 2 tablespoons lowfat sour cream
- ¼ teaspoon garlic or onion powder
- ⅛ teaspoon ground white pepper
- ¼ cup chopped chives or green onions (green part only)
- ⅛ teaspoon paprika

1. Place whole, unpeeled potatoes and bouillon in a pot and cover with water; bring to boil over high heat. Decrease heat to medium and cook until potatoes are tender, about 20 minutes; drain.
2. Peel potatoes, if desired, and mash. *NOTE: A potato ricer makes the smoothest and fluffiest potatoes, but a food mill, potato masher, or electric mixer also work. Avoid overmixing, particularly with a mixer, which can produce gluey, gummy potatoes.*
3. Add butter and mix; gradually stir in milk and sour cream. Mix in garlic powder, pepper, and green onions; sprinkle with paprika and serve.

   NOTE: For the best consistency, serve as soon as possible. However, you can prepare the dish the day before, cover, and refrigerate. Bring to room temperature before reheating:
   - *Microwave:* Cover and microwave, stirring every 2 minutes, until heated through, about 5 minutes.
   - *Bake:* Cover and bake in a preheated 350°F (180°C) oven about 20 minutes, or until heated through.

TOTAL SODIUM AND FAT BY INGREDIENT

Sodium:
- 2 lb russet potatoes - 51mg
- 2 t LS chicken bouillon - 10mg
- ½ c LF milk - 53mg
- 2 T LF sour cream - 15mg
- ¼ t garlic powder - 1mg

Fat (Sat Fat):
- 2 lb russet potatoes - 1g (0g)
- ¼ c NSA butter - 46g (29g)
  or NSA margarine - 36g (14g)
- ½ c LF milk - 3g (1g)
- 2 T LF sour cream - 3g (2g)

Brands used/alternatives:
Herb Ox NSA Chicken Bouillon
Daisy Light Sour Cream
Simple Truth 2% Milk

NUTRITIONAL INFO PER SERVING: Calories 221, Fat 9g (Saturated Fat 5g), Cholesterol 24mg, Carbohydrates 33g (Fiber 2g, Sugar 29g), Sodium 22mg

---

VARIATION

ROASTED GARLIC MASHED POTATOES
1. Roast 1-2 heads of garlic (see *Roasting Garlic*, pg 249); once cooled, squeeze out cooked cloves. Add to potatoes before mashing; proceed as directed.

NUTRITIONAL INFO PER SERVING: Calories 222, Fat 9g (Saturated Fat 5g), Cholesterol 24mg, Carbohydrates 33g (Fiber 2g, Sugar 29g), Sodium 22mg

FRIED POTATO PATTIES
1. Use up leftover potatoes by shaping into 3-inch patties and frying in 1 tablespoon unsalted butter over medium heat until brown on both sides.

NUTRITIONAL INFO PER SERVING: Calories 238, Fat 11g (Saturated Fat 6g), Cholesterol 29mg, Carbohydrates 33g (Fiber 2g, Sugar 29g), Sodium 22mg

---

Recipe Notes
1 – Yukon gold potatoes have a creamier flavor; russets mash fluffier. For added taste and texture, do not peel before mashing.

Scalloped Potatoes with Sun-Dried Tomato Pesto

Sodium Per Serving – 113mg   Serves 8

My neighbor, Gigi Wooldridge, gave me this recipe. I've eliminated most of the salt and made a few other changes, but I think you'll enjoy these flavorful scalloped potatoes. Although you can purée the pesto in a blender, a food processor works best. You can substitute Sun-Dried Tomato Pesto (pg 136) for the pesto ingredients below.

- 8 small red or Yukon Gold potatoes, thinly sliced (about 3 pounds)
- 4 oz Swiss cheese, shredded (about 1 cup)
- 2 oz Cheddar cheese, shredded (about ½ cup)
- 1 cup *Chicken Broth (pg 208)* or unsalted chicken broth
- 1 teaspoon LS chicken bouillon

Pesto:
- 1 cup oil-packed sun-dried tomatoes, undrained
- ½ cup fresh basil
- 3 tablespoons grated Parmesan cheese
- 2 garlic cloves, smashed and coarsely chopped
- ¼ teaspoon garlic powder
- ⅛ teaspoon ground black pepper

1. Preheat oven to 350°F (180°C). Coat a 2-quart casserole or baking dish with nonstick cooking spray.
2. *To make the pesto:* Place the tomatoes, basil, Parmesan, garlic, garlic powder, and pepper in a food processor or blender; pulse until a smooth paste. (If too dry, add a little olive oil while the machine is running.)
3. Mix the pesto with the potatoes and arrange half the potatoes in the bottom of a prepared casserole dish. Mix the two cheeses together; spread half on the potatoes and reserve the remaining cheese. Top with the rest of the potatoes.
4. Mix the chicken broth and bouillon together; pour over potatoes. Cover with foil and bake in a preheated oven for 30 minutes; remove foil and spread remaining cheese on top. Bake for 20 to 25 minutes more, until potatoes are tender.

NUTRITIONAL INFO PER SERVING: Calories 339, Fat 14g (Sat Fat 4g), Chol 21mg, Carb 42g (Fiber 3g, Sugar 7g), Sodium 113mg (121mg with NSA chicken broth)

TOTAL SODIUM AND FAT BY INGREDIENT

Sodium:
- 1 c sun-dried tomatoes - 80mg
- ½ c basil - 1mg
- 3 T Parmesan cheese - 90mg
- 2 garlic cloves - 1mg
- ¼ garlic powder - 1mg
- 3 lb red potatoes - 168mg
- 4 oz Swiss cheese - 200mg
- 2 oz Cheddar cheese - 340mg
- 1 c *Chicken Broth* - 20mg
  or LS chicken broth - 85mg
- 1 t LS chicken bouillon - 5mg

Fat (Sat Fat):
- 1 c dried tomatoes - 48g (0g)
- 3 T Parmesan - 6g (3g)
- 3 lb red potatoes - 2g (1g)
- 4 oz Swiss cheese - 38g (20g)
- 2 oz Cheddar - 18g (12g)

Brands used/alternatives:
Jeff's Naturals Sun-Dried Tomatoes
365 Whole Foods 3 Cheese Blend
Great Value Swiss Cheese
Kraft Cheddar Cheese
Pacific Foods Organic Unsalted Chicken Stock
Herb Ox NSA Chicken Bouillon

Asparagus with Tarragon Vinaigrette

Sodium Per Serving – 14mg Serves 4

This dish is a perennial favorite and goes nicely with grilled entrées.

- **20–24 asparagus spears, trimmed**
- **1 tablespoon tarragon or white wine vinegar**
- **1 tablespoon olive oil**
- **¼ teaspoon Dijon-style mustard**
- **½ teaspoon dried tarragon**
- **¼ teaspoon garlic powder**
- **⅛ teaspoon ground black pepper**

1. Cook asparagus by any method desired (see *Cooking Asparagus*, pg 243, for preparation methods).
2. Mix together vinegar, oil, mustard, tarragon, garlic powder, and pepper; pour over asparagus, gently stirring to coat. Serve immediately.

NUTRITIONAL INFO PER SERVING: Calories 48, Fat 4g (Saturated Fat 0g), Cholesterol 0mg, Carbohydrates 6g (Fiber 2g, Sugar 1g), Sodium 14mg

Souffled Sweets

Sodium Per Serving – 29mg Serves 8

This is a holiday favorite with our family, even the finicky eaters, who love the slightly sweet, orange flavor.

- **4 yams or red-skinned sweet potatoes (about 2 pounds)[1]**
- **3 tablespoons unsalted butter or margarine**
- **¼ cup orange juice**
- **⅓ cup sugar**
- **2 teaspoons LS chicken bouillon**
- **1 teaspoon vanilla extract**
- **¼ teaspoon garlic or onion powder**
- **⅛ teaspoon ground white pepper**
- **3 egg whites, beaten until stiff peaks form**

1. Preheat oven to 400°F (200°C). Coat a 2-quart casserole or baking dish with nonstick cooking spray.
2. Pierce potatoes in several places with a fork; place on baking sheet and bake for 45 to 50 minutes, or until soft. Remove and let cool slightly.
3. Reduce oven temperature to 350°F (180°C).
4. When potatoes are cool enough to handle, peel and mash; mix with butter. Stir in orange juice, sugar, bouillon, vanilla, garlic powder, and white pepper. Potatoes should have the consistency of mashed potatoes; if too dry, add more orange juice.
5. Gently fold in egg whites; pour into the prepared baking dish. Bake, uncovered, for 30 to 35 minutes, until top begins to turn golden brown.

NUTRITIONAL INFO PER SERVING: Calories 181, Fat 4g (Sat Fat 3g), Chol 11mg, Carb 33g (Fiber 4g, Sugar 8g), Sodium 29mg

Recipe Notes

1 – Even though similar, sweet potatoes and yams are from different species. In the U.S. there are two common sweet potatoes: a pale skinned and a darker orange variety. Although the latter is called a yam, to the rest of the world, it's a sweet potato.

You can use canned sweet potatoes, but I think freshly baked tastes best. If using canned, there is no need to cook them first.

TOTAL SODIUM AND FAT BY INGREDIENT

ASPARAGUS TARRAGON
Sodium:
- 20 asparagus - 44mg
- ¼ t Dijon mustard - 10mg
- ¼ t garlic powder - 1mg

Fat (Sat Fat):
- 20 asparagus - 1g (0g)
- 1 T olive oil - 14g (2g)

Brands used/alternatives:
Gold's Dijon Mustard

SOUFFLED SWEETS
Sodium:
- 4 yams - 58mg
- ¼ c orange juice - 1mg
- 2 t LS chicken bouillon - 10mg
- ¼ t garlic powder - 1mg
- 3 egg whites - 164mg

Fat (Sat Fat):
- 4 yams - 1g (0g)
- 3 T NSA butter - 35g (22g)
- or NSA margarine - 27g (11g)

Brands used/alternatives:
Herb Ox NSA Chicken Bouillon

CREAMED SPINACH

Sodium Per Serving – 111mg   Serves 8

People on low-sodium diets should normally avoid creamed spinach. A half-cup serving is high in sodium (about 335mg). This lightened up version is not only rich and creamy, but also low in sodium.

- 3 tablespoons unsalted butter or margarine
- ¼ cup all-purpose flour
- 1 cup lowfat milk
- 1 teaspoon olive oil
- ¼ cup finely chopped onion
- 2 (10-oz) packages frozen chopped spinach, thawed and water squeezed out[1]
- ½ cup lowfat sour cream
- ¼ teaspoon garlic or onion powder
- ⅛ teaspoon ground white pepper
- ¼ teaspoon freshly ground nutmeg[2]

1. *To make white sauce:* Melt butter in a saucepan over medium heat; add flour. Cook, stirring constantly, until flour begins to change to a golden color, about 2 minutes. Slowly add milk, stirring constantly, until mixture becomes thick and smooth; set aside.
2. Heat oil in a skillet over medium heat; add onions. Cook, stirring frequently, until onions are translucent, 2 to 3 minutes; set aside.
3. Cook spinach according to package directions until almost done; decrease heat to medium-low. Stir in white sauce, sour cream, garlic powder, and pepper; cook until well blended and heated through, 4 to 5 minutes. Top with nutmeg and serve.

NUTRITIONAL INFO PER SERVING: Calories 129, Fat 7g (Sat Fat 4g), Chol 19mg, Carb 13g (Fiber 3g, Sugar 3g), Sodium 111mg

Recipe Notes

1 – I have found that some brands have a chemical taste that may adversely affect this dish. Because of this, I usually purchase frozen organic or cook 24 oz fresh spinach (use any cooking method).

2 – You can use pre-ground nutmeg, but I think the taste of freshly ground nutmeg is far superior.

TOTAL SODIUM AND FAT BY INGREDIENT

Sodium:
½ c flour - 1mg
1 cup 2% milk - 105mg
¼ c onion - 2mg
20 oz spinach - 720mg
½ c LF sour cream - 60mg
1 t garlic powder - 1mg

Fat (Sat Fat):
3 T NSA butter - 35g (24g)
  or NSA margarine - 27g (11g)
1 cup 2% milk - 5g (3g)
1 t olive oil - 5g (0g)
½ c LF sour cream - 10g (6g)

Brands used/alternatives:
Birds Eye C&W Chopped Baby Spinach
Simple Truth 2% Milk
Daisy Light Sour Cream

Squash & Apple Gratin

Sodium Per Serving – 87mg Serves 8

This is my low-salt version of a recipe that a neighbor brought to a potluck dinner. The combination of apples and squash with the cheesy bread crumbs is a perfect accompaniment to most fish, meat, or poultry dishes.

- 1 tablespoon olive oil
- 3 tablespoons unsalted butter or margarine, divided
- 3 leeks, sliced (white & light green parts)[1]
- ½ cup apple juice or cider
- ½ cup lowfat milk
- 3 tablespoons lowfat sour cream
- 2 teaspoons fresh thyme, chopped, or ½ teaspoon dried
- 1 teaspoon ground cinnamon
- ½ teaspoon ground allspice
- ¼ teaspoon garlic powder
- ¼ teaspoon ground black pepper
- 2 apples, such as Braeburn, Fuji, or Jazz, peeled, cored, and thinly sliced
- 2 pounds butternut squash, peeled, quartered and thinly sliced (about 2½-3 cups)[2]

Topping:
- 1½ cups LS bread crumbs
- 2 tablespoons unsalted butter or margarine, melted
- 1 teaspoon fresh thyme, chopped, or ¼ teaspoon dried
- 4 oz Swiss cheese, shredded (about 1 cup)
- 2 oz lowfat Cheddar cheese, shredded (about ½ cup)

1. Preheat oven to 350°F (180°C). Coat a 2-quart gratin or baking dish with nonstick cooking spray.
2. Heat oil and 1 tablespoon butter in a large skillet over medium heat; add leeks. Cook, stirring frequently, until lightly browned, about 10 minutes; add apple juice and cook 2 minutes. Add milk, sour cream, remaining teaspoon fresh thyme, cinnamon, allspice, garlic powder, and pepper; stir well and set aside.
3. In another skillet, melt remaining 2 tablespoons butter over medium heat; add apples. Cook, gently turning, until most slices are brown and limp, about 10 minutes; add to leek mixture.
4. *For the topping:* Combine bread crumbs and butter in a bowl; mix in 1 teaspoon fresh thyme, Swiss, and Cheddar cheeses. Set aside.
5. Combine squash with the leek and apple mixtures; place in a prepared gratin dish and sprinkle with bread crumb topping. Bake, uncovered, in a preheated oven for 1 hour, or until the crust is golden brown.
6. Remove and let sit 15 minutes before serving.

NUTRITIONAL INFO PER SERVING: Calories 328, Fat 18g (Sat Fat 10g), Chol 42mg, Carb 38g (Fiber 6g, Sugar 11g), Sodium 87mg

Recipe Notes
1 – For information on cleaning and storing leeks, see *Leeks*, pg 249.
2 – Substitute sweet potatoes or yams for the squash.

TOTAL SODIUM AND FAT BY INGREDIENT

Sodium:
- 4 oz Swiss cheese - 200mg
- 2 oz LF Cheddar cheese - 340mg
- 3 leeks - 54mg
- ½ c apple juice - 4mg
- ½ c LF milk - 53mg
- 3 T LF sour cream - 23mg
- 1 t cinnamon - 1mg
- ½ t allspice - 1mg
- 2 apples - 4mg
- 2 lb squash - 21mg

Fat (Sat Fat):
- 5 T NSA butter - 58g (36g) or NSA margarine - 45g (18g)
- 4 oz Swiss cheese - 36g (20g)
- 2 oz LF Cheddar - 18g (12g)
- 1 T olive oil - 14g (2g)
- 3 leeks - 1g (0g)
- ½ c LF milk - 3g (2g)
- 3 T LF sour cream - 8g (5g)
- 2 apples - 1g (0g)
- 2 lb squash - 1g (0g)

Brands used/alternatives:
4C Salt Free Bread Crumbs
Great Value Swiss Cheese
Kraft Cheddar Cheese
Simple Truth 2% Milk
Daisy Light Sour Cream

Tomato, Onion & Goat Cheese Tart

Sodium Per Serving – 61mg   Serves 6

This tart is a great summertime treat when made with fresh, juicy tomatoes from the garden. Serve it on the side or as a main course. The tart ingredients also make a great topping for a yummy pizza.

- 1 *Basic Pie Crust (pg 205)* or LS pie crust
- 1 tablespoon olive oil
- ½ large sweet onion, thinly sliced
- ¼ teaspoon garlic powder
- ⅛ teaspoon ground black pepper
- 3–4 large tomatoes, cored and cut crosswise in ¼-inch thick slices
- 2 garlic cloves, finely minced
- 4 oz goat cheese[1]
- 2–3 tablespoons chopped fresh basil leaves

1. Preheat oven to 350ºF (180ºC).
2. Prick crust with a fork, line bottom of shell with aluminum foil and pour pie weights into crust to hold its shape while baking (see *Pie Weights*, pg 252, for additional info); bake in a preheated oven for 10 minutes. Remove weights and foil; return to oven and bake 10 minutes more, or until crust is golden brown. Remove and let cool.
3. Meanwhile, heat oil in a skillet over medium heat; add onions, garlic powder, and pepper. Cook, stirring frequently, until onions are translucent, about 5 minutes. Let cool slightly.
4. Spread onions on the bottom of the precooked crust; arrange tomatoes, slightly overlapping, on top of the onions. Sprinkle with garlic and cheese; top with basil. Broil tart about 6 inches from heat for 3 minutes, or until cheese starts to melt.

NUTRITIONAL INFO PER SERVING: Calories 317, Fat 19g (Saturated Fat 6g), Cholesterol 10mg, Carbohydrates 32g (Fiber 1g, Sugar 6g), Sodium 61mg (102mg with LS pie crust)

VARIATION
Tomato, Leek & Cheese Tart

1. In place of onions, substitute 2 thinly sliced leeks (white and some green parts) and add 1 tablespoon unsalted butter to the skillet. Cook leeks, stirring frequently, until softened, about 10 minutes; proceed as directed.

NUTRITIONAL INFO PER SERVING: Calories 343, Fat 21g (Sat Fat 7g), Chol 15mg, Carb 34g (Fiber 3g, Sugar 6g), Sodium 64mg (106mg with LS pie crust)

Recipe Notes

1 – Goat cheese has a wide range of sodium, from 50mg-140mg an oz, depending on the type (soft, semi-soft, etc). If you're not a fan of goat cheese, use fresh mozzarella (85mg an oz). Be sure to check the label, as some brands are packaged in brine, which increases the amount of sodium.

TOTAL SODIUM AND FAT BY INGREDIENT

Sodium:
- 1 *Basic Pie Crust* - 150mg
  - or LS pie crust - 400mg
- ½ sweet onion - 13mg
- 1 t garlic powder - 1mg
- 3 tomatoes - 18mg
- 2 garlic cloves - 1mg
- 4 oz goat cheese - 180mg

Fat (Sat Fat):
- 1 *Basic Pie Crust* - 74g (28g)
  - or LS pie crust - 64g (28g)
- 1 T olive oil - 14g (2g)
- 3 tomatoes - 1g (0g)
- 4 oz goat cheese - 24g (6g)

Brands used/alternatives:
Vermont Creamery Herb Goat Cheese
Marie Callender's Pie Shell

QUICK REFRIED BEANS

Sodium Per Serving – 10mg   Makes 2 cups

Canned refried beans average 530mg sodium per half a cup. The following is a good low-salt substitute to use in tacos, burritos, or bean dips.

- 1 (15-oz) can NSA kidney beans, drained[1]
- ½ cup *Chicken Broth (pg 208)* or unsalted chicken broth
- 1 teaspoon LS chicken bouillon
- 1 tablespoon olive oil
- 1 tablespoon unsalted butter or margarine
- ½ cup finely minced sweet onion
- 1 garlic clove, finely minced
- 1 teaspoon ground cumin
- ½ teaspoon garlic or onion powder
- ½ teaspoon ground black pepper
- Pinch cayenne pepper
- Swiss cheese, shredded (optional)

1. In a small bowl, mash beans and 2 tablespoons chicken broth using a potato masher, ricer, or wooden spoon, adding more broth as needed until smooth and creamy. Set aside.
2. Heat oil and butter in a skillet over medium heat; add onions. Cook, stirring frequently, until onions are golden brown and caramelized, about 5 minutes.
3. Add garlic; cook, stirring constantly, until you smell the garlic, 1 to 2 minutes. Decrease heat to medium; stir in beans, cumin, garlic powder, black pepper, and cayenne. Cook, stirring occasionally, until heated through, about 5 minutes. Sprinkle cheese on top and serve.

NUTRITIONAL INFO PER SERVING: Calories 164, Fat 7g (Saturated Fat 2g), Cholesterol 8mg, Carbohydrates 19g (Fiber 7g, Sugar 2g), Sodium 10mg (18mg with LS chicken broth)

VARIATION
REFRIED BLACK BEANS

1. Substitute 1 (15-oz) can NSA black beans for the kidney beans and increase the cumin to 1½ teaspoons; proceed as directed.

NUTRITIONAL INFO PER SERVING: Calories 165, Fat 7g (Sat Fat 2g), Chol 8mg, Carb 19g (Fiber 7g, Sugar 2g), Sodium 11mg (19mg with NSA chicken broth)

Recipe Notes
1 – Canned kidney beans average 370mg sodium per ½ cup, 50% less salt varieties have about 220mg, and NSA, 35mg (visit *LowSaltFoods.com* for LS brands).

TOTAL SODIUM AND FAT BY INGREDIENT

Sodium:
- 15 oz NSA kidney beans - 18mg
- ½ c *Chicken Broth* - 10mg
  or NSA chicken broth - 43mg
- 1 t LS chicken bouillon - 5mg
- ½ c sweet onion - 4mg
- 1 garlic clove - 1mg
- 1 t cumin - 4mg

Fat (Sat Fat):
- 1 T olive oil - 14g (2g)
- 1 T NSA butter - 12g (7g)
  or NSA margarine - 9g (4g)

Brands used/alternatives:
Kuner's NSA Red Kidney Beans
Pacific Foods Organic Unsalted Chicken Stock
Herb Ox NSA Chicken Bouillon

Killer Cowboy Beans

Sodium Per Serving – 75mg Serves 16

While visiting friends in Placerville, California, I tasted the most delicious beans at a cowboy poetry reading, unfortunately they were loaded with sodium and fat. When I got home, I tried to duplicate the taste, and this is the result, but without the salt and fat. The beans are extremely hot and spicy, if you want less heat, cut back on the jalapeños.

- 1 tablespoon olive oil
- 1 pound lean ground turkey or beef
- ¼ teaspoon garlic powder
- ⅛ teaspoon ground black pepper
- 1 sweet onion, chopped
- 1 green bell pepper, chopped
- 4 garlic cloves, finely minced
- 3 (15-oz) cans NSA black beans[1]
- 3–4 jalapeños, chopped[2]
- 2 (4-oz) cans diced green chiles
- 1 (28-oz) can crushed tomatoes in purée
- 1 (15-oz) can NSA diced tomatoes
- 1 (8-oz) can NSA tomato sauce or purée (about 1 cup)
- 1 cup NSA ketchup
- 2 cups *Chicken Broth (pg 208)* or unsalted chicken broth
- 2 teaspoons LS chicken bouillon
- 3 tablespoons NSA chili powder[3]
- 2 teaspoons ground cumin
- 2 teaspoons dried oregano
- 1 teaspoon NSA spicy seasoning mix, such as taco, Cajun, or barbecue[4]

1. Heat oil in a large pot over medium heat; add meat. Cook, stirring frequently and crumbling with a fork (you want little bits of meat, not chunks), until no longer pink, about 10 minutes; add onion and bell pepper. Cook, stirring frequently, until onion has softened, about 4 minutes; decrease heat to medium-low.
2. Add remaining ingredients and simmer, covered, for 1 hour.

NUTRITIONAL INFO PER SERVING: Calories 198, Fat 2g (Sat Fat 0g), Chol 14mg, Carb 32g (Fiber 9g, Sugar 11g), Sodium 75mg (83mg with NSA chicken broth)

Recipe Notes

1 – Instead of canned beans, use dried beans (see *Cooking Dried Beans*, pg 243). A 16-oz package yields about 5–6 cups cooked beans.

2 – See *Chile Peppers*, pg 251, for information on heat levels and handling hot peppers.

3 – Most chili powders contain sodium (26mg per tsp). Look for brands without salt listed in the ingredients.

4 – You can use one of several unsalted spicy seasonings often found in Cajun or barbecue rubs. Try *Dash* (formerly *Mrs. Dash*) salt-free taco seasoning or, if your market has a Hispanic section, check the dried spices for NSA seasonings.

TOTAL SODIUM AND FAT BY INGREDIENT

Sodium:
- 1 lb ground turkey - 280mg or ground beef - 395mg
- 1 sweet onion - 27mg
- 1 bell pepper - 4mg
- 4 garlic cloves - 2mg
- 45 oz NSA black beans - 53mg
- 8 oz green chiles - 360mg
- 28 oz crushed tomatoes - 260mg
- 15 oz NSA diced tomatoes - 53mg
- 8 oz NSA tomato sauce - 20mg or tomato purée - 60mg
- 1 c NSA ketchup - 80mg
- 2 c *Chicken Broth* - 40mg or NSA chicken broth - 170mg
- 2 t LS chicken bouillon - 10mg
- 2 t cumin - 7mg

Fat (Sat Fat):
- 1 T olive oil - 14g (2g)
- 1 lb lean ground turkey - 8g (2g) or ground beef - 17g (7g)
- 2 c *Chicken Broth* - 1g (0g) or NSA chicken broth - 0g (0g)
- 2 T NSA chili powder - 4g (1g)

Brands used/alternatives:
Jennie-O 99% Lean Ground Turkey
Kuner's NSA Black Beans
La Preferida Organic Diced Green Chiles
Cento Crushed Tomatoes
Simple Truth Organic NSA Diced Tomatoes
Pomi Tomato Sauce
Heinz NSA Ketchup
Pacific Foods Organic Unsalted Chicken Stock
Herb Ox Chicken Bouillon
Dash Salt-Free Taco Seasoning

GRAINS & RICE

HERBED COUSCOUS

Sodium Per Serving – 16mg · Serves 6

Couscous, originating in North Africa, is made of semolina, the same durham wheat from which many pasta noodles are made. It takes little time to prepare and is a delicious alternative to rice or potatoes. Fresh herbs make the difference in this colorful dish.

- 2 cups *Chicken Broth (pg 208)* or unsalted chicken broth
- 1 teaspoon LS chicken bouillon
- 1 ribbon lemon peel[1]
- 1½ cups uncooked couscous[2]
- 1–2 tablespoons lemon juice
- 1 tablespoon unsalted butter or margarine
- 2 shallots, finely minced[3]
- 1 red bell pepper, chopped
- 4 green onions, thinly sliced
- ¼ cup each chopped fresh basil and parsley
- ¼ teaspoon black pepper

1. Place chicken broth, bouillon, and lemon peel in a saucepan over medium-high heat; bring to a boil. Remove lemon peel; stir in couscous and lemon juice. Cover and remove from heat; let stand until all liquid is absorbed, about 5 minutes.
2. Meanwhile, melt butter in a skillet over medium heat; add shallots. Cook, stirring frequently, until golden brown, about 5 minutes.
3. Fluff couscous with a fork, breaking up any lumps; stir in shallots, bell pepper, green onions, basil, and parsley. Season with pepper and serve.

NUTRITIONAL INFO PER SERVING: Calories 100, Fat 2g (Saturated Fat 1g), Cholesterol 7mg, Carbohydrates 17g (Fiber 2g, Sugar 3g), Sodium 16mg (38mg with unsalted broth)

VARIATIONS

SUN-DRIED TOMATO-BASIL COUSCOUS
1. Stir in ½ cup drained and chopped oil-packed sun-dried tomatoes before serving.

NUTRITIONAL INFO PER SERVING: Calories 130, Fat 4g (Sat Fat 1g), Chol 7mg, Carb 17g (Fiber 2g, Sugar 4g), Sodium 20mg (26mg with NSA chicken broth)

COUSCOUS WITH DRIED APRICOTS & PINE NUTS
1. Stir in ½ cup chopped dried apricots and ½ cup toasted pine nuts before serving.

NUTRITIONAL INFO PER SERVING: Calories 246, Fat 14g (Sat Fat 3g), Chol 7mg, Carb 27g (Fiber 5g, Sugar 9g), Sodium 31mg (37mg with NSA chicken broth)

TOTAL SODIUM AND FAT BY INGREDIENT

Sodium:
- 2 c *Chicken Broth* - 40mg
  or NSA chicken broth - 170mg
- 1 t LS chicken bouillon - 5mg
- 1½ c couscous - 14mg
- 2 shallots - 5mg
- 1 red bell pepper - 5mg
- 4 green onions - 10mg
- ¼ c basil - 8mg

Fat (Sat Fat):
- 2 c *Chicken Broth* - 1g (0g)
  or NSA chicken broth - 0g (0g)
- 1½ c couscous - 1g (0g)
- 1 T NSA butter - 12g (7g)
  or NSA margarine - 9g (4g)

Brands used/alternatives:
Pacific Foods Organic Unsalted Chicken Stock
Herb Ox NSA Chicken Bouillon

Recipe Notes
1 – Lemon peel adds flavor to the broth. Use a zester or knife to remove about an inch of the peel (avoid the bitter white membrane).
2 – This dish uses the more familiar Moroccan or quick-cooking couscous, which looks like tiny golden pellets. Israeli or pearl couscous has larger pearl-sized granules and is usually boiled instead of steamed. If using the latter, boil for 8 minutes and drain; proceed as directed.
3 – Shallots look like small onions and have a mild garlic flavor. For additional preparation and storage info, see *Shallots*, pg 253.

RISOTTO

Sodium Per Serving – 57mg   Serves 4

This basic risotto takes about 30 minutes to prepare. Unlike steamed rice, which can be left unattended, risotto requires you to stir it every few minutes.

- **1 tablespoon olive oil**
- **1 tablespoon unsalted butter or margarine**
- **½ sweet onion, finely chopped**
- **1 cup arborio rice**[1]
- **½ cup dry white wine or vermouth**
- **4–5 cups *Chicken Broth (pg 208)* or unsalted chicken broth**
- **1 tablespoon LS chicken bouillon**
- **¼ cup Parmesan cheese, freshly grated**

1. Heat oil and butter in a saucepan over medium heat; add onion. Cook, stirring frequently, until onion softens; add rice, stirring until the rice is coated with the oil. Add wine and cook, stirring frequently, until most of the wine is absorbed.
2. Add chicken broth in ½ cup increments, stirring frequently after each addition until liquid is absorbed. Continue adding the broth and allowing liquid to absorb, until rice is creamy and tender, about 20 minutes. Stir in Parmesan and serve.

NUTRITIONAL INFO PER SERVING: Calories 284, Fat 9g (Sat Fat 3g), Chol 18mg, Carb 40g (Fiber 1g, Sugar 3g), Sodium 57mg (122mg with NSA chicken broth)

VARIATION
LEMON RISOTTO

1. Before serving, stir in 1 tablespoon fresh lemon juice, 2 teaspoons grated lemon peel, and 1 tablespoon chopped fresh Italian parsley.

NUTRITIONAL INFO PER SERVING: Calories 286, Fat 9g (Sat Fat 3g), Chol 18mg, Carb 41g (Fiber 1g, Sugar 4g), Sodium 58mg (123mg with NSA chicken broth)

TOTAL SODIUM AND FAT BY INGREDIENT

RISOTTO
Sodium:
- ½ sm sweet onion - 7mg
- ½ c white wine - 6mg
- 4 c *Chicken Broth* - 80mg
  - or NSA chicken broth - 340mg
- 1 T LS chicken bouillon - 15mg
- ¼ c Parmesan - 120mg

Fat (Sat Fat):
- 1 T olive oil - 14g (2g)
- 1 T NSA butter - 12g (7g)
  - or NSA margarine - 9g (4g)
- 4 c *Chicken Broth* - 1g (0g)
  - or NSA chicken broth - 0g (0g)
- ¼ c Parmesan - 6g (5g)

Brands used/alternatives:
- Pacific Foods Organic Unsalted Chicken Stock
- Herb Ox NSA Chicken Bouillon

BASIC STEAMED RICE
Sodium:
- 1 T LS chicken bouillon - 15mg

Fat (Sat Fat):
- 2 c white rice - 0g (0g)
  - or brown rice - 6g (0g)

Brands used/alternatives:
- 365 Whole Foods 3 Cheese Blend

BASIC STEAMED RICE

Sodium Per Serving – 3mg   Serves 6

This is a basic, never fail steamed rice recipe. Adding chicken bouillon to the water gives the rice more flavor.

- **2 cups rice**[1]
- **4 cups water**
- **1 tablespoon LS chicken bouillon**

1. Combine all ingredients in a saucepan and bring to a boil over high heat. Decrease heat to low; cover, and simmer until rice is tender and all liquid is absorbed, about 45 minutes. (If rice is done, but some liquid remains, adjust lid so that steam can escape from the pan; continue to cook until all liquid is absorbed.) Fluff with a fork and serve.

NUTRITIONAL INFO PER SERVING: Calories 218, Fat 0g (Saturated Fat 0g), Cholesterol 0mg, Carbohydrates 49g (Fiber 1g, Sugar 1g), Sodium 3mg

Recipe Notes
1 – Use any kind of rice, but the type determines the cooking time and amount of water that is used (see *Rice Preparation*, pg 253, for more info).

Rice Pilaf with Pecans & Currants
Sodium Per Serving – 18mg Serves 6

This delicious pilaf is quick and easy to prepare.

- 2 tablespoons unsalted butter or margarine
- 2 shallots, chopped[1]
- 1 cup uncooked rice[2]
- 1 carrot, shredded
- ⅓ cup currants or raisins
- 1 teaspoon finely shredded orange peel
- ¼ teaspoon ground cinnamon
- ¼ teaspoon onion powder
- ¼ teaspoon ground black pepper
- ⅛ teaspoon cayenne pepper
- 2 cups *Chicken Broth (pg 208)* or unsalted chicken broth
- 2 teaspoons LS chicken bouillon
- ¼ cup pecans or almonds, toasted, coarsely chopped

1. Melt butter in a saucepan over medium heat; add shallots. Cook, stirring frequently, until shallots soften, 2 to 3 minutes; add rice. Cook, stirring frequently, until rice begins to turn golden, 3 to 4 minutes.
2. Stir in carrot, currants, orange peel, cinnamon, onion powder, black pepper, and cayenne; mix thoroughly.
3. Stir in chicken broth and bouillon; bring to a boil. Decrease heat to low and simmer, covered, until liquid is absorbed and rice is tender, about 45 minutes. Fluff with a fork and stir in pecans; serve.

NUTRITIONAL INFO PER SERVING: Calories 233, Fat 7g (Saturated Fat 3g), Cholesterol 12mg, Carbohydrates 39g (Fiber 4g, Sugar 11g), Sodium 18mg (40mg with unsalted broth)

VARIATION
Wild Rice & Cranberry Pilaf
1. Replace ½ cup of the uncooked rice with ½ cup wild rice; decrease currants to ¼ cup and add ¼ cup dried cranberries. Proceed as directed.

NUTRITIONAL INFO PER SERVING: Calories 222, Fat 7g (Sat Fat 3g), Chol 12mg, Carb 37g (Fiber 4g, Sugar 17g), Sodium 19mg (41mg with NSA chicken broth)

Recipe Notes
1 – Shallots look like small onions and have a mild flavor, somewhere between an onion and garlic (see *Shallots*, pg 253, for additional info).
2 – Use any kind of rice, but the type determines the cooking time and amount of water that is used (see *Rice Preparation*, pg 253, for more info).

TOTAL SODIUM AND FAT BY INGREDIENT
Sodium:
- 2 shallots - 10mg
- 1 carrot - 42mg
- ⅓ c currants - 6mg
- 2 c *Chicken Broth* - 40mg
  or NSA chicken broth - 170mg
- 2 t NSA chicken bouillon - 10mg

Fat (Sat Fat):
- 2 T NSA butter - 23g (14g)
  or NSA margarine - 18g (7g)
- ¼ c pecans - 20g (2g)
- 2 c *Chicken Broth* - 1g (0g)
  or NSA chicken broth - 0g (0g)

Brands used/alternatives:
Pacific Foods Organic Unsalted Chicken Stock
Herb Ox NSA Chicken Bouillon

STUFFINGS

Dried Fruit & Curry Rice Dressing

Sodium Per Serving – 11mg   Serves 10–12

This dressing is great as a stuffing or side dish. It's full of flavor and goes very well with poultry or fish dishes.

- 1½ cups long-grain white and brown rice
- 2 cups *Chicken Broth (pg 208)* or unsalted chicken broth
- 2 teaspoons LS chicken bouillon
- 1 cup water
- 2 tablespoons unsalted butter or margarine, melted
- ½ sweet onion, chopped
- 1 celery stalk, chopped
- 1 garlic clove, minced
- ½ teaspoon garlic powder
- ½ teaspoon ground black pepper
- ½ teaspoon dried thyme
- 1 apple, cored and diced
- 1 tablespoon curry powder[1]
- ½ cup dried prunes, chopped
- ½ cup dried apricots, chopped
- ¼ cup raisins or currants[2]
- ¼ cup almonds or pecans, chopped and toasted[3]

1. In a large saucepan, combine rice, chicken broth, bouillon, and water; bring to a boil over high heat. Decrease heat to medium-low; cover and cook until rice is done, 35 to 40 minutes. If not using right away, cover and refrigerate until ready to use; reheat in the microwave.
2. Meanwhile, melt butter in a large skillet over medium heat; add onion, celery, garlic, garlic powder, pepper, and thyme. Cook, stirring frequently, until onion is translucent, about 4 minutes; add apples and curry. Cook, stirring frequently, until apples begin to soften, 2 to 3 minutes; mix into rice.
3. Stir in prunes, apricots, raisins, and almonds, mixing well. Cool slightly and use as a stuffing or serve immediately as a side dish.

NUTRITIONAL INFO PER SERVING: Calories 200, Fat 5g (Sat Fat 2g), Chol 8mg, Carb 38g (Fiber 3g, Sugar 12g), Sodium 11mg (24mg with NSA chicken broth)

Recipe Notes
1 – I like a little heat in this dressing and use a hot curry powder, but a mild type works just as well (see *Curry Powder*, pg 247, for additional info).
2 – For variety, substitute dried cranberries or cherries for the raisins.
3 – Toasting nuts intensifies their flavor, see *Toasting Nuts*, pg 250, for toasting methods.

TOTAL SODIUM AND FAT BY INGREDIENT

Sodium:
- 2 c *Chicken Broth* - 40mg
  or NSA canned broth - 170mg
- 2 t LS chicken bouillon - 10mg
- ½ sweet onion - 7mg
- 1 celery stalk - 32mg
- 1 garlic clove - 1mg
- ½ t garlic powder - 1mg
- 1 apple - 2mg
- 1 T curry - 5mg
- ½ c prunes - 2mg
- ½ c dried apricots - 7mg
- ¼ c raisins - 5mg

Fat (Sat Fat):
- ¾ c brown rice - 5g (0g)
- 2 c *Chicken Broth* - 1g (0g)
  or NSA chicken broth - 0g (0g)
- 2 T NSA butter - 23g (14g)
  or NSA margarine - 18g (7g)
- 1 T curry - 1g (0g)
- ¼ cup almonds - 17g (2g)

Brands used/alternatives:
- *Pacific Foods* Organic Unsalted Chicken Stock
- *Herb Ox* NSA Chicken Bouillon

Rice Stuffing with Almonds & Olives

Sodium Per Serving – 41mg Serves 4

This yummy side dish is great with poultry dishes, especially Herb Roasted Game Hens (pg 101), and cooks up in less than 30 minutes.

- 2 tablespoons unsalted butter or margarine
- ½ cup uncooked rice[1]
- 1¼ cups *Chicken Broth (pg 208)* or unsalted chicken broth
- 1 teaspoon LS chicken bouillon
- 1 egg, beaten[2]
- 2 tablespoons minced ripe olives
- ¼ cup slivered almonds
- 2 tablespoons LS bread crumbs

1. Melt butter in a skillet over medium-high heat; add rice. Cook, stirring frequently, until golden brown, about 4 to 5 minutes; stir in chicken broth and bouillon. Decrease heat to low; cover and simmer until rice is cooked, about 20 minutes.
2. Stir in egg, olives, almonds, and bread crumbs; cook, stirring frequently, until egg sets up and is no longer runny. Use as a stuffing or side dish.

NUTRITIONAL INFO PER SERVING: Calories 209, Fat 12g (Sat Fat 4g), Chol 17mg, Carb 31g (Fiber 2g, Sugar 1g), Sodium 41mg (62mg with NSA chicken broth)

Recipe Notes

1 – I like to use a medium-grain brown rice, but any type will work.

2 – To keep fat to a minimum, use an egg substitute. See *Eggs and Egg Substitutes*, pg 23, for a comparison of fat and sodium in eggs and egg substitutes.

TOTAL SODIUM AND FAT BY INGREDIENT

Sodium:
- 1¼ c *Chicken Broth* - 25mg or LS chicken broth - 108mg
- 1 t LS chicken bouillon - 5mg
- 1 egg - 55mg
- 2 T ripe olives - 80mg

Fat (Sat Fat):
- 2 T NSA butter - 23g (14g) or NSA margarine - 18g (7g)
- 1¼ c *Chicken Broth* - 4g (0g) or LS chicken broth - 0g (0g)
- 1 egg - 3g (0g)
- 2 T ripe olives - 3g (0g)
- ¼ c almonds - 17g (2g)
- 2 T LS bread crumbs - 1g (0g)

Brands used/alternatives:
- *Pacific Foods* Organic Unsalted Chicken Stock
- *Herb Ox* NSA Chicken Bouillon
- *Mario* LS Black Olives
- *4C* Salt Free Bread Crumbs

Herbed Bread Stuffing with Dried Cranberries

Sodium Per Serving – 43mg   Makes 12 cups

This flavorful stuffing is perfect for the holidays or anytime you have chicken, turkey, or pork. For variety, substitute other dried fruits for the cranberries.

- 1 loaf *Everyday Multigrain Bread (pg 194)*, without sunflower seeds, or 1 (24-oz) loaf LS bread, cubed and toasted (about 10 cups)[1]
- 2 tablespoons unsalted butter or margarine
- 1 large sweet onion, chopped
- 3 celery stalks, finely chopped
- ¼ teaspoon garlic powder
- ¼ teaspoon ground black pepper
- 1 garlic clove, finely minced
- 1 teaspoon dried sage
- ½ teaspoon dried rosemary, crumbled
- ½ teaspoon dried thyme
- 1 cup chopped dried cranberries[2]
- 1–1½ cups *Chicken Broth (pg 208)* or unsalted chicken broth
- 1 egg, beaten[3]

1. Preheat oven to 325ºF (160ºC). Adjust oven shelf to middle level. Coat a 3-quart casserole dish with nonstick cooking spray.
2. Spread the bread cubes in a shallow baking pan; bake until dry and a light golden color, about 25 minutes. Remove and cool; then transfer to a large bowl.
3. Meanwhile, melt butter in a large skillet over medium heat; add onion, celery, garlic powder, and pepper. Cook, stirring frequently, until onions are translucent, 3 to 4 minutes; add garlic and cook, stirring frequently, until you smell the garlic, 1 to 2 minutes. Remove from heat; stir in sage, rosemary, and thyme.
4. Add onion mixture to the bread cubes and toss lightly; stir in cranberries, chicken broth, and egg, mixing well. *NOTE:* Use 1 cup broth if you like it dry or all the broth if you want it moist.
5. Transfer to prepared casserole dish, cover with foil; bake in the middle of a preheated oven for 30 minutes. Remove foil and bake until stuffing is heated through and golden brown, about 30 minutes longer.

NOTE: You can assemble stuffing the day before, cover, and refrigerate. Bring to room temperature before baking.

NUTRITIONAL INFO PER SERVING: Calories 271, Fat 5g (Sat Fat 3g), Chol 46mg, Carb 51g (Fiber 3g, Sugar 17g), Sodium 43mg (48mg with NSA chicken broth)

Recipe Notes
1 – Although LS bread is harder to find, *Food for Life* Ezekiel 4:9 bread (75mg a slice) is widely available. Using this bread raises the sodium in the stuffing to 144mg a serving.
2 – Substitute dried cherries for the cranberries.
3 – To keep fat to a minimum, use an egg substitute. See *Eggs and Egg Substitutes*, pg 23, for a comparison of fat and sodium in eggs and egg substitutes.

TOTAL SODIUM AND FAT BY INGREDIENT

Sodium:
- 1 loaf *Multigrain Bread* - 286mg or LS bread - 1,500mg
- 1 sweet onion - 27mg
- 3 celery stalks - 96mg
- ¼ t garlic powder - 1mg
- 1 garlic clove - 1mg
- 1 c dried cranberries - 8mg
- 1 c *Chicken Broth* - 20mg or LS chicken broth - 35mg
- 1 t NSA chicken bouillon - 5mg
- 1 egg - 70mg

Fat (Sat Fat):
- 1 loaf *Multigrain Bread* - 36g (17g) or LS bread - 10g (0g)
- 2 T NSA butter - 23g (14g) or NSA margarine - 18g (7g)
- 1 egg - 5g (2g)

Brands used/alternatives:
- *Food for Life* Ezekiel 4:9 Bread
- *Pacific Foods* Organic Unsalted Chicken Stock
- *Herb Ox* NSA Chicken Bouillon

BREAKFAST & LUNCH

BREAKFAST

The Mixup 178
Sausage Mixup. 178
Night Before Western Souffle 179
Bacon & Vegetable Frittata. 180
Breakfast Tacos 181
Quiche Lorraine 182
Potato Crusted Breakfast Pizza 183
Sausage & Potato Crusted Morning Pizza 183
Apricot Stuffed French Toast 184
Blueberry Pancakes. 185
Potato Pancakes 185

SANDWICHES & WRAPS

Tuna Sandwiches. 186
Open-Face Avocado-Tuna Grill 186
Roast Beef & Blue Cheese Wraps 187
Curried Chicken Salad Sandwich 187
Veggie Sandwiches with Hummus 188
Cream Cheese, Avocado & Veggie Sandwich 188
Open-Face Melted Cheese & Avocado Sandwich 188
Sloppy Joes 189

ANYTIME QUICKIES

Yogurt Gruel with Granola & Nuts. 190
Fresh Fruit Smoothie 190

BREAKFAST

THE MIXUP

Sodium Per Serving – 107mg Serves 4

We have this breakfast almost every weekend. Just about any vegetables work—green onions, asparagus, zucchini, roasted red peppers, tomatoes, and spinach—but the following is our favorite combination.

- **1 tablespoon olive oil**
- **2 small red potatoes, diced**
- **½ teaspoon dried basil[1]**
- **¼ teaspoon garlic powder**
- **⅛ teaspoon black pepper**
- **Pinch cayenne (optional)**
- **½ cup chopped sweet onion**
- **1 cup sliced mushrooms**
- **½ cup broccoli florets, cut into pieces**
- **¼ cup diced red bell pepper**
- **4 eggs, beaten with 1–2 tablespoons water or milk[2]**
- **2 oz Swiss cheese, shredded (about ½ cup)**
- **LS salsa (optional)[3]**
- **Avocado slices (optional)**

1. Heat oil in a skillet over medium heat; add potatoes, basil, garlic powder, pepper, and cayenne. Cook, stirring occasionally, until potatoes begin to brown, about 5 minutes.
2. Stir in onions, mushrooms, broccoli, and red pepper; cover and cook, stirring occasionally, until potatoes are tender, about 4-5 minutes.
3. Pour eggs over the potato mixture; once eggs begin to set, add cheese. Decrease heat to medium-low; cover and cook until cheese is melted, 2 to 3 minutes. Serve with salsa and avocado.

NUTRITIONAL INFO PER SERVING: Calories 233, Fat 13g (Saturated Fat 5g), Cholesterol 224mg, Carbohydrates 18g (Fiber 2g, Sugar 2g), Sodium 107mg

---

VARIATION
SAUSAGE MIXUP

1. Add about 2 oz lower sodium breakfast sausage patties or links[4] (cut into small chunks) with the onions and mushrooms; proceed as directed.

NUTRITIONAL INFO PER SERVING: Calories 260, Fat 15g (Sat Fat 5g), Chol 237mg, Carb 18g (Fiber 2g, Sugar 3g), Sodium 232mg

---

TOTAL SODIUM AND FAT BY INGREDIENT

Sodium:
- 1 med red potato - 20mg
- ¼ t garlic powder - 1mg
- ½ c sweet onion - 4mg
- 1 c mushrooms - 4mg
- ½ c broccoli - 15mg
- ¼ c red bell pepper - 1mg
- 4 eggs - 284mg
- 2 oz Swiss cheese - 100mg

Fat (Sat Fat):
- 1 T olive oil - 14g (2g)
- 4 eggs - 19g (6g)|
- 2 oz Swiss cheese - 18g (10g)

Brands used/alternatives:
Great Value Swiss Cheese
Frog Ranch Salsa

Recipe Notes

1 – Don't leave out the basil... it takes this dish from ordinary to exceptional!

2 – To keep fat to a minimum, use an egg substitute. See *Eggs and Egg Substitutes*, pg 23, for a comparison of fat and sodium in eggs and egg substitutes.

3 – Any LS tomato-based salsa works. Also, mango or peach salsa is a nice accompaniment to the eggs and usually is low in sodium. Look for products with 80mg or less sodium per 2 tbsp (visit LowSaltFoods.com for a list of brands).

4 – A few manufacturers, such as *Al Fresca, Shelton's,* and *Bilinski's,* offer lower sodium chicken sausages. Generally, links have less salt than patties, and sweet sausages are lower in sodium. The *Sausage Mixup* uses *Al Fresca* Apple Maple Chicken Sausage Links (150mg a link).

Night Before Western Souffle

Sodium Per Serving – 172mg Serves 10–12

This delicious make-ahead breakfast soufflé is one of my most requested recipes. Salsa, particularly a sweet salsa like peach or mango, goes well with this dish. Make it the night before and bring it to room temperature before putting it in the oven.

- **8 slices *Everyday Multigrain Bread* (pg 194) or LS bread, torn into pieces[1]**
- **8 oz sliced mushrooms (about 6½ cups)**
- **½ sweet onion, chopped**
- **1 (4-oz) can diced green chiles**
- **1 red bell pepper, chopped**
- **1 (15-oz) NSA whole corn, drained**
- **2 lower sodium breakfast sausage patties or links, cut into small chunks (about 2 oz)[2]**
- **4 eggs[3]**
- **2 cups lowfat milk**
- **½ teaspoon garlic powder**
- **½ teaspoon paprika**
- **½ teaspoon ground black pepper**
- **¼ teaspoon dried sage**
- **¼ teaspoon dried thyme**
- **4 oz Swiss cheese, shredded (about 1 cup)**
- **2 oz Cheddar cheese, shredded (about ½ cup)**
- **1 tomato, chopped**

1. Coat a rectangular baking dish with nonstick cooking spray. Cover bottom with bread pieces; spread mushrooms on top. Continue layering with onions, green chiles, bell pepper, and corn; finish with crumbled sausage on top of veggies.
2. Combine eggs, milk, garlic powder, paprika, pepper, sage, and thyme; pour over veggies. Cover and refrigerate overnight.
3. Preheat oven to 350ºF (180ºC).
4. Bring soufflé to room temperature; top with cheeses and tomato. Bake, covered, for 1 hour. Let stand 5 minutes before cutting into squares. Serve with salsa, if desired.

NUTRITIONAL INFO PER SERVING: Calories 285, Fat 12g (Sat Fat 6g), Chol 121mg, Carb 30g (Fiber 2g, Sugar 8g), Sodium 172mg

Recipe Notes

1 – Visit LowSaltFoods.com for a current list of low sodium bread.
2 – Although most breakfast sausage has too much sodium for a low-salt diet, a few manufacturers, such as *Al Fresca*, *Shelton's*, and *Bilinski's*, offer lower sodium chicken sausages. Generally, links have less salt than patties, and sweet sausages are lower in sodium.
3 – To keep fat to a minimum, use an egg substitute. See *Eggs and Egg Substitutes*, pg 23, for a comparison of fat and sodium in eggs and egg substitutes.

TOTAL SODIUM AND FAT BY INGREDIENT

Sodium:
- 8 sl *Multigrain Bread* - 143mg or LS bread - 600mg
- 8 oz mushrooms - 11mg
- ½ sweet onion - 7mg
- 4 oz green chiles - 180mg
- 1 red bell pepper - 5mg
- 15 oz NSA corn - 35mg
- 2 oz sausage - 300mg
- 4 eggs - 284mg
- 2 c LF milk - 210mg
- ½ t garlic powder - 1mg
- 4 oz Swiss cheese - 200mg
- 2 oz LF Cheddar cheese - 340mg
- 1 tomato - 6mg

Fat (Sat Fat):
- 8 sl *Multigrain* - 29g (11g) or LS bread - 8g (0g)
- 8 oz mushrooms - 1g (0g)
- 15 oz NSA corn - 5g (0g)
- 2 oz sausage - 8g (3g)
- 4 eggs - 19g (6g)
- 2 c LF milk - 10g (6g)
- 4 oz Swiss - 36g (20g)
- 2 oz LF Cheddar - 18g (12g)

Brands used/alternatives:
- *Food for Life* Ezekiel 4:9 Bread
- *La Preferida* Organic Diced Green Chiles
- *Libby's Naturals* NSA Whole Kernel Sweet Corn
- *Al Fresco* Apple Maple Chicken Breakfast Sausage Links
- *Simple Truth* 2% Milk
- *Great Value* Swiss Cheese
- *Kraft* Cheddar Cheese

Bacon & Vegetable Frittata

Sodium Per Serving – 168mg | Serves 4

I liken a frittata to an omelet pizza, all the ingredients are slowly cooked in the skillet and served as a large round omelet. This is my basic frittata; vary the ingredients by adding different vegetables, cheeses, and meat.

- 1 teaspoon olive oil
- 2 slices lower sodium turkey bacon, cut into small pieces[1]
- ½ cup chopped sweet onion
- ½ red bell pepper, chopped
- ½ zucchini, chopped
- ¼ teaspoon garlic powder
- ⅛ teaspoon ground black pepper
- 1½ cups spinach leaves, coarsely chopped
- 6 eggs[2]
- ¼ teaspoon hot pepper sauce, such as *Tabasco*
- 2 oz Swiss cheese, shredded (about ½ cup)
- 1–2 tomatoes chopped
- 1–2 tablespoons chopped fresh basil

1. Heat oil in a large nonstick skillet over medium heat; add bacon and cook until lightly browned, 3 to 4 minutes. Add onion, bell pepper, zucchini, garlic powder, and pepper; cook, stirring frequently, until vegetables have softened, about 5 minutes. Add spinach and cook, stirring constantly, until wilted, about 1 minute.
2. In a bowl, whisk eggs with hot pepper sauce and pour over vegetable mixture; decrease heat to medium-low. Cover and cook, without stirring, until eggs are set, about 5 minutes; sprinkle eggs with cheese, tomatoes, and basil. Cover and cook until cheese has melted, 2 to 3 minutes. Cut into wedges and serve.

NUTRITIONAL INFO PER SERVING: Calories 201, Fat 14g (Sat Fat 5g), Chol 332mg, Carb 6g (Fiber 1g, Sugar 3g), Sodium 168mg

Recipe Notes

1 – Several manufacturers offer low sodium bacon. Visit *LowSaltFoods.com* for a list of brands.

2 – To keep fat to a minimum, use an egg substitute. See *Eggs and Egg Substitutes*, pg 23, for a comparison of fat and sodium in eggs and egg substitutes.

TOTAL SODIUM AND FAT BY INGREDIENT

Sodium:
- 2 sl LS turkey bacon - 80mg
- ½ sm sweet onion - 4mg
- ½ red bell pepper - 2mg
- ½ zucchini - 10mg
- ¼ t garlic powder - 1mg
- 1½ c spinach - 36mg
- ¼ t hot pepper sauce - 9mg
- 6 eggs - 426mg
- 2 oz Swiss cheese - 100mg
- 1 tomato - 6mg

Fat (Sat Fat):
- 1 t olive oil - 5g (1g)
- 2 sl LS turkey bacon - 2g (1g)
- 6 eggs - 29g (10g)
- 2 oz Swiss cheese - 18g (10g)

Brands used/alternatives:
- *Butterball* Lower Sodium Turkey Bacon
- *Great Value* Swiss Cheese

Breakfast Tacos

Sodium Per Serving – 104mg Serves 6

This yummy alternative to scrambled eggs is baked instead of fried. Use corn or low-sodium flour tortillas.

- 1 tablespoon olive oil
- 2 small red potatoes, diced (about 1 cup)
- ¼ teaspoon NSA chili powder[1]
- ¼ teaspoon garlic or onion powder
- ⅛ teaspoon dried cumin
- ⅛ teaspoon dried oregano
- ⅛ teaspoon ground black pepper
- ½ red or green bell pepper, chopped
- 2 green onions, chopped (white and green parts)
- 4 eggs, beaten with 2 tablespoons lowfat milk or water[2]
- 4 oz Swiss cheese, shredded (about ½ cup)
- 12 corn or 6 LS flour tortillas[3]

Optional garnishes:
- **Chopped tomato**
- **Chopped onion**
- *Guacamole (pg 28)*
- **LS salsa**[4]
- **Chopped cilantro**

1. Preheat oven to 350°F (180°C).
2. Heat oil in a skillet over medium heat; add potatoes, chili powder, garlic powder, cumin, oregano, and black pepper. Cook, stirring frequently, until potatoes begin to brown, about 5 minutes.
3. Stir in red pepper and onions; cover and cook, stirring occasionally, until potatoes are tender, 5 to 8 minutes.
4. Pour eggs over the potato mixture; once eggs begin to set, stir gently and continue cooking until eggs are done.
5. Equally divide egg mixture and fill each tortilla; top with cheese, fold in half, and place in a baking dish. Bake in a preheated oven for 10 to 15 minutes, until lightly browned and crisp. Serve with chopped tomato, onion, guacamole, salsa, and cilantro.

NUTRITIONAL INFO PER TACO (without garnishes): Calories 276, Fat 11g (Sat Fat 4g), Chol 151mg, Carb 132g (Fiber 3g, Sugar 3g), Sodium 104mg (169mg with LS flour tortillas)

Recipe Notes

1 – Surprisingly, chili powder contains sodium (26mg per teaspoon). Look for brands without salt listed in the ingredients.

2 – To keep fat to a minimum, use an egg substitute. See *Eggs and Egg Substitutes*, pg 23, for a comparison of fat and sodium in eggs and egg substitutes.

3 – When it comes to tortillas, fresh corn have the least sodium (11mg per 6-inch tortilla vs 364mg for an 8-inch flour). Shelf-stable shells average 80mg each.

4 – Most bottled salsas average 256mg sodium per 2 tbsp, a few LS varieties have 60mg or less (visit LowSaltFoods.com for a list of products).

TOTAL SODIUM AND FAT BY INGREDIENT

Sodium:
- 2 red potatoes - 61mg
- ½ red bell pepper - 1mg
- 2 green onions - 8mg
- ⅛ t cumin - 1mg
- 4 eggs - 280mg
- 2 T LF milk - 14mg
- 4 oz Swiss cheese - 40mg
- 12 corn tortillas - 40mg
  - or 4 LS flour tortillas - 340mg

Fat (Sat Fat):
- 1 T olive oil - 14g (2g)
- 4 eggs - 20g (6g)
- 2 T LF milk - 1g (0g)
- 4 oz Swiss cheese - 32g (20g)
- 8 corn tortillas - 8g (0g)
  - or 4 LS flour - 14g (6g)

Brands used/alternatives:
- *Simple Truth* 2% Milk
- *Great Value* Swiss Cheese
- *Mission* Corn Tortillas
  - or *La Banderita* LS Flour Tortillas

QUICHE LORRAINE

Sodium Per Serving – 166mg   Serves 6

Quiche Lorraine is a French classic served for breakfast, lunch, or dinner. Although traditionally high in salt, I've reduced the amount significantly using low-sodium bacon and Swiss cheese.

- 1 *Basic Pie Crust (pg 205)* or LS pie crust
- 1 tablespoon olive oil
- 1 tablespoon unsalted butter or margarine
- 1½ pounds red potatoes, shredded
- ½ cup chopped sweet onions
- ¼ teaspoon garlic or onion powder
- ⅛ teaspoon ground black pepper
- 4 slices lower sodium turkey bacon, crisply cooked and crumbled[1]
- 4 oz Swiss cheese, shredded (about 1 cup)
- 4 eggs[2]
- 1 cup lowfat milk
- ¼ teaspoon Worcestershire sauce
- 2 tablespoons all-purpose flour
- ½ teaspoon dry mustard
- ¼ teaspoon dried basil
- ⅛ teaspoon cayenne pepper
- Tomato slices (optional)

1. Preheat oven to 350°F (180°C).
2. Prick crust with a fork, line bottom of shell with aluminum foil and pour pie weights into crust to hold its shape while baking (see *Pie Weights*, pg 252, for more info); bake in a preheated oven for 10 minutes. Remove weights and foil; return to oven and bake 10 minutes more, or until crust is golden brown. Remove and let cool.
3. Heat oil and butter in a large skillet over medium-high heat; add potatoes, onions, garlic powder, and black pepper. Cook, stirring frequently, until potatoes are lightly browned, about 4 minutes; stir in bacon and remove from heat.
4. Spoon potato mixture into partially-baked pie crust; sprinkle with cheese.
5. Beat eggs slightly; mix with milk, Worcestershire sauce, flour, mustard, basil, and cayenne. Pour over potatoes.
6. Bake in a preheated oven for 45 minutes or until a knife inserted in the center comes out clean. Remove from oven and let stand 15 minutes; cut into wedges and serve. Garnish with tomato slices.

NUTRITIONAL INFO PER SERVING: Calories 534, Fat 28g (Sat Fat 11g), Chol 169mg, Carb 55g (Fiber 3g, Sugar 7g), Sodium 166mg (208mg with LS pie crust)

Recipe Notes

1 – Several manufacturers offer low sodium bacon. Visit *LowSaltFoods.com* for a list of LS products. You can also substitute 2 oz LS sausage, broken into chunks.

2 – To keep fat to a minimum, use an egg substitute. See *Eggs and Egg Substitutes*, pg 23, for a comparison of fat and sodium in eggs and egg substitutes.

VARIATION

Instead of a flour crust, layer thin slices of sliced yam or sweet potato on the bottom of the pie plate. This reduces the sodium per serving by 24mg (yam) or 19mg (sweet potato).

TOTAL SODIUM AND FAT BY INGREDIENT

Sodium:
- 1 *Basic Pie Crust* - 150mg
  or LS pie crust - 400mg
- 1½ lb red potatoes - 82mg
- ½ c sweet onion - 4mg
- ¼ t garlic powder - 1mg
- 4 sl LS turkey bacon - 160mg
- 4 oz Swiss cheese - 200mg
- 4 eggs - 284mg
- 1 c LF milk - 105mg
- ¼ t Worcestershire - 5mg

Fat (Sat Fat):
- 1 *Basic Pie Crust* - 74g (28g)
  or LS pie crust - 64g (28g)
- 1 T olive oil - 14g (2g)
- 1 T NSA butter - 12g (7g)
  or NSA margarine - 9g (4g)
- 1½ lb red potatoes - 1g (0g)
- 4 sl LS turkey bacon - 4g (1g)
- 4 oz Swiss cheese - 36g (20g)
- 4 eggs - 19g (6g)
- 1 c LF milk - 5g (3g)

Brands used/alternatives:
Butterball Lower Sodium Turkey Bacon
Great Value Swiss Cheese
Simple Truth 2% Milk
Robbie's Worcestershire Sauce
Marie Callender's Pie Shell

Potato Crusted Breakfast Pizza

Sodium Per Serving – 97mg   Serves 6

The potatoes, arranged in concentric circles, act as the crust for this morning dish and creates a beautiful presentation for a brunch or buffet. And the best part... it's ready in 30 minutes.

- 2 tablespoons olive oil, divided
- 2 medium red potatoes, thinly sliced
- ½ teaspoon Tuscan spice mix, divided[1]
- ¼ teaspoon garlic powder, divided
- ⅛ teaspoon ground black pepper, divided
- ½ medium sweet onion, sliced
- 2–3 garlic cloves, finely minced
- 1 cup mixed veggies, sliced or cut into bite-size pieces[2]
- 4 eggs mixed with 2 tablespoons lowfat milk or water[3]
- 1 green onion, chopped (white/green parts)
- 1 tomato, chopped
- 4 oz Swiss cheese, shredded (about 1 cup)
- 1 roasted red pepper[4]
- Parsley (optional)

1. Preheat oven to 350ºF (180ºC).
2. Rub a large oven-proof skillet with 1 tablespoon oil. Arrange potatoes on the bottom of the skillet in a circular design beginning on the outside and working toward the center (each slice overlapping the last). Sprinkle half the Tuscan spice mix, half the garlic powder, and half the pepper over the potatoes. Place potatoes over medium heat and fry until potatoes are golden brown on the bottom (do not turn), about 5 minutes.
3. Meanwhile, heat remaining 1 tablespoon oil in another skillet over medium heat; add onion, garlic, mixed veggies, and remaining Tuscan spice mix, garlic powder, and pepper. Cook, stirring frequently, until veggies are tender. Remove from heat; mix in eggs and milk. Pour over potatoes and top with cheese, green onions, and tomatoes; arrange red pepper slices on top in a spoke-like pattern.
4. Bake in a preheated oven for 10 to 15 minutes, until eggs are set. Remove and place on a platter; sprinkle with parsley and serve.

NUTRITIONAL INFO PER SERVING: Calories 254, Fat 15g (Sat Fat 5g), Chol 158mg, Carb 20g (Fiber 3g, Sugar 6g), Sodium 97mg

VARIATION
Sausage & Potato Crusted Morning Pizza
1. Cut into small chunks 2 lower sodium breakfast sausage patties or links (about 2 oz) and cook with the mixed vegetables; proceed as directed.

NUTRITIONAL INFO PER SERVING: Calories 271, Fat 16g (Sat Fat 6g), Chol 162mg, Carb 20g (Fiber 3g, Sugar 5g), Sodium 136mg

Recipe Notes
1 – Tuscan spice blends are found in most supermarkets. To make your own, mix together equal amounts of dried rosemary, sage, thyme, and basil.
2 – Use a combination of veggies, such as broccoli, corn, mushrooms, and zucchini.
3 – To keep fat to a minimum, use an egg substitute. See *Eggs and Egg Substitutes*, pg 23, for a comparison of eggs and egg substitutes.
4 – Substitute bottled roasted red sweet peppers, cut into strips (see *Roasting Peppers*, pg 251, for roasting info).

TOTAL SODIUM AND FAT BY INGREDIENT

Sodium:
- 2 red potatoes - 42mg
- ¼ t garlic powder - 1mg
- ½ c sweet onion - 13mg
- 2 garlic clove - 1mg
- 1 c mixed veggies - 20mg
- 4 eggs - 284mg
- 2 T LF milk - 13mg
- 1 green onion - 2mg
- 1 tomato - 6mg
- 1 roasted red pepper - 2mg
- 4 oz Swiss cheese - 200mg

Fat (Sat Fat):
- 2 T olive oil - 28g (4g)
- 2 red potatoes - 1g (0g)
- 1 c mixed veggies - 1g (0g)
- 4 eggs - 20g (6g)
- 2 T LF milk - 1g (0g)
- 4 oz Swiss Cheese - 36g (20g)
- 1 roasted red pepper - 4g (1g)

Brands used/alternatives:
Birds Eye C&W Ultimate Petite Mixed Veggies
Great Value Swiss Cheese
Simple Truth 2% Milk

APRICOT STUFFED FRENCH TOAST

Sodium Per Serving – 136mg   Serves 8

This recipe was given to me some time ago and although the original had too much salt, I've managed to remove most of it and still keep its wonderful decadence. It is perfect for a special occasion breakfast or brunch. Filled with a cream cheese-apricot mixture and topped with an apricot sauce, it is both delicious and easy to make. I like to use mascarpone and a lowfat cream cheese to keep both fat and sodium to a minimum.

- ½ cup chopped dried apricots
- ¾ cup orange juice, divided
- ⅔ cup apricot jam (preferably fruit sweetened)
- 4 oz mascarpone[1]
- 4 oz lowfat cream cheese[1]
- ¼ cup chopped pecans or almonds, toasted[2]
- 16 slices *No Knead French Bread (pg 192)* or LS bread
- 4 eggs[3]
- ¼ cup lowfat or nonfat milk
- 3–4 tablespoons sugar
- 1 tablespoon grated orange zest
- 1 teaspoon vanilla extract
- 2 tablespoons unsalted butter or margarine

1. In a small saucepan over medium-high heat, mix together apricots and ¼ cup orange juice; place on medium-high and bring to a boil. Reduce heat to low and simmer 10 minutes; remove and cool to room temperature.
2. *For the apricot syrup:* In another small saucepan over medium-high heat, combine jam and remaining ½ cup orange juice; bring to a boil. Cook, stirring occasionally, until thickened to a syrup consistency, about 3 minutes; remove from heat and let cool slightly.
3. In a small bowl, combine mascarpone, cream cheese, pecans, and dried apricot mixture. Equally divide filling and spread on 8 slices of bread; top with remaining bread, making 8 sandwiches.
4. Combine eggs, milk, sugar, orange zest, and vanilla. Dip each sandwich into the egg mixture; turn, until both sides are coated.
5. Melt butter in a skillet or griddle over medium-high heat; fry sandwiches until brown on both sides. Serve with apricot syrup.

NUTRITIONAL INFO PER SERVING: Calories 523, Fat 20g (Sat Fat 11g), Chol 148mg, Carb 73g (Fiber 3g, Sugar 22g), Sodium 136mg (280mg with LS bread)

Recipe Notes

1 – Mascarpone, known as Italian cream cheese, is low in sodium, but high in fat (see *Cream Cheese Comparison*, pg 247, for more info).
2 – See *Toasting Nuts*, pg 250, for toasting options.
3 – To keep fat to a minimum, use an egg substitute. See *Eggs and Egg Substitutes*, pg 23, for a comparison of fat and sodium in eggs and egg substitutes.

TOTAL SODIUM AND FAT BY INGREDIENT

Sodium:
- ½ c apricots - 7mg
- ¾ c orange juice - 2mg
- 4 oz mascarpone cheese - 40mg
- 4 oz cream cheese - 300mg or LF cream cheese - 480mg
- 16 sl *No Knead Bread* - 307mg or LS bread - 1,440mg
- ¼ c LF milk - 27mg
- 4 eggs - 284mg

Fat (Sat Fat):
- 4 oz mascarpone - 56g (40g)
- 4 oz cream cheese - 36g (24g) or LF cream cheese - 24g (14g)
- ¼ c pecans - 20g (2g)
- 16 sl *No Knead Bread* - 17g (8g) or LS bread - 12g (0g)
- ¼ c LF milk - 1g (1g)
- 4 eggs - 19g (6g)
- 2 T NSA butter - 23g (16g) or NSA margarine - 18g (7g)

Brands used/alternatives:
BelGioioso Mascarpone Cheese
Great Value Neufchâtel Cheese
Signature Select Wheat Bread
Simple Truth 2% Milk

BLUEBERRY PANCAKES

Sodium Per Serving – 76mg Serves 4–6

Packaged pancake mixes average 562mg sodium a serving. By using, no-salt-added baking powder, you can make thick, dense pancakes that are low in sodium... and so delicious!

- 1½ cups all-purpose or whole-wheat flour
- ¼ cup sugar
- 2 tablespoons NSA baking powder[1]
- 2 eggs, lightly beaten[2]
- 1½ cups lowfat milk
- ½ teaspoon vanilla extract
- ¼ teaspoon ground cinnamon
- 1 tablespoon unsalted butter or margarine, melted
- 1 cup fresh or frozen blueberries

1. In a large bowl, mix together flour, sugar, and baking powder.
2. In another bowl, beat eggs, milk, vanilla, cinnamon, and butter; gradually add to flour.
3. Heat a lightly oiled griddle or skillet over medium heat. Working in batches, pour batter onto griddle, using ¼ cup batter for each pancake. Top each pancake with 6–8 blueberries; cook until browned on both sides, about 2 minutes a side. Serve with syrup or jam.

NUTRITIONAL INFO PER SERVING: Calories 303, Fat 8g (Saturated Fat 4g), Cholesterol 121mg, Carbohydrates 47g (Fiber 1g, Sugar 10g), Sodium 76mg

POTATO PANCAKES

Sodium Per Serving – 31mg Serves 4–6

Serve these potato pancakes anytime; plus, they are easy to fix and taste great.

- 1 pound Yukon gold or russet potatoes, grated and moisture squeezed out
- 1 egg, lightly beaten[2]
- ½ sweet onion, chopped
- 1 teaspoon all-purpose flour
- ¼ teaspoon onion powder
- ⅛ teaspoon ground black pepper
- 1 tablespoon olive oil
- 1 tablespoon unsalted butter or margarine
- 2 cups applesauce

1. Mix together potatoes, egg, onion, flour, onion powder, and pepper.
2. Heat oil and butter in a skillet over medium heat; cook potatoes until browned on both sides, about 5 minutes per side. Serve with applesauce.

NUTRITIONAL INFO PER SERVING: Calories 295, Fat 8g (Sat Fat 3g), Chol 60mg, Carb 54g (Fiber 4g, Sugar 27g), Sodium 31mg

Recipe Notes

1 – See *Baking Powder/Baking Soda*, pg 243, for info on NSA baking powder.
2 – To keep fat to a minimum, use an egg substitute. See *Eggs and Egg Substitutes*, pg 23, for a comparison of fat and sodium in eggs and egg substitutes.

TOTAL SODIUM AND FAT BY INGREDIENT

BLUEBERRY PANCAKES
Sodium:
1½ c flour - 4mg
2 eggs - 142mg
1½ c LF milk - 158mg
1 c blueberries - 2mg
Fat (Sat Fat):
1½ c flour - 2g (0g)
2 eggs - 10g (3g)
1½ c LF milk - 8g (5g)
1 T NSA butter - 12g (7g)
 or NSA margarine - 9g (4g)
Brands used/alternatives:
Hain Featherweight Baking Powder
Simple Truth 2% Milk

POTATO PANCAKES
Sodium:
1 lb potatoes - 45mg
1 egg - 71mg
½ sm sweet onion - 7mg
Fat (Sat Fat):
1 lb potatoes - 1g (0g)
1 egg - 5g (2g)
1 T NSA butter - 12g (7g)
 or NSA margarine - 9g (4g)
1 T olive oil - 14g (2g)
Brands used/alternatives:
Motts Applesauce

SANDWICHES & WRAPS

TUNA SANDWICHES

Sodium Per Serving – 134mg   Makes 3 sandwiches

This is one of our favorite sandwiches. It's light and flavorful and not loaded with mayonnaise.

- 1 (6.5-oz) can LS tuna (albacore)
- 2 tablespoons minced onion
- 1 tablespoon sweet pickle relish
- 2 tablespoons mayonnaise
- 2 tablespoons plain lowfat yogurt
- 6 slices *Everyday Multigrain Bread (pg 194)* or LS bread
- Lettuce leaves
- Tomato slices

1. Mix together tuna, onion, pickle relish, mayonnaise, and yogurt. NOTE: If tuna is too dry for your taste, add 1-2 tablespoons more yogurt.
2. Spread one-third mixture on 3 slices of bread; top with lettuce, tomato, and remaining bread.

NUTRITIONAL INFO PER SANDWICH: Calories 384, Fat 10g (Saturated Fat 2g), Cholesterol 23mg, Carbohydrates 54g (Fiber 3g, Sugar 5g), Sodium 134mg (179 with LS bread)

VARIATION

OPEN-FACE AVOCADO-TUNA GRILL

1. Spread prepared tuna filling equally on 3 slices of bread. Top with sliced avocado and 1 slice Swiss cheese. Broil about 5 inches from heat until cheese melts, 2 to 3 minutes. NOTE: The bread will be soft; if you want it toasted, do so before adding the tuna and broiling.

NUTRITIONAL INFO PER SANDWICH: Calories 421, Fat 21g (Sat Fat 7g), Chol 36mg, Carb 34g (Fiber 5g, Sugar 4g), Sodium 153mg (165mg with LS bread)

TOTAL SODIUM AND FAT BY INGREDIENT

Sodium:
- 6.5 oz NSA tuna - 65mg
- 2 T onion - 2mg
- 1 T pickle relish - 60mg
- 2 T mayonnaise - 140mg
  or lite mayonnaise - 200mg
- 2 T LF yogurt - 9mg
- 6 sl *Everyday Multigrain* - 115mg
  or LS bread - 600mg
- 3 lettuce leaves - 4mg
- 3 sl tomato - 6mg

Fat (Sat Fat):
- 6.5 oz NSA tuna - 1g (0g)
- 2 T mayonnaise - 22g (3g)
  or lite mayonnaise - 9g (1g)
- 2 T LF yogurt - 1g (0g)
- 6 sl *Multigrain* - 6g (3g)
  or LS bread - 4g (0g)

Brands used/alternatives:
Bumble Bee LS Albacore in Water
Heinz Sweet Pickle Relish
Kraft Real Mayo
Fagé 2% Greek Yogurt
Food for Life Ezekiel 4:9 Bread

Roast Beef & Blue Cheese Wraps

Sodium Per Serving – 219mg Serves 4

This is perfect for leftover beef; the horseradish and blue cheese add a zesty flavor to this delicious wrap. For a milder taste, use Swiss cheese. This filling also is good on sandwiches or in pitas.

- 1 oz Stilton blue cheese, crumbled[1]
- 1–1½ tablespoons prepared horseradish
- 1 tablespoon mayonnaise
- 2 tablespoons lowfat sour cream
- ½ teaspoon Dijon mustard
- ½ teaspoon garlic powder
- ½ teaspoon black pepper
- ½ small sweet onion, thinly sliced
- 4 (1-oz) slices roast beef
- 1 roasted red pepper, sliced
- 4 LS flour tortillas or wraps[2]

1. Mix together blue cheese, horseradish, mayonnaise, sour cream, mustard, garlic powder, and pepper. Divide equally and spread on each tortilla; layer onions, beef, and red peppers. Roll up and cut in half diagonally.

NUTRITIONAL INFO PER SERVING: Calories 263, Fat 11g (Sat Fat 4g), Chol 31mg, Carb 27g (Fiber 3g, Sugar 4g), Sodium 219mg

Curried Chicken Salad Sandwich

Sodium Per Serving – 118mg Serves 4

This goes together quickly with leftover chicken. Serve on low-salt bread, in a pita pocket, or roll up in a low-sodium flour tortilla. The filling also makes a yummy salad when served on romaine leaves.

- 2 cups cooked chicken, diced
- 1 apple, diced
- ½ cup cashews, chopped
- 1 celery stalk, diced
- ¼ cup currants or raisins
- 2 tablespoons lowfat mayo
- 2 tablespoons lowfat plain yogurt
- 2 tablespoons LS mango chutney[3]
- ⅛ teaspoon black pepper
- ½–1 teaspoon curry powder[4]
- 8 slices *Everyday Multigrain Bread (pg 194)* or LS bread

1. Mix together all ingredients, except bread. Evenly divide and spread on bread.

NUTRITIONAL INFO PER SERVING: Calories 712, Fat 25g (Sat Fat 7g), Chol 102mg, Carb 90g (Fiber 8g, Sugar 25g), Sodium 118mg (219 with LS bread)

Recipe Notes

1 – Stilton is milder and firmer than other blue cheeses, and has less sodium.
2 – Most flour tortillas are high in sodium (335mg per 10-inch tortilla), however, several low-carb varieties have less than 125mg per tortilla.
3 – Mango chutney averages 70mg-170mg sodium or more per tbsp (visit LowSaltFoods.com for a list of LS brands).
4 – A sweet, hot curry goes well with this (see *Curry Powder*, pg 247, for more info).

TOTAL SODIUM AND FAT BY INGREDIENT

ROAST BEEF WRAPS
Sodium:
- 1 oz Stilton cheese - 220mg
- 1 T horseradish - 60mg
- 1 T lite mayonnaise - 50mg
- 2 T LF sour cream - 15mg
- ½ t Dijon mustard - 20mg
- ½ t garlic powder - 1mg
- ½ sweet onion - 7mg
- 4 oz beef - 160mg
- 1 roasted red bell pepper - 2mg
- 4 LS flour tortillas - 340mg

Fat (Sat Fat):
- 1 oz Stilton cheese - 9g (6g)
- 1 T horseradish - 2g (0g)
- 1 T lite mayonnaise - 11g (2g)
- 2 T LF yogurt - 3g (2g)
- 4 oz beef - 6g (2g)
- 4 LS flour tortillas - 14g (6g)

Brands used/alternatives:
Clausen Blue Stilton Cheese
Beaver Cream Horseradish
Chosen Foods Classic Mayo w/ Avocado Oil
Daisy Light Sour Cream
Gold's Dijon Mustard
Boar's Head LS Sliced Roast Beef
La Banderita LS Tortillas
Tumaro's Ancient Grain Wraps

CURRIED CHICKEN SANDWICH
Sodium:
- 2 c chicken - 120mg
- 1 apple - 2mg
- 1 celery stalk - 32mg
- ¼ c currants - 4mg
- 2 T lite mayonnaise - 100mg
- 2 T LF yogurt - 5mg
- 2 T mango chutney - 20mg
- ½ t curry - 1mg
- 8 sl *Multigrain Bread* - 191mg or LS bread - 600mg

Fat (Sat Fat):
- 2 c chicken - 12g (5g)
- ½ c NSA cashews - 26g (5g)
- 2 T lite mayonnaise - 22g (3g)
- 8 sl *Multigrain Bread* - 39g (15g) or LS bread - 4g (0g)

Brands used/alternatives:
Tyson All Natural Chicken Breasts
Chosen Foods Classic Mayo w/ Avocado Oil
Two Good Plain Yogurt
Stonewall Kitchen Mango Chutney
Food for Life Ezekiel 4:9 Bread

Veggie Sandwiches with Hummus

Sodium Per Serving – 141mg   Serves

This healthy vegetarian sandwich is great with leftover hummus and raw vegetables.

- **1 cup *Spicy Roasted Red Pepper Hummus* (pg 26) or LS prepared hummus**
- **8 slices *Olive-Sage Bread* (pg 194) or LS sandwich bread**
- **½ cucumber, sliced**
- **6–8 mushrooms, sliced**
- **½ red bell pepper, sliced**
- **4 slices sweet onion**
- **1–2 tomatoes, sliced**
- **4 slices Swiss cheese**
- **2 cups alfalfa sprouts or shredded lettuce[1]**

1. Spread 2 tablespoons hummus on each slice of bread; top 4 slices with layers of cucumber, mushrooms, bell pepper, onion, tomato, cheese, and alfalfa sprouts. Cover with remaining bread slices and serve. *NOTE:* This is also good with melted cheese. Remove sprouts and the bread slice on top. Place cheese on 4 slices; broil for 2 to 3 minutes until cheese melts. Top with sprouts and remaining bread; serve.

NUTRITIONAL INFO PER SERVING: Calories 635, Fat 22g (Saturated Fat 9g), Cholesterol 66mg, Carbohydrates 95g (Fiber 13g, Sugar 15g), Sodium 141mg (244mg with LS bread)

VARIATIONS

Cream Cheese, Avocado & Veggie Sandwich

1. Omit the hummus and use ½ cup whipped cream cheese; spread 2 tablespoons on 4 slices of bread. Proceed as directed, omitting the Swiss cheese and adding sliced avocado instead. NOTE: Spread a little mustard or aoili on the remaining bread before placing on top.

NUTRITIONAL INFO PER SANDWICH: Calories 639, Fat 28g (Sat Fat 13g), Chol 86mg, Carb 77g (Fiber 8g, Sugar 12g), Sodium 140mg (243mg with LS bread)

Open-Face Melted Cheese & Avocado Sandwich

1. To make 4 open-face sandwiches, omit the sprouts and 4 pieces of bread. Slice a large avocado and evenly divide, placing one-fourth on each veggie sandwich.
2. Top with a slice of Swiss cheese and broil for 2 to 3 minutes until cheese melts; serve.

NUTRITIONAL INFO PER SANDWICH: Calories 482, Fat 23g (Sat Fat 7g), Chol 43mg, Carb 65g (Fiber 13g, Sugar 12g), Sodium 119mg (171mg with LS bread)

TOTAL SODIUM AND FAT BY INGREDIENT

Sodium:
- 1 c *Red Pepper Hummus* - 196mg or prepared hummus -
- 8 sl *Olive-Sage Bread* - 191mg or LS bread - 600mg
- ½ cucumber - 3mg
- 6 mushrooms - 1mg
- ½ red bell pepper - 2mg
- ½ sweet onion - 2mg
- 1 tomato - 6mg
- 4 sl Swiss cheese - 160mg
- 2 c alfalfa sprouts - 4mg

Fat (Sat Fat):
- 8 sl *Olive Bread* - 39g (15g) or LS bread - 4g (0g)
- 1 c Hummus - 25g (3g)
- 4 sl Swiss cheese - 24g (16g)
- 2 c alfalfa sprouts - 1g (0g)

Brands used/alternatives:
Great Value Sliced Swiss
Food for Life Ezekiel 4:9 Bread
Oasis Roasted Red Pepper Hommus

Recipe Notes

1 – Coleslaw or coleslaw mix is a tasty substitute for the sprouts and it adds a bit of crunch.

SLOPPY JOES

Sodium Per Serving – 126mg   Serves 4

This childhood favorite is not only fast and easy, but it also tastes delicious.

- **1 pound ground turkey or beef[1]**
- **½ small sweet onion, thinly sliced**
- **1 green bell pepper, chopped**
- **1 celery stalk, finely chopped**
- **¾ cup *Chili Sauce (pg 214)* or LS salsa**
- **¼ cup NSA ketchup**
- **1 tablespoon Worcestershire sauce**
- **1 teaspoon prepared mustard**
- **¼ teaspoon garlic powder**
- **⅛ teaspoon ground black pepper**
- **4 *Hamburger Buns (see pg 196)* or LS buns[2]**

1. In a large pot or Dutch oven over medium heat, add turkey, onion, bell pepper, and celery; cook, stirring frequently until meat is no longer pink, about 5 minutes. Drain any liquid or fat from the meat.
2. Add *Chili Sauce*, ketchup, Worcestershire, mustard, garlic, and pepper; decrease heat to medium-low and simmer, uncovered. Stir as needed until mixture has thickened to a chili-like consistency, 35 to 45 minutes.
3. Equally divide meat mixture and pour over buns.

NUTRITIONAL INFO PER SERVING (WITH GROUND TURKEY): Calories 526, Fat 12g (Saturated Fat 3g), Cholesterol 55mg, Carbohydrates 75g (Fiber 5g, Sugar 25g), Sodium 126mg (395mg with ground beef)

Recipe Notes
1 – For less fat and sodium, use lean ground turkey breast.
2 – Store-bought buns average 206mg a roll; there are a few LS brands with less than 140mg but they're not available everywhere.

TOTAL SODIUM AND FAT BY INGREDIENT

Sodium:
- 1 lb lean ground turkey - 157mg or ground beef - 395mg
- ½ sweet onion - 7mg
- 1 green bell pepper - 4mg
- 1 celery stalk - 32mg
- ¾ c *Chili Sauce* - 22mg
- ¼ c ketchup - 20mg
- 1 T Worcestershire - 20mg
- ¼ t garlic powder - 1mg
- 4 *Hamburger Buns* - 241mg or LS bun - 500mg

Fat (Sat Fat):
- 1 lb lean ground turkey - 11g (2g) or ground beef - 17g (7g)
- ¾ c *Chili Sauce* - 1g (0g)
- 4 *Hamburger Buns* - 35g (8g) or LS bun - 16g (8g)

Brands used/alternatives:
Jennie-O 99% Lean Turkey
Heinz NSA Ketchup
Robbie's Worcestershire
Gold's LS New York Deli Mustard
King's Hawaiian Hamburger Buns
Frog Ranch Salsa

ANYTIME QUICKIES

Yogurt Gruel with Granola & Nuts

Sodium Per Serving – 58mg   Serves 2

My late father-in-law loved this so much, he ate it nearly every day for either breakfast or lunch. Vary it by using different flavors of yogurt or fruit.

- **12 oz nonfat vanilla or plain Greek yogurt**
- **1 cup fresh fruit, cut into bite-size chunks (such as, an apple, peach, berries, grapes, or banana)**
- **½ cup lowfat granola**[1]
- **⅓ cup unsalted nuts, chopped (optional)**[2]

1. Mix yogurt with fruit; sprinkle with granola and nuts.

NUTRITIONAL INFO PER SERVING: Calories 311, Fat 11g (Saturated Fat 2g), Cholesterol 10mg, Carbohydrates 40g (Fiber 4g, Sugar 18g), Sodium 58mg

Fresh Fruit Smoothie

Sodium Per Serving – 2mg   Serves 2

These are the best smoothies, they're thick and delicious, a meal in itself. Just about any fruit works, but this is our favorite combination.

- **¾–1 cup orange juice**[3]
- **1 peach, quartered**
- **1 banana, cut in half**
- **½ cup fresh or frozen berries**

1. Place all ingredients in a blender and pulse until smooth; pour into glasses and serve.

NUTRITIONAL INFO PER SERVING: Calories 150, Fat 1g (Sat Fat 0g), Chol 0mg, Carb 37g (Fiber 4g, Sugar 26g), Sodium 2mg

Recipe Notes

1 – *Kind* Healthy Grains Oats & Honey Granola is our favorite granola topping. It has 15mg sodium and 2.5g fat in ⅓ cup.

2 – Use any favorite nut or combination of nuts. For added flavor, toast the nuts (see *Toasting Nuts*, pg 250).

3 – The lesser amount makes a thick smoothie; if you like it thinner, increase the orange juice to 1 cup.

TOTAL SODIUM AND FAT BY INGREDIENT

YOGURT & GRANOLA & NUTS
Sodium:
- 12 oz LF yogurt - 90mg
- 1 c fruit - 3mg
- ½ c granola - 23mg

Fat (Sat Fat):
- ½ c granola - 4g (0g)
- ⅓ c NSA nuts - 17g (3g)

Brands used/alternatives:
- *Dannon* Light & Fit Vanilla Yogurt
- *Kind* Healthy Grains Oats & Honey Granola

FRESH FRUIT SMOOTHIE
Sodium:
- ¾ c orange juice - 2mg
- 1 banana - 1mg
- ½ c berries - 1mg

BREADS & BAKED GOODS

BREADS, BUNS & DOUGHS

No Knead French Bread.............. 192
Rosemary Herb Bread 193
Everyday Multigrain Bread 194
Olive-Sage Bread................... 194
Quick Herbal Flatbread & Pizza Crust.. 195
Hamburger Buns................... 196
Cinnamon Rolls.................... 196
Mango Bread 197

OTHER BAKED GOODS

Cornbread 198
Jalapeño Cornbread 198
Herbed Buttermilk Biscuits.......... 199
Lemon Currant Scones.............. 200
Orange Currant Scones 200
Chocolate Chip Scones.............. 200
Blueberry Muffins 201
Poppy Seed Muffins with Lemon Glaze. 202
    Lemon Glaze.................... 202

BREADS, BUNS & DOUGHS

No Knead French Bread

Sodium Per Serving – 19mg • Makes two 6-inch loaves (16 slices)

This tasty French bread requires no kneading. Allow about 5 hours until the bread comes out of the oven. Makes one large loaf or two 6" round loaves.

- 1 tablespoon active dry yeast[1]
- 1¾ cups lukewarm water, divided
- 4 cups all-purpose or bread flour
- 1 tablespoon sugar
- ⅛ teaspoon salt (optional)[2]
- 1 tablespoon unsalted butter or margarine, melted

1. Dissolve yeast in 1 cup lukewarm water.
2. While yeast softens, sift flour, sugar, and salt together; stir in dissolved yeast. Gradually add remaining ¾ cup water, adding just enough until dough holds together; mix with a spoon or a mixer *(see Bread Making Without a Machine, pg 244)*, until dough is soft and sticky. Cover with a clean cloth, place in a warm spot, and let rise until double its size, 2 to 3 hours.
3. Punch down and hit a few times with your fist to remove air bubbles. Divide into two portions and place in two well-greased 6-inch round baking dishes (or make one large loaf and place in a well-greased loaf pan).
4. Cover with a clean cloth and let rise to the top of the baking dish; brush with melted butter. Bake in a preheated oven at 400°F (200°C) for 1 hour, or until golden brown. Let cool before slicing.

Bread Machine Method:

1. *For one large loaf:* Place ingredients in the bread machine according to manufacturer's directions; start on normal or basic cycle.

   IMPORTANT: Because the amount of humidity affects the wetness or dryness of the dough, after a few minutes into the first cycle, check the consistency of the dough. If necessary, add more flour or water until dough holds together, but is still sticky.

   NOTE: To eliminate the hole in the bottom of the bread caused by the paddle, gently lift out the dough at beginning of bake cycle. Remove paddle and return dough to the machine; continue with bake cycle.

2. *For two small loaves:* Follow directions for one loaf, except start on dough cycle instead of normal cycle. When cycle is finished, remove dough and divide into two portions and place in two well-greased 6-inch round baking dishes. Cover and let rise to the top of the baking dish; bake as directed.

NUTRITIONAL INFO PER SLICE: Calories 125, Fat 1g (Saturated Fat 1g), Cholesterol 2mg, Carbohydrates 25g (Fiber 1g, Sugar 1g), Sodium 19mg

Recipe Notes

1 – Be sure the yeast is not past its expiration date. Fresh yeast will produce a higher, lighter loaf.

2 – I think a little salt is needed for flavor, but the bread tastes good without it. Each slice without salt has 1mg sodium. For added information, see *Why Is Salt Used in Bread?*, pg 245.

TOTAL SODIUM AND FAT BY INGREDIENT

Sodium:
- 1 pkg yeast - 6mg
- 4 c flour - 10mg
- ⅛ t salt - 291mg

Fat (Sat Fat):
- 1 pkg yeast - 1g (0g)
- 4 c flour - 5g (1g)
- 1 T NSA butter - 12g (7g)
  or NSA margarine - 9g (4g)

Rosemary Herb Bread

Sodium Per Serving – 18mg Makes a 1½ pound loaf (12 servings)

Here is another great bread machine recipe that I often serve at family holiday festivities. Plus, it makes the best sandwiches with leftover turkey or meatloaf.

- **1 tablespoon unsalted butter or margarine**
- **⅓ cup chopped sweet onion**
- **3 cups bread flour**[1]
- **1½ tablespoons powdered buttermilk**[2]
- **1 cup water**[2]
- **1 tablespoon dried basil**
- **1 tablespoon dried rosemary, crumbled**
- **1½ tablespoons sugar**
- **Pinch salt (optional)**[3]
- **1 tablespoon active dry yeast**

1. Melt butter in a small skillet over medium heat; add onion and cook, stirring frequently, until onions are translucent, 4 to 5 minutes. Let cool slightly.
2. Place flour, buttermilk powder, water, basil, rosemary, sugar, salt, and yeast in bread machine according to manufacturer's directions. Start on *normal* or *basic* cycle.
3. After 5 minutes into the first cycle, check the consistency of the dough. If necessary, add more flour or water until dough holds together, but is still sticky.

   NOTE: To eliminate hole in the bottom of the bread from the paddle, gently lift out the dough at beginning of bake cycle. Remove paddle and return dough to the machine; continue on the bake cycle.
4. Let bread cool before slicing.

NUTRITIONAL INFO PER SLICE: Calories 138, Fat 1g (Saturated Fat 1g), Cholesterol 3mg, Carbohydrates 27g (Fiber 1g, Sugar 2g), Sodium 18mg

Recipe Notes

1 – Bread flour is made specifically for bread making and has more gluten in it, which produces a larger, more-structured loaf than with all-purpose flour.

2 – Substitute 1 cup nonfat or lowfat milk for the powdered buttermilk and water.

3 – Although I usually add a pinch of salt, this bread tastes fine without it (each slice without salt is 6mg). For added information, see *Why Is Salt Used in Bread?*, pg 245.

TOTAL SODIUM AND FAT BY INGREDIENT

Sodium:
⅓ c sweet onion - 1mg
1½ T dried buttermilk - 53mg
3 c bread flour - 8mg
1 T basil - 2mg
1 T rosemary - 3mg
Pinch salt - 146mg
1 T yeast - 6mg

Fat (Sat Fat):
1 T NSA butter - 12g (7g)
  or NSA margarine - 9g (4g)
1½ T dried buttermilk - 1g (0g)
3 c bread flour - 4g (1g)
1 T yeast - 1g (0g)
1 T rosemary - 1g (0g)

Brands used/alternatives:
Bob's Red Mill Buttermilk Powder

Everyday Multigrain Bread

Sodium Per Serving – 24mg Makes a 1½ pound loaf (12 serv)

This healthy multigrain bread is ideal for sandwiches. Although the directions are for a bread machine, you can also make this without one (see Bread Making Without a Machine, pg 245).

- ⅓ cup 8-grain cereal
- ½ cup lowfat milk
- ½ cup water
- 1 egg, lightly beaten[1]
- 2½ cups bread flour
- ¾ cup whole wheat flour
- 2 tablespoons unsalted butter or margarine
- 2 tablespoons honey
- Pinch salt (optional)[2]
- ⅓ cup raw, unsalted sunflower seeds
- 4 teaspoons active dry yeast

1. Place all ingredients in bread machine according to machine directions. Start on *light crust* setting. Let cool before slicing. *NOTE: To eliminate hole in the bottom of the bread from the paddle, gently lift out the dough at beginning of bake cycle. Remove paddle and return dough to the machine; continue on the bake cycle.*

NUTRITIONAL INFO PER SLICE: Calories 200, Fat 5g (Sat Fat 2g), Chol 24mg, Carb 33g (Fiber 2g, Sugar 4g), Sodium 24mg (12mg sodium without salt)

Olive-Sage Bread

Sodium Per Serving – 16mg   Makes a 1½ pound loaf (12 serv)

One of our favorite Italian restaurants, Cafe Juanita in Kirkland, Washington, serves a delicious olive-sage bread. My version tastes almost as good and is made either in a bread machine or by hand.

- 3 cups bread flour[3]
- 1½ tablespoons buttermilk powder + 1 cup water[4]
- 3 tablespoons chopped ripe olives
- 2 tablespoons dried sage
- 1½ tablespoons sugar
- 1 tablespoon active dry yeast

1. Place all ingredients in bread machine and start on *light crust* setting. Let cool before slicing. (See *NOTE* in previous recipe to eliminate hole in bottom of bread.)

NUTRITIONAL INFO PER SLICE: Calories 129, Fat 1g (Sat Fat 0g), Chol 0mg, Carb 25g (Fiber 0g, Sugar 1g), Sodium 16mg

Recipe Notes

1 – To keep fat to a minimum, use an egg substitute. See *Eggs and Egg Substitutes*, pg 23, for a comparison of fat and sodium in eggs and egg substitutes.

2 – I think a little salt is needed for flavor, but tastes good without it. For added information, see *Why Is Salt Used in Bread?*, pg 245.

3 – Bread flour is made specifically for bread making, has more gluten, and produces a larger, more-structured loaf than all-purpose flour.

4 – Substitute 1 cup lowfat buttermilk for the powdered buttermilk and omit the water.

TOTAL SODIUM AND FAT BY INGREDIENT

EVERYDAY MULTIGRAIN
Sodium:
½ c 2% milk - 53mg
1 egg - 71mg
2½ c bread flour - 6mg
¾ c whole wheat flour - 2mg
2 T honey - 2mg
Dash salt - 146mg
⅓ c sunflower seeds - 1mg
4 t yeast - 8mg
Fat (Sat Fat):
⅓ c 8-grain cereal - 2g (0g)
½ c nonfat milk - 0g (0g)
  or LF milk - 3g (1g)
1 egg - 5g (2g)
2½ c bread flour - 3g (1g)
¾ c whole wheat flour - 2g (1g)
2 T NSA butter - 23g (14g)
  or NSA margarine - 18g (7g)
½ c sunflower seeds - 21g (2g)
4 t yeast - 1g (0g)
Brands used/alternatives:
Bob's Red Mill 8-Grain Hot Cereal
Simple Truth 2% Milk

OLIVE-SAGE BREAD
Sodium:
1½ T dried buttermilk - 53mg
3 c bread flour - 8mg
3 T c ripe olives - 120mg
1 T yeast - 6mg
Fat (Sat Fat):
1½ T dried buttermilk - 1g (0g)
3 c bread flour - 7m (1g)
3 T c ripe olives - 3g (0g)
1 T yeast - 1g (0g)
Brands used/alternatives:
Bob's Red Mill Buttermilk Powder
Mario LS Black Olives

Quick Herbal Flatbread & Pizza Crust

Sodium Per Serving – 36mg | Makes 8 flatbreads

Flatbreads are popular in middle eastern culture. This version uses herbs and spices to make a delicious bread that also makes the best pizza crust.

- 3½ cups all-purpose or bread flour[1]
- ⅓ cup cornmeal
- 2 teaspoons sugar
- 2 teaspoons active dry yeast
- ½ teaspoon garlic powder
- ½ teaspoon dried oregano
- ½ teaspoon dried rosemary, crumbled
- ½ teaspoon dried thyme
- ¼ teaspoon ground black pepper
- Pinch salt (optional)[2]
- ½ cup lowfat milk
- 2 tablespoons olive oil
- 1 egg, lightly beaten[3]
- ½ cup warm water
- 2 tablespoons unsalted butter or margarine, melted

1. In a large bowl, mix together flour, cornmeal, sugar, yeast, garlic powder, oregano, rosemary, thyme, black pepper, and salt. Add milk, oil, egg, and warm water; stir until a soft dough forms.
2. Turn out onto floured work surface and knead 5 to 10 minutes; cover and let rest one hour. Divide into 8 portions and roll out each into 8-inch round pieces.
3. Use one of the following methods to cook:
   - **Baking:** Place on a baking sheet and brush with butter. Bake in a preheated oven at 400ºF (200ºC) for 10 to 12 minutes, or until golden brown.
   - **Frying:** Heat a cast-iron skillet over high heat until very hot. Place one flatbread in skillet; cook 1 to 2 minutes per side until just browned. Keep warm; repeat with remaining flatbread
   - **Broiling:** Brush with butter or water and broil 3 inches from the heat until browned, about 3 minutes; turn and brown on other side.

NUTRITIONAL INFO PER FLATBREAD: Calories 302, Fat 8g (Sat Fat 3g), Chol 35mg, Carb 55g (Fiber 2g, Sugar 2g), Sodium 36mg

Recipe Notes

1 – Replace some white flour with ½ to 1 cup whole wheat flour. This makes a denser dough.

2 – I think a little salt is needed for taste, but is equally good without it (each flatbread without salt is 18mg).

3 – To keep fat to a minimum, use an egg substitute. See *Eggs and Egg Substitutes*, pg 23, for a comparison of fat and sodium in eggs and egg substitutes.

TOTAL SODIUM AND FAT BY INGREDIENT

Sodium:
- 3½ c flour - 10mg
- 2 t yeast - 4mg
- ½ t garlic powder - 1mg
- Pinch salt - 146mg
- ½ c LF milk - 53mg
- 1 egg - 70mg

Fat (Sat Fat):
- 3½ c flour - 5g (1g)
- ⅓ c cornmeal - 2g (0g)
- ½ c LF milk - 3g (2g)
- 2 T olive oil - 28g (4g)
- 1 egg - 5g (2g)
- 2 T NSA butter - 23g (14g)
  - or NSA margarine - 18g (7g)

Brands used/alternatives:
Simple Truth 2% Milk

Hamburger Buns

Sodium Per Serving – 60mg   Makes 8 buns

These are the best-tasting light and fluffy buns. You won't believe how easy they are to make. Use your bread machine to do the kneading, then simply divide into balls, flatten and bake. You will never eat store-bought again!

- 2 cups bread flour
- 1 cup whole wheat flour[1]
- ⅛ teaspoon salt (optional)[2]
- 2 tablespoons honey[3]
- 3 tablespoons canola oil
- 1 cup lowfat milk
- 1 egg, lightly beaten[4]
- 2 teaspoons active dry yeast[5]
- 1 tablespoon unsalted butter or margarine, melted (optional)
- Dried onion or sesame seeds (optional)

1. Place bread flour, whole wheat flour, salt, honey, oil, milk, egg, and yeast in bread machine per manufacturer's instructions; select dough setting.
2. When cycle is finished, remove dough and place on floured work surface; punch down dough and divide into 8 equal pieces. Form into balls, then flatten into a smooth, even 3½-inch circle. Place on a lightly greased baking sheet; cover with a damp towel and let rise 30 minutes until double in size.
3. Brush tops with melted butter and sprinkle with dried onions or sesame seeds. Bake in a preheated 350°F (180°C) oven for 10 to 15 minutes, or until lightly brown.

NUTRITIONAL INFO PER SERVING: Calories 269, Fat 9g (Saturated Fat 2g), Cholesterol 33mg, Carbohydrates 41g (Fiber 2g, Sugar 6g), Sodium 60mg (24mg without salt)

VARIATION
Cinnamon Rolls

1. Omit the honey and mix 3 tablespoons sugar with ¼ teaspoon ground cinnamon. Roll out dough onto a floured surface until it is about 10 x 12 inches.
2. Increase the butter to 2 tablespoons and brush dough with the melted butter. Sprinkle with the sugar/cinnamon mixture.
3. Roll up tightly and cut into 10 buns. Place on a lightly greased baking sheet; cover with a damp towel and let rise 30 minutes.
4. Bake in a preheated 350°F (180°C) oven, about 15 minutes, or until lightly brown. Ice with *Cream Cheese Frosting (pg 240)*, if desired.

NUTRITIONAL INFO PER ROLL (without frosting): Calories 284, Fat 10g (Sat Fat 3g), Chol 37mg, Carb 42g (Fiber 2g, Sugar 7g), Sodium 60mg (24mg without salt)

TOTAL SODIUM AND FAT BY INGREDIENT

Sodium:
- 2 c bread flour - 5mg
- 1 c whole wheat flour - 2mg
- ⅛ t salt - 291mg
- 2 T honey - 2mg
- 1 egg - 71mg
- 1 c LF milk - 105mg
- 2 t yeast - 4mg
- 1 T dried onion - 1mg

Fat (Sat Fat):
- 2 c bread flour - 2g (0g)
- 1 c w/w flour - 3g (0g)
- 3 T canola oil - 42g (3g)
- 1 egg - 5g (2g)
- 1 c LF milk - 5g (3g)
- 1 T NSA butter - 12g (7g)
- or NSA margarine - 9g (4g)

Brands used/alternatives:
Simple Truth 2% Milk

Recipe Notes

1 – Instead of whole wheat, use bread flour (see *Flour Comparison*, pg 248, for sodium content in flours).
2 – I think a little salt is needed for taste, but it tastes good without it (each bun without salt is 26mg).
3 – Instead of honey, use 1–2 tablespoons sugar, plus 1–2 tbsp water.
4 – To keep fat to a minimum, use an egg substitute. See *Eggs and Egg Substitutes*, pg 23, for a comparison of fat and sodium in eggs and egg substitutes.
5 – Be sure the yeast is not past its expiration date. Fresh yeast will produce higher, lighter buns.

Mango Bread

Sodium Per Serving – 30mg Approximately 12 slices

This updated family recipe was given to me years ago by an elderly Hawaiian woman, whose grandmother made this bread for the early missionaries. It is absolutely delicious, especially with fresh coconut (if you have the time and don't mind the added work).

- **2 cups all-purpose flour**
- **1½ tablespoons NSA baking powder[1]**
- **½ cup sugar**
- **2 teaspoons ground cinnamon**
- **2 cups diced mango**
- **¾ cup canola or vegetable oil**
- **1 tablespoon lemon or lime juice**
- **1 teaspoon vanilla extract**
- **½ cup raisins**
- **½ cup chopped walnuts**
- **½ cup freshly grated coconut or packaged coconut flakes[2]**
- **3 eggs, slightly beaten[3]**

1. Preheat oven to 350°F (180°C). Lightly oil and flour a 9 x 5-inch loaf pan.
2. In a large bowl, sift together flour and baking powder; add sugar and cinnamon. Make a well in the center and add remaining ingredients, stirring just enough to mix. Pour into prepared pan and bake for 15 minutes, lower heat to 325° (180°C) and bake for 45 to 55 minutes, or until a toothpick inserted in center comes out clean.

NUTRITIONAL INFO PER SLICE: Calories 313, Fat 19g (Sat Fat 3g), Chol 54mg, Carb 34g (Fiber 2g, Sugar 15g), Sodium 30mg

Recipe Notes

1 – See *Baking Powder/Baking Soda*, pg 243, for NSA baking powder info.

2 – Sweetened flakes average 5mg per 0.5 oz, sweetened, 30mg. Sweetened will make a sweeter bread.

3 – To keep fat to a minimum, use an egg substitute. See *Eggs and Egg Substitutes*, pg 23, for a comparison of fat and sodium in eggs and egg substitutes.

TOTAL SODIUM AND FAT BY INGREDIENT

Sodium:
- 2 c flour - 5mg
- ½ c sugar - 1mg
- 2 t cinnamon - 1mg
- 2 c mango - 3mg
- ½ c raisins - 9mg
- ½ c walnuts - 1mg
- ½ c fresh/unsweet coconut - 9mg or sweetened flakes - 121mg
- 3 eggs - 213mg

Fat (Sat Fat):
- 2 c flour - 2g (0g)
- 2 c mango - 1g (0g)
- ¾ c canola oil - 164g (12g)
- ½ c walnuts - 39g (4g)
- ½ c frsh/unsw coconut - 12g (11g) or sweet coconut - 14g (12g)
- 3 eggs - 15g (5g)

Brands used/alternatives:
Hain Featherweight Baking Powder

OTHER BAKED GOODS

CORNBREAD

Sodium Per Serving – 46mg | Makes 15 squares

My mother-in-law loved this cornbread. It is slightly sweet and is the perfect accompaniment to a bowl of bean soup or chili.

- 1 cup yellow cornmeal
- 1 cup all-purpose flour
- 2½ tablespoons NSA baking powder[1]
- ½ cup unsalted butter or margarine, at room temperature
- ½ cup sugar
- 3 eggs[2]
- ⅓ cup lowfat milk
- ¼ cup lowfat sour cream
- 1 (15-oz) can NSA cream-style corn
- 1 (4-oz) can diced green chiles
- 4 oz Swiss cheese, shredded (about 1 cup)

1. Preheat oven to 350°F (180°C). Lightly grease a 9x13 baking dish.
2. In a large bowl, combine cornmeal, flour, and baking powder.
3. In another bowl, cream together the butter and sugar; beat in eggs, one at a time. Stir in milk, sour cream, corn, chiles, and Swiss cheese; add to cornmeal mixture, stirring until smooth.
4. Pour batter into prepared baking dish; bake in preheated oven for 45 minutes, or until a toothpick inserted in the center comes out clean. Cut into 15 squares.

NUTRITIONAL INFO PER SQUARE: Calories 191, Fat 11g (Saturated Fat 6g), Cholesterol 67mg, Carbohydrates 19g (Fiber 1g, Sugar 3g), Sodium 46mg

---

VARIATION
JALAPEÑO CORNBREAD

1. Substitute 1–2 seeded and chopped jalapeños for the chiles; proceed as directed. *NOTE: If you like it spicy add ¼ cup LS salsa to the batter before baking.*

NUTRITIONAL INFO PER SQUARE: Calories 206, Fat 11g (Sat Fat 6g), Chol 67mg, Carb 23g (Fiber 1g, Sugar 7g), Sodium 34mg (40mg with LS salsa)

Recipe Notes

1 – Baking powder has 488mg sodium per tsp. *Ener-G* and *Hain Featherweight* make a salt-free baking powder. I find that doubling the amount called for in a recipe gives the best results.

2 – To keep fat to a minimum, use an egg substitute. See *Eggs and Egg Substitutes*, pg 23, for a comparison of fat and sodium in eggs and egg substitutes.

TOTAL SODIUM AND FAT BY INGREDIENT

Sodium:
- 1 c flour - 3mg
- 3 eggs - 213mg
- 15 oz NSA cream corn - 35mg
- 4 oz green chiles - 180mg
- 4 oz Swiss cheese - 200mg
- ⅓ c LF milk - 35mg
- ¼ c LF sour cream - 30mg

Fat (Sat Fat):
- 1 c cornmeal - 6g (0g)
- 1 c flour - 1g (0g)
- ½ c NSA butter - 92g (58g) or NSA margarine - 72g (28g)
- 3 eggs - 15g (5g) or
- 15 oz NSA cream corn - 4g (0g)
- 2 oz Swiss cheese - 36g (20g)
- ⅓ c LF milk - 2g (1g)
- ¼ c LF sour cream - 5g (3g)

Brands used/alternatives:
- *Hain Featherweight* Baking Powder
- *Simple Truth* 2% Milk
- *Daisy Light* Sour Cream
- *Del Monte* NSA Creamed Corn
- *La Preferida* Organic Diced Green Chiles
- *Great Value* Swiss Cheese

Herbed Buttermilk Biscuits

Sodium Per Serving – 31mg | Makes 12 biscuits

These light and fluffy biscuits are delicious with soups and stews or with Country Gravy (pg 81) on top. For variety, add other spices, such as sage and rosemary.

- 2 cups all-purpose flour
- 2 tablespoons NSA baking powder[1]
- 1 tablespoon sugar
- 1/8 teaspoon salt (optional)[2]
- 1/2 cup unsalted butter or margarine
- 1/2 cup lowfat milk, mixed with 1/4 teaspoon lemon juice, let sit for 5 to 10 minutes[3]
- 2 tablespoons lowfat sour cream
- 1 cup chopped chives or green onions (green part only)
- 1/4 teaspoon dried basil
- 1/4 teaspoon garlic powder
- 1/4 teaspoon dried tarragon
- 1/4 teaspoon dried thyme
- 1/8 teaspoon ground black pepper

1. Preheat oven to 425°F (220°C).
2. In a large bowl, combine flour, baking powder, sugar, and salt; cut in butter until mixture resembles coarse granules. *NOTE: This step goes quickly using a food processor.*
3. Stir in the milk and sour cream, mixing until just combined and dough sticks together (if too dry, add a little more milk).
4. Form dough into a ball and place on a lightly floured surface; flatten into an 8-inch round, about 1/2-inch thick. Cut into rounds, using a 2-inch diameter cutter. Repeat, gathering and flattening dough scraps and cutting out biscuits, until all dough is used.
5. Place biscuits on a baking sheet; bake in a preheated oven for 15 to 20 minutes, or until golden brown. *NOTE: If not serving immediately, wrap cooled biscuits in aluminum foil and store at room temperature. Rewarm in a preheated oven at 350°F (175°C) for 5 to 10 minutes, or until heated through.*

NUTRITIONAL INFO PER BISCUIT: Calories 156, Fat 8g (Saturated Fat 5g), Cholesterol 22mg, Carbohydrates 18g (Fiber 0g, Sugar 2g), Sodium 31mg

Recipe Notes

1 – See *Baking Powder/Baking Soda*, pg 243, for salt-free baking powder info.
2 – While I think these taste best with a little bit of salt, it can be omitted without too much loss of flavor (each biscuit without salt is 7mg).
3 – Substitute reduced fat buttermilk for the milk and lemon (this increases the sodium to 40mg per biscuit).

TOTAL SODIUM AND FAT BY INGREDIENT

Sodium:
- 2 c flour - 5mg
- 1/8 t salt - 291mg
- 1/2 c LF milk - 53mg
- 2 T LF sour cream - 15mg
- 1 c chives - 1mg
- 1/4 t garlic powder - 1mg

Fat (Sat Fat):
- 2 c flour - 2g (0g)
- 1/2 c NSA butter - 92g (58g)
  or NSA margarine -72g (28g)
- 1/2 c LF milk - 3g (2g)
- 2 T LF sour cream - 3g (2g)

Brands used/alternatives:
Hain Featherweight Baking Powder
Simple Truth 2% Milk
Daisy Light Sour Cream

Lemon Currant Scones

Sodium Per Serving – 20mg   Makes 8 scones

Warm scones and coffee, what a way to relax on a Sunday morning. These light and moist scones are quick to fix with a food processor. Make several hours ahead of time, cool completely before storing in an air-tight container.

- 2¼ cups all-purpose flour
- 1½ tablespoons NSA baking powder[1]
- 4 tablespoons sugar
- ¼ cup unsalted butter or margarine
- 1 egg[2]
- ½ cup lowfat milk
- 2 tablespoon lowfat sour cream
- 1 teaspoon vanilla extract
- 1 tablespoon grated lemon peel
- ½ cup dried currants or raisins

1. Preheat oven to 400ºF (200ºC). Lightly grease a baking sheet or line with aluminum foil or parchment paper.
2. In a large bowl, combine flour, baking powder, and sugar. Cut the butter into the flour using a pastry blender or two knives, until mixture resembles coarse granules.
3. In a small bowl, combine egg, milk, sour cream, vanilla, lemon peel, and currants; add to dry ingredients. Mix until dough comes together in a moist, sticky clump.
4. With floured hands, form dough into a ball. Place on a lightly floured surface and flatten into a 8-inch round, about ¾ inch thick. Using a floured knife, slice in 8 wedges. Place scones on a prepared baking sheet; bake in a preheated oven for 20 minutes, or until golden brown. Serve warm or at room temperature.

NUTRITIONAL INFO PER SCONE: Calories 265, Fat 7g (Saturated Fat 3g), Cholesterol 44mg, Carbohydrates 48g (Fiber 2g, Sugar 17g), Sodium 20mg

VARIATIONS

Orange Currant Scones

1. Instead of lemon peel, substitute 1 tablespoon orange peel.

NUTRITIONAL INFO PER SCONE: Calories 265, Fat 7g (Sat Fat 3g), Chol 44mg, Carb 48g (Fiber 2g, Sugar 17g), Sodium 20mg

Chocolate Chip Scones

1. Instead of currants, add ½ cup miniature semisweet chocolate morsels and replace the lemon peel with 1 tablespoon grated orange peel.

NUTRITIONAL INFO PER SCONE: Calories 296, Fat 12g (Sat Fat 6g), Chol 44mg, Carb 46g (Fiber 1g, Sugar 8g), Sodium 19mg

TOTAL SODIUM AND FAT BY INGREDIENT

Sodium:
- 2¼ c flour - 6mg
- 4 tbsp sugar -1mg
- 1 egg - 71mg
- ½ c LF milk - 53mg
- 2 T LF sour cream - 25mg
- ½ c currants - 6mg or raisins - 9mg

Fat (Sat Fat):
- 2¼ c flour - 3g (1g)
- ¼ c NSA butter - 46g (19g) or NSA margarine - 36g (14g)
- 1 egg - 5g (2g)
- ½ c LF milk - 3g (2g)
- 2 T LF sour cream - 3g (2g)

Brands used/alternatives:
Hain Featherweight Baking Powder
Simple Truth 2% Milk
Daisy Light Sour Cream

Recipe Notes

1 – See *Baking Powder/Baking Soda*, pg 243, for salt-free baking powder info.

2 – To keep fat to a minimum, use an egg substitute. See *Eggs and Egg Substitutes*, pg 23, for a comparison of fat and sodium in eggs and egg substitutes.

BLUEBERRY MUFFINS

Sodium Per Serving – 17mg   Makes 12 muffins

Most muffins are very high in sodium (averaging 505mg per medium-size muffin). This is because of the baking powder and baking soda used in most recipes. This version uses no-salt-added baking powder. Although they won't rise as high as you may be accustomed, they will taste yummy. If using fresh or thawed blueberries, mixing them with a little flour before adding to the batter keeps it from turning blue.

- 2 cups all-purpose flour
- 1 tablespoon plus 1 teaspoon NSA baking powder[1]
- ¼ teaspoon ground cinnamon
- 1 cup sugar
- ⅓ cup unsalted butter or margarine
- 2 eggs, beaten[2]
- ½ teaspoon vanilla extract
- ½ cup lowfat milk[3]
- ½ teaspoon lemon juice[3]
- 2 cups fresh or frozen blueberries

1. Preheat oven to 400°F (200°C). Line muffin pan with paper liners. *NOTE: These muffins tend to stick to the muffin pan and the liners help lessen this. For the liners to peel off cleanly from the muffins, spray the liners with nonstick cooking spray.*
2. In a bowl, combine the flour, baking powder, and cinnamon. *NOTE: If using fresh or thawed frozen berries, set ¼ cup flour mixture aside.*
3. In another large bowl, cream the sugar and butter until light and fluffy; beat in the eggs, one at a time. Mix in vanilla; add flour mixture and buttermilk, mixing until combined.
4. Mix reserved flour mixture with blueberries to keep them from bleeding into the batter and turning it blue. Fold blueberries into the muffin batter.
5. Pour into muffin cups and bake in a preheated oven for 20 to 25 minutes, or until golden brown and tops spring back when lightly touched.

NUTRITIONAL INFO PER MUFFIN: Calories 215, Fat 6g (Saturated Fat 3g), Cholesterol 50mg, Carbohydrates 37g (Fiber 1g, Sugar 16g), Sodium 17mg

Recipe Notes

1 – See *Baking Powder/Baking Soda*, pg 243, for salt-free baking powder info.
2 – To keep fat to a minimum, use an egg substitute. See *Eggs and Egg Substitutes*, pg 23, for a comparison of fat and sodium in eggs and egg substitutes.
3 – Substitute ½ cup lowfat buttermilk instead of the milk and lemon juice. This increases the sodium to 23mg in each muffin.

TOTAL SODIUM AND FAT BY INGREDIENT

Sodium:
- 2 c flour - 5mg
- 1 c sugar - 2mg
- 2 eggs - 142mg
- ½ c LF milk - 53mg
- 2 c blueberries - 3mg

Fat (Sat Fat):
- 2 c flour - 2g (0g)
- ⅓ c NSA butter - 48g (19g)
  or NSA margarine - 61g (25g)
- 2 eggs - 10g (3g)
- ½ c LF milk - 3g (2g)
- 2 c blueberries - 1g (0g)

Brands used/alternatives:
Hain Featherweight Baking Powder
Simple Truth 2% Milk

Poppy Seed Muffins with Lemon Glaze

Sodium Per Serving – 22mg   Makes 12 muffins

These moist muffins have a sweet, lemony glaze that taste just like what you'd buy at the bakery.

- **2 cups all-purpose flour**
- **1½ tablespoons NSA baking powder[1]**
- **2 tablespoons poppy seeds**
- **½ cup (1 stick) unsalted butter or margarine**
- **⅔ cup sugar**
- **2 eggs[2]**
- **¾ cup lowfat milk**
- **¼ cup lowfat sour cream**
- **1 teaspoon vanilla extract**
- **1 teaspoon finely grated lemon peel**
- ***Lemon Glaze (recipe follows)***

1. Preheat oven to 375ºF (190ºC). Place liners in a muffin tin or coat pan with nonstick cooking spray.
2. In a bowl, combine flour, baking powder, and poppy seeds; set aside.
3. In another bowl, cream the butter and sugar until light and fluffy; beat in eggs, one at a time. Stir in milk, sour cream, and vanilla.
4. Fold half the flour into the wet ingredients, mixing until just combined; repeat with remaining flour. Don't overmix.
5. Divide evenly into 12 muffin cups; bake in a preheated oven for 20 to 25 minutes, or until golden brown and a toothpick inserted in the center comes out clean. Remove from oven and let cool 5 minutes; dunk muffin tops into *Lemon Glaze* or drizzle over the tops. Let cool before eating.

NUTRITIONAL INFO PER MUFFIN: Calories 223, Fat 10g (Saturated Fat 6g), Cholesterol 58mg, Carbohydrates 30g (Fiber 0g, Sugar 30g), Sodium 22mg

Lemon Glaze

Sodium Per Serving – 0mg   Makes ¾ cup

This sweet glaze is delicious over sweet breads, scones, or muffins.

- **⅔ cup sugar**
- **Juice of 1 lemon (about 3 tablespoons)**

1. In a saucepan over medium heat, combine sugar and lemon juice; cook, stirring frequently, until sugar is dissolved. Drizzle over baked items or dunk while still warm; allow to cool before eating.

NUTRITIONAL INFO PER TABLESPOON: Calories 43, Fat 0g (Sat Fat 0g), Chol 0mg, Carb 11g (Fiber 0g, Sugar 11g), Sodium 0mg

Recipe Notes

1 – See *Baking Powder/Baking Soda*, pg 243, for salt-free baking powder info.

2 – To keep fat to a minimum, use an egg substitute. See *Eggs and Egg Substitutes*, pg 23, for a comparison of fat and sodium in eggs and egg substitutes.

TOTAL SODIUM AND FAT BY INGREDIENT

POPPY SEED MUFFINS

Sodium:
- 2 c flour - 5mg
- 2 T poppy seeds - 6mg
- 2 eggs - 142mg
- ¾ LF milk - 79mg
- ¼ LF sour cream - 30mg

Fat (Sat Fat):
- 2 c flour - 2g (0g)
- 2 T poppy seeds - 8g (0g)
- ½ c NSA butter - 92g (58g)
   or NSA margarine - 72g (28g)
- 2 eggs - 10g (3g)
- ¾ LF milk - 4g (2g)
- ¼ LF sour cream - 5g (3g)

Brands used/alternatives:
- *Hain Featherweight* Baking Powder
- *Simple Truth* 2% Milk
- *Daisy Light* Sour Cream

BASICS, CONDIMENTS & SAUCES

BASIC STUFF

Herbed Garlic Croutons............. 204
Basic Pie Crust..................... 205
Egg Roll Wraps 205
Basic Crepes...................... 206
Dessert Crepes.................... 206
Blender Mayonnaise 207
Chipotle Mayonnaise 207
Basil Mayonnaise.................. 207
Chicken Broth 208
Beef Broth........................ 208
Low-Sodium Pickles 209

RELISHES, SALSAS & SAUCES

Cranberry-Orange Relish with Grand
    Marnier 210
Fresh Corn Relish 210
Mango Salsa...................... 211
Pineapple-Mango Salsa 211
Black Bean-Mango Salsa 211
Mucho Caliente Fresh Tomato Salsa ... 212
Tex-Mex Hot Sauce................ 212
Texas-Style Barbecue Sauce.......... 213
Chili Sauce 214
Sherried Raisin Sauce.............. 215
Blackberry Wine Sauce............. 215
Blender Hollandaise 216
Orange Hollandaise Sauce 216
Bearnaise Sauce 216

BASIC STUFF

Herbed Garlic Croutons

Sodium Per Serving – 22mg Makes 4 cups (16 servings)

Once you taste these croutons, you'll never use store-bought again. For a buttery taste, coat with butter-flavored spray. Store croutons in an airtight container for up to a week.

- 3 tablespoons olive oil
- 1 tablespoon grated Parmesan cheese
- 1 tablespoon garlic powder
- 1 tablespoon Italian seasoning[1]
- 1/8 teaspoon onion powder
- 1/8 teaspoon ground black powder
- 1 loaf *No Knead French Bread (pg 192)* or 8 slices LS bread, cubed (about 4 cups)[2]

1. In a large bowl, mix olive oil with Parmesan, garlic powder, Italian seasoning, onion powder, and pepper; stir in bread cubes, mixing well until bread is well coated. *NOTE: You can also add all ingredients to a large container with a lid and shake until well coated.*
2. To toast croutons:
   - *Oven method:* Preheat oven to 350ºF (180ºC). Spread on a baking sheet and spray with butter-flavored spray; bake until lightly brown and crisp, 15 to 20 minutes.
   - *Stove-top method:* Melt 1 tablespoon unsalted butter in a large skillet over medium heat; toast croutons, tossing and stirring frequently, until golden brown and crisp, about 4 to 5 minutes. *CAUTION: The croutons can easily burn using this method, so watch them carefully.*

NUTRITIONAL INFO PER SERVING: Calories 150, Fat 4g (Saturated Fat 1g), Cholesterol 2mg, Carbohydrates 25g (Fiber 1g, Sugar 0g), Sodium 22mg

Recipe Notes

1 – Instead of Italian seasoning, use 1 teaspoon dried basil, 1 teaspoon dried oregano, and 1 teaspoon dried thyme.

2 – *Rosemary Herb Bread (pg 193)* is also nice to use for croutons. If using, omit Italian seasoning.

TOTAL SODIUM AND FAT BY INGREDIENT

Sodium:
- 1 T Parmesan cheese - 30mg
- 1 T garlic powder - 5mg
- 1 T Italian seasoning - 2mg
- 1 loaf *No Knead French* - 307mg
- 5 butter-flavored sprays - 5mg

Fat (Sat Fat):
- 3 T olive oil - 42g (6g)
- 1 T Parmesan - 2g (1g)
- 1 T Italian seasoning - 1g (0g)
- 1 loaf *No Knead French* - 17g (8g)
- 5 butter-flavored sprays - 1g (0g)

Brands used/alternatives:
365 Whole Foods 3 Cheese Blend
Food for Life Ezekiel 4:9 Bread

BASIC PIE CRUST

Sodium Per Serving – 19mg Serves 8

If you can't find a premade pie crust with less than 80mg sodium a serving, this is a good alternative.

- **1½ cups all-purpose flour**
- **1 tablespoon sugar**
- **Pinch salt (optional)[1]**
- **½ cup unsalted butter or margarine[2]**
- **3 tablespoons cold water**

1. *To prepare crust:*
   - **By hand:** In a large bowl, mix together flour, sugar, and salt. Using a pastry blender or two knives, cut the butter into the flour until mixture resembles coarse granules. Stir in water, 1 tablespoon at a time, mixing after each addition until a dough forms.
   - **With a food processor:** Place all ingredients in a food processor and pulse until dough starts to pull away from the sides. *NOTE: Do not overwork or crust will be tough.*
2. Place dough on a floured surface and roll out to an 11-inch circle. Place in a 9-inch pie plate and flute edges; cover and refrigerate until ready to use.

NUTRITIONAL INFO PER SERVING: Calories 171, Fat 9g (Saturated Fat 4g), Cholesterol 0mg, Carbohydrates 19g (Fiber 0g, Sugar 2g), Sodium 19mg (0mg without salt)

EGG ROLL WRAPS

Sodium Per Serving – 28mg Makes 8 wrappers

Egg roll wrappers are a great substitute for puff pastry or pie dough in turnover recipes. Just spread your favorite filling on the wrapper, either fold in half on the diagonal or roll up jelly roll style; then fry or bake until golden brown.

- **2 cups all-purpose flour**
- **1 egg, mixed with ⅓ cup water**
- **Pinch salt (optional)[1]**

1. In a large bowl, mix flour and salt; make a well in the center of the bowl. Add egg, mixing well; if dough is too dry, add a little water until dough holds together.
2. Dust the working surface lightly with cornstarch or flour; knead the dough until it is smooth and pliable. Cover with a damp cloth and let rest for 1 hour. Cut dough into 8 pieces; roll each piece into an 7x7-inch paper-thin square, adding flour as needed. *NOTE:* Use a ruler or straight edge to trim side. If making wonton wraps, cut each piece into 4 equal squares (3.5"x3.5").
3. *To store:* Lightly dust each side with cornstarch to keep from sticking together; wrap in plastic and store in refrigerator or freezer.

NUTRITIONAL INFO PER WRAPPER: Calories 123, Fat 1g (Sat Fat 0g), Chol 26mg, Carb 24g (Fiber 0g, Sugar 0g), Sodium 28mg (10mg without salt)

> **TOTAL SODIUM AND FAT BY INGREDIENT**
>
> **BASIC PIE CRUST**
> *Sodium:*
>   1½ c flour - 4mg
>   Pinch salt - 146mg
> *Fat (Sat Fat):*
>   1½ c flour - 2g (0g)
>   ½ c NSA butter - 92g (58g)
>   or NSA margarine - 72g (28g)
>
> **EGG ROLL WRAPS**
> *Sodium:*
>   1 egg - 71mg
>   2 c flour - 5mg
>   Pinch salt - 146mg
> *Fat (Sat Fat):*
>   1 egg - 5g (2g)
>   2 c flour - 2g (0g)

Recipe Notes

1 – While I think a tiny bit of salt enhances flavor, it tastes almost as good without it.
2 – I often use margarine instead of butter to keep the fat down. Use regular margarine if NSA is not available and eliminate the salt.

Basic Crepes

Sodium Per Serving – 54mg

Makes 8–10 crepes

Making crepes is like making pancakes... quick and easy! Use these in place of egg roll wrappers or tortillas; fill with anything from meat and vegetables to strawberries and cream cheese.

- **1 cup all-purpose flour**
- **2 teaspoons sugar**
- **Pinch salt (optional)[1]**
- **2 eggs[2]**
- **1 tablespoon unsalted butter or margarine, melted**
- **1⅓ cups lowfat milk**

1. Mix together all ingredients, either with a whisk or electric mixer; if batter is too thick, add 1–2 tablespoons more milk or water. Cover and refrigerate for 30 minutes to 1 hour.
2. Coat a 7 or 8-inch nonstick skillet with nonstick cooking spray and place over medium heat. *NOTE: The correct temperature (400ºF or 204ºC) is important to cooking crepes properly. Depending on your cooktop, you may have to adjust the heat up or down, until you get the correct temperature.*
3. Pour 2–3 tablespoons batter into skillet and swirl to coat the bottom; cook until the edges start to turn golden, about 1 minute. Loosen sides with spatula and turn; cook until golden brown, about 30 to 45 seconds. Transfer to a plate and repeat with remaining batter, adding more nonstick cooking spray, as needed.

NUTRITIONAL INFO PER CREPE: Calories 108, Fat 4g (Saturated Fat 2g), Cholesterol 60mg, Carbohydrates 14g (Fiber 0g, Sugar 3g), Sodium 54mg

---

VARIATION
Dessert Crepes
1. Increase sugar to 2 tablespoons and add ¼ teaspoon vanilla extract to the batter; proceed as directed.

NUTRITIONAL INFO PER CREPE: Calories 109, Fat 4g (Sat Fat 2g), Chol 60mg, Carb 14g (Fiber 0g, Sugar 2g), Sodium 54mg

TOTAL SODIUM AND FAT BY INGREDIENT
Sodium:
- 1 c flour - 3mg
- Pinch salt - 146mg
- 2 eggs - 142mg
- 1⅓ c LF milk - 140mg

Fat (Sat Fat):
- 1 c flour - 1g (0g)
- 2 eggs - 10g (3g)
- 1 T NSA butter - 12g (7g)
  or NSA margarine - 9g (4g)
- 1⅓ c LF milk - 7g (3g)

Recipe Not
1 – While I think these taste best with a little salt, they are equally good without (each crepe without salt is 49mg).
2 – To keep fat to a minimum, use an egg substitute. See *Eggs and Egg Substitutes*, pg 23, for a comparison of fat and sodium in eggs and egg substitutes.

BLENDER MAYONNAISE
Sodium Per Serving – 15mg · Makes about 1½ cups

Once you've tried homemade mayonnaise, you won't want to use the commercial brands again. I've had this recipe for ages, unfortunately I do not know where it came from, so I cannot give credit to the creator.

- 1 egg[1]
- 2 tablespoons lemon juice or vinegar
- ½ teaspoon sugar
- ½ teaspoon dry mustard
- ¼ teaspoon garlic powder
- ⅛ teaspoon paprika (optional)
- Pinch cayenne pepper
- ⅛ teaspoon salt (optional)
- 1 cup canola or vegetable oil

1. In a blender or food processor, combine egg, lemon juice, sugar, mustard, garlic powder, paprika, cayenne, and salt; pulse at low speed until blended. Increase speed to high; slowly add oil in a steady stream, blending until smooth and creamy. If necessary, stop blender or processor and scrape down the sides. Keep refrigerated in a tightly covered jar for up to a month.

NUTRITIONAL INFO PER 1 TABLESPOON: Calories 84, Fat 9g (Saturated Fat 1g), Cholesterol 9mg, Carbohydrates 0g (Fiber 0g, Sugar 0g), Sodium 15mg

---

VARIATIONS
Use flavored mayonnaise in sandwiches, on vegetables, and fish cakes.

CHIPOTLE MAYONNAISE
1. Add 1 tablespoon chipotle chile paste[2] or chipotle chiles in adobo sauce (these are canned smoked jalapeños in tomato sauce, found in the Hispanic section of many supermarkets) to the ingredients in the blender or food processor; pulse until smooth.

NUTRITIONAL INFO PER SERVING: Calories 85, Fat 9g (Saturated Fat 1g), Cholesterol 9mg, Carbohydrates 0g (Fiber 0g, Sugar 0g), Sodium 16mg (18mg using chipotles in adobo)

BASIL MAYONNAISE
1. Place ¼ cup fresh basil and ½ cup *Blender Mayonnaise* in a blender or food processor and pulse until smooth; add to remaining *Blender Mayonnaise* and stir until well mixed.

NUTRITIONAL INFO PER SERVING: Calories 84, Fat 9g (Saturated Fat 1g), Cholesterol 9mg, Carbohydrates 0g (Fiber 0g, Sugar 0g), Sodium 15mg

---

Recipe Notes
1 – For a richer taste, substitute 2 medium egg yolks for the egg. This decreases the sodium to 13mg in each tbsp.
2 – I use *Gran Luchito* Chipotle Chile Paste, available at Walmart and Amazon. It has a wonderful smoky flavor and only has 15mg sodium per tbsp (versus 70mg-130mg for chipotles in adobo sauce).

TOTAL SODIUM AND FAT BY INGREDIENT
Sodium:
 1 egg - 71mg
 ⅛ t salt - 291mg
Fat (Sat Fat):
 1 egg - 5g (2g)
 1 c canola oil - 218g (16g)

Chicken Broth

Sodium Per Serving – 20mg   Makes about 8 cups

A good broth is far superior to any bouillon or canned broth and is very useful in low-salt cooking. Not only does it add lots of flavor and nutrients, but it has very little sodium. The secret to a good, flavorful broth is browning the bones and vegetables before making the broth. Once the broth is completely chilled, freeze in paper cups in varying amounts (¼ cup to 1 cup) for later use. You can also make the broth in a crock pot—place all ingredients in the pot, cover and cook on low heat for 8 hours or overnight. This recipe works for either beef or chicken.

- 1 tablespoon olive oil
- 3–4 pounds chicken parts, such as necks, backs, wings, bones, and carcasses[1]
- ¼ teaspoon garlic powder
- ⅛ teaspoon ground black pepper
- 2 onions, unpeeled and quartered
- 3 celery stalks, including tops, chopped in 1-inch chunks
- 3 carrots, chopped in 1-inch chunks
- 3 quarts water
- 4 garlic cloves, 2 whole and 2 crushed
- 6 fresh parsley sprigs[2]
- 6 fresh thyme sprigs[2]
- 6–8 black peppercorns
- 4 whole cloves
- 3 bay leaves

1. Brown the bones and vegetables either on the stove-top or in the oven:
   - *Stove-top browning*: Heat oil in a 6-quart or larger pot over medium heat; add bones and sprinkle with garlic powder and pepper. Cook, turning occasionally, until browned on all sides, about 15 minutes. Remove bones and set aside. In the same pot, add onions, celery, and carrots; cook, stirring frequently, until vegetables are a golden brown, about 10 minutes. Return bones to pot; decrease heat to low and proceed as directed in Step 2 below.
   - *Oven browning:* Place chicken parts and vegetables in a roasting pan and bake, uncovered, in a preheated oven at 450ºF (230ºC) until chicken and vegetables are brown, about 30 minutes. Remove from oven and drain off fat; place browned bones and vegetables in a large pot or Dutch oven over low heat.
2. Add water, garlic, parsley, thyme, cloves, bay leaves, and peppercorns; cover, and simmer for 3 hours, occasionally skimming the froth from the top of the broth. *CAUTION: The froth contains impurities that should be removed, not stirred back into the broth.*
3. Strain the broth through a colander and discard solids; strain again through a fine-mesh sieve or cheesecloth-lined colander. If using right away, refrigerate, uncovered, until slightly cooled, then remove fat that has formed on top. If not using right away, refrigerate until thoroughly chilled, then remove fat. Cover and refrigerate for up to a week or pour into paper cups in varying amounts (such as ¼ cup, ½ cup, and 1 cup) and freeze up to 3 months.

NUTRITIONAL INFO PER 1 CUP (values are approximates): Calories 15, Fat 0g (Saturated Fat 0g), Cholesterol 6mg, Carbohydrates 1g (Fiber 0g, Sugar 0g), Sodium 20mg

---

VARIATION
Beef Broth
1. Instead of chicken parts, add 3–4 pounds meaty beef bones (such as shanks and neck bones); proceed as directed.

NUTRITIONAL INFO PER 1 CUP: Calories 13, Fat 0g (Saturated Fat 0g), Cholesterol 0mg, Carbohydrates 0g (Fiber 0g, Sugar 0g), Sodium 20mg

---

Recipe Notes
1 – Use cooked carcasses, raw parts, or a combination of both.
2 – Although I think the flavor of homemade broth is much better using fresh herbs, you can substitute 2 tsp dried parsley and 2 tsp dried thyme for the fresh sprigs.

Low-Sodium Pickles

Sodium Per Serving – 3mg   Makes about 2½ quarts, about 20 servings

This is an old recipe from an unknown source that contains no salt. According to my friend, Sally, who is a master canner, you can leave salt out of fresh-packed or quick-processed pickles. However, when salt is omitted, you must have either the same amount or more of vinegar as water, or it must contain only vinegar. However, fermented pickles must have salt to kill unwanted organisms. Allow two days to prepare, as the cucumbers soak overnight in cold water.

- 20–25 small pickling cucumbers (3 to 4 inches in length)
- 1-2 garlic cloves per quart[1]
- 3 fresh dill heads (4-inch diameter) or 1–2 tablespoons dill seed per quart
- 1 tablespoon whole mixed pickling spice per quart
- 6 peppercorns per quart
- 2 teaspoons whole mustard seed per quart
- 1 slice fresh horseradish root per quart (optional)[2]
- 7½ cups white vinegar
- 7½ cups water
- ¼ cup sugar[3]

1. Scrub cucumbers with a brush until clean. Cover with cold water and let sit overnight; drain.
2. Sterilize several quart and/or pint jars. Place garlic, dill, peppercorns, pickling spice, mustard seed, and horseradish into hot sterilized jars; pack cucumbers into the jars.
3. In a saucepan over medium-high heat, combine the vinegar, water, and sugar; bring to boil, stirring constantly, until sugar is dissolved. Pour over cucumbers, leaving ½-inch head space.
4. Wipe jar rims with a towel dipped in hot water; place lid on jar and seal tightly. Lower jars into a 180°F (82°C) water bath and process for 30 minutes. *NOTE: Use a thermometer to be sure water stays at 180°F (82°C).*
5. Carefully remove jars and cool thoroughly. Check seals by pressing the center of each lid; if it stays down, the jar is sealed. Store in a cool dry place for up to 1 year. If lid is not sealed, refrigerate for up to 3 weeks.

NUTRITIONAL INFO PER SERVING: Calories 37, Fat 0g (Saturated Fat 0g), Cholesterol 0mg, Carbohydrates 5g (Fiber 1g, Sugar 4g), Sodium 3mg

Recipe Notes

1 – For a stronger garlic flavor, use 2 cloves per quart.
2 – Horseradish adds a little zip and helps overcome the lack of salt. If you like the taste of horseradish, add a second piece per quart.
3 – Sugar substitutes are not recommended, as the pickles have an undesirable flavor and are mushy instead of crisp.

To Sterilize Jars:

There are two basic ways to sterilize jars:
- Place empty jars in water and bring to a boil for 10 minutes. Remove and drain.
- Place lids and jars in a preheated oven at 225°F (110°C) for 10 minutes. Turn off oven and leave jars inside until ready to use.

NOTE: Use tempered glass jars designed for canning, not jars from store-bought products, such as pickle or mayonnaise jars.

TOTAL SODIUM AND FAT BY INGREDIENT

Sodium:
20 cucumbers - 20mg
1 garlic clove - 1mg
2 t mustard seed - 1mg
1 sl horseradish - 6mg
7½ c white vinegar - 36mg
¼ c sugar - 1mg

Fat (Sat Fat):
20 cucumbers - 1g (0g)
2 t mustard seed - 1g (0g)

RELISHES, SALSAS & SAUCES

Cranberry-Orange Relish with Grand Marnier

Sodium Per Serving – 2mgMakes 2 cups

This relish is a family favorite during the holidays. We like it on the tart side, but if you like it sweeter, add more sugar. For best results, use a food processor.

- 1 (12-oz) bag cranberries, frozen
- 1 unpeeled navel orange, cut into chunks, or 2 unpeeled tangerines, quartered
- ½ cup unsalted dry roasted hazelnuts or macadamia nuts
- ¾ cup sugar
- 3–4 tablespoons Grand Marnier or orange liqueur

1. In a food processor, pulse frozen cranberries, oranges, and nuts together until coarsely ground. (Depending on the size of your processor, you may have to do this in several batches.) Transfer to a bowl and stir in sugar and Grand Marnier, mixing well. Refrigerate at least an hour; stir before serving.

NUTRITIONAL INFO PER ¼ CUP: Calories 133, Fat 5g (Saturated Fat 0g), Cholesterol 0mg, Carbohydrates 19g (Fiber 2g, Sugar 16g), Sodium 2mg

Fresh Corn Relish

Sodium Per Serving – 5mgMakes 4 cups

This light and refreshing relish is great with poultry, fish, and in tacos. You can serve it right away, but allowing it to chill for an hour enhances the flavor.

- 2½ cups fresh or frozen corn (about 4 ears)[1]
- ½ sweet onion, chopped
- 1 tomato, seeded and chopped
- 1 red bell pepper, chopped
- ½ cup chopped fresh cilantro
- 1 jalapeño, seeded, chopped[2]
- ¼ cup fresh lime or lemon juice
- 2 teaspoons extra-virgin olive oil
- ½ teaspoon ground cumin

1. Combine all ingredients; cover and refrigerate for 1 hour; stir before serving.

NUTRITIONAL INFO PER ½ CUP: Calories 91, Fat 2g (Sat Fat 0g), Chol 0mg, Carb 20g (Fiber 3g, Sugar 5g), Sodium 5mg

Recipe Notes

1 – For even more flavor, use roasted corn (see *Roasting Corn*, pg 253).

2 – On a scale of 1 to 5, jalapeños are a 3, with most of the heat contained in the seeds and veins.

CAUTION: When handling hot chiles, wear rubber gloves, as the oils of the pepper are very potent. Use a piece of plastic wrap or a sandwich bag to hold the pepper. If you should touch the pepper with your bare fingers, wash your hands thoroughly and be sure to keep your fingers away from your eyes or you'll be in sheer agony!

TOTAL SODIUM AND FAT BY INGREDIENT

CRANBERRY-ORANGE RELISH
Sodium:
- 12 oz cranberries - 3mg
- 1 orange - 1mg
- ½ c hazelnuts - 0mg or macadamia nuts - 3mg

Fat (Sat Fat):
- ½ c hazelnuts - 38g (3g) or macadamia nuts - 50g (8g)

FRESH CORN RELISH
Sodium:
- 2½ c corn - 20mg or frozen corn - 60mg
- ½ sweet onion - 7mg
- 1 tomato - 6mg
- 1 red bell pepper - 5mg
- ½ c cilantro - 4mg
- ½ t cumin - 2mg

Fat (Sat Fat):
- 2½ c corn - 4g (0g) or frozen corn - 8g (0g)
- 2 t olive oil - 9g (1g)

Brands used/alternatives:
Birds Eye Steamfresh Super Sweet Corn

Mango Salsa

Sodium Per Serving – 2mg Makes 3 cups

This salsa is a great accompaniment to grilled fish, poultry, or pork. It also is delicious as a dip for tortilla chips.

- 2 mangos, peeled and cubed[1]
- ½ sweet onion, chopped
- ½ red bell pepper, chopped
- ¼ cup chopped fresh cilantro
- 2 tablespoons fresh lime or lemon juice
- 1 jalapeño or serrano pepper, seeded and chopped[2]

1. Combine all ingredients; cover and refrigerate for 1 hour. Stir before serving.

NUTRITIONAL INFO PER ¼ CUP: Calories 41, Fat 0g (Saturated Fat 0g), Cholesterol 0mg, Carbohydrates 10g (Fiber 1g, Sugar 9g), Sodium 2mg

---

VARIATIONS

Pineapple-Mango Salsa
1. Add ½ cup crushed pineapple (drained); proceed as directed.

NUTRITIONAL INFO PER ¼ CUP: Calories 46, Fat 0g (Saturated Fat 0g), Cholesterol 0mg, Carbohydrates 11g (Fiber 1g, Sugar 10g), Sodium 3mg

Black Bean-Mango Salsa
1. Add 1 (15-oz) can NSA black beans (drained and rinsed); proceed as directed.

NUTRITIONAL INFO PER ¼ CUP: Calories 73, Fat 0g (Saturated Fat 0g), Cholesterol 0mg, Carbohydrates 16g (Fiber 4g, Sugar 9g), Sodium 3mg

---

Recipe Notes

1 – If the mango is not very ripe, mix in 1 teaspoon sugar with the salsa.
2 – On a scale of 1 to 5, jalapeños are a 3, with most of the heat contained in the seeds and veins.

CAUTION: When handling hot chiles, wear rubber gloves, as the oils of the pepper are very potent. Use a piece of plastic wrap or a sandwich bag to hold the pepper. If you should touch the pepper with your bare fingers, wash your hands thoroughly and be sure to keep your fingers away from your eyes or you'll be in sheer agony!

TOTAL SODIUM AND FAT BY INGREDIENT

Sodium:
2 mangos - 7mg
½ sweet onion - 13mg
½ red bell pepper - 2mg
¼ c cilantro - 2mg

Fat (Sat Fat):
2 mangos - 3g (1g)

Mucho Caliente Fresh Tomato Salsa

Sodium Per Serving – 4mg | Makes 2 cups

Simple and delicious; tastes just like the fresh salsa you'll find in Mexico.

- 2 tomatoes, chopped[1]
- 2–5 jalapeño or serrano chile peppers, seeded and chopped[2]
- ½ sweet onion, chopped
- ½ cup chopped fresh cilantro
- 1½ teaspoons fresh lime juice

1. Combine all ingredients; cover and refrigerate for 1 hour. Stir before serving.

NUTRITIONAL INFO PER ¼ CUP: Calories 11, Fat 0g (Saturated Fat 0g), Cholesterol 0mg, Carbohydrates 3g (Fiber 1g, Sugar 2g), Sodium 4mg

Tex-Mex Hot Sauce

Sodium Per Serving – 22mg | Makes 4 cups

This salsa is briefly cooked and then puréed

- 2 pounds Roma or plum tomatoes, peeled and crushed or 1 (28-oz) can LS crushed tomatoes[3]
- 2 teaspoons garlic powder
- 1 tablespoon fresh lime or lemon juice
- 1 teaspoon cayenne pepper
- ½ teaspoon ground cumin
- 1 small sweet onion, chopped
- 2–10 jalapeño or serrano chile peppers, seeded and chopped[2]
- ½ cup chopped fresh cilantro
- ⅛ teaspoon salt (optional)[4]

1. In a saucepan over medium-high heat; add all ingredients, mixing well. Bring to a boil; continue cooking 10 minutes. Remove from heat and let cool slightly.
2. Place half the tomato mixture in a blender or food processor; pulse until a smooth consistency. Mix with remaining tomato mixture and refrigerate until ready to use. Will keep for up to a week in a covered container in the refrigerator or store in the freezer for later use.

NUTRITIONAL INFO PER 2 TABLESPOONS: Calories 16, Fat 0g (Sat Fat 0g), Chol 0mg, Carb 4g (Fiber 1g, Sugar 2g), Sodium 22mg (4mg without salt)

Recipe Notes

1 – Roma or plum tomatoes are preferred, as they are less watery. You can use other varieties, but will produce a thinner, watery salsa.

2 – The pungency of chile peppers vary by the type of pepper, growing conditions, and time of year. Start with 2 peppers and add more until desired heat. *NOTE: The heat will intensify the longer the salsa sits.* See Chile Peppers, pg 251, for info on handling peppers.

3 – *To peel tomatoes:* Bring a pot of water to a boil; place tomatoes in water for 10 seconds to loosen skins. Remove skins and crush.

4 – I think a little salt enhances the flavor of this salsa, but is equally good without it. If using canned crushed tomatoes, omit the salt.

TOTAL SODIUM AND FAT BY INGREDIENT

MUCHO CALIENTE SALSA
Sodium:
- 2 tomatoes - 12mg
- ½ sweet onion - 13mg
- ½ c cilantro - 4mg

Fat (Sat Fat):
- 2 tomatoes - 1g (0g)

TEX-MEX HOT SALSA
Sodium:
- 2 lb tomatoes - 45mg or LS crushed tomatoes - 260mg
- 2 t garlic powder - 4mg
- 1 t cumin - 2mg
- 1 sm sweet onion - 13mg
- ½ c cilantro - 4mg
- ⅛ t salt - 291mg

Fat (Sat Fat):
- 2 lb tomatoes - 2g (0g) or LS crushed tomatoes - 0g (0g)

Brands used/alternatives:
Cento Crushed Tomatoes

Texas-Style Barbecue Sauce

Sodium Per Serving – 28mg Makes 3 cups

There are many regional styles of barbecue sauce, from hot and tangy to sweet and spicy. This tangy sauce is smoky-hot and slightly sweet. It cooks up in 30 minutes and will keep up to 2 weeks in an airtight container in the refrigerator.

- 1 tablespoon olive oil
- ½ cup chopped onion
- 3-4 garlic cloves, minced
- 2-4 tablespoons chipotle chile paste or chipotle peppers in adobo sauce[1]
- 2 cups NSA ketchup
- 2 tablespoons Worcestershire sauce
- ½ cup apple cider vinegar
- ½ cup sugar
- 1 tablespoon molasses
- 1 tablespoon instant coffee, preferably espresso[2]
- 1 tablespoon NSA chili powder[3]
- 1 teaspoon mustard powder
- 1 teaspoon garlic powder
- 1 teaspoon onion powder

1. Place all ingredients in a large pot and bring to a boil over medium-high heat; decrease heat to medium low. Cook, stirring often, until the sauce has thickened to the desired consistency, about 30 minutes.
2. Let cool completely before placing in jars with tight-fitting lids. Will keep up to 2 weeks in the refrigerator.

NUTRITIONAL INFO PER ¼ CUP: Calories 121, Fat 2g (Sat Fat 0g), Chol 0mg, Carb 26g (Fiber 1g, Sugar 21g), Sodium 28mg (58mg with chipotle peppers in adobo)

Recipe Notes

1 – I use *Gran Luchito* Chipotle Chile Paste, available at Walmart and Amazon. It has a wonderful smoky flavor and only has 15mg sodium per tbsp (versus 70mg-130mg for chipotles in adobo sauce).

2 – The stronger the flavor of the instant coffee, the better the sauce.

3 – Most chili powders contain sodium (26mg per tsp); look for brands without salt listed in the ingredients.

TOTAL SODIUM AND FAT BY INGREDIENT

Sodium:
- ½ sweet onion - 3mg
- 3 garlic cloves - 2mg
- 2 T chipotle chile paste - 30mg or chipotle in adobo - 140mg
- 2 c NSA ketchup - 160mg
- 2 T Worcestershire - 120mg
- ½ c sugar - 1mg
- 1 T molasses - 15mg
- 1 T instant coffee - 1mg
- 1 t garlic powder - 2mg
- 1 t onion powder - 2mg

Fat (Sat Fat):
- 1 T olive oil - 14g (2g)
- 1 T chipotle chile paste - 3g (0g) or chipotle in adobo - 1g (0g)
- 1 T NSA chili powder - 1g (0g)
- 1 t mustard powder - 1g (0g)

Brands used/alternatives:
Gran Luchito Chipotle Chile Pas
Herdez Chipotles in Adobo
Heinz NSA Ketchup
Robbie's Worcestershire
The Spice Hunter Chili Powder

CHILI SAUCE

Sodium Per Serving – 7mg Makes 2 cups

Most bottled chili sauce is loaded with sodium (456mg per 2 tablespoons). This low-salt version simmers for a couple of hours on the stove. Use on meatloaf, chicken, or as a substitute for ketchup. This will keep for many months in the refrigerator in a container with a tight-fitting lid.

- **4 large ripe tomatoes, chopped, or 1 (28-oz) can NSA diced tomatoes**
- **1 small sweet onion, chopped (about 1 cup)**
- **½ cup chopped red bell pepper**
- **½ cup chopped green bell pepper**
- **⅓ cup sugar**
- **¼ cup cider vinegar**
- **½ teaspoon ground allspice**
- **½ teaspoon ground cinnamon**
- **½ teaspoon ground cloves**
- **¼ teaspoon ground black pepper**
- **¼ teaspoon mustard powder**
- **¼ teaspoon crushed red chile flakes**

1. Place all ingredients in a large pot and bring to a boil over medium-high heat; decrease heat to medium low. Stirring often, cook, uncovered, until the sauce has thickened to the desired consistency, 2 to 3 hours (this will depend on the juiciness of the tomatoes used).
2. After 2 hours, check for sweetness, and add more sugar, if needed. Let cool completely before placing in jars with tight-fitting lids.

NUTRITIONAL INFO PER ¼ CUP: Calories 63, Fat 0g (Sat Fat 0g), Chol 0mg, Carb 15g (Fiber 2g, Sugar 12g), Sodium 7mg

---

TOTAL SODIUM AND FAT BY INGREDIENT

Sodium:
- 4 tomatoes - 36mg or
- 28-oz diced tomatoes - 105mg
- 1 sm sweet onion - 13mg
- ½ c red bell pepper - 1mg
- ½ c green bell pepper - 1mg
- ⅓ c sugar - 1mg
- ½ t allspice - 1mg
- ½ t cloves - 3mg
- ¼ t dried chili flakes - 1mg

Fat (Sat Fat):
- 4 tomatoes - 2g (0g) or
- 28-oz diced tomatoes - 0g (0g)

Brands used/alternatives:
Simple Truth Org Diced Tomatoes

SHERRIED RAISIN SAUCE

Sodium Per Serving – 4mg | Makes 2 cups

This luscious, sweet sauce is an old family recipe served over pork or vegetables, such as carrots.

- ¾ cup raisins
- 1½ cups water
- ½ cup sugar
- 1½ tablespoons cornstarch
- ¼ teaspoon ground cloves
- 1 tablespoon unsalted butter or margarine
- ½ cup dry sherry

1. Combine raisins and water in a saucepan; simmer over low heat for 10 minutes.
2. Mix together sugar, cornstarch, and cloves; stir into raisins; cook, stirring constantly, until clear and thickened, about 5 minutes. Stir in butter and sherry; heat through and serve warm.

NUTRITIONAL INFO PER ¼ CUP: Calories 121, Fat 2g (Saturated Fat 1g), Cholesterol 4mg, Carbohydrates 27g (Fiber 1g, Sugar 21g), Sodium 4mg

BLACKBERRY WINE SAUCE

Sodium Per Serving – 1mg | Makes 2 cups

This tangy berry sauce is the perfect accompaniment to salmon, chicken, or pork.

- 2 cups blackberries, fresh or frozen
- ¼ cup water
- ¼ cup sugar
- ¼ cup red wine vinegar
- 1 tablespoon unsalted butter or margarine
- ¼ cup minced onions or shallots
- ¼ cup dry red wine
- ¼ teaspoon garlic powder

1. Place blackberries in a blender or food processor and pulse until puréed. *NOTE:* If you want this free of seeds, strain purée through a fine-mesh sieve.
2. Combine water and sugar in a saucepan over medium-high heat; cook, stirring frequently, until reduced to a thick syrup, 6 to 8 minutes. Remove from heat; stir in vinegar and set aside.
3. Melt butter in a skillet over medium-high heat; add onions. Cook, stirring frequently, until golden brown, 2 to 3 minutes. Add wine and garlic powder; cook until most of the liquid evaporates, 6 to 8 minutes.
4. Add berry purée and cook, stirring occasionally, until reduced by half, about 6 to 8 minutes. Stir in syrup mixture; serve warm or cold.

NUTRITIONAL INFO PER ¼ CUP: Calories 56, Fat 2g (Sat Fat 1g), Chol 4mg, Carb 10g (Fiber 2g, Sugar 8g), Sodium 1mg

---

TOTAL SODIUM AND FAT BY INGREDIENT

SHERRIED RAISIN SAUCE
Sodium:
- ¾ c raisins - 14mg
- ½ c sugar - 1mg
- 1½ T cornstarch - 1mg
- ¼ t cloves - 2mg
- ½ c sherry - 11mg

Fat (Sat Fat):
- ¾ c raisins - 1g (0g)
- 1 T NSA butter - 12g (7g)
  or NSA margarine - 9g (4g)

BLACKBERRY WINE SAUCE
Sodium:
- 2 c blackberries - 2mg
- ¼ c sugar - 2mg
- ¼ c onions - 2mg

Fat (Sat Fat):
- 2 c blackberries - 1g (0g)
- 1 T NSA butter - 12g (7g)
  or NSA margarine - 9g (4g)

Blender Hollandaise

Sodium Per Serving – 19mg   Makes about 1 cup

This lightened-up hollandaise is simply divine; pour over asparagus, fish, or eggs. This does not hold very well, so make just before ready to serve.

- **3 egg yolks**
- **Juice of ½ lemon (about 1½ tablespoons)**
- **1½ teaspoons Dijon-style mustard**
- **2 drops Worcestershire sauce**
- **⅛ teaspoon hot pepper sauce, such as Tabasco**
- **¼ cup unsalted butter, melted**

1. Place all ingredients except butter in a blender. While motor is running, slowly add butter until sauce is thick and creamy. Serve immediately.

NUTRITIONAL INFO PER ¼ CUP: Calories 144, Fat 15g (Saturated Fat 8g), Cholesterol 138mg, Carbohydrates 1g (Fiber 0g, Sugar 0g), Sodium 19mg

---

VARIATION
Orange Hollandaise Sauce

1. Instead of lemon juice, use freshly squeezed orange juice.

NUTRITIONAL INFO PER ¼ CUP: Calories 145, Fat 15g (Saturated Fat 8g), Cholesterol 138mg, Carbohydrates 1g (Fiber 0g, Sugar 1g), Sodium 19mg

---

Bearnaise Sauce

Sodium Per Serving – 16mg   Makes about 1 cup

The difference between Bearnaise and Hollandaise is Bearnaise has herbs and shallots, Hollandaise does not, but has more lemon. Serve it over asparagus, grilled meats, or with artichokes.

- **¼ cup white wine vinegar**
- **¼ cup white wine**
- **1 shallot, finely minced**
- **1 tablespoon minced fresh tarragon or chervil (or 1 teaspoon dried)**
- **⅛ teaspoon black pepper**
- **⅛ teaspoon onion powder**
- **½ teaspoon Dijon-style mustard**
- **3 egg yolks**
- **¼ cup unsalted butter, melted**

1. In a saucepan over medium heat, add vinegar, wine, shallot, tarragon, pepper, and onion powder. Cook, stirring frequently, until reduced to 2 tablespoons. Strain through a fine-mesh sieve.
2. Place eggs and mustard in a blender and add strained vinegar/wine sauce. While motor is running, slowly add butter until sauce is thick and creamy. Serve immediately.

NUTRITIONAL INFO PER ¼ CUP: Calories 163, Fat 15g (Sat Fat 8g), Chol 138mg, Carb 3g (Fiber 0g, Sugar 1g), Sodium 16mg

---

TOTAL SODIUM AND FAT BY INGREDIENT

BLENDER HOLLANDAISE
Sodium:
- 3 egg yolks - 25mg
- 1½ t Dijon mustard - 45mg
- 2 drops Worcestershire - 3mg
- ⅛ t Tabasco - 4mg

Fat (Sat Fat):
- 3 egg yolks - 14g (5g)
- ¼ c NSA butter - 46g (29g)

Brands used/alternatives:
- Gold's Dijon Mustard
- Robbie's Worcestershire

BEARNAISE SAUCE
Sodium
- ¼ c white wine - 3mg
- 1 shallot - 5mg
- 1 T tarragon - 1mg
- 3 egg yolks - 25mg
- ½ t Dijon mustard - 30mg

Fat (Sat Fat):
- 3 egg yolks - 14g (5g)
- ¼ c NSA butter - 46g (29g)

Brands used/alternatives:
- Gold's Dijon Mustard

DESSERTS & SWEETS

PIES, TARTS & TORTES

Pecan Pie with Bourbon Creme 218
    Bourbon Creme 218
Absolutely The Best Berry Pie 219
Pumpkin Pie with Amaretto Creme 220
Brandied Pumpkin Pie 220
    Amaretto Creme 220
Light Apple Tart 221
Fresh Strawberry Tart 222
Brandied Apricot Almond Tart 222
Chocolate Decadence Torte 223

CAKES & CHEESECAKES

Lemon Curd-Mascarpone Cake 224
Carrot Cake 225
Pound Cake 226
Cream Cheese Pound Cake 226
Sponge Cake 226
Pumpkin Cheesecake 227
Cheesecake with Northwest Berry
    Sauce 228
Chocolate Chip Cheesecake 229

CRISPS, STRUDELS & TURNOVERS

Apple Strudel 230
Berry Strudel 230
Peach & Blueberry Crisp 231
Apple Turnovers 232
Apricot-Peach Turnovers 232
Dried Cherry-Almond Turnovers 233
Cream Cheese & Jam Turnovers 233

PUDDINGS & CUSTARDS

Bread Pudding with Whiskey Sauce 234
Crème Brûlee 235
Grand Marnier Brûlèe 235
Brandied Mocha Brûlèe 235

FRUIT DESSERTS

Ice Cream with Blueberries & Grand
    Marnier 236
Strawberry & Amaretto Parfait 236

COOKIES

Shortbread Cookies 237
Hazelnut Shortbread Cookies 237
Chocolate Chip Cookies 238
No-Flour Peanut Butter Cookies 238

FILLINGS, FROSTINGS & TOPPINGS

Lemon Curd 239
Orange Curd 239
Lime Curd 239
Cream Cheese Frosting 240
Chocolate Cream Cheese Frosting 240
Grandma's Italian Frosting 241
Northwest Berry Sauce 241

PIES, TARTS & TORTES

PECAN PIE WITH BOURBON CREME

Sodium Per Serving – 39mg　　　　　　　　　　　　　　　　　Serves 8

This great-tasting pie is made with maple syrup instead of corn syrup. Although rich and luscious, it is not too sweet. Topping this with the bourbon creme sends it over the top!

- 1 *Basic Pie Crust (pg 205)* or LS pie crust
- 1½ cups pecan halves
- 1 cup sugar
- 3 tablespoons unsalted butter or margarine, melted
- 2 eggs, beaten[1]
- ½ cup maple syrup[2]
- 2 tablespoons brewed strong coffee or espresso[3]
- 1 tablespoon molasses
- 1 tablespoon all-purpose flour
- 1 teaspoon vanilla extract
- 1½ cups *Bourbon Creme (recipe follows)*

1. Preheat oven to 350ºF (180ºC).
2. Place pecans in the bottom of an unbaked pie crust.
3. In a large bowl, mix together the sugar, butter, eggs, maple syrup, coffee, molasses, flour, and vanilla; pour over the pecans.
4. Bake in a preheated oven for 50 to 60 minutes, until a knife inserted in the center comes out clean. Remove and cool completely.

NUTRITIONAL INFO PER SERVING: Calories 523, Fat 31g (Saturated Fat 9g), Cholesterol 64mg, Carbohydrates 59g (Fiber 2g, Sugar 30g), Sodium 39mg (70mg with LS pie crust)

BOURBON CREME

Sodium Per Serving – 0mg　　　　　　　　　　　　　　　　　Serves 8

This simple, yet delicious topping is also good on bread pudding, fruit compote, sweet potato pie, or apple tarts.

- 1½ cups lowfat whipped topping
- 1–1½ tablespoons bourbon or whiskey

1. Mix whipped topping with bourbon and serve with pie.

NUTRITIONAL INFO PER SERVING: Calories 27, Fat 2g (Sat Fat 1g), Chol 0mg, Carb 2g (Fiber 0g, Sugar 2g), Sodium 0mg

Recipe Notes

1 – To keep fat to a minimum, use an egg substitute. See *Eggs and Egg Substitutes*, pg 23, for a comparison of fat and sodium in eggs and egg substitutes.

2 – Use sugar-free maple syrup to keep the sugar low. Be careful, many varieties have a load of sodium (100mg or more).

3 – I like to keep a jar of instant espresso on hand for recipes that call for coffee. Use 2 tbsp hot water to 1 tsp instant coffee granules.

TOTAL SODIUM AND FAT BY INGREDIENT

PECAN PIE
Sodium:
- 1 *Basic Pie Crust* - 150mg or LS pie crust - 400mg
- 1 c sugar - 2mg
- 2 eggs - 142mg
- 1 T molasses - 15mg

Fat (Sat Fat):
- 1 *Basic Pie Crust* - 74g (28g) or LS pie crust - 64g (28g)
- 1½ c pecans - 120g (12g)
- 2 eggs - 10g (3g)
- 3 T NSA butter - 35g (22g) or NSA margarine - 27g (11g)
- 1½ c *Bourbon Creme* - 12g (6g)

Brands used/alternatives:
Marie Callender's Pie Shell

BOURBON CREME
Fat (Sat Fat):
- 1½ c LF whip topping - 12g (6g)

ABSOLUTELY THE BEST BERRY PIE

Sodium Per Serving – 27mg Serves 6

The secret to a great berry pie is that it have a fresh fruit taste that is not masked with a lot of sugar. The following recipe is a family favorite; use any fresh, frozen, or combination of berries.

- **1** *Basic Pie Crust (pg 205)* **or LS pie crust**
- **5 cups fresh or frozen berries, such as blackberries, blueberries, strawberries, raspberries, or any combination**
- **2–3 tablespoons cornstarch**[1]
- **¼ teaspoon ground cinnamon**
- **1 tablespoon lemon juice**
- **1 cup sugar**
- **½ teaspoon almond extract**

1. Preheat oven to 350°F (180°C). Adjust oven shelf to lowest level.
2. Prick crust with a fork; line bottom of shell with aluminum foil. Pour pie weights into the pie crust to hold its shape while baking (for info on pie weights, see *Pie Weights, pg 252*). Bake for 5 minutes in a preheated oven; remove weights and bake 5 minutes more. Remove from oven and let cool slightly. *NOTE: If using a refrigerated or frozen pie crust, this step is not necessary.*
3. In a large bowl, gently mix the berries with cornstarch until well coated. *NOTE:* Use cornstarch only if using frozen berries and allow fruit to stand 15 to 20 minutes until partially thawed.
4. Add sugar, lemon juice, almond extract, and cinnamon; gently toss until well mixed. Pour into prepared pie crust; place on lowest oven shelf and bake in a preheated oven for 40 to 45 minutes until crust is golden brown. Remove and let cool before serving.

NUTRITIONAL INFO PER SERVING: Calories 440, Fat 13g (Sat Fat 5g), Chol 0mg, Carb 80g (Fiber 3g, Sugar 48g), Sodium 27mg (68mg with LS pie crust)

Recipe Notes
1 – If using frozen or very juicy berries, use all 3 tbsp cornstarch.

TOTAL SODIUM AND FAT BY INGREDIENT

AMARETTO CREME
Sodium:
 1 T amaretto - 1mg
Fat (Sat Fat):
 1½ c LF topping - 12g (6g)

THE BEST BERRY PIE
Sodium:
 1 *Basic Pie Crust* - 150mg
  or LS pie crust - 400mg
 5 c blackberries - 8mg
 1 c sugar - 2mg
Fat (Sat Fat):
 1 *Basic Pie Crust* - 74g (28g)
  or LS pie crust - 56g (16g)
Brands used/alternatives:
 Marie Callender's Pie Shell

Pumpkin Pie with Amaretto Creme

Sodium Per Serving – 76mg Serves 6

A traditional pumpkin pie has about 349mg sodium per serving. Mine has been lightened up—both in fat and sodium. But you won't miss either, as you enjoy this creamy, spicy traditional favorite. Top with Amaretto Creme for a fine ending to any holiday dinner.

- **1 *Basic Pie Crust (pg 205)* or LS pie crust**
- **1 (15-oz) can pumpkin**
- **1 cup lowfat sour cream**
- **1 cup sugar**
- **2 eggs, beaten[1]**
- **¼ cup lowfat milk or fat free half-and-half**
- **1 teaspoon vanilla extract**
- **1 teaspoon ground cinnamon**
- **½ teaspoon ground ginger**
- **½ teaspoon ground nutmeg**
- **1½ cups *Amaretto Creme (recipe follows)***

1. Preheat oven to 350ºF (180ºC).
2. Prick crust with a fork; line bottom of shell with aluminum foil. Pour pie weights into the pie crust to hold its shape while baking (see *Pie Weights*, pg 252, for info). Bake for 5 minutes in a preheated oven; remove weights and bake 5 minutes more. Remove shell from oven and let cool slightly. *NOTE: If using a refrigerated or frozen pie crust, this step is not necessary.*
3. Meanwhile, in a large bowl, mix together all ingredients and pour into prepared crust.
4. Place pie on lowest oven shelf; bake for about 1 hour. Pie is ready if it no longer wiggles when pan is shaken. Remove and let cool. *NOTE: Pie continues to cook as it cools; cracking means it cooked too long.*

NUTRITIONAL INFO PER SERVING: Calories 503, Fat 20g (Sat Fat 8g), Chol 85mg, Carbs 71g (Fiber 2g, Sugar 43g), Sodium 76mg (118mg with LS pie crust)

VARIATION
Brandied Pumpkin Pie

1. Add ¼ cup brandy to the pumpkin mixture before pouring into the pie crust. Omit the *Amaretto Creme* and top with lowfat whipped topping or ice cream.

NUTRITIONAL INFO PER SERVING: Calories 507, Fat 19g (Sat Fat 8g), Chol 85mg, Carb 71g (Fiber 2g, Sugar 41g), Sodium 76mg (118mg with LS pie crust)

Amaretto Creme

Sodium Per Serving – 0mg Serves 8

This yummy topping is also good on bread pudding, fruit compote, or peach tart.

- **1½ cups lowfat whipped topping**
- **1–1½ tablespoons amaretto or other almond-flavored liqueur**

1. Mix together the whipped topping and amaretto. Spoon on top of pie and serve.

NUTRITIONAL INFO PER SERVING: Calories 29, Fat 2g (Sat Fat 1g), Chol 0mg, Carb 2g (Fiber 0g, Sugar 2g), Sodium 0mg

Recipe Notes
1 – To keep fat to a minimum, use an egg substitute. See *Eggs and Egg Substitutes*, pg 23, for a comparison of fat and sodium in eggs and egg substitutes.

TOTAL SODIUM AND FAT BY INGREDIENT

PUMPKIN PIE WITH CREME
Sodium:
- 1 *Basic Pie Crust* - 150mg
  or LS pie crust - 400mg
- 15 oz pumpkin - 18mg
- 1 c LF sour cream - 120mg
- 1 cup sugar - 2mg
- 2 eggs - 142mg
- ¼ c LF milk - 26mg
  or FF half-and-half - 60mg
- 1½ c *Amaretto Creme* - 1mg

Fat (Sat Fat):
- 1 *Basic Pie Crust* - 74g (28g)
  or LS pie crust - 64g (28g)
- 15 oz pumpkin - 2g (0g)
- 1 c LF sour cream - 20g (12g)
- 2 eggs - 10g (3g)
- ¼ c LF milk - 1g (1g)
  or FF half-and-half - 2g (1g)
- 1½ c *Amaretto Creme* - 12g (6g)

Brands used/alternatives:
Daisy Light Sour Cream
Simple Truth 2% Milk
Marie Callender's Pie Shell

AMARETTO CREME
Sodium:
- 1 T amaretto - 1mg

Fat (Sat Fat):
- 1½ c LF topping - 12g (6g)

Light Apple Tart

Sodium Per Serving – 26mg Serves 6

This light and refreshing tart is the perfect ending to a wonderful meal and is a great favorite whenever I entertain. The secret is keeping the taste of sugar to a minimum, which allows the flavor of the apples to come through.

- **1 *Basic Pie Crust (see pg 205)* or LS pie crust**
- **3 apples, such as Braeburn, Jazz, or Fuji, peeled and thinly sliced[1]**
- **½ cup sugar**
- **1½ tablespoons all-purpose flour**
- **¼ teaspoon ground cinnamon**
- **2 tablespoons unsalted butter or margarine**

1. Preheat oven to 425°F (220°C). Adjust oven shelf to lowest level.
2. Place pie crust in a 9-inch tart pan with a removable base, pressing dough into the bottom and up the fluted sides of the pan.
3. Arrange apple slices in a circular design. There will be 3 layers of alternating varieties.
4. Mix together sugar, flour, cinnamon, and butter. If using a processor, pulse until well mixed; sprinkle evenly over the apples.
5. Bake on the lowest oven rack for 40 to 45 minutes, until crust is golden brown. Remove and cool before serving.

NUTRITIONAL INFO PER SERVING: Calories 381, Fat 16g (Saturated Fat 7g), Cholesterol 10mg, Carbohydrates 57g (Fiber 3g, Sugar 28g), Sodium 26mg (68mg with LS pie crust)

Recipe Notes

1 – Many cooks prefer using tart apples, such as Pippin, Gravenstein, or Granny Smith, that require a lot of sugar. In this particular tart, I like to use apples with a sweet-tart taste, so I can add less sugar.

TOTAL SODIUM AND FAT BY INGREDIENT

Sodium:
- 1 *Basic Pie Crust* - 150mg
  - or LS pie crust - 400mg
- 3 apples - 5mg
- ½ c sugar - 1mg

Fat (Sat Fat):
- 1 *Basic Pie Crust* - 74g (28g)
  - or LS pie crust - 64g (28g)
- 3 apples - 1g (0g)
- 2 T NSA butter - 23g (14g)
  - or NSA margarine - 18g (7g)

Brands used/alternatives:
Marie Callender's Pie Shell

Fresh Strawberry Tart

Sodium Per Serving – 28mg   Serves 6

This quick and easy tart makes the most beautiful presentation. Everyone wants to eat this first and save dinner for later. Use fresh strawberries for the best results.

- **1 Basic Pie Crust (pg 205) or LS pie crust**
- **1 cup fruit juice (such as apple or berry)**
- **¾ cup sugar**
- **2½ tablespoons cornstarch**
- **5 cups fresh strawberries, halved**
- **Lowfat whipped topping (optional)**

1. Preheat oven to 350ºF (180ºC).
2. Prick crust with a fork; line bottom of shell with aluminum foil. Pour pie weights into the pie crust to hold its shape while baking (for info on pie weights, see *Pie Weights*, pg 252). Bake for 10 minutes in a preheated oven; remove weights and bake 10 minutes more. Remove from oven and let cool slightly. NOTE: If using a refrigerated or frozen pie crust, this step is not necessary.
3. *For the glaze:* In a small saucepan over medium-high heat, add fruit juice, sugar, and cornstarch. Cook, stirring frequently, until glaze thickens to a syrupy consistency, about 5 minutes; remove and let cool.
4. Pour a few tablespoons glaze into the cooked crust to cover the bottom. Arrange strawberries cut side down with the largest berries on the bottom and the smallest filling in the holes on top.
5. Cover strawberries with remaining glaze; refrigerate for 2-3 hours. Serve with whipped topping.

NUTRITIONAL INFO PER SERVING: Calories 395, Fat 15g (Saturated Fat 6g), Cholesterol 0mg, Carbohydrates 62g (Fiber 3g, Sugar 31g), Sodium 28mg (69mg with LS pie crust)

Brandied Apricot Almond Tart

Sodium Per Serving – 49mg   Serves 8

This very rich tart recipe is from a friend from Seattle, who enjoyed a version of this at Place Pigalle in Pike Place Market. The combination of dried apricots and almonds is a wonderful treat for the palate.

- **1 Basic Pie Crust (pg 205) or LS pie crust**
- **2 cups dried apricots, chopped**
- **⅓ cup brandy or rum**
- **1 cup sliced almonds**
- **¼ cup sugar**
- **¼ cup unsalted butter or margarine**
- **½ cup apricot preserves**
- **3 eggs or egg substitute, slightly beaten**
- **½ teaspoon almond extract**

1. Preheat oven to 350ºF (180ºC).
2. Prick crust with a fork; line bottom of shell with aluminum foil. Follow pie weights instructions in Step 2 of the previous recipe.
3. Soak apricots in brandy for 15-20 minutes; drain, reserve liquid. Sprinkle apricots in prepared pie crust.
4. In a bowl, mix together almonds, sugar, butter, apricot preserves, and reserved brandy; beat in eggs, one at a time, add almond extract. Pour batter over the apricots. Bake in a preheated oven for 1 hour, until almonds are golden brown. Let cool and serve with cream, if desired.

NUTRITIONAL INFO PER SERVING: Calories 505, Fat 26g (Sat Fat 8g), Chol 94mg, Carb 59g (Fiber 4g, Sugar 35g), Sodium 49mg (80mg with LS pie crust)

TOTAL SODIUM AND FAT BY INGREDIENT

FRESH STRAWBERRY TART
Sodium:
- 1 Basic Pie Crust - 150mg or LS pie crust - 400mg
- 1 c fruit juice - 8mg
- 2½ T cornstarch - 1mg
- 5 c strawberries - 8mg

Fat (Sat Fat):
- 1 Basic Pie Crust - 74g (28g) or LS pie crust - 64g (28g)
- 5 c strawberries - 3g (0g)
- 2½ c LF whip topping - 12g (6g)

Brands used/alternatives:
Marie Callender's Pie Shell

BRANDIED APRICOT TART
Sodium:
- 1 Basic Pie Crust - 150mg or LS pie crust - 400mg
- 2 c dried apricots - 26mg
- ¼ c sugar - 1mg
- 3 eggs - 213mg

Fat (Sat Fat):
- 1 Basic Pie Crust - 74g (28g) or LS pie crust - 64g (28g)
- 2 c dried apricots -1g (0g)
- 1 c almonds - 68g (6g)
- ¼ c NSA butter - 46g (29g) or NSA margarine - 36g (14g)
- 3 eggs - 15g (5g)

Brands used/alternatives:
Marie Callender's Pie Shell

Chocolate Decadence Torte

Sodium Per Serving – 9mg Serves 16

Chocolate lovers beware, this torte may be addicting! This no-bake dessert is another of my most-requested recipes. Although it contains a lot of fat, it is so rich that a little goes a long ways.

Crust:
- **2 cups dry roasted unsalted pecans[1]**
- **½ teaspoon ground cinnamon**
- **¼ cup unsalted butter or margarine, melted**

Filling:
- **½ cup unsalted butter or margarine, at room temperature**
- **½ cup sugar**
- **2 eggs[2]**
- **1 teaspoon vanilla extract**
- **1 (12-oz) package chocolate morsels, melted[3]**
- **2 tablespoons lowfat whipped topping**

1. *For the crust:* Place nuts and cinnamon in processor and pulse until nuts are finely ground; slowly add butter. Press into bottom of springform pan.
2. *For the filling:* Combine butter and sugar; beat until light and fluffy. Mix in eggs, one at a time, and vanilla; beat 2 minutes. Mix in melted chocolate; fold in whipped topping. Pour into crust and refrigerate until firm, about 4 to 6 hours.

NUTRITIONAL INFO PER SERVING: Calories 315, Fat 25g (Saturated Fat 10g), Cholesterol 27mg, Carbohydrates 22g (Fiber 3g, Sugar 17g), Sodium 9mg

Recipe Notes

1 – Substitute almonds, walnuts, or a combination of nuts.
2 – To keep fat to a minimum, use an egg substitute. See *Eggs and Egg Substitutes*, pg 23, for a comparison of fat and sodium in eggs and egg substitutes.
3 – I often make this torte sugar free, using a sugar substitute and sugar free chocolate chips. It is delicious and always goes fast at our annual community club bake sale!

TOTAL SODIUM AND FAT BY INGREDIENT

Sodium:
½ c sugar - 1mg
2 eggs - 142mg

Fat (Sat Fat):
2 c pecans - 160g (16g)
¾ c NSA butter -138g (87g)
  or NSA margarine - 108g (42g)
2 eggs - 10g (3g)
10 oz choc chips - 96g (60g)
2 T LF topping - 1g (1g)

CAKES & CHEESECAKES

Lemon Curd-Mascarpone Cake

Sodium Per Serving – 45mg   Serves 12

This is my adaptation of a decadently rich, but light cake that appeared in Bon Appetite. Although I've removed most of the sodium, it is still absolutely yummy. The best compliment came from a professional cake maker who asked for my recipe.

- **2 cups all-purpose flour**
- **1½ tablespoons NSA baking powder[1]**
- **½ cup (1 stick) unsalted butter or margarine, softened**
- **1½ cups sugar**
- **2 eggs[2]**
- **1 cup lowfat milk**
- **1½ teaspoons vanilla extract**

Frosting and Filling:
- **12 oz mascarpone[3]**
- **⅓ cup sugar**
- **1½ cups *Lemon Curd (pg 239)* or 1 (12-oz) jar lemon curd, divided**
- **1 cup lowfat whipped topping**
- **Sliced almonds (optional)**

1. Preheat oven to 350ºF (180ºC). Lightly oil and flour the inside of two 8" round cake pans.
2. *For the cake:* Sift together the flour and baking powder; set aside.
3. In a large bowl, beat butter and sugar together until light and creamy. Beat in the eggs, one at a time; add vanilla. Alternately mix in the flour mixture and milk, beating until smooth.
4. Pour into prepared cake pans; bake in a preheated oven for 35 to 40 minutes, until a toothpick inserted into the center of the cake comes out clean. Remove and let cool before frosting.
5. *For the frosting:* Beat together mascarpone and sugar until smooth, add ½ cup lemon curd; fold in whipped topping.
6. *To assemble:* Place one cake layer on plate; spread with one-third of the mascarpone mixture. Top with remaining 1 cup lemon curd. Place second cake layer on top; spread remaining frosting on sides and top of cake.
7. Cover the sides of the cake with sliced almonds, leaving the top free of nuts (This takes a lot of time, but makes a gorgeous presentation.), or sprinkle almonds all over the cake. Refrigerate for several hours; bring to room temperature before serving.

NUTRITIONAL INFO PER SERVING: Calories 540, Fat 31g (Sat Fat 18g), Chol 127mg, Carb 63g (Fiber 1g, Sugar 45g), Sodium 45mg

Recipe Notes
1 – For information on NSA baking powder, see *Baking Powder/Baking Soda*, pg 243.
2 – To keep fat to a minimum, use an egg substitute. See *Eggs and Egg Substitutes*, pg 23, for a comparison of fat and sodium in eggs and egg substitutes.
3 – Mascarpone, or "Italian cream cheese", is creamier and richer than American cream cheese. Although it has more fat, it is low in sodium.

TOTAL SODIUM AND FAT BY INGREDIENT

Sodium:
- 2 c flour - 5mg
- 1½ + ⅓ c sugar - 4mg
- 2 eggs - 142mg
- 1 c LF milk - 105mg
- 12 oz mascarpone - 120mg
- 1½ c *Lemon Curd* - 161mg or 12-oz lemon curd - 0mg

Fat (Sat Fat):
- 2 c flour - 2g (0g)
- ½ c NSA butter - 92g (58g) or NSA margarine - 72g (28g)
- 2 eggs - 10g (3g)
- 1 c LF milk - 5g (3g)
- 12 oz mascarpone - 168g (120g)
- 1½ c *Lemon Curd* - 57g (22g) or 12-oz lemon curd - 36g (27g)
- 1 c whipped topping - 8g (4g)
- ½ c sliced almonds - 34g (3g)

Brands used/alternatives:
Hain Featherweight Baking Powder
Simple Truth 2% Milk
BelGioioso Mascarpone Cheese
Bonne Maman Lemon Curd

CARROT CAKE

Sodium Per Serving – 28mg   Serves 12

This carrot cake is moist and full of flavor. Most commercial carrot cakes have way to much sodium for a low-salt diet. Not only is this cake low in sodium, it's moist and full of flavor.

- 1½ cups all-purpose flour
- 1½ teaspoons ground cinnamon
- 1 tablespoon NSA baking powder[1]
- ½ teaspoon ground cloves
- 2 eggs[2]
- 1 cup sugar
- ⅔ cup vegetable or canola oil
- 1½ teaspoons vanilla extract
- 1½ cups grated carrots (about 2 large)
- ¾ cup crushed pineapple, drained
- ⅓ cup unsweetened coconut (optional)[3]
- ½ cup walnuts, toasted and chopped[4]
- **Cream Cheese Frosting (pg 240)**

1. Preheat oven to 350°F (180°C). Lightly oil and flour the inside of a 9x13x2-inch rectangular baking dish, or two 9-inch cake pans.
2. Sift together the flour, cinnamon, baking powder, and cloves; set aside.
3. In a large bowl, beat eggs, one at a time, with sugar until smooth and creamy; slowly add oil, beating until well mixed. Stir in vanilla.
4. Gradually add the flour mixture, beating until smooth; stir in carrots, pineapple, coconut, and walnuts.
5. Pour into prepared baking dish or cake pans; bake in a preheated oven for 1 hour, or until a toothpick inserted into the center of the cake comes out clean. Remove and let cool before frosting.

NUTRITIONAL INFO PER SERVING (without frosting): Calories 308, Fat 18g (Saturated Fat 3g), Cholesterol 37mg, Carbohydrates 36g (Fiber 3g, Sugar 21g), Sodium 28mg

Recipe Notes

1– For more info, see *Baking Powder/Baking Soda*, pg 243.
2 – To keep fat to a minimum, use an egg substitute. See *Eggs and Egg Substitutes*, pg 23, for a comparison of fat and sodium in eggs and egg substitutes.
3 – The sodium in coconut depends on whether it's sweetened or not; unsweetened averages 10mg an ounce, sweetened has 60mg.
4 – For directions to toast nuts, see *Toasting Nuts*, pg 250.

TOTAL SODIUM AND FAT BY INGREDIENT

Sodium:
- 1½ c flour - 4mg
- 1½ t cinnamon - 1mg
- 2 eggs - 142mg
- 1½ c carrots - 64mg
- ¾ c pineapple - 15mg
- ½ c coconut - 107mg
- ½ c walnuts - 1mg

Fat (Sat Fat):
- 1½ c flour - 2g (0g)
- 2 eggs - 10g (3g)
- ⅔ c vegetable oil - 145g (11g)
- ⅓ c coconut - 19g (19g)
- ½ c walnuts - 39g (4g)

Brands used/alternatives:
Hain Featherweight Baking Powder

Pound Cake

Sodium Per Serving – 39mg   Serves 14

We use pound cake in lots of ways. It's delicious on its own, or you can top it with a lemon glaze or fresh fruit, like strawberries. Some pound cake recipes use baking powder and salt to make it rise, but this one doesn't. Instead, it gets its volume from air that's mixed in when you beat the batter. Use ingredients that are at room temperature which helps get more air into the batter.

- 1½ cups (3 sticks) unsalted butter or margarine, softened
- 3 cups sugar
- 6 eggs
- 1 tablespoon lemon extract
- 2 teaspoons vanilla extract
- 3 cups all-purpose flour
- 1 cup lowfat milk

1. Preheat oven to 350ºF (180ºC). Lightly oil and flour the inside of a 5x9x3-inch loaf pan or bundt pan.
2. In a large bowl, beat the butter and sugar together until light and creamy; add eggs, one at a time, beating until smooth and creamy. Stir in lemon and vanilla extracts; alternately mix in flour and milk, stirring until well mixed.
3. Pour into prepared pan; bake in a preheated oven for 1 hour and 15 minutes, or until a toothpick inserted in the center comes out clean. Remove and let cool.

NUTRITIONAL INFO PER SERVING: Calories 474, Fat 22g (Sat Fat 13g), Chol 92mg, Carb 65g (Fiber 0g, Sugar 44g), Sodium 39mg

---

VARIATION
Cream Cheese Pound Cake

1. Add 8 oz cream cheese to the butter and sugar; proceed as directed.

NUTRITIONAL INFO PER SERVING: Calories 526, Fat 28g (Sat Fat 17g), Chol 107mg, Carb 65g (Fiber 0g, Sugar 45g), Sodium 82mg

---

Sponge Cake

Sodium Per Serving – 13mg   Serves 14

This is a basic sponge cake recipe with a hint of lemon. Add a frosting of your choice or serve it with fresh fruit.

- 8 egg yolks
- 1 cup sugar
- ¼ cup water
- 2 teaspoons lemon juice
- 1 teaspoon finely grated lemon peel or ½ teaspoon lemon extract
- 1 cup all-purpose flour
- 2 egg whites
- ½ teaspoon cream of tartar

1. Preheat oven to 350ºF (180ºC). Lightly oil and flour the inside of a 9x5x3-inch loaf or tube pan.
2. In a large bowl, beat egg yolks until thick and lemon colored. Gradually beat in the sugar, mixing well between additions. Add water, lemon peel, and lemon juice; mix in flour.
3. In another bowl, beat the egg whites and cream of tartar until stiff, but not dry; gently fold into the cake batter. Pour into prepared pan.
4. Bake in a preheated oven for 1 hour or until a toothpick inserted into the center of the cake comes out clean; remove from oven and let cool.

NUTRITIONAL INFO PER SERVING: Calories 122, Fat 3g (Saturated Fat 1g), Cholesterol 105mg, Carbohydrates 22g (Fiber 0g, Sugar 14g), Sodium 13mg

---

TOTAL SODIUM AND FAT BY INGREDIENT

POUND CAKE
Sodium:
- 3 c sugar - 2mg
- 6 eggs - 426mg
- 1 T lemon extract - 1mg
- 3 c flour - 8mg
- 1 c LF milk - 105mg

Fat (Sat Fat):
- 1½ c NSA butter - 276g (173g) or NSA margarine - 192g (36g)
- 6 eggs - 30g (9g)
- 3 c flour - 4g (1g)
- 1 c LF milk - 5g (3g)

Brands used/alternatives:
- *Simple Truth* 2% Milk

SPONGE CAKE
Sodium:
- 8 egg yolks - 66mg
- 1 c sugar - 2mg
- 1 c flour - 3mg
- 2 egg whites - 110mg
- ½ t cream of tartar - 1mg

Fat (Sat Fat):
- 2 egg yolks - 36g (13g)
- 1 c flour - 1g (0g)

Pumpkin Cheesecake

Sodium Per Serving – 100mg Serves 16

This is a luscious cheesecake that is the perfect ending to a holiday dinner. Allow at least 5 hours for the cheesecake to set up before serving.

Crust:

1 cup ladyfingers or shortbread cookies (about 5 oz)[1]

¼ cup coarsely ground almonds or pecans

⅓ cup unsalted butter or margarine, melted

Filling:

8 oz mascarpone[2]

16 oz regular or lowfat cream cheese[3]

1 cup sugar

3 eggs, lightly beaten[4]

1 teaspoon vanilla extract

1 (15-oz) can 100% pure pumpkin

1 teaspoon ground cinnamon

¼ teaspoon ground nutmeg

⅛ teaspoon ground allspice

Topping:

1 cup whipped cream topping

1. Preheat oven to 350°F (180°C). Adjust oven rack to lowest position.
2. *For the crust:* In a food processor, pulse ladyfingers and almonds until coarse; add butter and pulse until well mixed. Press into bottom of springform pan. Bake in a preheated oven for 10 minutes; remove and let cool slightly.
3. *For the filling:* Cream together the mascarpone, cream cheese, and sugar; beat in eggs. Add vanilla, pumpkin, and spices; pour into cookie crust.
4. Bake on the lowest oven rack for 1 hour; turn off heat and let sit another 30 minutes. Remove from oven and let cool.
5. Cover and refrigerate at least 5 hours or overnight. Remove springform rim and top cheesecake with whipped topping before serving.

NUTRITIONAL INFO PER SERVING: Calories 299, Fat 24g (Sat Fat 13g), Chol 101mg, Carb 22g (Fiber 1g, Sugar 18g), Sodium 100mg

Recipe Notes

1 – I prefer using Italian ladyfingers, also called Savoiardi. They are a drier, finger-shaped sponge cake and are very low in sodium.

2 – Mascarpone, or "Italian cream cheese", is creamier and richer than American cream cheese. Although it has more fat, it is low in sodium.

3 – To reduce fat and keep sodium to a minimum, use a lower fat alternative or combine with regular cream cheese. See *Cream Cheese Comparison*, pg 247, for more info.

4 – To keep fat to a minimum, use an egg substitute. See *Eggs and Egg Substitutes*, pg 23, for a comparison of fat and sodium in eggs and egg substitutes.

TOTAL SODIUM AND FAT BY INGREDIENT

Sodium:
- 1 c ladyfingers - 80mg
- 8 oz mascarpone - 80mg
- 16 oz cream cheese - 1,200mg
  or LF cream cheese - 1,680mg
- 1 c sugar - 2mg
- 3 eggs - 213mg
- 15-oz pumpkin - 18mg

Fat (Sat Fat):
- 1 c ladyfingers - 4g (4g)
- ¼ c almonds - 17g (2g)
- ⅓ c NSA butter - 61g (25g)
  or margarine - 48g (19g)
- 8 oz mascarpone - 112g (80g)
- 16 oz cream cheese - 160g (96g)
  or LF cream cheese - 96g (56g)
- 3 eggs - 15g (5g)
- 15-oz pumpkin - 2g (0g)
- 1 c whipped topping - 8g (4g)

Brands used/alternatives:

Matilde Vicenzi Ladyfingers
BelGioioso Mascarpone Cheese
Green Valley Lactose-Free Cream Cheese
Great Value Neufchâtel Cheese

Cheesecake with Northwest Berry Sauce

Sodium Per Serving – 104mg
Serves 16

Most cheesecakes have loads of fat and sodium. Although lightened up, this adaptation is both rich and creamy, and paired with the berry sauce, makes a beautiful presentation. Prepare the day before to allow the cheesecake to set up.

Crust:
- **1 cup ladyfingers (about 5 oz)**[1]
- **¼ cup pecans or walnuts**
- **⅓ cup unsalted butter or margarine, melted**
- **1 tablespoon sugar**
- **½ teaspoon ground cinnamon**

Filling:
- **8 oz mascarpone**[2]
- **16 oz regular or lowfat cream cheese**[3]
- **¾ cup lowfat sour cream**
- **1 cup sugar**
- **3 eggs, lightly beaten**[4]
- **1 teaspoon vanilla extract**
- **½ teaspoon almond extract**
- **1 teaspoon lemon juice**

Topping:
- **Northwest Berry Sauce (pg 241), chilled**

1. Preheat oven to 350ºF (180ºC).
2. *For the crust:* In a food processor, pulse ladyfingers and pecans until coarse. Add butter, sugar, and cinnamon; pulse until mixed well. Press into bottom of springform pan. Bake for 10 minutes; remove and let cool.
3. *For the filling:* Cream together the mascarpone, cream cheese, and sugar. Beat in eggs; mix in vanilla, almond extract, and lemon juice. Pour over cookie crust.
4. Bake on the lowest oven rack in a preheated oven for 1 hour; turn off heat and let sit another 30 minutes. Remove from oven and let cool.
5. Cover tightly and refrigerate at least 5 hours or overnight before serving. Remove springform rim; spread *Northwest Berry Sauce* on top of cheesecake.

NUTRITIONAL INFO PER SERVING: Calories 322, Fat 24g (Sat Fat 14g), Chol 105mg, Carb 24g (Fiber 1g, Sugar 22g), Sodium 104mg

Recipe Notes

1 – I prefer using Italian ladyfingers, also called Savoiardi. They are a drier, finger-shaped sponge cake and are very low in sodium.

2 – Mascarpone, or "Italian cream cheese", is creamier and richer than American cream cheese. Although it has more fat, it's low in sodium.

3 – To reduce fat and keep sodium to a minimum, use a lower fat alternative or combine with regular cream cheese. See *Cream Cheese Comparison*, pg 247, for more info.

5 – To keep fat to a minimum, use an egg substitute. See *Eggs and Egg Substitutes*, pg 23, for a comparison of fat and sodium in eggs and egg substitutes.

TOTAL SODIUM AND FAT BY INGREDIENT

Sodium:
- 1 c ladyfingers - 80mg
- 8 oz mascarpone - 80mg
- 16 oz cream cheese - 1,200mg
  or LF cream cheese - 1,680mg
- ¾ c LF sour cream - 90mg
- 1 c sugar - 2mg
- 3 eggs - 213mg
- NW Berry Sauce - 3mg

Fat (Sat Fat):
- 1 c ladyfingers - 4g (4g)
- ¼ c pecans - 20g (2g)
- ⅓ c NSA butter - 61g (25g)
  or NSA margarine - 48g (19g)
- 8 oz mascarpone - 112g 80g)
- 16 oz cream cheese - 160g (96g)
  or LF cream cheese - 96g (56g)
- ¾ c LF sour cream - 15g (9g)
- 3 eggs - 15g (5g)
- NW Berry Sauce - 1g (0g)

Brands used/alternatives:
- *Matilde Vicenzi* Ladyfingers
- *BelGioioso* Mascarpone Cheese
- *Green Valley* Lactose-Free Cream Cheese
- *Great Value* Neufchâtel Cheese
- *Daisy* Light Sour Cream

CHOCOLATE CHIP CHEESECAKE

Sodium Per Serving – 112mg					Serves 16

This is a luscious cheesecake that is the perfect ending to any family dinner. Allow at least 5 hours for the cheesecake to set up before serving.

Crust:

1½ cups Danish butter or shortbread cookies, coarsely ground (about 6 oz)

¼ cup unsalted butter or margarine, melted

Filling:

16 oz regular or lowfat cream cheese[1]

8 oz mascarpone[2]

1 cup sugar

3 eggs, lightly beaten[3]

½ cup lowfat sour cream

1 teaspoon vanilla extract

1 (6-oz) package chocolate chips

1. Preheat oven to 350°F (180°C). Adjust oven rack to lowest position.
2. *For the crust:* Mix together the cookie crumbs and melted butter. Add enough butter to hold the crumbs together. Press into bottom of springform pan and bake in a preheated oven for 10 minutes. Remove from oven and let cool slightly.
3. *For the filling:* Cream together cream cheese, mascarpone, and sugar. Beat in eggs; stir in sour cream and vanilla. Mix in chocolate chips; pour into cookie crust.
4. Bake on the lowest rack in a preheated oven for 1 hour; turn off heat and let sit another 30 minutes. Remove from oven and let cool.
5. Cover tightly and refrigerate at least 5 hours or overnight before serving.

NUTRITIONAL INFO PER SERVING: Calories 355, Fat 27g (Sat Fat 17g), Chol 103mg, Carb 28g (Fiber 1g, Sugar 22g), Sodium 112mg

Recipe Notes

1 – To reduce fat and keep sodium to a minimum, use a lower fat alternative or combine with regular cream cheese. See *Cream Cheese Comparison*, pg 247, for more info.

2 – Mascarpone, or "Italian cream cheese", is creamier and richer than American cream cheese. Although it has more fat, it's low in sodium.

3 – To keep fat to a minimum, use an egg substitute. See *Eggs and Egg Substitutes*, pg 23, for a comparison of fat and sodium in eggs and egg substitutes.

TOTAL SODIUM AND FAT BY INGREDIENT

Sodium:
1½ c cookies - 240mg
8 oz mascarpone - 80mg
16 oz cream cheese - 1,200mg
  or LF cream cheese - 1,680mg
1 c sugar - 2 mg
3 eggs - 213mg
½ c LF sour cream - 60mg

Fat (Sat Fat):
1½ c cookies - 48g (39g)
¼ NSA butter - 46g (19g)
  or NSA margarine - 36g (14g)
8 oz mascarpone - 112g (80g)
16 oz cream cheese - 160g (96g)
  or LS cream cheese - 96g (56g)
3 eggs - 15g (5g)
½ c LF sour cream - 10g (6g)
6 oz chocolate chips - 48g (30g)

Brands used/alternatives:
Royal Dansk Danish Butter Cookies
BelGioioso Mascarpone Cheese
Green Valley Lactose-Free Cream Cheese
Great Value Neufchâtel Cheese
Daisy Light Sour Cream

CRISPS, STRUDELS & TURNOVERS

Apple Strudel

Sodium Per Serving – 77mg   Makes 2 strudels / Serves 8

This is one of my husband's favorite desserts. This yummy strudel goes together quickly with packaged phyllo dough and is made even better with the cream cheese frosting. To ensure flakiness, melted butter or margarine is usually brushed on each layer of the phyllo dough.

- 8 sheets phyllo dough[1]
- ¼ cup unsalted butter or margarine, melted
- 2 apples, sliced, such as Braeburn, Jazz, or Fuji
- 2 tablespoons sugar
- ½ teaspoon ground cinnamon
- ⅛ teaspoon ground nutmeg
- ⅓ cup chopped walnuts
- ¼ cup raisins
- ½ cup *Cream Cheese Frosting (pg 240)*

1. Preheat oven to 350ºF (180ºC). Coat a baking sheet with nonstick cooking spray.
2. Place one sheet of phyllo dough on work surface with the long side facing you; brush lightly with butter. Place a second sheet on top and brush lightly again. Repeat with third and fourth sheets. *NOTE: To keep fat to a minimum, I sometimes spray the sheets with butter-flavored cooking spray. It still taste good, but butter makes for a flakier strudel.*
3. Spread half the apples in the center of the dough to within ½ inch of the edges. Evenly sprinkle one-half the sugar, cinnamon, nutmeg, walnuts, and raisins over the apples. Roll up jelly-roll style, tucking in sides.
4. Repeat with remaining phyllo dough and ingredients, making a second strudel.
5. Place strudels, seam side down, on prepared baking sheet. Brush the tops and sides with remaining butter. Cut two or three 1-inch diagonal vents in the top of each strudel. Bake for 20 to 25 minutes, until golden brown. Remove and cool.
6. Cover with *Cream Cheese Frosting* and serve.

NUTRITIONAL INFO PER SERVING: Calories 253, Fat 14g (Saturated Fat 6g), Cholesterol 29mg, Carbohydrates 31g (Fiber 2g, Sugar 20g), Sodium 77mg

---

VARIATION
Berry Strudel
1. Instead of apples, mix 2 cups blueberries or blackberries with 1 tablespoon cornstarch; proceed as directed.

NUTRITIONAL INFO PER SERVING: Calories 260, Fat 14g (Sat Fat 6g), Chol 29mg, Carb 31g (Fiber 2g, Sugar 19g), Sodium 77mg

Recipe Notes
1 – Phyllo (also spelled fillo) dough is paper-thin pastry found in the frozen foods section. To keep the dough from drying out, working quickly is essential; cover sheets with a damp towel until ready to use.

TOTAL SODIUM AND FAT BY INGREDIENT

Sodium:
- 8 sheets phyllo dough - 300mg
- 2 apples - 4mg
- ⅓ c walnuts - 1mg
- ¼ c raisins - 10mg
- 1 c *Cr Cheese* Frosting - 281mg

Fat (Sat Fat):
- 8 sheets phyllo - 2g (0g)
- ¼ c NSA butter 46g (19g) or NSA margarine - 36g (14g)
- 2 apples - 1g (0g)
- ⅓ c walnuts - 26g (2g)
- 1 c *Cr Cheese* Frosting - 24g (16g)

Brands used/alternatives:
Athens Phyllo Dough

Peach & Blueberry Crisp

Sodium Per Serving – 2mg Serves 8

Peaches and blueberries are a delicious combination. I'm sure you'll love this crisp that uses both.

- **4 cups blueberries, fresh or frozen**
- **2 large peaches, sliced, or 2½ cups frozen sliced peaches**
- **¼ cup sugar**
- **2 tablespoons cornstarch**
- **½ teaspoon ground cinnamon**
- **¼ teaspoon ground nutmeg**

Topping:
- **¾ cup all-purpose flour**
- **⅓ cup unsalted butter or margarine**
- **¼ cup sugar**
- **1 teaspoon ground cinnamon**
- **½ teaspoon ground allspice**
- **½ cup chopped pecans or walnuts[1]**

1. Preheat oven to 350ºF (180ºC). Coat the inside of an 8-inch square baking dish with nonstick cooking spray.
2. Combine berries, peaches, sugar, cornstarch, cinnamon, and nutmeg. Pour into prepared baking dish. Cover with foil and bake in a preheated oven for about 1 hour, or until juices bubble. Remove from oven.
3. *For the topping:* Meanwhile, mix together the topping ingredients:

    In a food processor – Place flour, butter, sugar, cinnamon, and allspice in food processor; pulse until crumbly. Add nuts and pulse just enough times to incorporate the nuts.

    By hand – Mix together flour, cinnamon, and allspice; set aside. Cream together the butter and sugar; add flour mixture; mixing well. Stir in nuts.
4. Sprinkle topping evenly over the baked fruit; return to oven and bake, uncovered, for 30 minutes, or until the topping is golden brown. Cool slightly and serve.

NUTRITIONAL INFO PER SERVING: Calories 289, Fat 13g (Sat Fat 4g), Chol 20mg, Carb 49g (Fiber 4g, Sugar 24g), Sodium 2mg

Recipe Notes

1 – Toasted nuts add more flavor (see *Toasting Nuts*, pg 250, for several ways to toast nuts).

TOTAL SODIUM AND FAT BY INGREDIENT

Sodium:
- 4 c blueberries - 6mg
- ½ c sugar - 1mg
- 2 T cornstarch - 1mg
- ¾ c flour - 4mg
- ½ t allspice - 1mg

Fat (Sat Fat):
- 4 c blueberries - 2g (0g)
- 2½ c peaches - 1g (0g)
- ¾ c flour - 2g (0g)
- ⅓ c NSA butter - 61g (25g)
    or NSA margarine - 48g (19g)
- ½ c pecans - 40g (4g)
    or walnuts - 39g (3g)

Apple Turnovers

Sodium Per Serving – 66mg   Makes 4 turnovers

Once I discovered low-salt egg roll wrappers, I've found many uses for them, including these quick and delicious individual pies. Here are several of our favorite fillings, each makes four pies.

- **2 apples, such as Braeburn, Jazz, or Fuji, peeled and diced**
- **2-3 tablespoons sugar**
- **1/2 teaspoon ground cinnamon**
- **4 LS egg roll wraps or *Egg Roll Wraps* (pg 205)**
- **Oil, for frying**

1. In a small saucepan over low heat, add apples, sugar, and cinnamon. Cook, stirring frequently, until apples are soft, about 5 minutes; mash with a fork to make a thick applesauce. Divide mixture and spread on one side of wrappers; moisten 2 adjacent edges with water. Fold in half on the diagonal, forming a triangle. Press edges together with a fork.

2. Add oil to a frying pan over medium-high heat until it sizzles when a drop of water is added. Fry turnovers until golden brown, about 2 to 3 minutes per side. Drain on paper towels. If desired, sprinkle with confectioner's sugar or finely ground sugar. *NOTE:* To finely grind, place sugar in a blender or food processor and pulse until a fine powder.

NUTRITIONAL INFO PER TURNOVER*: Calories 143, Fat 0g (Sat Fat 0g), Chol 0mg, Carb 34g (Fiber 2g, Sugar 16g), Sodium 66mg (29mg with *Egg Roll Wraps*)   *Does not include oil for frying

Apricot-Peach Turnovers

Sodium Per Serving – 67mg   Makes 4 turnovers

This is a quick to prepare turnover using dried fruit.

- **1/4 cup chopped dried apricots**
- **1/4 cup chopped dried peaches**
- **1 tablespoon sugar**
- **4 LS egg roll wraps or *Egg Roll Wraps* (pg 205)**
- **Oil, for frying**

1. In a small saucepan over low heat, add apricots, peaches, sugar, and enough water to cover the fruit. Cook, stirring frequently, until fruit is soft, about 5 minutes. Divide mixture and spread on one side of wrappers; moisten 2 adjacent edges with water. Fold in half on the diagonal, forming a triangle, and press edges together with a fork.

2. Add oil to a frying pan over medium-high heat until it sizzles when a drop of water is added. Fry turnovers until golden brown, about 2 to 3 minutes per side. Drain on paper towels. If desired, sprinkle with confectioner's sugar or finely ground sugar. *NOTE:* To finely grind, place sugar in a blender or food processor and pulse until a fine powder.

NUTRITIONAL INFO PER TURNOVER*: Calories 122, Fat 0g (Saturated Fat 0g), Cholesterol 0mg, Carbohydrates 28g (Fiber 1g, Sugar 11g), Sodium 67mg (29mg with *Egg Roll Wraps*)   *Does not include oil for frying

---

TOTAL SODIUM AND FAT BY INGREDIENT

APPLE TURNOVERS
Sodium:
- 2 apples - 4mg
- 4 LS egg roll wraps - 260mg
  or *Egg Roll Wraps* - 148mg

Fat (Sat Fat):
- 4 LS egg roll wraps - 0g (0g)
  or 4 *Egg Roll Wraps* - 5g (1g)

Brands used/alternatives:
Twin Dragon Egg Roll Wrapper

APRICOT-PEACH TURNOVERS
Sodium:
- 1/4 c dried apricots - 3mg
- 1/4 c dried peaches - 3mg
- 4 LS egg roll wraps - 260mg
  or *Egg Roll Wraps* - 148mg

Fat (Sat Fat):
- 4 LS egg roll wraps - 0g (0g)
  or 4 *Egg Roll Wraps* - 5g (1g)

Brands used/alternatives:
Twin Dragon Egg Roll Wrapper

Dried Cherry-Almond Turnovers

Sodium Per Serving – 129mg　　　　　　　　　　　　　　　　　　　　Makes 4 turnovers

Here is another yummy turnover filled with cream cheese, nuts, and dried fruit.

- **6 tablespoons whipped cream cheese**
- **1 tablespoon sugar**
- **¾ cup dried cherries or dried cranberries**
- **2 tablespoons slivered almonds, chopped**
- **4 LS egg roll wraps or *Egg Roll Wraps* (pg 205)**
- **Oil, for frying**

1. Mix together cream cheese and sugar. Divide and spread on one side of each wrapper; top with cherries and almonds. Moisten 2 adjacent edges with water; fold in half on the diagonal, forming a triangle. Press edges together with a fork.
2. Add oil to a frying pan over medium-high heat until it sizzles when a drop of water is added. Fry turnovers until golden brown, about 2 to 3 minutes per side. Drain on paper towels. If desired, sprinkle with confectioner's sugar or finely ground sugar. *NOTE:* To finely grind, place sugar in a blender or food processor and pulse until a fine powder.

NUTRITIONAL INFO PER TURNOVER*: Calories 243, Fat 5g (Saturated Fat 2g), Cholesterol 11mg, Carbohydrates 45g (Fiber 2g, Sugar 22g), Sodium 129mg (91mg with *Egg Roll Wraps*)　*Does not include oil for frying

Cream Cheese & Jam Turnovers

Sodium Per Serving – 129mg　　　　　　　　　　　　　　　　　　　　Makes 4 turnovers

Here is another cream cheese-based turnover that is made with your favorite jam.

- **6 tablespoons whipped cream cheese**
- **¾ cup fruit jam (such as apricot, raspberry, or strawberry)**
- **4 LS egg roll wraps or *Egg Roll Wraps* (pg 205)**
- **Oil, for frying**

1. Evenly divide cream cheese and spread on one side of each wrapper; top with one-fourth jam. Moisten 2 adjacent edges with water; fold in half on the diagonal, forming a triangle. Press edges together with a fork.
2. Add oil to a frying pan over medium-high heat until it sizzles when a drop of water is added. Fry turnovers until golden brown, about 2 to 3 minutes per side. Drain on paper towels. If desired, sprinkle with confectioner's sugar or finely ground sugar. *NOTE:* To finely grind, place sugar in a blender or food processor and pulse until a fine powder.

NUTRITIONAL INFO PER TURNOVER*: Calories 228, Fat 3g (Sat Fat 2g), Chol 11mg, Carb 47g (Fiber 0g, Sugar 28g), Sodium 129mg (91mg with *Egg Roll Wraps*)　*Does not include oil for frying

---

TOTAL SODIUM AND FAT BY INGREDIENT

DRIED CHERRY TURNOVERS
Sodium:
　6 T whip cream cheese - 255mg
　4 LS egg roll wraps - 260mg
　　or *Egg Roll Wraps* - 111mg
Fat (Sat Fat):
　6 T whip cream cheese - 12g (8g)
　2 T almonds - 9g (1g)
　4 LS egg roll wraps - 0g (0g)
　　or 4 *Egg Roll Wraps* - 4g (1g)
Brands used/alternatives:
Philadelphia Whip Cream Cheese
Good & Gather Dried Cherries
Twin Dragon Egg Roll Wrapper

CREAM CHEESE TURNOVERS
Sodium:
　6 T whip cream cheese - 255mg
　4 LS egg roll wraps - 260mg
　　or *Egg Roll Wraps* - 111mg
Fat (Sat Fat):
　6 T whip cream cheese - 12g (8g)
　4 LS egg roll wraps - 0g (0g)
　　or 4 *Egg Roll Wraps* - 4g (1g)
Brands used/alternatives:
Philadelphia Whip Cream Cheese
Twin Dragon Egg Roll Wrapper

PUDDINGS & CUSTARDS

BREAD PUDDING WITH WHISKEY SAUCE

Sodium Per Serving – 73mg   Serves 10–12

I love bread pudding, but it is usually full of fat, sugar, and sodium. This lightened up version is so decadent, you'll never miss the bad stuff.

- ½ cup raisins or currants
- ¼ cup whiskey or bourbon[1]
- 1 loaf *No Knead French Bread (pg 192)* or LS sweet bread, broken into pieces[2]
- 1½ cups lowfat milk
- ½ cup half-and-half or whipping cream
- 2 tablespoons unsalted butter or margarine, melted
- 3 eggs[3]
- 1 cup sugar
- 1 teaspoon vanilla extract
- ¼ teaspoon ground cinnamon
- ⅛ teaspoon ground nutmeg

Whiskey Sauce:
- ¼ cup (½ stick) unsalted butter or margarine
- ½ cup sugar
- 2 tablespoons lowfat whipped topping
- 2–4 tablespoons whiskey or bourbon[1]

1. Preheat oven to 350ºF (180ºC). Coat the inside of 9x13-inch baking dish with nonstick cooking spray.
2. Soak raisins in ¼ cup whiskey for 30 minutes.
3. Place bread in a large bowl. In another bowl, mix together milk, half-and-half, 2 tablespoons butter, eggs, sugar, vanilla, cinnamon, and nutmeg; pour over bread. Stir in raisins/whiskey mixture and let sit for 15 to 20 minutes to allow the bread to absorb the whiskey mixture.
4. Transfer to prepared baking dish; bake in a preheated oven for about 45 minutes, or until pudding is set and a knife inserted in the center comes out clean.
5. *For the Whiskey Sauce:* Melt ¼ cup butter in a saucepan over low heat; stir in sugar, whipped topping, and whiskey. Heat through; serve pudding with warm sauce on top.

NUTRITIONAL INFO PER SERVING: Calories 418, Fat 12g (Sat Fat 6g), Chol 92mg, Carb 67g (Fiber 2g, Sugar 27g), Sodium 73mg (172mg with LS sweet bread)

Recipe Notes

1 – For an alcohol-free pudding, soak the raisins in ¼ cup water and 2-3 tbsp rum or brandy extract. In the whiskey sauce, substitute 1–2 tbsp rum or brandy extract for the alcohol.

2 – Use a LS sweet bread, such as cinnamon-raisin, and reduce raisins to ¼ cup and omit the cinnamon in the recipe. *Food for Life's Ezekiel* bread is the most widely available low sodium bread (Cinnamon-Raisin has 65mg a slice).

3 – To keep fat to a minimum, use an egg substitute. See *Eggs and Egg Substitutes*, pg 23, for a comparison of fat and sodium in eggs and egg substitutes.

TOTAL SODIUM AND FAT BY INGREDIENT

Sodium:
- ½ c raisins - 9mg
- 1 loaf *No Knead Bread* - 307mg or LS sweet bread - 1,300mg
- 1½ c LF milk - 158mg
- ½ c half-and-half - 40mg
- 3 eggs - 213mg
- ⅔ c sugar - 1mg

Fat (Sat Fat):
- 1 loaf French Bread - 17g (8g) or LS sweet bread - 0g (0g)
- 1½ c LF milk - 8g (5g)
- ½ c half-and-half - 14g (8g)
- 2 T + ¼ c NSA butter - 69g (33g) or NSA margarine - 54g (21g)
- 3 eggs - 15g (5g)
- 2 T whipped topping - 1g (1g)

Brands used/alternatives:
Simple Truth 2% Milk
Organic Valley Half and Half
Food for Life Ezekiel Cinnamon-Raisin Bread

CRÈME BRÛLÉE

Sodium Per Serving – 32mg | Serves 6

No gourmet cookbook would be complete without a recipe for crème brûlée (or burnt creme). This luscious custard is the perfect ending to a special meal. Allow at least 3 hours before serving for custard to chill. You can also prepare the custard the day before, cover, and keep refrigerated until ready to serve.

- **2 cups half-and-half or heavy whipping cream**
- **⅓ cup sugar**
- **4 large egg yolks**
- **1 teaspoon vanilla extract or 1 vanilla bean[1]**
- **4 teaspoons sugar[2]**

1. Preheat oven to 300°F (150°C). Arrange six 6-oz ramekins in a large roasting pan.
2. In a saucepan over medium heat, add half-and-half and sugar; cook, stirring frequently, until sugar is dissolved, about 5 minutes. Remove from heat.
3. In a medium bowl, beat egg yolks and vanilla; gradually add warm cream, stirring constantly.
4. Fill ramekins equally with custard. Pour enough hot water into the roasting pan to come halfway up the sides of the ramekins. Bake for 30 to 45 minutes, until custard is set. Remove and refrigerate at least 3 hours.
5. Before serving, sprinkle sugar over each custard, spreading evenly to the edges. Use a kitchen torch, or place ramekins under a preheated broiler, until sugar has melted and browned, about 2 minutes.

NUTRITIONAL INFO PER SERVING: Calories 199, Fat 12g (Saturated Fat 6g), Cholesterol 149mg, Carbohydrates 17g (Fiber 0g, Sugar 17g), Sodium 32mg

---

VARIATIONS

GRAND MARNIER BRÛLÉE

1. Mix 2 tbsp Grand Marnier or other orange-flavored liqueur with the yolks, before adding the warm cream; proceed as directed.

NUTRITIONAL INFO PER SERVING: Calories 163, Fat 12g (Saturated Fat 6g), Cholesterol 149mg, Carbohydrates 4g (Fiber 0g, Sugar 4g), Sodium 32mg

BRANDIED MOCHA BRÛLÉE

1. Add 1½ tsp instant coffee granules[3] and 1 tbsp brandy to the simmering cream; whisk until coffee is dissolved; proceed as directed.

NUTRITIONAL INFO PER SERVING: Calories 156, Fat 12g (Saturated Fat 6g), Cholesterol 148mg, Carbohydrates 4g (Fiber 0g, Sugar 4g), Sodium 32mg

---

Recipe Notes

1 – *Using vanilla bean:* Combine half-and-half, sugar, and whole vanilla bean; cook, stirring frequently, until sugar is dissolved, about 5 mins. Remove from heat and split vanilla bean lengthwise; scrape out seeds. Stir seeds into the warm half-and-half; proceed as directed. See *Vanilla Beans*, pg 254, for storage info.

2 – Crème brûlée traditionally has a burnt sugar crust which is achieved by torching a thin layer of sugar. If you want to lower the sugar content, I've found that Splenda works well, as there usually isn't enough sweetener in the other substitutes to cover the top.

3 – I like to keep a jar of instant espresso on hand for recipes that call for coffee, as the flavor is a little stronger than regular coffee.

TOTAL SODIUM AND FAT BY INGREDIENT

Sodium:
2 c half-and-half - 160mg
  or whipping cream - 160mg
⅓ c sugar - 1mg
4 egg yolks - 33mg

Fat (Sat Fat):
2 c half-and-half - 56g (32g)
  or whipping cream - 160g (112g)
4 egg yolks - 18g (6g)

Brands used/alternatives:
Organic Valley Half and Half

FRUIT DESSERTS

ICE CREAM WITH BLUEBERRIES & GRAND MARNIER

Sodium Per Serving – 30mg Serves 4

This is a simple, yet elegant dessert and the added Grand Marnier is exquisite. For a beautiful presentation, place in a tall parfait or wine glass. If you want to jazz it up even more, add toasted pecans before serving.

- **1 cup fresh blueberries[1]**
- **¼ cup Grand Marnier or other orange-flavored liqueur**
- **4 scoops lowfat vanilla ice cream**

1. Soak blueberries in Grand Marnier for 15 minutes or more.
2. Place a scoop of ice cream in a glass goblet, top with one-fourth of the blueberries and Grand Marnier mixture. Serve with *Shortbread Cookies (pg 237)*, if desired.

NUTRITIONAL INFO PER SERVING: Calories 159, Fat 3g (Saturated Fat 2g), Cholesterol 10mg, Carbohydrates 22g (Fiber 3g, Sugar 13g), Sodium 30mg

STRAWBERRY & AMARETTO PARFAIT

Sodium Per Serving – 37mg Serves 4

If you love strawberries and chocolate, you'll enjoy this quick and delicious dessert.

- **4 scoops lowfat vanilla ice cream**
- **1 cup strawberries, hulled and sliced**
- **4–8 tablespoons LS chocolate syrup**
- **4 tablespoons Amaretto or other almond-flavored liqueur[2]**
- **Whipped cream (optional)**

1. Place a scoop of ice cream in a glass goblet; top with ¼ cup strawberries, 1 tablespoon Amaretto, and 1–2 tablespoons chocolate sauce. Top with whipped topping and serve.

NUTRITIONAL INFO PER SERVING: Calories 233, Fat 4g (Sat Fat 3g), Chol 10mg, Carb 38g (Fiber 4g, Sugar 25g), Sodium 37mg

Recipe Notes
1 – Sliced strawberries or pears also are nice with Grand Marnier.
2 – Amaretto pairs well with raspberries, blueberries, or sliced peaches, too.

TOTAL SODIUM AND FAT BY INGREDIENT

ICE CREAM WITH BERRIES
Sodium:
 1 c blueberries - 2mg
 4 scoops LF ice cream - 120mg
Fat (Sat Fat):
 1 c blueberries - 1mg (0mg)
 4 scoops LF ice cream - 12g (8g)
Brands used/alternatives:
 Dreyer's (Edy's) Slow Churn Vanilla Ice Cream

STRAWBERRY PARFAIT
Sodium:
 4 scoops LF ice cream - 120mg
 1 c strawberries - 2mg
 4 T Amaretto - 8mg
 ¼ c LS chocolate sauce - 20mg
Fat (Sat Fat):
 4 scoops LF ice cream - 12g (8g)
 1 c strawberries - 1mg (0mg)
 4 T whipped cream - 4g (4g)
Brands used/alternatives:
 Dreyer's (Edy's) Slow Churn Vanilla Ice Cream
 Hershey's Chocolate Syrup

COOKIES

Shortbread Cookies

Sodium Per Serving – 0mg Makes 16 cookies

The secret to these tender, melt-in-your mouth cookies is not overworking the dough. To reduce the fat, I use half butter and half margarine.

- 1 stick unsalted butter, at room temperature
- 1 stick unsalted margarine, at room temperature
- ½ cup sugar
- 2 teaspoons vanilla extract
- 2 cups all-purpose flour

1. Preheat oven to 350°F (180°C).
2. Cream together butter, margarine, sugar, and vanilla until light and fluffy; gradually add flour, mixing well, until it forms a soft dough. *NOTE:* To make dough easier to handle, cover and refrigerate for 30 minutes.
3. Form into small balls, place on a baking sheet, 1 inch apart; flatten with a fork. Bake in a preheated oven for 15 to 20 minutes, or until lightly browned.

NUTRITIONAL INFO PER COOKIE: Calories 164, Fat 10g (Saturated Fat 5g), Cholesterol 15mg, Carbohydrates 16g (Fiber 0g, Sugar 4g), Sodium 0mg

VARIATION

Hazelnut Shortbread Cookies

1. Add ½ cup ground hazelnuts to the dough; proceed as directed.

NUTRITIONAL INFO PER COOKIE: Calories 187, Fat 13g (Saturated Fat 6g), Cholesterol 15mg, Carbohydrates 17g (Fiber 0g, Sugar 4g), Sodium 0mg

TOTAL SODIUM AND FAT BY INGREDIENT

Sodium:
- 5 tbsp sugar - 1mg
- 2 c flour - 5mg

Fat (Sat Fat):
- ½ c NSA butter - 92g (58g)
- ½ c NSA margarine - 72g (28g)
- 2 c flour - 2g (0g)

Chocolate Chip Cookies

Sodium Per Serving – 3mg   Makes 4 dozen

These are some of the best low-salt cookies you'll ever eat... see if you don't agree.

- **1 stick unsalted butter or margarine**
- **1½ cups sugar**
- **½ teaspoon vanilla extract**
- **½ teaspoon almond extract**
- **2 eggs[1]**
- **2 cups all-purpose flour**
- **2 teaspoons NSA baking powder[2]**
- **1 (6-oz) package semi-sweet chocolate chips**
- **½ cup unsalted chopped walnuts**

1. Preheat oven to 350ºF (180ºC).
2. In a large bowl, beat butter, sugar, vanilla, and almond extract until creamy; beat in eggs, one at a time.
3. In another bowl, combine flour and baking powder; gradually add to the creamed mixture, mixing well after each addition. Gently stir in chocolate morsels and walnuts.
4. Using a tablespoon, drop dough onto a baking sheet; bake in a preheated oven for 12 to 15 minutes, until golden brown.

NUTRITIONAL INFO PER COOKIE: Calories 81, Fat 4g (Saturated Fat 2g), Cholesterol 14mg, Carbohydrates 11g (Fiber 0g, Sugar 6g), Sodium 3mg

No-Flour Peanut Butter Cookies

Sodium Per Serving – 3mg   Makes 2 dozen

A similar version of this recipe is popping up all over, due to the popularity of low-carb diets. Not only are these low in carbs, but also low in sodium.

- **1 cup unsalted crunchy peanut butter**
- **1 egg[1]**
- **1 cup sugar**
- **1 teaspoon vanilla extract**

1. Preheat oven to 350ºF (180ºC).
2. Mix together all ingredients. Drop by heaping teaspoons onto a baking sheet; flatten each cookie slightly with a fork.
3. Bake in a preheated oven for 15 minutes, or until golden brown. Cookies will crisp up as they cool.

NUTRITIONAL INFO PER COOKIE: Calories 70, Fat 6g (Sat Fat 1g), Chol 9mg, Carb 11g (Fiber 1g, Sugar 9g), Sodium 3mg

Recipe Notes

1 – To keep fat to a minimum, use an egg substitute. See *Eggs and Egg Substitutes*, pg 23, for a comparison of fat and sodium in eggs and egg substitutes.

2 – For more info, see *Baking Powder/Baking Soda*, pg 243.

TOTAL SODIUM AND FAT BY INGREDIENT

CHOCOLATE CHIP COOKIES
Sodium:
- 1 c sugar - 2mg
- 2 eggs - 142mg
- 2 c flour - 5mg
- ½ c walnuts - 1mg

Fat (Sat Fat):
- ½ c NSA butter - 92g (58g)
  or NSA margarine - 72g (28g)
- 2 eggs - 10g (3g)
- 2 c flour - 2g (0g)
- 1 c chocolate chips - 48g (30g)
- ½ c walnuts - 39g (4g)

NO-FLOUR PB COOKIES
Sodium:
- 1 egg - 70mg
- 1 c sugar - 2mg

Fat (Sat Fat):
- 1 c NSA peanut but - 128g (24g)
- 1 egg - 5g (2g)

Brands used/alternatives:
Adams 100% Natural Crunchy Unsalted Peanut Butter
Hain Featherweight Baking Powder

FILLINGS, FROSTINGS & TOPPINGS

LEMON CURD

Sodium Per Serving – 13mg   Makes about 2 cups

If you've never made lemon curd, you're in for a treat. It tastes similar to the filling in lemon meringue pie and is easy to make. Use it as a spread on breads and muffins, as a filling for lemon tarts, or between cake layers. This also makes a great hostess or Christmas gift, just ladle into decorative jars and seal (will keep for up to a week in the refrigerator).

4 teaspoons (about 4 lemons) finely grated lemon peel (use the finest grate)
2/3 cup fresh lemon juice (about 4 lemons)
3 eggs[1]
1 cup sugar
1/3 cup unsalted butter, melted

1. Place the lemon peel, lemon juice, eggs, and sugar in a blender; whirl until well mixed. While blender is running, slowly add the melted butter.
2. Pour into saucepan and cook over medium heat, stirring constantly, until it thickens to the consistency of pudding, about 5 minutes. Ladle into sterilized jars, screw on lids, and let cool. Keep refrigerated up to a week.

NUTRITIONAL INFO PER 2 TABLESPOONS: Calories 96, Fat 5g (Saturated Fat 2g), Cholesterol 50mg, Carbohydrates 14g (Fiber 0g, Sugar 13g), Sodium 13mg

---

VARIATIONS

ORANGE CURD
1. Use orange instead of lemon for the peel and juice.

NUTRITIONAL INFO PER 2 TABLESPOONS: Calories 98, Fat 5g (Saturated Fat 2g), Cholesterol 50mg, Carbohydrates 14g (Fiber 0g, Sugar 13g), Sodium 13mg

LIME CURD
1. Use lime instead of lemon for the peel and juice.

NUTRITIONAL INFO PER 2 TABLESPOONS: Calories 96, Fat 5g (Saturated Fat 2g), Cholesterol 50mg, Carbohydrates 14g (Fiber 0g, Sugar 13g), Sodium 13mg

---

Recipe Notes
1 – Do not use egg substitutes. I've tried using them to make the curd, but the texture and consistency of the curd is unsatisfactory. Real eggs and butter are a must!

TOTAL SODIUM AND FAT BY INGREDIENT

Sodium:
3 eggs - 213mg
1 c sugar - 2mg

Fat (Sat Fat):
3 eggs - 15g (5g)
1/3 c NSA butter - 61g (25g)
  or NSA margarine - 48g (19g)

Cream Cheese Frosting
Sodium Per Serving – 50mg   Makes 1½ cups

This creamy, slightly sweet frosting is delicious on strudels, turnovers, cinnamon rolls, and carrot cakes.

8 oz regular or lowfat cream cheese[1] **1 teaspoon vanilla extract**
¾ cup sugar

1. Mix cream cheese and sugar together until well blended and creamy; stir in vanilla. Spread on baked item; refrigerate until ready to use.

NUTRITIONAL INFO PER 2 TABLESPOONS: Calories 109, Fat 7g (Saturated Fat 4g), Cholesterol 17mg, Carbohydrates 13g (Fiber 0g, Sugar 13g), Sodium 50mg

---

VARIATION

Chocolate Cream Cheese Frosting

1. Add 2 tablespoons chocolate sauce and refrigerate 15 minutes or more before using to allow frosting to set up.

NUTRITIONAL INFO PER 2 TABLESPOONS: Calories 117, Fat 7g (Saturated Fat 4g), Cholesterol 17mg, Carbohydrates 15g (Fiber 0g, Sugar 15g), Sodium 51mg

---

Recipe Notes

1 – To reduce fat and keep sodium to a minimum, use a lower fat alternative or combine with regular cream cheese. See *Cream Cheese Comparison*, pg 247, for more info.

TOTAL SODIUM AND FAT BY INGREDIENT

Sodium:
  8 oz cream cheese - 600mg or
  LF cream cheese - 840mg
  ½ c sugar - 2mg

Fat (Sat Fat):
  8 oz cream cheese - 80g (48g) or
  LF cream cheese - 48g (28g)

Brands used/alternatives:
  Green Valley Lactose-Free Cream Cheese
  Great Value Neufchâtel Cheese

Grandma's Italian Frosting

Sodium Per Serving – 7mg   Makes 2 cups

Although high in fat, I must share my Italian grandmother's luscious frosting. It is absolutely the best... wonderfully rich, creamy, and not too sweet!

- 1 cup 2% or whole milk
- 5 tablespoons all-purpose flour
- 1 stick unsalted butter or margarine, at room temperature
- ½ cup shortening
- 1 cup sugar
- 1 tablespoon vanilla extract

1. In a small saucepan over medium heat, heat the milk and flour, stirring frequently, until a thick paste; remove and cool.
2. In a bowl, cream together the butter, shortening, and sugar; add the cooled flour mixture and beat until the consistency of whipped cream. Mix in vanilla and spread on cake; refrigerate until ready to use.

NUTRITIONAL INFO PER 2 TABLESPOONS: Calories 138, Fat 13g (Saturated Fat 6g), Cholesterol 20mg, Carbohydrates 6g (Fiber 0g, Sugar 4g), Sodium 7mg

Northwest Berry Sauce

Sodium Per Serving – 0mg   Makes about 2 cups

This yummy sauce is the perfect topping for cheesecake, ice cream, or pound cake. And to take it to the next level, I add a little brandy.

- 2 cups fresh or frozen blueberries, raspberries, blackberries, or any combination of berries
- ¼ cup sugar
- ⅛ teaspoon ground cinnamon
- Pinch freshly ground nutmeg
- 2 tablespoons brandy (optional)[1]
- 1 teaspoon cornstarch, mixed with 1 tablespoon water to make a paste

1. In a saucepan over medium heat, bring blueberries, sugar, cinnamon, nutmeg, and brandy to a boil; cook, stirring constantly, until sugar dissolves and juices from the berries release, 3 to 5 minutes.
2. Slowly add cornstarch paste, stirring constantly, until desired consistency (sauce will thicken as it cools). Serve warm or cold.

NUTRITIONAL INFO PER 2 TABLESPOONS: Calories 23, Fat 0g (Sat Fat 0g), Chol 0mg, Carb 4g (Fiber 0g, Sugar 3g), Sodium 0mg

Recipe Notes

1 – Grand Marnier or other orange-flavored liqueur also works. Although this delicious sauce does not need brandy, it does kick it up a notch.

TOTAL SODIUM AND FAT BY INGREDIENT

GRANDMA'S FROSTING
Sodium:
- 1 c 2% milk - 105mg
  or 1 c whole milk - 105mg
- 5 T flour - 1mg
- 1 T sugar - 1mg

Fat (Sat Fat):
- 1 c 2% milk - 5g (3g)
  or 1 c whole milk - 8g (5g)
- 5 T flour - 1g (0g)
- ½ c NSA butter - 92g (58g)
  or NSA margarine - 72g (28g)
- ½ c shortening - 103g (42g)

Brands used/alternatives:
Simple Truth 2% Milk

NORTHWEST BERRY SAUCE
Sodium:
- 2 c berries - 3mg

Fat (Sat Fat):
- 2 c berries - 1g (0g)

COOKING TIPS AND FOOD FACTS

ALCOHOL SUBSTITUTIONS

Red & White Wines

When substituting wine in a recipe, the best choice depends on the role wine plays in the dish—whether it's for acidity, sweetness, depth of flavor, or deglazing.

Each substitute comes with its own set of flavors, so consider what the wine is meant to add to your dish and choose accordingly. You may need to experiment with a combination of substitutes to achieve the desired flavor.

Here are some suggestions for non-alcoholic substitutes:

Non-alcoholic wine: You can also use non-alcoholic wines in place of their alcoholic counterparts, providing similar flavors without the alcohol content.

Grape juice: Use red grape juice for red wine or white grape juice for white wine. It has a similar flavor profile, but is sweeter; add a little vinegar or lemon juice to cut the sweetness.

Beef, chicken, or vegetable broth: Works well in soups, stews, and sauces; adds richness, but lacks the acidity of wine. Adding a little white wine vinegar or apple cider vinegar can add the desired acidity, but use sparingly.

Fruit or vegetable juice: You can use tomato, pomegranate, or apple juice, although they are sweeter and have distinct flavors that may work.

Keep in mind the following tips:

Acidity balance: When using sweeter substitutes, consider balancing the dish's acidity with a splash of vinegar or lemon juice.

Reduction: If a recipe calls for reducing the wine, your substitute should also be able to withstand reduction well. Juices may become too sweet when reduced, so adjusting quantities and adding water or broth might be necessary.

Fortified Wines

Non-alcoholic substitutions for fortified wines like Sherry, Madeira, and Marsala are achieved by mimicking their unique flavors with combinations of juices, broths, and other ingredients. By thoughtfully combining these ingredients, you can mimic the complex flavors.

Here are some suggestions for each type of fortified wine:

Sherry: Mix white grape juice with a splash of vinegar (apple cider or white wine vinegar) to mimic the acidity and depth of Sherry. Also, try non-alcoholic white wine with a bit of vinegar.

Madeira: Grape juice mixed with a small amount of brandy extract is a good substitute. Also, you can try a reduction of balsamic vinegar that is sweetened slightly with brown sugar,.

Marsala: White grape juice mixed with a little brandy extract tastes similar, but adjust the sweetness with a bit of sugar, if necessary. In desserts, mix apple juice with a drop of vanilla extract.

Port: Blend grape juice with a small amount of raspberry or blackberry syrup. Or mix cranberry juice with a bit of lemon juice will give a tart yet sweet taste similar to Port.

Keep in mind the following tips:

Acidity and sweetness: Adjust the balance of acidity and sweetness in your substitute to match the dish you're preparing. Add a splash of vinegar or lemon juice to reduce sweetness, or a bit of sugar or syrup to increase it.

Flavor depth: Non-alcoholic substitutes may lack the depth of flavor that alcohol provides. To enhance depth, consider adding a small amount of an extract, such as almond or vanilla, or a dash of spices.

Reduction: If the recipe calls for reducing the fortified wine, keep in mind that non-alcoholic substitutes may not reduce in the same way. Monitor the reduction closely to achieve the desired consistency without over-sweetening.

Experimentation: Finding the perfect non-alcoholic substitute might require some experimentation. Start with small amounts and adjust based on taste.

APPLES

Apples are high in fiber and potassium, have no fat, and are sodium free. They have many health benefits, including cancer prevention, cholesterol reduction, and reduced risk of stroke.

There are over 2,500 varieties of apples, some of the most popular are: Braeburn (sweet-tart), Fuji (sweet), Gala (sweet), Golden Delicious (mellow-sweet), Granny Smith (tart), McIntosh (tart), and Red Delicious (sweet).

Selection and Storage

Should be firm, shiny, and free of blemishes. Keep in plastic bags in the refrigerator up to six weeks. Apples stored in fruit bowls do not stay crisp for very long.

Preparation

To minimize browning, prepare just before using, or dip cut pieces into a solution of one part lemon juice and three parts water.

ASPARAGUS

Asparagus is high in folic acid, a good source of potassium, and low in sodium (3mg per cup). There is little taste difference between thick or thin stalks; thicker stalks are the most tender and thinner spears, which are picked early in the season, are more chewy.

Preparation

Select bright green firm stalks with compact tips. Snap off the tough ends with your hands; they will break naturally at the point that is tough and chewy. Or peel the tough outer skin with a vegetable peeler (not necessary if using thin stalks, only the ends need trimming). *NOTE: Prepare asparagus as soon as possible; the longer it sits, the tougher it becomes, regardless of size.*

Cooking Asparagus

There are several ways to cook asparagus:

Boil: Place in boiling water; cook 5 to 8 minutes. Do not overcook. Perfectly cooked asparagus is bright green and crisp-tender; it is not mushy.

Steam: Place asparagus in the upper half of a steamer over boiling water; cook 7 to 12 minutes.

Microwave: Place asparagus and 1–2 tablespoons water in a covered dish and microwave on high 3 to 4 minutes.

Roast: Drizzle a little olive oil on the asparagus and place in an oven-proof dish; roast in a preheated oven at 400°F (200°C) until tender, about 10 to 15 minutes (depending on thickness of spears).

Grill: Coat asparagus with 1–2 tablespoons olive oil (place asparagus and oil in a plastic bag, seal and roll asparagus in oil until well coated); place on a hot grill and cook for several minutes, turning once, until asparagus has softened enough to wiggle slightly when picked up with tongs.

Storage

Wrap asparagus in a damp cloth, place in a plastic bag with holes, and store in the refrigerator 3 to 4 days. To refresh, if wilted, remove ¼ inch from bottom and stand in water for 5 minutes.

Freezing: Blanch by boiling or microwaving 1 to 2 minutes, cool in ice water, and drain. Place in plastic bags and freeze up to 9 months. *NOTE: Do not defrost before cooking and do not refreeze.*

BAKING POWDER/BAKING SODA

Baking powder has 488mg sodium per teaspoon and baking soda has 1,259mg. A couple of manufacturers make a salt-free substitute for baking powder, *Hain Pure Foods Featherweight* and *Ener-G*. I find that doubling the amount called for in a recipe gives the best results. *Ener-G* also makes a salt-free baking soda that is free of potassium and aluminum.

BEANS
Canned beans

Most canned beans have large amounts of added salt, averaging anywhere from 350mg to 480mg per ½ cup serving. There are several brands of NSA beans with 35mg or less sodium per ½ cup serving) and low-salt varieties that contain 140mg. Although less salt products, such as "50% less salt," have reduced sodium, it is still too much at 260mg or more per serving.

NOTE: NSA beans do not need rinsing; rinse all others. Although rinsing removes some salt, it is not a significant amount.

Cooking Dried Beans

Wash and pick through 1 cup dried beans, discarding any foreign particles or flawed beans. Place in a heavy pot and add enough water to cover the beans; cover and soak 6 to 8 hours or overnight. Drain and rinse.

Return beans to the same pot and cover with 2 inches of water; stir in 1 tbsp (or 3 envelopes) LS chicken bouillon. Bring to a boil over high heat; decrease heat to low and simmer, partially covered, until tender, about 1 hour. Drain. Makes enough to equal one can of beans.

BEEF

Cuts of Beef

The best beef is marbled with very thin lines of fat; lower grades of beef have lots of marbling or none at all. The cut of beef determines the way it should be cooked and whether or not it needs marinating. The five main cuts of beef:

Chuck: Tough with lots of gristle, but most flavorful and economical; perfect for slow cooking, such as pot roasts. Popular cuts are arm, chuck, shoulder, and blade roasts or steaks.

Rib: Tender, juicy, and flavorful, does not need marinating; perfect for grilling or roasting. Popular cuts are rib and rib-eye steaks and roasts.

Loin: Most tender and expensive, does not need marinating and is ideal for grilling or broiling. Popular cuts are tenderloin, Porterhouse, T-bone, top loin (New York strip), filet mignon, top sirloin, and roast beef.

Round: Tough, but lean, best if marinated or slow cooked with liquid. Popular cuts are bottom round, London broil, round, top round, round tip, and rump roast.

Breast or Flank: Tough and fatty, best if marinated, then grilled or slow cooked. Popular cuts are brisket, short ribs, hanger, or skirt steaks.

BREAD CRUMBS

Two types of crumbs include bread crumbs, made from the entire loaf, including the crust, and Panko or "Japanese bread crumbs," made without the crust. They are lighter and crispier than regular crumbs and have no fat.

Bread crumbs are great for binding ingredients together, like meatloafs, and panko crumbs are best as a coating for foods like fried chicken or fish.

Homemade bread crumbs are easy to make. Use dry bread crumbs for breading and as a topping on pasta (instead of cheese); add soft bread crumbs to meatloafs (for a moister loaf) and as a topping on casseroles.

Preparation

Dry bread crumbs: For 1 cup bread crumbs, use 3–4 slices stale bread. If bread is not at least one day old, dry it in the oven. (Arrange slices in a single layer on a baking sheet; bake in a preheated oven at 250°F (121°C) until dry and crisp, 20 to 30 minutes.) Break into small pieces and place in a food processor or blender; pulse until desired coarseness. You can also make coarse crumbs with a knife or use a grater for very fine crumbs.

Soft bread crumbs: For 1 cup fresh crumbs, use 1–2 slices fresh bread. Break into small pieces and place in a food processor or blender; pulse until the desired coarseness.

Toasting Bread Crumbs

Heat 1 tbsp oil in a skillet over medium heat, add ½ cup dry crumbs. Cook, stirring frequently, until golden brown, about 2 minutes.

Storage

Store crumbs in an airtight container in the refrigerator for several weeks or in the freezer indefinitely.

BREAD MAKING

Without a Machine

Here are 3 ways to prepare your dough for the first rising. Once it has risen, proceed as directed in the recipe.

Electric Mixer: Using the flat beater, mix all the dough ingredients together at medium speed until the dough begins to get some shape, about 5 to 8 minutes. Change to the dough hook, once the dough is well mixed. Transfer to a lightly oiled bowl, cover and let rise.

Food processor: Place all ingredients in processor; pulse until dough is smooth and sticky, about 1 to 2 minutes. Transfer to a lightly oiled bowl, cover and let rise.

By hand: Place half the dry ingredients in a large bowl, forming a well in the center; pour in the wet ingredients. Mix with a wooden spoon, or your hands, until smooth; gradually add remaining flour until dough is stiff and workable. Transfer to a lightly oiled bowl, cover and let rise. *NOTE:* You may not use all the flour.

Why is Salt Used in Bread?

In addition to flavor, salt controls the fermentation of the yeast, preventing the bread from overrising during the initial risings. This is necessary so that there will be enough oomph for the final rise and during baking.

Although breads may be made without salt, to compensate for the loss of energy, a sweetener (which enhances yeast growth) is needed. Also, herbs and/or spices are often added for the loss of flavor the salt provides.

Depending on the bread, I like to use a tablespoon of sweetener and anywhere from a pinch to 1/8 teaspoon salt (a pinch adds about 155mg sodium to the whole loaf or about 13mg per slice, 1/8 teaspoon adds 291mg or about 18mg per slice).

Also, bread that is made without salt will have a coarser texture.

Broccoli

Broccoli is a member of the cabbage family and is an excellent source for potassium and vitamins C and A. High in fiber and low in sodium (29mg per cup), this nutritional powerhouse helps reduce the risk of cancer, heart disease, and other ailments.

Selection

Choose broccoli with compact floret clusters that are dark green, sage, or purple-green in color, depending on the variety. There should be no yellowing (indicates it's past its prime) and the stalks should be firm. A medium head of broccoli, will yield enough for 3 or 4 people. Both the stalk and floret can be eaten raw or cooked.

Preparation

Since the stalks take longer to cook than the florets, split stalks larger than 1 inch halfway up or cut into smaller uniform pieces. You can also cook the stalks for 2 to 3 minutes before adding the florets. To cook:

Microwave: Place florets in a covered dish with 1–2 tablespoons water and microwave on high 3 to 4 minutes. If cooking the whole stalk; place in a spoke pattern (with florets in the center), add 1–2 tablespoons water, and microwave on high 6 to 10 minutes.

Steam: Place broccoli in upper half of steamer over boiling water; cook, covered, 2 to 3 minutes. Remove lid to allow the strong odors to escape; replace lid and continue cooking 3 to 4 minutes.

Boil: Bring water to a boil; add broccoli, and cook 5 to 7 minutes.

Stir-fry: Cook over medium-high heat, stirring frequently, for 2 minutes; add a little water or broth, cover, and continue cooking 2 to 3 minutes.

Storage

Place in an open bag in the refrigerator for up 4 to 5 days. *To freeze:* Blanch by boiling or microwaving 1 to 2 minutes, cool in ice water, and drain. Place in plastic bags and freeze for up to a year.

Caramelizing Onions

Caramelizing brings out the natural sugars in onions. Use them to add richness to soups, entrées, and side dishes; as a topping on pizzas; and anywhere else cooked onions are specified. Make up extra and freeze (up to 3 months) for later use.

To caramelize onions, a combination of butter (or margarine) and oil is used to cook sliced onions until they turn a rich caramel color. Yellow onions are most often used, as they have less water than other onions, allowing for better caramelization. In some dishes where additional sweetness is desired, stir in 1–2 tsp sugar or sugar substitute. Three common ways to caramelize onions:

Stove-top slow-cook: Cook onions in butter (or margarine) and oil in a skillet over low heat for 30 to 45 minutes, stirring frequently, until they are dark brown and caramelized.

Quick caramelization: Some chefs speed up the process by cooking over high heat, but unless it's done properly, the onions can easily burn. Cook onions in butter (or margarine) and oil in a skillet over medium-high heat, stirring constantly. Scrap up onions and any browned bits that stick to the bottom of the pan, adding 1 to 2 tbsp water, while stirring constantly (this is called deglazing). Continue stirring and deglazing until onions are caramelized.

Slow-cooker method: Place onions and butter or margarine (1–2 tsp per onion) in the cooker, cover and cook on LOW for 10 to 12 hours, or until onions are dark brown.

CARROTS

Carrots are extremely versatile—they may be eaten raw or cooked in various way. Their sweet flavor also makes them a favorite in muffins, breads, and other desserts. Although carrots are low in calories and high in fiber, they also contain a lot of sodium (an average carrot has 50mg).

Parsnips are a good substitute for carrots in cooked dishes and have substantially less sodium (about 7mg in a 1/2 cup serving). *CAUTION: Do not eat raw parsnips, they contain toxins that are destroyed once they are cooked.*

Selection
Select carrots that are firm and uniform in color, avoid any that are cracked, have large green areas at the crown (a little green is okay), or are limp. If stems are attached, choose ones that are fresh-looking.

Storage
Wrap in a paper towel, place in a plastic bag, and store in the refrigerator up to a month. Do not place near fruits, like apples or pears, as they produce a gas that can make the carrots bitter.

CHICKEN AND TURKEY
Sodium and Fat Comparison (4 oz serving)

Chicken	Fat	SatFat	Sodium
Breast, no skin, meat only	3g	1g	51mg
Breast, with skin	10g	3g	71mg
Ground	9g	3g	68mg
Thigh, with skin	19g	5g	92mg
Thigh, no skin, meat only	5g	1g	107mg
Turkey			
Ground	9g	3g	66mg
Breast, no skin, meat only	2g	0g	128mg
Dark, no skin, meat only	3g	1g	140mg
Cornish game hen, half	24g	7g	102mg

Poaching Chicken

There are several ways to poach chicken:

Stove-top: In a large pot over medium-high heat, place chicken, 1 onion (peeled and quartered), 1 celery stalk (cut into large chunks, including leaves), 1 carrot (cut into large chunks), 4–5 parsley sprigs, 6 peppercorns, 1 tbsp fresh thyme or tarragon (or 1½ tsp dried), and 1 bay leaf. Add 2 cups LS chicken broth or canned broth and ½ cup white wine; bring to a boil. Decrease heat; cover, and simmer until chicken is tender and no longer pink inside, about 20 minutes

Oven: Place chicken with same stove-top ingredients above in a baking dish; cover and bake in a preheated oven at 425ºF (220ºC) for 20 minutes.

Microwave: Arrange chicken in a microwave-safe dish with the thickest portions toward the outside of the dish. Add 1 cup LS chicken broth, ½ cup white wine, 1 tbsp fresh thyme or tarragon (or 1½ tsp dried), and 1 tsp (or 1 envelope) LS chicken bouillon. Cover with a microwave-safe lid or plastic wrap. Microwave at 50% for 20 minutes.

After poaching, remove chicken and let cool slightly; prepare chicken as directed in the recipe. Strain the broth and freeze for other uses.

COCONUTS

Fresh coconuts purchased at the market are often rancid; consequently, choosing the right coconut can help reduce your odds of getting a bad one.

Selection and Storage

Feel the weight and gently shake it – a fresh coconut is very heavy and has lots of liquid inside that you can hear sloshing when shaken. Look for cracks and mold – the shell should be intact and free of cracks; any mold, mildew, or black spots, particularly around the 3 "eyes", indicates it's rancid.

Once the coconut is opened, separate the meat from the shell, peel the thin brown layer, and grate. One coconut yields about 3–3½ cups grated coconut. Store in the refrigerator 2 to 3 days in a sealed bag or jar.

Preparation

Most people drain the coconut prior to opening it, as it can get quite messy. To drain, pierce the eyes at the top of the shell with a knife or ice pick. The liquid should be fairly clear and smell fresh. If it is cloudy or smells bad, throw the coconut away. Once drained, there are several ways to open it:

Place in plastic bag and drop on pavement: It may take several drops, but will break in several pieces.

Gently tap the shell: Use a rock or hammer, tapping around the middle (or diameter) of the coconut until a crack forms; continue tapping until the shell breaks in half.

Bake drained coconut: Place in a preheated oven at 350ºF (180ºC) for about 25 minutes, remove and lightly tap the shell with a hammer until it breaks.

Freeze for an hour: Remove and lightly tap with a hammer until it breaks.

CREAM CHEESE

Comparison

Cream cheese has a lot of sodium, particularly lower fat and nonfat varieties, and is a good example of how manufacturers increase the salt when fat is removed. There are many types of cream cheese, a few include:

Mascarpone: Known as "Italian cream cheese", is richer and creamier than American cream cheese. It has more fat and very little sodium.

Neufchâtel: Has less fat and is comparable to light cream cheese. Use it in place of regular cream cheese in most recipes. There's little difference in taste, but has more sodium.

Whipped cream cheese: Simply, it's cheese whipped with air. It's less dense and not as rich as regular cream cheese, and has less sodium and half the fat. You can substitute it for regular cream cheese in many dishes that don't need richness and creaminess.

Cream cheese spread: Similar to whipped or light cream cheese, but are flavored.

Below are comparisons of a 1-oz serving:

	Fat	Sat Fat	Sodium
Mascarpone	13g	7g	15mg
Whipped cream cheese	4g	3g	85mg
Regular cream cheese	10g	6g	110mg
Neufchâtel	6g	4g	120mg
Cream cheese spread	8g	5g	124mg
Plant-based cream cheese	6g	0g	170mg
Fat free (FF)	0g	0g	252mg

To keep fat and sodium to a minimum, combine regular or whipped cream cheese with lower fat and/or sodium brands:

	Fat	Sat Fat	Sodium
½ reg & ½ mascarpone	12g	7g	63mg
½ regular & ½ whipped	7g	5g	98mg
½ regular & ½ Neufchâtel	8g	5g	115mg
½ regular & ½ FF	5g	3g	181mg

CURRY POWDER

Curry powder is a blend of herbs and spices and vary by region. There are thousands of curries, ranging from complex (up to 20 or more ingredients) to simple (4 or 5 components). Depending on the herbs and spices used, curry can vary greatly in flavor and heat—from hot and spicy to mild and sweet. Its distinctive yellow color comes from turmeric, the primary ingredient; other commonly used ingredients are cayenne pepper, ginger, coriander, fennel, chili powder, cumin, cloves, and cardamom.

Varieties

Commercial curry powder comes in two basic varieties—standard and Madras (the hottest).

Garam masala, used in Indian cooking, is another variety of curry.

Storage

Curry powder quickly loses its pungency. Store in an airtight container for up to 2 months.

EGG ROLL WRAPPERS

Although most egg roll wrappers average 180mg sodium, there are several LS brands (visit **LowSaltFoods.com** for a list). Each egg roll wrap is equal to 4 wonton wrappers. You'll find wraps in the produce section of many supermarkets and health food stores. If unable to find LS wrappers, they are easy to make from scratch (see *Egg Roll Wraps, pg 205*).

Egg roll wraps are also a great substitute in many recipes for puff pastry or pie dough. Just spread your favorite filling on the wrapper, either fold in half on the diagonal or roll up; then fry or bake until golden brown.

Folding Wontons

When used with wontons, the wrappers are easy to fold. Dip finger in water and rub onto two adjacent edges of the wrap. Fold in half on the diagonal to form a triangle; pinch together the wet edges to seal. Finish by folding two opposite points under to make a packet. (I like to use my thumb as a guide by placing my thumb under the wonton and folding the corners under.) NOTE: While making wontons, cover wrappers with a damp towel to keep from drying out.

EGGPLANT

Choose smooth skinned eggplants that are 3 to 6-inches in diameter and free of tan spots, scars, or wrinkles. They should feel heavy, have a bright green stem, and quickly return to normal when pressed with the thumb.

Many recipes suggest salting before cooking to draw out moisture and eliminate any bitter taste, but it's not necessary if you choose smaller, tender eggplants. Prick the skin in several places before baking to allow the steam to escape.

FISH AND SEAFOOD COMPARISON

There is a wide difference in the amount of sodium in fish and seafood species. Listed from least amount of sodium to the most, the following figures are based on a 3-oz serving of fresh fish:

Monkfish	15mg
Rainbow trout	28mg
Tuna	31mg
Pike, Northern	33mg
Walleye	43mg
Catfish, Wild	37mg
Farmed	45mg
Salmon:	
Chinook	40mg
Atlantic, farm	50mg
Pink	57mg
Smoked	667mg
Lox	1,700mg
Cod	46mg
Halibut	46mg
Sturgeon	46mg
Clams	48mg
Crayfish	53mg
Perch	53mg
Atlantic	64mg
Snapper	54mg
Orange Roughy	54mg
Freshwater	60mg
Sole (Flounder)	69mg
Mackerel:	
Pacific/Atlantic	75mg
King	134mg
Mahi Mahi	75mg
Swordfish	76mg
Pollack	78mg
Oysters, Pacific	90mg
Eastern	151mg
Shrimp	126mg
Scallops	137mg
Lobster, Spiny	150mg
Northern	252mg
Mussels	243mg
Crab:	
Blue	250mg
Dungeness	250mg
Alaskan King	711mg
Imitation	715mg
Abalone	256mg
Cuttlefish	316mg

Flour Comparison

Most flours have very little sodium, except for self-rising flour, which has added leavening agents. The following is the sodium content in a cup of several flours.

Cake flour	0mg
Rice flour, white	0mg
Rye flour	1mg
All-purpose flour	3mg
Whole wheat flour	6mg
Soy flour	11mg
Rice flour, brown	13mg
Potato flour	88mg
Self-rising flour	1,588mg

Garlic
Roasting

Roasting garlic mellows its flavor, giving a slightly sweet, creamy, non-bitter taste. Roast several heads at a time and use on pizzas, in sauces and vegetable dishes, as a spread on bread (when mixed with unsalted butter and Parmesan), or in recipes that call for garlic. Save any unused heads for later use.

To roast: Preheat the oven to 375ºF (190ºC). Cut the top third off each head of garlic; do not remove outer skins. Place the heads, cut sides up, in a small baking dish and drizzle a teaspoon of olive oil over the top of each head. Cover tightly or wrap in aluminum foil; roast in a preheated oven for 1 hour, or until cloves are soft and golden. Remove and let sit for 15 minutes, until cool enough to handle; squeeze out cloves (they should pop out easily).

Storage

Place unused cloves in a jar, add oil from the baking dish, cover and store in the refrigerator up to a week.

Jicama

Jicama is a large brown-skinned tuber that can weigh up to 5 pounds. The white meat has a mildly sweet flavor and is very crisp and crunchy, much like water chestnuts. It is good both raw and cooked and should be peeled before using. Available most of the year in many supermarkets; it will keep up to 2 weeks in the refrigerator.

Leeks

Leeks have a mild, onion-like flavor, but a little sweeter. They are available year round, but are at their peak in the spring and fall. Choose small to medium leeks with crisp, bright green leaves and a white bulb. Smaller leeks are the most tender.

Cleaning

Leeks contain a lot of hidden dirt and it's important to clean them thoroughly. Cut off the root end and the top leaves (which can be used in a stock or soup), leaving a little of the green. Slit the leeks in half lengthwise and wash the trapped dirt away by gently spreading the leaves apart and rinsing.

Storage

Wrap in a damp paper towel, place in a plastic bag, and store in the refrigerator up to a week.

Lentils

There are several kinds of lentils; all are high in protein and fiber, and have very little sodium. They have an earthy flavor and black lentils have the most flavor, but are harder to find. *CAUTION: Like beans, lentils can cause bloating and excessive gas.*

Preparation

Place lentils in a pot and cover lentils with water (no need to soak before cooking); bring to boil over high heat. Decrease heat to medium-low, cover, and simmer until tender (see below for cooking times). One cup dried beans equals 3 cups cooked.

Brown: Ready in 30 to 40 minutes.

French: Cooks up quickly, less than 30 minutes, and stays frim and nutty after cooking. Don't cook them in an iron pot or they will turn black.

Red: Turns a yellowish-beige when cooked, takes 15 to 20 mins cooking time until tender.

Lettuce/Other Salad Greens

There are dozens of lettuce varieties and most supermarkets carry anywhere from 4 to 12 different kinds. As far as nutrition, iceberg is the least nutritious; just about any other lettuce, particularly varieties with darker green leaves, is a better choice.

Lettuce varieties

There are 4 basic types of lettuce:

Butterhead: Includes Boston and Bibb lettuces, both have a mild, buttery flavor, but Bibb is more flavorful.

Iceberg: Crispiest of all lettuces, keeps well in the refrigerator (up to 2 weeks).

Looseleaf (such as Oakleaf, red and green leaf): Mild flavored with smooth or ruffled, green or red-edged leaves.

Romaine: Crunchy and flavorful, used most often in Caesar salads.

Other salad green varieties

Each has their own distinct flavor and provide added color and texture:

Arugula: Has a peppery, slightly bitter taste.

Belgian endive (French endive): Slightly bitter taste, turns bitter when exposed to light.

Curly endive (chicory): Generally has a slightly bitter flavor (use young inner leaves for salads).

Escarole: Slightly bitter flavor, but milder than Belgian or curly endive (use young inner leaves for salads).

Mâche: Prounounced mosh (also known as lamb's lettuce, field salad, corn salad), has a mild buttery flavor.

Radicchio: Slightly bitter taste, similar to Belgian endive; the purplish red and white leaves add lots of color to salads.

Spinach: Slightly bitter flavor, baby spinach is particularly good in salads.

Watercress: Flavor is peppery, mustard-like.

NOTE: *Mesclun is not a lettuce type, but a mixture of baby greens. There are many different combinations and often include arugula, fresee, mâche, mizuni, oakleaf, radicchio, and baby spinach.*

MELTING CHOCOLATE

Here are two ways to melt chocolate:

Microwave: Place in a microwave-safe container and microwave for 2 to 4 minutes at 50% power. Once chocolate appears shiny, remove and stir until completely melted.

Stove-top: Place chocolate in the top of double boiler over hot, near-boiling wate; stir until chocolate has melted.

MUSHROOMS

Mushrooms not only have a wide-range of textures and taste, but they also add an earthy quality to dishes. They are low in calories and nearly fat and sodium free. There are thousands of varieties, but the most commonly available in supermarkets are:

Button: Range in color from white to light brown and come in many sizes from small to large. They have a mild flavor that is enhanced by cooking.

Criminis: Related to button mushrooms, but are brown in color. Their taste is similar to buttons, but more flavorful.

Portobellos: Larger relatives of the button and cremini, reaching up to 4 or 5 inches in diameter. They have a meaty flavor, a firm texture, and are often used in place of meat in vegetarian dishes.

Wild varieties: Include shiitake (rich, woodsy flavor with a spongy texture), oyster (mild flavor with a soft, chewy texture), enoki (sweet and crisp), and porcini (one of the best tasting, usually sold dried and have a meaty, buttery flavor). Other wild varieties include maitakes, chanterelles, and morels.

Selection and Storage

Select firm, evenly-colored mushrooms that are tightly closed on the underside. Keep refrigerated in a paper bag 5 to 7 days (up to 2 weeks for shiitake).

Preparation

To prepare, trim off the stem bottom and wipe clean. If you must rinse them, do so quickly, as they absorb water.

NUTS

Toasting

Toasting intensifies the flavor of nuts; the amount of time it takes varies with the type and size of nuts. For instance, chopped nuts cook faster than whole. There are three common ways to toast nuts:

Oven: Spread nuts on a baking sheet and bake in a preheated oven at 350°F (180°C) until they start to brown, 5 to 10 minutes. Watch carefully, as they can quickly burn—once you smell them, take them out.

Stove-top: Spread nuts in a dry skillet. Cook over medium-low heat, stirring or shaking frequently, until they start to turn golden, 5 to 7 minutes.

Microwave: Spread nuts in one layer on microwave-safe plate. Microwave on high 1 minute; stir. Continue microwaving in 30 second intervals, until nuts are fragrant and golden. *NOTE: Nuts will continue to darken after they are removed.*

Sugared Nuts

Follow stove-top method above. Remove from heat and sprinkle with sugar (1 teaspoon per ¼ cup nuts) and a dash of cayenne pepper (if desired); mix well. Remove from skillet and let cool.

PASTA SHAPES

Pasta comes in a variety of shapes and sizes and each shape serves a different purpose. Pasta falls into the following general categories:

Long/straight (spaghetti, linguine, and vermicelli): Generally thinner varieties are for light sauces and the broader strips for thicker sauces.

Lasagna: Use in baked dishes or spread with filling and roll up.

Curly (fusilli and rotini spirals): Very versatile, use with most any sauce, soups, and salads.

Small tubular (elbow macaroni, penne, and ziti): Very versatile, use in soups, salads, and a variety of sauces.

Large tubular (manicotti and cannelloni): These are generally stuffed with cheese, meat, and/or vegetables.

Specialty (farfalle, shells, and orzo): Use in soups, salads, and with most sauces.

PEAS

Peas are typically classified as fresh, field, or pod:

Fresh peas: Small, round, and green; grown in a pod and generally harvested in the early summer. Also known by other names such as sweet pea, green pea, garden pea, or English pea. The fresh pea is eaten raw or used as an ingredient in salads, soups, stews, casseroles, and other dishes. Fresh peas are available as a raw podded pea, canned as a shelled pea, and frozen.

Field peas: Grown, dried, and then split or used whole for use in purées, soups, and dishes requiring thickening. Varieties of the field pea include the green and yellow pea (either split or whole), the chickpea, and the black-eyed pea.

Pod peas: Grown so that both the pod and the pea can be eaten either raw or cooked; examples are snow and sugar snap peas.

Split Peas

Also known as field peas, split peas come in yellow or green varieties (yellow peas are more earthier in taste than green), and are grown specifically for drying. Once dried they are split, hence the name split pea. They do not require presoaking before cooking.

To store: Place in an airtight container in a cool, dark place for up to a year.

PEPPERS

Roasting

Roasting intensifies the flavor of peppers and is far more flavorful than canned or bottled varieties.

In the broiler: Broil about 5 inches from the heat, turning frequently, until peppers are blackened on all sides, 10 to 15 minutes. Remove and cool.

Over a gas flame: Hold the pepper with tongs over a medium flame, turning as it blackens, about 10 to 15 minutes. Let cool.

Stove-top: In a cast-iron skillet over medium-high heat, cook pepper, turning frequently, until blackened on all sides, 10 to 15 minutes. Let cool.

NOTE: Once blackened, place peppers in a paper bag and let cool 15 minutes. Remove and peel; the skin easily pulls away from the peppers.

Chile Peppers

There are many kinds of chile peppers ranging from mild to extremely hot. Based on the Scoville heat unit (SHU), which measures the amount of heat in chile peppers, here are a few of the more popular varieties, listed from hottest to mildest:

Habanero: Hottest of all chile peppers, ranging from 200,000 to over 300,000 SHU

Cayenne: Very hot, especially red varieties, used in Cajun cooking, 8,000–100,000 SHU

Serrano: Hot, ranges from 7,000–25,000 SHU

Chipotle (smoked jalapeño): Hot, 10,000 SHU

Jalapeño: Moderately hot, fresh are usually hotter than canned, 3,500–25,000 SHU

New Mexican: Similar in size to Anaheims, but hotter, 4,500–5,000 SHU

Poblano (Ancho): Mild, great for stuffing, 2,500–3,000 SHU

Anaheim: Large mild chile, used for chile rellenos, 1,000–1,400 SHU

Banana pepper: Mild and sweet, 1-500 SHU

CAUTION: *When handling hot chiles, wear rubber gloves, as the oils of the pepper are very potent. A piece of plastic wrap or a sandwich bag also works to hold the pepper. If you touch the pepper with your bare fingers, wash your hands thoroughly and be sure to keep your fingers away from your eyes or you'll be in sheer agony!*

PIE WEIGHTS

Pie weights are reusable small ceramic or aluminum pellet-like weights used to keep an unfilled pie or tart crust from shrinking or forming bubbles during baking and are found in gourmet stores and some supermarkets. Another alternative, is using rice or beans, however, they have a short lifespan, as they may burn or become musty after repeated use.

For a prebaked crust: Prick shell with a fork in several places. Line the pie crust with a piece of aluminum foil or parchment paper; pour in 1 to 2 cups pie weights. Bake in a preheated oven at 350°F (180°C) for 20 minutes; remove the weights and foil. Bake for 10 minutes more, until edges are golden brown.

For partially baked crust: If the pie has a filling that will be baked further, follow the prebaked crust directions above, except reduce baking time to 5 to 10 minutes then remove weights and foil; bake another 5 to 10 minutes before filling.

POTATOES

Potatoes are one of the most versatile and popular vegetables. They are high in potassium (nearly twice as much as a banana), have no fat, and very little sodium.

Varieties

There are more than 100 kinds of potatoes, the most common supermarket varieties are:

Russet: Most popular potato, high in starch and cooks up light and fluffy; best for baking, mashing, roasting, and frying

White: Good all-purpose potato, with medium starch and creamy flavor, and hold their shape when cooked; use in most potato dishes.

Red: Low-starch potato with a firm texture; best in salads, roasting, steaming, or boiling (not recommended for mashing, may become sticky and gummy).

Yellow-flesh (Yukon Gold): Good all-purpose potato, creamy texture; use in most potato dishes.

Blue or purple: Medium starch potato with a nutty taste that is not as flavorful as other varieties; adds color to any potato dish.

Storage

Will keep for several weeks in a cool (45°F to 50°F), dark place. Do not store below 40°F (such as the refrigerator) or the starch will turn into sugar, changing the flavor. Avoid prolonged exposure to light, as potatoes will turn green and can be toxic. NOTE: *You can eat green potatoes, just cut away the green areas.*

RICE

Varieties and Sizes

Rice comes in brown and white varieties:

Brown: Contains the entire grain but without the husk; has a chewy, nutty taste with slightly more nutrients than white; takes twice as long to cook as white.

White: Without the husk, bran, and germ; is lighter and more tender in taste.

Rice is then classified by size:

Long-grain: Long, thin grains that cook up fluffy and don't stick together; best for side dishes.

Medium-grain: Shorter and fatter than long-grain; starchier than long-grain, but more fluffy than short-grain; good all-purpose rice.

Short-grain: Nearly round grains; high starch content, causing the grains to stick together; use in Asian cooking and risottos (arborio rice).

Brown and white rice also come in converted (has less nutrients than brown, but more than white) and instant varieties (is precooked and dehydrated, so it takes less time to cook, but lacks taste and texture). *NOTE: If you are watching carbohydrates, instant has half the carbs as other kinds of rice.*

Preparation

Generally, to cook rice, use 2 parts water to 1 part rice; white takes 20 to 30 minutes, brown about 45 minutes.

Storage

White rice keeps indefinitely in an airtight container in a cool, dark place, while brown rice will keep up to 6 months (store in refrigerator for a longer shelf life).

ROASTING BEETS

Roasting beets brings out their richness and intensifies the flavor. To roast, wash and trim beets (do not peel) and either wrap each in aluminum foil or place in a covered baking dish with 2 cups water. Bake in a preheated oven at 425°F (220°C) for 45 minutes to 1 hour (depending on size).

When cool enough to handle, remove skin and prepare according to recipe instructions.

WARNING: Be sure to wear gloves when handling the roasted beets, otherwise prepare for red hands.

ROASTING CORN

Pull back husks, remove silks, replace husks before roasting:

On the grill: Place on grill and roast, turning often, until husks are browned and corn is tender, 12 to 15 minutes.

In the oven: Bake at 350°F (180°C) for 40 minutes.

Stove-top: Remove kernels from cobs; heat a dry skillet over high heat. Add corn and cook, stirring and tossing constantly until corn begins to darken, about 4 minutes.

SHALLOTS

Shallots look like small onions, but are similar to garlic, as they separate into multiple cloves. They are mild in flavor, somewhere between an onion and garlic. Use shallots in place of onions in many recipes, as they add more flavor to most any dish.

Selection and Storage

Choose shallots with well-formed heads; avoid those that have started to sprout. Will keep for several months in a cool dry area.

Preparation

Remove the outer skin and cook the same as onions and garlic. *NOTE: If they go beyond light brown in color, they may taste bitter.*

SPINACH

Spinach is rich in cancer-fighting antioxidants and is a vitamin and mineral powerhouse. It is relatively fat free, but contains a significant amount of sodium (1 cup raw spinach has 24mg).

Selection

Choose spinach with deep green leaves that are unwilted and free of any yellowing.

Preparation

Wash spinach before using, as there may be dirt trapped between the leaves. Here are several ways to cook spinach:

Sauté: Place the spinach and a few drops of water in a pot; place over medium heat. Cover and cook, stirring frequently, until spinach wilts, about 4 to 5 minutes.

Steam: Place spinach in a steamer over boiling water and cook until wilted, 5 to 8 minutes

Microwave: Cover and place in microwave; cook on high until tender, 4 to 6 minutes.

Storage

Loosely pack unwashed spinach in a plastic bag and keep in the refrigerator for 3 or 4 days. *NOTE: Washed spinach will rot and decay quicker than unwashed.*

TOMATILLOS

A relative of the tomato, tomatillos look like green tomatoes, but have a thin papery husk. Their flavor is tart with a hint of lemon, and they are most often used to make green salsa (salsa verde).

Selection and Storage

Tomatillos are used most often in an unripened state. Choose firm tomatillos that are bright green with tight-fitting, unblemished husks; avoid those that are beginning to turn a light yellow, as they will be too ripe. Place in a paper bag and store in the refrigerator up to 4 weeks

Preparation

Before using, remove husk and wash to remove stickiness. There are several ways to cook tomatillos:

Boiling: Bring a pot of water to a boil over high heat; add peeled tomatillos and cook until soft but still whole, 3 to 4 minutes. *NOTE: Tomatillos will burst and get mushy if cooked too long.*

Grilling: Heat a skillet (preferably cast iron) over high heat; add whole tomatillos and grill, turning occasionally, until browned on all sides, about 5 minutes.

Roasting: Either place tomatillos in a pan and broil 2 inches from heat, turning until all sides are blistered and charred, 6 to 7 minutes; or place in a pan and roast in a preheated oven at 350°F (180°C) for 15 to 20 minutes..

TOMATO PASTE, PURÉE & SAUCE

When your recipe calls for tomato purée and all you have is tomato sauce or tomato paste, what do you do? Here are the differences between these three tomato products and how to use them interchangeably.

Tomato paste: Thick concentrated, strained tomatoes, average amount of sodium in 2 tbsp 20mg. Substitute with tomato purée or sauce, using twice as much as the recipe calls for and reducing another liquid in the recipe to compensate for the added liquid.

Tomato purée: Thinner than paste and has not been cooked down as long, average sodium is 10mg per ¼ cup. Substitute 3 parts tomato paste, plus 5 parts water. *NOTE: In Britain, tomato purée is the same as tomato paste in the U.S.*

Tomato sauce: Thinner than purée and is usually seasoned, average sodium is 280mg per ¼ cup (NSA brands have 10mg-20mg). Substitute tomato purée or use 3 parts tomato paste, plus 4 parts water.

VANILLA BEANS

Vanilla beans come from the vanilla planifolia orchid and their flavor varies depending on where they are grown. The most commonly available beans are called Bourbon and come from Madagascar. Other varieties are Mexican (more mellow than Bourbon) and Tahitian (more aromatic, but less flavorful than Bourbon).

Preparation

Depending on how much flavor you want, either use the whole bean or just a portion. To get the most flavor, slice the bean lengthwise and place it in the liquid you are flavoring. You can also scrape the seeds from the bean and place both the bean and seeds in the liquid. If you find the little black seeds offensive, strain through a fine mesh sieve.

Useage

Vanilla beans can be reused several times (unless a bean with the seeds removed was in hot cream, then little flavor is left). After using, rinse and dry the bean before storing (see below). Before throwing out spent beans, place them in a jar with sugar or coffee to add a hint of vanilla.

Storage

Beans will keep indefinitely in an airtight container in a cool, dark place, but may lose some flavor over time as they dry out. Discard any beans that are moldy.

INDEX

A
Abbreviations, 24
About The Recipes, 21-23
Alcohol Substitutions, 242
Almonds (see *Nuts*)
Appetizers, 25–38
　Dips & Spreads, 26-30
　Finger Foods, 31-38
Apples
　about, 243
　Desserts & Sweets
　　Apple Strudel, 230
　　Apple Turnovers, 232
　　Light Apple Tart, 221
　Side Dishes
　　Squash & Apple Gratin, 167
　Soups & Salads
　　Avocado, Apple, Dates & Jicama, 72
　　Chicken, Apple & Pecan Salad, 72
　　Curried Chicken Waldorf, 74
　　Curried Yam & Apple Bisque, 41
Apricots
　Breakfast & Lunch
　　Apricot Stuffed French Toast, 184
　Desserts & Sweets
　　Apricot-Peach Turnovers, 232
　　Brandied Apricot Almond Tart, 222
　Side Dishes
　　Couscous w/Dried Apricots & Pine Nuts, 171
Artichokes
　Main Dishes
　　Chicken Sausage w/Artichokes, 94
　　Creamy Artichokes, Mushrooms, Peas & Chicken, 91
　Soups
　　Artichoke & Leek Soup, 42
Asian Foods, 140-141
　folding wontons, 248
　Appetizers
　　Crispy Pork & Shrimp Wontons, 38
　　Spinach & Goat Cheese Wontons, 37
　Basics
　　Chinese Hot Mustard, 38
　　Egg Roll Wraps, 205
　Main Dishes
　　Moo Goo Gai Pan, 140
　　Shrimp Curry, 116
　　Sweet & Sour Pork, 141

Asparagus
　about, 243
　Main Dishes
　　Asparagus Chicken w/Cream Sauce, 93
　　Chicken in Mushroom-Asparagus-Tarragon Sauce, 89
　Side Dishes
　　Asparagus w/Tarragon Vinaigrette, 165
　　Caramelized Shallots & Asparagus, 152
　Soups
　　Creamy Asparagus Soup, 40
Avocado
　Appetizers
　　Guacamole, 28
　Breakfast & Lunch
　　Open-Face Avocado Tuna Grill, 186
　　Open-Face Melted Cheese & Avocado Sandwich, 188
　Main Dishes
　　Tostadas w/Chicken & Guacamole, 168
　Salads
　　Avocado, Apple, Dates & Jicama Salad, 72
　　Cobb Salad, 73
　　Green Goddess Dressing, 77
　　Mixed Greens w/Avocado & Orange, 68

B
Bacon
　Breakfast & Lunch
　　Bacon & Vegetable Frittata, 180
　Salads
　　Pea Salad w/Bacon & Cashews, 60
　　Spinach w/Warm Bacon Dressing, 71
　　Warm Bacon Dressing, 71
Baking powder/Baking soda, 243
Basics, Condiments & Sauces, 203-216
　Basic Stuff, 204-209
　Relishes, Salsas & Sauces, 210-216
Beans
　canned beans, 243
　cooking dried beans, 243
　Appetizers
　　Warm Bean Dip, 28
　Side Dishes
　　Killer Cowboy Beans, 170
　　Quick Refried Beans, 160
　　Refried Black Beans, 169
　　Succotash, 152
　Soups & Salads
　　Bean, Pepper & Chèvre Salad, 58
　　Bean, Pepper & Stilton Salad, 58
　　Black Bean & Pepper Salad, 58
　　Easy 4-Bean Soup, 55
　　Four Bean Salad, 59
　　Hearty Black Bean Soup, 54
　　Meaty Bean Soup, 55
　　Texas-Style Turkey Chili, 56
Beef, Veal, Lamb & Pork, 102-110
　cuts of beef, 244
　Appetizers
　　Crispy Pork & Shrimp Wontons, 38
　Main Dishes
　　Beef Quesadillas, 146
　　Beef Stroganoff, 106
　　Fruit Stuffed Pork Tenderloin, 110
　　Meatballs with Marinara Sauce, 132
　　Pan-Seared Steaks with Tarragon Shallot Sauce, 102
　　Pork Chops w/Raspberry Sauce, 109
　　Pot Roast, 105
　　Quick Fajitas, 143
　　Rib-Eye w/Brandied Mushrooms, 103
　　Sicilian Meatballs, 132
　　Steaks w/Wild Mushroom-Mustard Sauce, 104
　　Sweet & Sour Pork, 141
　　Top Sirloin with Mustard Sauce, 104
　　Veal Marsala, 107
　Soups
　　Beef Broth, 208
　　Borscht with Beef Broth, 44
　　Mighty Fine Borscht, 44
Beets
　roasting beets, 253
　Soups & Salads
　　Borscht with Beef Broth, 44
　　Mighty Fine Borscht, 44
　　Roasted Beet & Walnut Salad, 60
Bell peppers (sweet peppers)
　roasting peppers, 251

Appetizers
  Spicy Roasted Red Pepper Hummus, 26
Main Dishes & Sauces
  Chipotle Pepper Sauce, 124
  Red Pepper Coulis, 124
  Vegetable Strudel w/Red Pepper Coulis, 123
Soups & Salads
  Bean, Pepper & Chèvre Salad, 58
  Bean, Pepper & Stilton Salad, 58
  Black Bean & Pepper Salad, 58
Berries
Breakfast & Lunch
  Blueberry Muffins, 201
  Blueberry Pancakes, 185
Desserts & Sweets
  Absolutely The Best Berry Pie, 219
  Berry Strudel, 230
  Fresh Strawberry Tart, 222
  Northwest Berry Sauce, 241
  Peach & Blueberry Crisp, 231
  Strawberries & Amaretto Parfait, 236
Main Dishes
  Pork Chops with Raspberry Sauce, 109
  Raspberry Sauce, 109
Salad Dressings
  Raspberry Vinaigrette, 76
Biscuits, 223
Bread crumbs, 244
Breads & Baked Goods, 191-202
  bread making without a machine, 244
  Breads, Buns & Doughs, 192-197
  Other Baked Goods, 198-202
Breakfast & Lunch, 177-190
  Breakfast, 178-185
  Sandwiches & Wraps, 186-189
Broccoli
  about, 245
Side Dishes
  Broccoli in Lemon-Shallot Butter, 153
Soups
  Cheesy Broccoli Soup, 43
  Creamed Broccoli with Mandarin Oranges, 43
Broth, beef & chicken, 208
Buns, 220
Burritos (see *Hispanic Dishes*)
Butters
  Beurre Blanc Sauce, 137

  Lemon Butter Sauce, 131
  Orange Butter Sauce, 130

C
Cabbage
Salads
  Spicy Cole Slaw, 61
  Sweet & Sour Cole Slaw, 61
Cakes & Cheesecakes, 224-229
Carrots
  about, 246
Desserts & Sweets
  Carrot Cake, 225
Side Dishes
  Spicy Carrots with Currants, 155
  Carrots & Sugar Snap Peas in Thyme Sauce, 154
  Roasted Vegetables, 153
Soups
  Curried Carrot Soup, 46
  Fresh Carrot Potage, 46
Casseroles
Main Dishes
  Easy Fiesta Casserole, 142
Side Dishes
  Green Beans Supreme, 156
  Onion Casserole, 160
  Scalloped Potatoes with Sun-Dried Tomato Pesto, 164
  Squash 7 Apple Gratin, 167
Celery
Appetizers
  Celery with Pimento-Walnut Cheese, 31
  Chive-Cheese Stuffed Celery, 31
Cheesecakes (see *Cakes & Cheesecakes*)
Cherries
Desserts & Sweets
  Dried Cherry-Almond Turnovers, 233
Chicken (see *Poultry*)
Chickpeas (see *Beans*)
Chile peppers (see *Peppers*)
Chili
Main Dishes
  Chili Stuffed Potatoes, 130
Soups & Chili
  Texas-Style Turkey Chili, 56
Chipotle pepper (see *Peppers*)
Chocolate
  melting chocolate, 250

Baked Goods
  Chocolate Chip Scones, 200
Desserts & Sweets
  Chocolate Chip Cheesecake, 229
  Chocolate Chip Cookies, 238
  Chocolate Cream Cheese Frosting, 240
  Chocolate Decadence Torte, 223
Clams (see *Fish & Seafood*)
Coconuts, about, 246
Cookies, 237
Cooking Without Salt, 12-15
Corn
  roasting, 253
Baked Goods
  Jalapeño Cornbread, 198
Side Dishes & Relishes
  Corn, Leek & Snap Pea Sauté, 155
  Fresh Corn Relish, 210
  Succotash, 152
Cornish game hens (see *Poultry*)
Cornmeal/Polenta
  Creamy Polenta w/Mushroom Sauce, 125
Couscous, 171
Crab (see *Fish & Seafood*)
Cranberries
Relishes & Side Dishes
  Cranberry-Orange Relish with Grand Marnier, 234
  Herbed Bread Stuffing with Dried Cranberries, 176
  Wild Rice & Cranberry Pilaf, 173
Salads
  Spinach, Dried Cranberries & Chèvre Salad, 69
  Three-Layer Molded Salad, 64
Crepes, 206
Crisps, Strudels & Turnovers, 230-233
Croutons, 204
Currants (see *Raisins & Currants*)
Curry
  about, 247
Breakfast & Lunch
  Curried Chicken Salad Sandwich, 187
Main Dishes
  Shrimp Curry, 135
Side Dishes
  Dried Fruit & Curry Rice Dressing, 174

Soups & Salads
  Curried Carrot Soup, 46
  Curried Chicken Waldorf Salad, 74
  Curried Yam & Apple Bisque, 41
Custard (see *Puddings & Custards*)

D
Dairy Products, 23
  adding creaminess, 23
  cream cheese comparison, 247
  Dairy Products Comparison, 23
DASH diet, 9
Dessert Sauces/Toppings
  Amaretto Creme, 220
  Bourbon Creme, 218
  Northwest Berry Sauce, 241
  Whiskey Sauce, 234
Desserts & Sweets, 217-241
  Pies, Tarts & Tortes, 218-223
  Cakes & Cheesecakes, 224-229
  Crisps, Strudels, Turnovers, 230-233
  Puddings & Custards, 234-235
  Fruit Desserts, 236
  Cookies, 237
  Fillings, Frostings, Toppings, 238-241
Dips & Spreads, 26-30
Dressing (see *Stuffings*)

E
Edamame (see *Beans*)
Eggplant
  about, 248
  Chicken Tagine with Eggplant, 97
Eggs & Egg Substitutes, 22

F
Feta (see *Goat Cheese*)
Fillings, Frostings & Sauces, 238-241
Finger Foods, 31-38
Fish & Seafood, 111-120
  comparison of, 248
  Breakfast & Lunch
    Open-Face Avocado-Tuna Grill, 186
    Tuna Sandwich, 186
  Main Dishes
    Best Grilled Salmon, The, 113
    Broiled Salmon with Pesto, 112
    Crispy Pork & Shrimp Wontons, 38
    Crab Quiche, 119
    Grilled Fish Tacos, 149
    Grilled Mahi Mahi Almondine, 118
    Horseradish Grilled Salmon, 113
    Linguine with Clam Sauce, 137
    Orange Roughy in Creamy Leek Sauce, 112
    Red Snapper Beurre Meunière, 111
    Salmon Cakes, 114
    Salmon Tortilla Roll-Ups, 34
    Scallops w/Beurre Blanc Sauce, 120
    Shrimp Curry, 116
    Shrimp in Garlic Butter, 115
    Spicy Crab Stuffed Mushrooms, 33
    Tuna in Marsala Sauce, 117
  Soups
    Simply White Clam Chowder, 53
Food Labeling Guidelines, 11
Foods High In Sodium, 10
Frosting
  Chocolate Cream Cheese Frosting, 240
  Cream Cheese Frosting, 240
  Grandma's Italian Frosting, 241

G
Game hens (see *Poultry*)
Garbanzo beans (see *Beans*)
Garlic
  roasting, 249
  Basics
    Herbed Garlic Croutons, 204
  Main Dishes
    Shrimp in Garlic Butter, 115
  Salad Dressings
    Roasted Garlic Dressing, 76
  Side Dishes
    Roasted Garlic Mashed Potatoes, 163
Gelatin
  Three-Layer Molded Salad, 64
Goat cheese
  Appetizers
    Spinach & Goat Cheese Rolls, 35
  Main Dishes
    Herbed Goat Cheese, 84
    Herbed Goat Cheese Stuffed Chicken, 84
    Onion, Mushroom & Chèvre Tart, 122
  Side Dishes
    Tomato, Leek & Cheese Tart, 168
    Tomato, Onion & Goat Cheese Tart, 168
Grains (see *Couscous*)
Gravy (see *Sauces*)
Green beans, 156-157

H
Hazelnuts (filberts) (see *Nuts*)
Herbs & Spices, 16-17
Hispanic Dishes (see *Salsas & Hot Sauces*)
  Appetizers
    Guacamole, 28
    Jalapeño-Cheese Rolls, 36
    Spicy & Cheesy Tortilla Swirls, 34
    Warm Bean Dip, 28
  Breakfast & Lunch
    Breakfast Tacos, 205
  Main Dishes
    Beef Quesadillas, 146
    Chicken Burritos w/Tomatillo Sauce, 144
    Easy Fiesta Casserole, 142
    Grilled Fish Tacos, 149
    Quick Fajitas, 143
    Stuffed Quesadillas, 147
    Tostadas w/Chicken & Guacamole, 150
    Yummy Turkey Tacos, 148
  Side Dishes
    Quick Refried Beans, 169
    Refried Black Beans, 169
Hollandaise (see *Sauces*)
Hummus, 26

I
Ice cream desserts, 236
Icing (see *Frosting*)
Italian/Pasta
  pasta shapes, 251
  Main Dishes
    15-Minute Spaghetti, 131
    Broiled Salmon with Pesto, 112
    Creamy Mushroom Pasta, 134
    Lasagna with a Cinnamon Twist, 138
    Linguine with Clam Sauce, 137
    Marinara Sauce, 133
    Meatballs with Marinara Sauce, 132
    Pesto, Tomato & Fresh Mozzarella Pizza, 139
    Quick Pesto, 136
    Sicilian Meatballs, 132
    Sun-Dried Tomato Pesto, 136
    Turkey Sausage & Edamame Pasta, 135
    Vegetable Lasagna, 138
  Salads
    Mediterranean Pasta Salad, 66
  Side Dishes
    Scalloped Potatoes w/Sun-Dried Tomato Pesto, 164

Soups
   Minestrone, 51

J
Jalapeños (see *Peppers*)
Jam
Desserts & Sweets
   Cream Cheese & Jam Turnovers, 233
Jicama
  about, 249
Salads
   Avocado, Apple, Dates & Jicama Salad, 88

K
Kidney beans (see *Beans*)

L
Label Claims, 11
Lamb (see *Beef, Veal, Lamb & Pork*)
Lasagna (see *Italian/Pasta*)
Leeks
  about, 249
Main Dishes
   Orange Roughy in Creamy Leek Sauce, 112
Side Dishes
   Green Beans & Leeks in Tarragon Sauce, 157
   Corn, Leek and Snap Pea Sauté, 155
   Tomato, Leek & Cheese Tart, 168
Soups
   Artichoke & Leek Soup, 42
   Cream of Leek Soup, 47
   Mushroom-Leek Soup, 47
Lemon
Baked Goods
   Lemon Currant Scones, 200
   Poppy Seed Muffins w/Lemon Glaze, 202
   Lemon Glaze, 202
Desserts & Sweets
   Lemon Curd-Mascarpone Cake, 224
   Lemon Curd, 239
Sauces
   Lemon Butter Sauce, 115
Side Dishes
   Broccoli in Lemon-Shallot Butter, 153
   Lemon Risotto, 172
Lentils
  about, 249
  Grandma's Lentil Soup, 52
Lettuce/Other Salad Greens (see *Salads*)
  lettuce varieties, 249
Lima beans (see *Beans*)
Lime
Desserts & Sweets
   Lime Curd, 239
Low-Salt Lifestyle, 8-10
Low-Salt Tips to Reducing Sodium, 13, 15

M
Main Courses, 79-150
  Poultry, 80-101
  Beef, Veal, Lamb & Pork, 102-110
  Fish & Seafood, 111-120
  Meatless Dishes, 121-130
  Pasta Dishes & Pizza, 131-139
  Asian Entrées, 140-141
  Hispanic Dishes, 142-150
Mandarin oranges (see *Oranges*)
Mango
Baked Goods
   Mango Bread, 221
Salsa
   Black Bean-Mango Salsa, 235
   Mango Salsa, 235
   Pineapple-Mango Salsa, 235
Margarine and Butter, 22
Mayonnaise, 207
Measurements & Abbreviations, 24
Meatballs, 150
Meatless Dishes, 121-130
Meatloaf, 116
Mexican dishes (see *Hispanic Dishes*)
Muffins, 201-202
Mushrooms
  about, 249
Appetizers
   Mushroom Pâté with Port & Almonds, 30
   Spicy Crab Stuffed Mushrooms, 33
   Stuffed Mushrooms, 32
Main Dishes
   Chicken Breasts in Mushroom-Shallot Sauce, 91
   Chicken in Mushroom-Asparagus-Tarragon Sauce, 89
   Creamy-Mushroom Pasta, 134
   Creamy Mushroom Stuffed Potatoes, 130
   Creamy Artichokes, Mushrooms, Peas & Chicken, 91
   Creamy Polenta w/Mushroom Sauce, 125
   Crustless Spinach-Mushroom Quiche, 129
   Mushroom Chicken Paprikash, 87
   Onion, Mushroom & Chèvre Tart, 122
   Rib-Eye Steak w/Brandied Mushrooms, 103
   Steaks w/Wild Mushroom-Mustard Sauce, 104
Sauces
   Mushroom Sauce, 125
Side Dishes
   Wild Mushroom & Walnut Sauté, 158
   Wild Mushrooms in Madeira Sauce, 158
Soups
   Mushroom Bisque with Brandy, 45
   Mushroom-Leek Soup, 47

N
Nuts
  toasting, 250
Appetizers
   Celery with Pimento-Walnut Cheese, 31
   Mushroom Pâté with Port and Almonds, 30
Desserts & Sweets
   Brandied Apricot Almond Tart, 222
   Dried Cherry-Almond Turnovers, 233
   Pecan Pie with Bourbon Creme, 218
Main Dishes
   Grilled Mahi Mahi Almondine, 118
Side Dishes
   Rice Stuffing with Almonds & Olives, 175
   Rice Pilaf w/Pecans & Currants, 173

O
Olives
Baked Goods
   Olive-Sage Bread, 194
Side Dishes
   Rice Stuffing w/Almonds & Olives, 175
Onions
  caramelizing, 245
Appetizers
   Caramelized Onion Dip, 27
Main Dishes
   Onion, Mushroom & Chèvre Tart, 122

Side Dishes
  Caramelized Onion Tart, 159
  Caramelized Onion Tart with Parmesan, 159
  Onion Casserole, 160
  Peas & Onions au Gratin, 161
  Tomato, Onion & Goat Cheese Tart, 168
Soups
  French Onion Soup, 48

Oranges
Baked Goods
  Orange Current Scones, 200
Main Dishes
  Roasted Game Hens with Orange-Herb Sauce, 101
Salads & Salad Dressings
  Mixed Greens w/Avocado & Orange, 68
  Orange Vinaigrette, 75
Sauces & Sweets
  Orange Butter Sauce, 115
  Orange Curd, 239
  Orange Hollandaise Sauce, 216
Side Dishes
  Creamed Broccoli w/Mandarin Oranges, 43

P

Pancakes, 209
Pasta (see *Italian/Pasta***)**
Peaches
  Apricot-Peach Turnovers, 252
  Peach & Blueberry Crisp, 231
Peanut butter
  No-Flour Peanut Butter Cookies, 238
Pears
Salads
  Mâche, Pear & Toasted Walnut Salad, 68
  Spinach, Pear & Walnut Salad, 68
Peas
  about, 251
Side Dishes
  Carrots & Sugar Snap Peas in Thyme Sauce, 154
  Corn, Leek & Snap Pea Sauté, 155
  Gingered Peas & Carrots, 154
  Peas & Onions au Gratin, 161
Soups & Salads
  Pea Salad w/Bacon & Cashews, 69
  Spicy Split Pea Soup, 50

  Split Pea Soup, 50
Pecans (see *Nuts***)**
Peppers, Hot (also see *Bell Peppers***)**
  about, 251
Baked Goods
  Jalapeño-Cheese Rolls, 36
  Jalapeño Cornbread, 198
Basics
  Chipotle Mayonnaise, 207
Sauces
  Chipotle Pepper Sauce, 124
Soups
  Pumpkin Jalapeño Soup, 49
Pesto (see *Italian/Pasta***)**
Pickles, low-sodium, 209
Pie crust, 208
Pie weights, 252
Pies, Tarts & Tortes, 218-223
Pilaf (see *Rice***)**
Pineapple
Desserts & Sweets
  Carrot Cake, 225
Salsas & Hot Sauces
  Pineapple-Mango Salsa, 235
Pizza (also see *Italian/Pasta***)**
  Chicken, Spinach & Sun-Dried Tomato, 139
  Quick Herbal Flatbread & Pizza Crust, 195
  Pesto, Tomato & Fresh Mozzarella, 139
  Potato Crusted Breakfast Pizza, 183
  Sausage, Cheese & Potato Morning Pizza, 183
Polenta (see *Cornmeal/Polenta***)**
Pork (see *Beef, Veal, Lamb & Pork***)**
Potatoes
  about, 252
Breakfast & Lunch
  Mixup, The, 178
  Potato Crusted Breakfast Pizza, 183
  Potato Pancakes, 185
  Sausage, Cheese & Potato Morning Pizza, 183
Main Dishes
  Chili Stuffed Potatoes, 130
  Creamy Cheese Chicken Stuffed Potatoes, 130
  Creamy Mushroom Stuffed Potatoes, 130
  Stroganoff Stuffed Potatoes, 130

Salads
  Baked Potato Salad, 62
  German Potato Salad, 63
  Warm Potato Salad, 63
Side Dishes
  Baked Spicy French Fried Wedges, 154
  Baked Idahoes w/Caramelized Shallots, 162
  Fried Potato Patties, 163
  Pan-Roasted Potatoes, 161
  Perfect Mashed Potatoes, 163
  Roasted Garlic Mashed Potatoes, 163
  Roasted Vegetables, 153
  Scalloped Potatoes with Sun-Dried Tomato Pesto, 164
  Souffléd Sweets, 165
Poultry
  fat & sodium comparison, 246
  poaching chicken, 246
  Chicken Broth, 208
Breakfast & Lunch
  Curried Chicken Salad Sandwich, 187
Main dishes
  Asparagus Chicken w/Cream Sauce, 93
  Chicken Breasts w/Shallot Sauce, 90
  Chicken Breasts in Mushroom-Shallot Sauce, 91
  Chicken Burritos w/Tomatillo Sauce, 144
  Chicken Diane, 82
  Chicken in Mushroom-Asparagus-Tarragon Sauce, 89
  Chicken Paprika with Tomato Cream Sauce, 87
  Chicken Piccata, 83
  Chicken Piri Piri, 92
  Chicken Pot Pie, 92
  Chicken Sausage with Artichokes, 94
  Chicken, Spinach & Sun-Dried Tomato Pizza, 139
  Chicken Stroganoff, 95
  Chicken Tagine with Eggplant, 97
  Coq Au Vin, 99
  Creamy Artichokes, Mushrooms, Peas and Chicken, 91
  Creamy Cheesy Chicken, 85
  Creamy Cheese Chicken Stuffed Potatoes, 130

Creamy Mushroom Stuffed Potatoes, 130
Feta-Stuffed Chicken, 85
Fried Chicken, 80
Fried Chicken w/Country Gravy, 81
Herbed Goat Cheese Stuffed Chicken, 84
Herb Roasted Game Hens, 101
Marsala Chicken, 88
Mushroom Chicken Paprikash, 87
Oven-Baked Chicken, 80
Rich & Creamy Chicken Stroganoff, 95
Roasted Game Hens with Orange-Herb Sauce, 101
Sun-Dried Tomato Chicken, 86
Sweet & Sour Turkey Meatloaf, 100
Tostadas w/Chicken & Guacamole, 150
Turkey Sausage & Edamame Pasta, 135
Tuscan Chicken Stew, 96
Yummy Turkey Tacos, 148
Salads
Chicken, Romaine & Stilton Salad, 67
Chicken Caesar, 70
Cobb Salad, 73
Curried Chicken Waldorf, 74
Soups & Chili
Texas-Style Turkey Chili, 56
Puddings & Custards, 234-235
Pumpkin
Desserts & Sweets
Pumpkin Cheesecake, 227
Pumpkin Pie w/Amaretto Creme, 220
Soups
Pumpkin Jalapeño Soup, 49

Q
Quiche
Breakfast & Lunch
Quiche Lorraine, 182
Main Dishes
Crab Quiche, 119
Crustless Spinach-Mushroom Quiche, 129

R
Raisins & Currants
Baked Goods
Lemon Currant Scones, 200
Orange Currant Scones, 200
Sauces
Sherried Raisin Sauce, 215
Side Dishes
Rice Pilaf w/Pecans & Currants, 173
Spicy Carrots with Currants, 155
Raspberries (see *Berries*)
Reducing sodium, 12-15
Refried beans (see *Beans*)
Relishes, 210
Rice (also see *Couscous*)
about, 252
Sides Dishes
Basic Steamed Rice, 172
Dried Fruit & Curry Rice Dressing, 174
Lemon Risotto, 172
Rice Pilaf w/Pecans & Currants, 173
Rice Stuffing w/Almonds & Olives, 125
Risotto, 172
Wild Rice & Cranberry Pilaf, 173
Roasting beets, 253
Roasting corn, 253

S
Salad Dressings, 70, 71, 75-77
Salads & Salad Dressings, 57-77
Side Salads, 58-66
Tossed Salads, 67-71
Main Curse Salads, 72-74
Salad Dressings, 75-78
Salmon (see *Fish & Seafood*)
Salsas & Hot Sauces
Black Bean-Mango Salsa, 211
Fresh Corn Relish, 210
Mango Salsa, 211
Mucho Caliente Fresh Tomato Salsa, 212
Pineapple-Mango Salsa 211
Tex-Mex Hot Sauce, 212
Tomatillo Sauce, 145
Sandwiches & Wraps, 186-189
Sauces, Marinades & Gravies
Bearnaise Sauce, 216
Beurre Blanc Sauce, 120
Blackberry Wine Sauce, 215
Blender Hollandaise, 207
Cheese Sauce, 128
Chili Sauce, 214
Chipotle Pepper Sauce, 124
Country Gravy, 81
Lemon Butter Sauce, 115
Marinara Sauce, 133
Mushroom Sauce, 125
Mushroom-Shallot Sauce, 91
Mustard Sauce, 104
Orange Butter Sauce, 115
Orange Hollandaise Sauce, 216
Piri Piri Sauce, 92
Quick Pesto, 136
Raspberry Sauce, 109
Red Pepper Coulis, 124
Shallot Sauce, 90
Sherried Raisin Sauce, 215
Sun-Dried Tomato Pesto, 136
Tarragon-Shallot Sauce, 102
Texas-Style Barbecue Sauce, 213
Tomatillo Sauce, 145
Wild Mushroom-Mustard Sauce, 104
Sausage
Breakfast & Lunch
Night Before Western Soufflé, 179
Sausage, Cheese & Potato Morning Pizza, 183
Sausage Mixup, 178
Main Dishes
Turkey Sausage & Edamame Pasta, 135
Chicken Sausage with Artichokes, 94
Scones, 200
Seafood Chowders, 53
Shallots
about, 253
Main Dishes
Chicken Breasts with Shallot Sauce, 90
Green Beans in Shallot Sauce, 157
Mushroom-Shallot Sauce, 91
Pan-Seared Steaks with Tarragon Shallot Sauce, 102
Salads & Salad Dressings
Shallot Vinaigrette, 76
Sauces
Shallot Sauce, 90
Side Dishes
Baked Idahoes w/Caramelized Shallots, 162
Broccoli in Lemon-Shallot Butter, 153
Caramelized Shallots & Asparagus, 152
Shrimp (see *Fish & Seafood*)

Side Dishes, 151-176
  Vegetables & Legumes, 152-170
  Grains & Rice, 171-173
  Stuffings, 174-176

Snap peas
  Carrots & Sugar Snap Peas in Thyme Sauce, 154
  Corn, Leek & Snap Pea Sauté, 155

Sodium/Salt
  Cooking Without Salt, 12-15
  Foods High in Sodium, 10
  Sodium & Hypertension, 9
  Sodium in Commonly Used Foods, 18-19
  Which Foods Have Less Sodium?, 20

Soups & Chili, 39-56
  Vegetable Soups, 40-52
  Seafood Chowders, 53-54
  Bean Soups & Chili, 55-56

Soybeans (see *Edamame*)
Spaghetti (see *Italian/Pasta*)
Spices & Herbs, 16-17
Spinach
  about, 253
  Appetizers
    Cheesy Leek & Spinach Rolls, 35
    Spinach & Feta Wontons, 37
    Spinach & Goat Cheese Rolls, 35
  Main Dishes
    Chicken, Spinach & Sun-Dried Tomato Pizza, 139
  Salads & Salad Dressings
    Spinach, Dried Cranberries & Chèvre Salad, 69
    Spinach, Pear & Walnut Salad, 68
    Spinach w/Warm Bacon Dressing, 71
  Side Dishes
    Creamed Spinach, 166
    Crustless Spinach-Mushroom Quiche, 129

Squash
  Squash & Apple Gratin, 167

Strawberries (see *Berries*)
Stuffings, 198–200
Sun-dried tomatoes
  Main Dishes
    Chicken, Spinach & Sun-Dried Tomato Pizza, 139
    Sun-Dried Tomato Chicken, 86
    Sun-Dried Tomato Pesto, 136
  Side Dishes
    Scalloped Potatoes w/Sun-Dried Tomato Pesto, 165
    Sun-Dried Tomato-Basil Couscous, 171

Sweet potatoes & yams
  Side Dishes
    Roasted Vegetables, 153
    Souffléd Sweets, 165
  Soups
    Curried Yam & Apple Bisque, 41

T

Tacos (see *Hispanic Dishes*)
Toasting nuts, 250
Tofu
  Crustless Spinach-Mushroom Quiche, 129
Tomatillos
  about, 254
  Condiments & Sauces
    Chicken Burritos w/Tomatillo Sauce, 144
    Tomatillo Sauce, 145
Tomatoes
  tomato paste, purée & sauce, 254
  Condiments & Sauces
    Mucho Caliente Fresh Tomato Salsa, 212
  Main Dishes
    Chicken Paprika w/Tomato Cream, 87
    Pesto, Tomato & Fresh Mozzarella Pizza, 139
    Tomato, Leek & Cheese Tart, 168
    Tomato, Onion & Goat Cheese Tart, 168
Tuna (see *Fish & Seafood*)
Turkey (see *Poultry*)

V

Vanilla beans, about, 254
Veal (see *Beef, Veal, Lamb & Pork*)
Vegetable Soups, 40-52
Vegetarian (see *Meatless Dishes*)

W

Which Foods Have Less Sodium?, 20
Wine, fortified, 14
Wraps, 187

Y

Yogurt
  Breakfast & Lunch
    Yogurt Gruel w/Granola & Nuts, 190
  Salads
    Fruit Salad with Vanilla Yogurt, 65
    Grand Marnier Fruit Salad, 65

www.ingramcontent.com/pod-product-compliance
Lightning Source LLC
LaVergne TN
LVHW081527060526
838200LV00045B/2030